Foreword by Don Tapscott

e-Business 2.0
Roadmap for Success

Second Edition of the e-Business Bestseller!

"Marcia and Ravi provide a wealth of information about the key technologies that are enabling new business models...Once you've read this book you'll know why all business will soon be e-business."
—From the Foreword by Don Tapscott

Dr. Ravi Kalakota
Author of *Frontiers of Electronic Commerce* and *Electronic Commerce: A Manager's Guide*

Marcia Robinson

Praise for
e-Business 2.0:
Roadmap for Success

I work for a system integrator specializing in e-business. Many of my coworkers have read the first edition of this book and they have recommended it. I can't wait to get the second edition published since it will continue to help us explain these concepts to our many consultants. I definitely enjoyed this book and will recommend it to others.

DIONE MCBRIDE
E-COMMERCE AND eCRM PRACTICES
DIRECTOR/TECHNICAL ARCHITECT,
E-COMMERCE AND eCRM PRACTICES,
CAMBRIDGE TECHNOLOGY PARTNERS, INC.

This book is part treatise—offering annotations of the best and the worst of e-business practices; part encyclopedia—defining the ubiquitous buzzwords; and part survival guide for executives and practitioners needing an expert hand to hold in the brave new world of the e-economy. Kalakota and Robinson have written the seminal and definitive compendium.

JILL DYCHÉ
PARTNER, BASELINE CONSULTING GROUP

If there is one book on e-business you must read, this is it.

AMRIT TIWANA
RESEARCHER,
J. MACK ROBINSON COLLEGE OF BUSINESS,
DEPARTMENT OF COMPUTER
INFORMATION SYSTEMS,
AUTHOR OF *THE KNOWLEDGE MANAGEMENT TOOLKIT* (PRENTICE HALL, 1999)
AND *THE ESSENTIAL GUIDE TO KNOWLEDGE* (PRENTICE HALL, 2000)

e-Business 2.0

Addison-Wesley Information Technology Series
Capers Jones and David S. Linthicum, Consulting Editors

The information technology (IT) industry is in the public eye now more than ever before because of a number of major issues in which software technology and national policies are closely related. As the use of software expands, there is a continuing need for business and software professionals to stay current with the state of the art in software methodologies and technologies. The goal of the Addison-Wesley Information Technology Series is to cover any and all topics that affect the IT community: These books illustrate and explore how information technology can be aligned with business practices to achieve business goals and support business imperatives. Addison-Wesley has created this innovative series to empower you with the benefits of the industry experts' experience.

For more information point your browser to
http://www.awl.com/cseng/series/it/

Sid Adelman, Larissa Terpeluk Moss, *Data Warehouse Project Management.* ISBN: 0-201-61635-1

Wayne Applehans, Alden Globe, and Greg Laugero, *Managing Knowledge: A Practical Web-Based Approach.* ISBN: 0-201-43315-X

Michael H. Brackett, *Data Resource Quality: Turning Bad Habits into Good Practices.* ISBN: 0-201-71306-3

James Craig and Dawn Jutla, *e-Business Readiness: A Customer-Focused Framework* ISBN: 0-201-71006-4

Gregory C. Dennis and James R. Rubin, *Mission-Critical Java™ Project Management: Business Strategies, Applications, and Development.* ISBN: 0-201-32573-X

Kevin Dick, *XML: A Manager's Guide.* ISBN: 0-201-43335-4

Jill Dyché, *e-Data: Turning Data into Information with Data Warehousing.* ISBN: 0-201-65780-5

Dr. Nick V. Flor, *Web Business Engineering: Using Offline Activites to Drive Internet Strategies.* ISBN: 0-201-60468-X

David Garmus and David Herron, *Function Point Analysis: Measurement Practices for Successful Software Projects.* ISBN: 0-201-69944-3

Capers Jones, *Software Assessments, Benchmarks, and Best Practices.* ISBN: 0-201-48542-7

Capers Jones, *The Year 2000 Software Problem: Quantifying the Costs and Assessing the Consequences.* ISBN: 0-201-30964-5

Ravi Kalakota and Marcia Robinson, *e-Business 2.0: Roadmap for Success* ISBN: 0-201-72165-1

David S. Linthicum, *B2B Application Integration: e-Business-Enable Your Enterprise* ISBN: 0-201-70936-8

Sergio Lozinsky, *Enterprise-Wide Software Solutions: Integration Strategies and Practices.* ISBN: 0-201-30971-8

Patrick O'Beirne, *Managing the Euro in Information Systems: Strategies for Successful Changeover.* ISBN: 0-201-60482-5

Mai-lan Tomsen, *Killer Content: Strategies for Web Content and E-Commerce.* ISBN: 0-201-65786-4

Bill Wiley, *Essential System Requirements: A Practical Guide to Event-Driven Methods.* ISBN: 0-201-61606-8

Ralph R. Young, *Effective Requirements Practices.* ISBN: 0-201-70912-0

Bill Zoellick, *Web Engagement: Connecting to Customers in e-Business.* ISBN: 0-201-65766-X

e-Business 2.0

Roadmap for Success

Ravi Kalakota and Marcia Robinson

Addison-Wesley

Boston • San Francisco • New York • Toronto
Montreal • London • Munich • Paris • Madrid • Capetown
Sydney • Tokyo • Singapore • Mexico City

The publisher offers discounts on this book when ordered in quantity for special sales. For more information, please contact:

Pearson Education Corporate Sales Division
One Lake Street
Upper Saddle River, NJ 07458
(800) 382-3419
corpsales@pearsontechgroup.com

Visit AW on the Web: www.awl.com/cseng/

Library of Congress Cataloging-in-Publication Data

Kalakota, Ravi.
        e-Business 2.0 : roadmap for success / Ravi Kalakota and Marcia Robinson.
            p.   cm.—(Addison-Wesley information technology series)
    Rev. ed. of e-Business. c1999.
    Includes bibliographical references and index.
    ISBN 0-201-72165-1
    1. Electronic commerce.   I. Robinson, Marcia, 1964–   II. Kalakota, Ravi.
E-Business.   III. Title.   IV. Series
    HF5548.32.K348 2000
    658.8'4—dc21   00-048518

ISBN 0-201-72165-1
Text printed on recycled paper
1 2 3 4 5 6 7 8 9 10 — MA — 0403020100
First printing, November 2000

This book is dedicated to:

Shelby and Jaima
—MMR

Vijay and Vinod
—RK

Contents

Foreword

New Business Models and the Creation of Wealth

Throughout the twentieth century, wealth was created by the integrated Industrial Age corporation. A clear model of the firm was established, along with many assumptions. Organizations were structured as hierarchies with reporting relationships and an internal economy. Marketing-based print and broadcast technologies became central to revenue generation. Manufacturing plants and processes that had many similarities across industries were established.

Understandably, the traditional starting point for strategic business thinking had been the individual corporation. But in the digital economy, that is no longer appropriate. A new form of value creation is becoming the basis for competitive strategy. We're entering the era of the business web, or b-web. The b-web is any system—of suppliers, distributors, service providers, infrastructure providers, and customers— that uses the Internet as the basis for business communications and transactions.

The key to competing in the digital economy is business model innovation that exploits the power of business webs. Industry by industry, business webs are destroying the old model of the firm.

To fully appreciate the fundamental realignments under way in the economy, we must reach back to the early writings of the Nobel laureate economist, Ronald Coase. More than six decades ago, Coase posed the question, "Why do firms exist?" If the marketplace is so efficient, why not have each worker, each step in the production process, act as independent buyer and seller? Coase cited *transaction costs* as the basis of contradiction between the theoretical agility of the market and the durability of the firm. Firms incur transaction costs when, instead of using their own internal resources, they go out to the market for products or services.

Transaction costs have three parts, which together, or even individually, can be prohibitive.

Search costs. Finding what you need takes time, resources, and out-of-pocket costs (such as travel). Determining whether to trust a supplier adds more costs.
Contracting costs. If every exchange requires a unique, separate price negotiation and contract, the costs can be totally out of whack with the value of the deal.
Coordination costs. This is the cost of coordinating resources and processes. In Coase's time, innovations like the telephone and the telegraph made it easier for distant firms to coordinate their activities.

The vertically integrated Industrial Age corporations developed to sidestep these costs. This is why Henry Ford's company—the first archetypal Industrial Age firm—didn't just build cars; it owned rubber plantations to produce raw materials for tires and marine fleets for shipping materials on the Great Lakes.

As communication tools got better and cheaper, transaction costs dropped. Firms began to specialize. With the Internet's arrival, many transaction costs are plunging to zero. Now, large and diverse sets of people scattered around the world can cheaply and easily gain real-time access to the information they need to make safe decisions and coordinate complex activities.

A company can add knowledge value to a product or service through innovation, enhancement, cost reduction, or customization, at each step in its life cycle. Often, specialists do a better value-adding job than vertically integrated firms. In the digital economy, the notion of a separate, electronically negotiated deal at each step of the value cycle becomes a reasonable, often compelling, proposition.

New business models based on networks are the new keys to competitiveness and wealth creation. This is why Ravi Kalakota and Marcia Robinson's book is timely. The term e-business began as a marketing slogan for technology companies. It is now a central theme at the heart of business strategy. However, most managers still view e-business and e-commerce as the buying and selling of goods on the Internet. Ravi and Marcia show how it is much more than this. They provide a wealth of information about the key technologies that are enabling new business models, as well as some helpful practical advice on how to get from there to here.

Once you've read this book you'll know why all business will soon be e-business.

Don Tapscott
Chairman
Digital 4Sight
September 2000

Preface

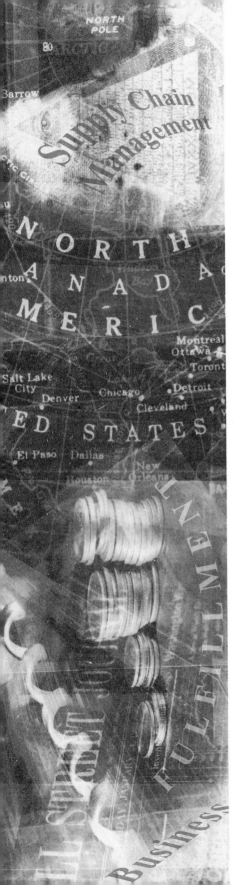

e-Commerce is changing the shape of competition, the dynamics of the customer relationship, the speed of fulfillment, and the nature of leadership. In the face of change, is your management

- Willing to cannibalize its existing channels with a risky, untested new one?

- Creating a click-and-mortar service infrastructure that gives customers the same experience through all the channels?

- Digitizing the supply chain and linking up with competitors to reduce costs further?

Managers and companies everywhere are at a crossroad. With so many ways to go, which road will lead to success? What roadblocks will need to be navigated? Which business models, management strategies, and tactics will ensure success? What will the characteristics of the next generation of business applications be, and which vendors will lead in delivering them? To whom can managers turn for help? If you're losing sleep over these questions, you've picked up the right book. We'll help you find the road to take to learn the fundamentals of business built on a digital foundation. If these questions are not of paramount importance to you, get used to mediocre business performance.

In these days of frequent and rapid change, skill in designing and changing complex "digital corporations" is a significant advantage. This advantage is highlighted throughout the book. To achieve an edge, management must be able to create complex service models built on technology—"e-service" designs. Simple designs offer no advantage and are easily copied. This book is about the discipline needed to create complex infrastructure choices, which are central to any modern firm. This book, based on several years of researching, consulting, managing, and growing e-business start-ups, tackles two nagging questions.

- Why are some companies relentlessly successful at e-commerce while others flounder? What are the successful businesses doing differently to solve customer problems or pain?

- How are successful companies, both old and new, moving from traditional applications to the new breed of integrated, e-business application architectures?

Through detailed case studies and analysis, this book examines the e-business blueprint, offering step-by-step guidance in choosing and implementing the right application strategies to survive the e-commerce onslaught and to succeed. The thesis of the book is that durable application frameworks can guide you through the e-business chaos. Business models change. Technology changes. But application infrastructure design principles endure.

What This Book Is About

Managers of established companies are struggling to comprehend this new phenomenon: e-commerce. But already, the next wave—e-business—is reaching shore. Intensified competition and new e-commerce opportunities are pressing traditional companies to build e-business models that are flexible, fast moving, and customer focused. In other words, the core of the enterprise itself is undergoing a metamorphosis from e-commerce to e-business.

e-Business is the complex fusion of business processes, enterprise applications, and organizational structure necessary to create a high-performance business model. The message is simple: Without a transition to an e-business foundation, e-commerce cannot be executed effectively. Considering the inevitability of moving toward an e-business foundation, senior management is being galvanized into tactical action. Those who fail will pay a high price.

One point deserves emphasis: Choosing to pursue e-business is not easy. e-Business is not a slogan. It is not a public relations campaign. It cannot be grafted onto or integrated into a company's normal business-as-usual operating philosophy. Going "e" is a central act that shapes every subsequent plan and decision a company makes, coloring the entire organization, from its competencies to its culture. e-Business, in effect, defines what a company does and, therefore, what it is.

If they seriously want to develop effective strategies for competing in the new economy, managers must understand the fundamental structure of the next-generation e-corporation built on an interconnected web of enterprise applications. We wrote this book to provide a master blueprint for building an innovative e-corporation that can survive and thrive in the digital world.

What Makes This Book Different

Many books have been written about how the old economic rules of scale, scope, efficiency, market share, and vertical integration are no longer sufficient. New rules must be applied, and that requires new organizational capabilities. Managers everywhere understand the urgency; they're itching to get going and to make change happen.

Unfortunately, first-generation e-commerce strategy books were long on vision but short on detail. It's easy to talk about the e-commerce future, but the real management challenge is to make it happen in a systematic way without derailing existing business. What does this mean to top management? If customers are moving online, the whole information technology (IT) investment paradigm must shift toward creating an integrated e-business model.

The focus of this book is practical: helping senior management plan for and manage e-business investments. The first step is to design a comprehensive e-commerce strategy and then to evaluate prospective line-of-business application framework investments on the basis of how well the technology or application advances the strategy. Companies often make the mistake of focusing first on e-commerce applications and only then trying to bend a strategy around this outline. To succeed, managers must have a strong e-business strategy in place *before* considering specific e-commerce application investments. Otherwise, most e-commerce efforts are doomed to fail.

But what do these internal e-business architectures and investments look like? The answer is the focus of this book, the first to look at the problem of structural migration: how to transform an old company into a new agile e-corporation. This book provides a unique view of the next-generation, integrated enterprise and the line-of-business application investments necessary to compete. We highlight the critical elements—business processes, back-office and front-office applications, and strategy—that managers need to be successful in the digital economy.

In other words, corporations involved in e-commerce must rethink their visions of the future. Understanding how to lead one's company into the e-commerce arena requires a new point of view about integration and the business design. We offer step-by-step navigation of the uncharted e-business terrain. Executives and consultants everywhere need this guide to navigate the information economy.

Who Should Read This Book

Many managers are so focused on the details of e-business that they fail to see the vast structural change in how the application infrastructure is being put together. Virtually every business discipline is affected by e-commerce and e-business application architectural efforts. Management needs to learn that the real challenge surrounding e-business is the task of making it happen. This book focuses on the business architecture that managers must build in order to achieve e-business success.

For firms in mature industries, such as automotive, insurance, and retail, that are trying to move in new directions, this book offers critical insights. For market leaders, such as Home Depot and FedEx, this book offers insights for sustaining their leadership. For entrepreneurs managing start-ups, this book highlights the key issues on which those businesses will succeed or fail. Its timeliness and insights into the changes in organizational practice make this book appealing to a broad management market:

- Senior management and strategic planners charged with developing business strategies

- Consultants helping corporate executives shape their companies' competitive future

- Information technology managers leading their teams with strategic decisions

This book is a must-read for all managers, consultants, entrepreneurs, and business school students who have been discussing and reading about e-commerce and who are interested in knowing how they can capitalize on the next wave of business innovation.

How This Book Is Organized

We start by dissecting the critical practices of companies that have pursued an e-business operating model to reach the top. We then extract examples of the sharpest thinking in business today. What emerges is a clear picture of the kinds of companies that will be tomorrow's stars and the strategies that will help them retain the market leader moniker.

The first five chapters describe a new e-business design composed of building blocks called *enterprise applications.* Market leaders are developing intricate e-models resting on a set of intertwined enterprise apps—customer relationship solutions, enterprise resource planning systems, order management solutions, or supply chain solutions—and then building their strategies around that set. Each enterprise app demands a distinct strategic fusion of customer-centric processes, information systems, management systems, and culture.

Most managers are apprehensive about tackling strategic fusion issues because they represent such a formidable task, one that transcends the organizational structure and line-of-business considerations. This book offers a way to structure this widespread strategy problem, slice it into manageable pieces, and create actionable plans that can be executed quickly.

Chapters 6 through 11 explore the various e-business design elements in the new e-corporation. The goal is to identify clear, rational, strategic design choices that are responsive to evolving customer needs. Each chapter ends with a Memo to the CEO that provides a set of normative questions that must be answered convincingly if the building blocks of strategic integration are to be constructed effectively and profitably.

The last three chapters are prescriptive, focusing on the challenges of becoming digital by describing the design process and explaining how to undertake it. In today's business environment, the stakes are high and failure is swift and ruthless. How an organization mobilizes itself into constructive action will determine its survival and ultimate success. In these chapters, we describe in great detail how the choice of an e-business strategy and application infrastructure must be made, we provide help in identifying the right choices, and we detail the means for implementing it. We do everything but make the choice for you. That's your job.

Acknowledgments

Because this book contains information on many companies struggling with their e-business initiatives, we would like to thank them all for their hard work as they continue to tackle this tough issue.

We have learned much through our consulting engagements and extend thanks to the many people we have talked to: in particular, David Dingott, Frances Frei, Kemal Kocksal, Alex Lowy, Shirish Netke, S. P. Reddy, Kirk Reiss, Mohan Sawhney, Don Tapscott, David Ticoll, Nagesh Vempaty, Richard Welke and Peter Zencke.

Thanks to the many people at Addison-Wesley who made this book possible: in particular, our editor, Mary O'Brien. Many thanks to our reviewers, who took time out of their busy schedules to read through the manuscript page by page and indicate areas that needed attention. To Lorna Gentry and Keith Gribble, thank you for your patience and expertise in editing and improving our book. We appreciate the long hours and honest feedback that made this book much better.

Thanks to our family and friends: in particular, Bill and Judy Robinson, whom we miss every day; Shelley Cicero and Roby Robinson, who brighten our day; and Lynn Lorenc, who always makes us smile.

Ravi Kalakota
kalakota@mindspring.com
www.ebstrategy.com

Marcia M. Robinson
marcia.robinson@mindspring.com
www.ebstrategy.com

CHAPTER ONE

Moving from e-Commerce to e-Business

What to Expect

New economy, new tools, new rules. Few concepts have revolutionized business more profoundly than e-commerce. Simply put, the streamlining of interactions, products, and payments from customers to companies and from companies to suppliers is causing a seismic upheaval in corporate boardrooms. Managers in the new millennium are being forced to reexamine traditional definitions of value, competition, and service.

To compete effectively in the e-commerce world, a company must structurally transform its internal foundation. This structural change requires a company to develop an innovative e-business strategy, focusing on speed to market and breakthrough execution. This structural change requires large-scale process changes, focusing on reducing variation and handoffs. At the same time, companies must also develop a potent e-business infrastructure oriented toward continuous service improvement and ceaseless innovation.

In this chapter, we'll look at the mechanics of e-business: what it is, its corporate and economic impacts, and how it is radically changing business processes. A core component of successful e-business practice is assessing and redesigning how your firm provides value to its customers. This chapter includes the steps we recommend for disaggregating these components of customer value and reaggregating them into the value chains that support the e-business model.

- Why can consumers buy a $999 built-to-order PC from Dell online but not a customized $3,000 color copier from Xerox?

- Why can you trade stocks and options online through Charles Schwab but not go online to view or make changes to your Cigna or Kaiser health insurance plan?

- Why does it take only a few minutes to choose a flight, buy an airline ticket, and reserve a hotel room and car through Microsoft Expedia but twice as long to speak with an American or United travel agent?

- How can FedEx and UPS make it easy for customers to track their packages, create airbills, and schedule pickups on the Web, but banks cannot tell their customers the status of online bill payments made to the local phone company?

- Why is it that Cisco can overhaul its product line every 2 years, but Kodak cannot seem to deliver rapid innovations to meet changing customer requirements?

What makes some companies successful in the digital economy? Visionary companies understand that current business designs are insufficient to meet the challenges of doing business in the e-commerce era. If you take a close look at such leading businesses as Intel, Dell, Nokia, Cisco, and GE, you'll find a new business design, one that emphasizes a finely tuned integration of customer needs, technology, and processes. These companies use technology to streamline operations, boost brands, improve customer loyalty, and, ultimately, drive profit growth.

In today's connected, computerized, and communicating world, visionary firms are setting new rules within their industries via new e-business designs and interenterprise processes. These companies have integrated operations to support changing customer requirements, realizing that the e-customers' needs, tastes, and expectations are transforming the shape of the enterprise. The visionary firms also realize that the next wave of customer-centric innovation requires the fusion of business designs, processes, applications, and systems on an unprecedented scale.

We call this customer-oriented integration *e-business,* the organizational foundation needed to support business in the Net economy. This forces the management of traditional companies to ask four questions.

- *How will e-commerce change our customer priorities?*

- *How can we construct a business design to meet these new customer priorities?*

- *What kind of new applications infrastructure do we need to orchestrate the new business design?*

- *What short-term and long-term investments in people, partners, and technology must we make to survive, let alone thrive, in this new environment?*

Are You Ready?

As you look around your company, what problems preoccupy senior management? What are your firm's current priorities: long-term market share versus short-term profits, revenue growth versus cost reduction? What high-profile projects have either been initiated or recently proposed to accomplish these priorities? In light of these priorities, and the projects intended to achieve them, how do you feel about the digital future? Analyze your company's ability to compete with new entrants that don't have your company's baggage: legacy applications, calcified processes, bureaucratic controls, and inflexible business models.

As you continue your analysis, ask yourself questions about your corporate strategy. Does my senior management have a clear understanding of how our industry is being shaped by new and unconventional rivals? Do senior managers suffer from flawed assumptions or blind spots in interpreting industry-level changes? Does senior management see these changes as a threat or as an opportunity? Is senior management willing to make changes to the company business model before it's too late? Is senior management setting the right priorities to be the rule makers rather than rule takers in the e-commerce era?

What is your top management's mindset? Is it one of a sprinter or of a long-distance runner in pursuing new technologies? Does senior management think that catching up to today's industry leaders will be easy? If so, beware: The reality is often the reverse. The companies leading today's e-commerce revolution move quickly and stake out significant market positions early. Cisco, for instance, moved in a decade from an obscure company into a market leader. Companies like Cisco make it very difficult—and expensive—for slow-moving, traditional firms to catch up, much less overtake them.

Be brutally honest about your company's readiness to change. Does senior management understand the implementation side of strategy? Do the company leaders know that the entire business platform is being transformed by new technology—a new generation of enterprise applications—that tightly integrates internal and external processes? Does senior management understand the risks, challenges, and difficulties in integrating and implementing these complex enterprise applications necessary for an e-business enterprise to operate success-fully? Does top management understand what it takes to build interenterprise, technology-supported processes, such as supply chain management, that form the backbone of e-business?

Thoughtfully answering the preceding questions will help you shape the cor-porate transformation that occurs with the enterprise-wide implementation of new technology and business processes. In this chapter, our goal is to make the logic of e-business explicit and comprehensible so everyone on your man-agement team can participate in creating the new infrastructure required by e-business. Many enlightened managers are better than one. An understanding of technology and its role in your firm's future must be made accessible to all management, not reserved, as is sometimes the case, for only an anointed few who have managed to penetrate technology's thick fog and hype. Let us help you to begin this educational process and to get started in linking today's business with tomorrow's technology.

Linking Today's Business with Tomorrow's Technology

It's happening right before our eyes: a vast and rapid reconfiguration of business on an unprecedented scale. Conventional wisdom says that e-commerce is an economic solvent. It dissolves old business models, changes the cost structure, and rearranges links among buyers, sellers, and everyone in between. What is only now becoming clear is that e-commerce is a relationship solvent as well, melting traditional boundaries between companies' partners and customers, changing the nature of relationships. Simply put, e-commerce is a potent socio-economic chemical that reacts with everything it touches.

However, the impact of e-commerce is happening in phases. In its first phase (1994–1997), e-commerce was about presence: making sure that everybody had a Web site, meeting the demand that every company, large or small, get out there and have at least something on the Internet. People weren't quite sure why they were doing it, but they knew that they had to have an online presence.

The second phase (1997–2000) of e-commerce was about transactions—buy-ing and selling over digital media. The focus in this phase was on order flow and gross revenue. Some of that was the matching of buyers and sellers who never would have found each other in the past. Some of it was simply taking transactions that would have been done through paper purchase orders and saying that this business was done on the Internet, although the meaning of that change was quite trivial. But in this phase, the announcements were all about order flow at any cost: why-sell-it-when-you-can-give-it-away business models. As a result, many of the first movers in this phase, such as Value America, are either gasping, have gasped their last breath, or are flailing about in a sea of red ink.

Today, e-commerce is entering the third phase (2000–?), with a focus on how the Internet can impact profitability. And profitability is not about increasing gross revenues but rather increasing gross margins. We call this phase *e-business*, and it includes all the applications and processes enabling a company to service a business transaction. In addition to encompassing e-commerce, e-business includes both front- and back-office applications that form the core engine for modern business. Thus, e-business is not just about e-commerce transactions or about buying and selling over the Web; it's the overall strategy of redefining old business models, with the aid of technology, to maximize customer value and profits. To paraphrase *Business Week*, "Forget B2B or B2C, E-business is about P2P—path to profitability."[1]

In the first two phases of the Internet era, it seemed that the future would belong to upstarts, such as eToys, and that technology would trump experience. Now, it is evident that experience, distribution, and margins are worth something after all. It was inevitable that we would go through these phases. All technologies go through a honeymoon period, and eventually you get down to the bottom line: How is technology really going to affect business?

Why is e-business a big deal? CEOs everywhere are faced with shareholder demands for double-digit revenue growth, no matter what the business environment. CEOs have already reengineered, downsized, and cut costs. Consequently, they are investigating new strategic initiatives to deliver results, and many are looking to technology to transform the business model—in other words, harnessing the power of e-business.

What is driving e-business? Every day, more and more individuals and companies worldwide are linked electronically. This digital binding of consumers and companies in a low-cost way is as significant a technological advance as the invention of the steam engine, electric power generation, telephone, or the assembly line. The resulting democratization of information resulting from this digital revolution casts aside the stodgy old conventions of business built on information asymmetry.[2]

The rules of the business game are being rewritten to be the rules of e-business, as listed in Table 1.1. In the pages that follow, we discuss each rule in greater detail. Let's start by looking at the first rule of e-business:

> ▶ *Technology is no longer an afterthought in forming business strategy but rather the cause and driver.*

Technology is no longer the Rodney Dangerfield of business. Technology has made it to the executive floor. Although the effect of technology on business strategy may not be clear initially, it's relentless and cumulative, like the effects of water over time. Technological change comes in waves, and just as the ocean erodes the shore, so too technology erodes strategies, causing business models to behave in ways difficult to predict. Consequently, e-business is not something that conventional, risk-averse businesses can ignore.

Indeed, e-commerce poses the most significant challenge to the business model since the advent of computing itself. Although the computer has increased business speed, it hasn't fundamentally altered the business foundation, but e-commerce has. *If any entity in the value chain begins doing business electronically, companies up and down the value chain must follow suit or risk being substituted or*

Table 1.1: Ten Rules of e-Business

Rule 1	Technology is no longer an afterthought in forming business strategy but rather the cause and driver.
Rule 2	The ability to streamline the structure of information and to influence and control its flow is a dramatically more powerful and cost-effective service than is that of moving and manufacturing physical products.
Rule 3	Inability to overthrow the dominant, outdated business design often leads to business failure.
Rule 4	Using e-commerce, companies can listen to their customers and become "the cheapest," "the most familiar," or "the best."
Rule 5	Don't use technology just to create the product. Use technology to innovate, entertain, and enhance the entire experience surrounding the product: from selecting and ordering to receiving and service.
Rule 6	The business design of the future increasingly uses reconfigurable e-business models to best meet customers' needs.
Rule 7	The goal of new business designs is for companies to create flexible outsourcing alliances that not only off-load costs but also make customers ecstatic.
Rule 8	For urgent e-business projects, it's easy to minimize application infrastructure needs and to focus on the glitzy front-end apps. The oversight can be costly in more ways than one.
Rule 9	The ability to plan an e-business infrastructure course swiftly and to implement it ruthlessly are key to success. Ruthless execution is the norm.
Rule 10	The tough task for management is to align business strategies, processes, and applications quickly, correctly, and all at once. Strong leadership is imperative.

excluded from the chain's transactions. Therefore, rethinking and redesigning your company's business model is not merely an option. It's the first step to profiting—even surviving—in the e-business information era.

Are executives at large companies aware that the impact of these changes is of seismic proportions? Some are, but most aren't. The majority of executives are too busy dealing with, and reacting to, current operational problems to think of the future. Time is tight; resources are tighter. Those executives who see the future and the coming technological changes but ignore their magnitude are likewise at risk. Those executives can't afford to sit around inventing elegant strategies and then try to execute them through a series of flawless decisions. To do so is to fail, dooming their business. In order for executives everywhere to operate successfully in the new age of e-business, business itself must be seen differently. As John Seely Brown, chief scientist of Xerox, puts it, "Seeing differently means learning to question the framework through which we view and frame competition, competencies and business models."[3] If the current paradigm is one of reacting to short-term business problems and ignoring the long-term problem of the future, executives must step outside that paradigm, which weaves intricate, "best-laid" plans based on a skewed view of what the future entails.

Maintaining the status quo is not a viable option. Unfortunately, too many companies develop a pathology of reasoning, learning, and attempting to innovate only in their own comfort zones. It's as if management views the coming changes and asks, "What will my new office space look like?" when instead they should ask, "Will the building be standing once the quake passes?" The first step to seeing differently is to understand that e-business is about structural transformation.

Defining e-Business: Structural Transformation

If e-commerce innovation is revolutionizing the rules of business, resulting in structural transformation, where do we see the effects? We see them in the growing pace of application innovation, the development of new distribution channels, and the competitive dynamics that continue to baffle even the smartest managers.

Are most companies organized to deal with structural change? Not really. Virtually every business today is stretched to the limit, attempting to maintain viability and profitability in the face of unparalleled uncertainty and change. And no relief is in sight. For example, the encyclopedia marketplace has undergone radical change. Thanks to the Internet, Encyclopaedia Britannica has been forced to place much of its product on the Web for free. Yes, free—a huge step for the tradition-bound company, which hadn't made a change in operation since the mid 1990s, when it put its products on CD-ROMs.[4]

As technological innovations permeate more and more business processes, structural transformation becomes more difficult to manage because the issues of change play out on a much grander scale. Explosive, virginal markets are popping up everywhere as the Internet transforms old industries—financial services, retailing, industrial distribution—and creates new ones—portals, Internet service providers, application service providers. Increasingly, the structural changes are not found just in tangible assets, such as processes and products but also in intangibles, such as branding, customer relationships, supplier integration, and the flexible aggregation of key information assets. This transition from the tangibles to the intangibles of business value leads to the second rule of e-business:

> *The ability to streamline the structure of information and to influence and control its flow is a dramatically more powerful and cost-effective service than is that of moving and manufacturing physical products. The information surrounding a product or service is more important than the product or service itself.*

This second rule of e-business is the core driver of structural transformation. Unfortunately, few companies have developed the necessary information-centric business designs required to deal with the issues of continuous business change and innovation. Changing the flow of information requires changing not just the product mix but also, and perhaps more important, the business ecosystem in which companies compete.

Managing during a period of structural transformation is difficult. For example, in the 1980s, IBM and Digital Equipment Corporation (DEC) were positioned to own the PC market, but they did nothing when upstarts Compaq, Dell, and Gateway took the market by storm. Why? Because their commitment and attention were directed elsewhere. Even as late as the early 1990s, DEC's official line was that PCs represented a niche market with only limited growth potential. DEC dug itself into a hole from which it was impossible to escape and consequently was acquired by Compaq, a company it could have bought many times over in the 1980s. DEC's management made two significant mistakes. First, in the late 1980s, it didn't proactively transform the business design to rely less on midrange computers and to focus more on the PC and the coming client/server revolution. Second, in the mid 1990s, management was reluctant to fully embrace the Internet as a "bet-the-company" future trend.

Most companies have a terrible time cannibalizing their existing business structures in order to reallocate assets to compete directly with e-start-ups. For instance, if you're Toys "R" Us, it's difficult to ignore existing assets—1,000+ retail stores—in order to compete directly with eToys. This same challenge is playing out again and again in industry after industry. The big dilemma facing management today is how to trigger the spark of innovation in the current business models, allowing the firm to compete seriously in the new economy. Unless it develops an explicit strategy to accommodate the structural transformation implied by the e-commerce revolution, an enterprise will find itself scrambling, working harder and faster just to stay afloat and survive.

High Transformation Stakes

Why do successful firms fail? The marketplace is cruel to companies that don't adapt to change. History shows that organizations best positioned to seize the future rarely do. As Alvin Toffler pointed out in *Future Shock,* either we do not respond at all, or we do not respond quickly or effectively enough to the change occurring around us. He called our paralysis in the face of demanding change "future shock." Too often, senior managers fail to anticipate change and become overconfident, or they lack the ability to implement change and fail to manage change successfully.

Remember CompuServe and Prodigy? Their stories are another example of market leaders that did not transform quickly enough. Founded in 1969, CompuServe offered thousands of unique content areas to its subscribers, including unmatched business and professional resources, industry-renowned forum areas, the latest in news and information, and searchable databases. Prodigy erupted onto the scene in 1990 as a joint venture of Sears and IBM. At its peak, Prodigy had 2 million subscribers and innovative services that even today would be considered cutting edge. Both Prodigy and CompuServe were superbly positioned to take advantage of the Internet.

Unfortunately, both stumbled. They watched as America Online, a nimble, aggressive competitor a fraction of their size, seized the Internet and took away market share. While Prodigy and CompuServe were hamstrung by internal management problems, AOL was carpet-bombing the United States with floppy disks. In no time, AOL's management built a powerful brand and outexecuted the competition. In 1995, with losses mounting, Sears tried to sell its stake in Prodigy. IBM was willing to buy but thought that the price was too steep. Finally, in 1996, the two companies sold Prodigy to its employees. In 1998, CompuServe was sold by parent H&R Block to AOL.

Of the five big consumer online services in 1994, four were owned by large corporations: Prodigy—Sears and IBM; Delphi—News Corp.; GEnie—General

Electric; and CompuServe—H&R Block. The fifth, independent AOL, would ultimately beat them all. Online players that have taken on corporate partners, such as CNET with NBC, InfoSeek with Disney, and Excite@Home with AT&T, should learn from history.[5]

The cases of CompuServe and Prodigy illustrate the greatest threat companies face: adjusting to nonstop change in order to sustain growth. Continuous change means that organizations must manufacture a healthy discomfort with the status quo, develop the ability to detect emerging trends more quickly than the competition, make rapid decisions, and be agile enough to create new business models. In other words, to thrive, companies must live in a state of perpetual transformation, continuously creating fundamental change, improvement, and innovation. This observation leads us to the third rule of e-business:

> *Inability to overthrow the dominant, outdated business design often leads to business failure.*

Changes in business design combined with the pressures of time to market and new technology create serious management challenges. In today's environment, the survival of a company depends on its ability to anticipate, gauge, and respond quickly to changing customer demands. If a company's business design is faulty or built on old assumptions, no amount of patchwork will do any good. Standing still and fantasizing about silver-bullet solutions results only in heartbreak when none is forthcoming; working harder and longer using an outdated business model results only in company-wide frustration and fear. Neither approach is realistic for addressing an issue so fundamental to the future of any enterprise: *How should a company be designed in order to handle the serious challenges presented by new competitors?*

Value Chain Disaggregation and Reaggregation

The value of any business is in the needs it serves, not in the products it offers. In this "back-to-the-basics" philosophy, disaggregation of the value chain allows firms to separate the means, or products, from the ends, or customer needs. Disaggregation requires identifying, valuing, and nurturing the true core of the business: the underlying needs satisfied by the company's products and services. This approach enables managers to disassemble old structures, rethink core capabilities, and identify new forms and sources of value.

Intel, with its continual innovation in chip design and manufacturing, is a prime example of the disaggregation and reaggregation strategy. Disaggregation is a crucial tool for industry leaders, such as Intel, because successful organizations may need to abandon old paradigms—systems, strategies, products—while these assets possess equity. The foresight to cannibalize a working business design takes courage because it's risky, but the payoff can be enormous.

The objective of reaggregation is to either lower cost or enhance differentiation between a firm and its competitors. Reaggregation, by reorienting the business toward a renewed vision of the needs it serves, enables businesses to streamline the entire value chain. Reaggregation also helps create an unparalleled customer experience that satisfies specific needs while offering the customer far more. Customers can find their interactions with a business less sterile, more engaging, and even intriguing as they encounter an array of support, services, and sensitivity never before experienced.

Successful reaggregated business designs depend on a well-integrated set of enterprise software applications. These "killer apps" represent the new technological backbone of the modern corporation and will soon be the standard for companies seeking to compete in the new era. Using technology to reaggregate the value chain is fundamental to the emergence of the digital economy.

Reaggregation enables new entrants to compete differently, even though they're competing with the same scope of activities as well-established leaders. Amazon.com, for example, reaggregated the value chain to perform individual activities differently, although it offers the same scope of activities as leader Barnes & Noble.

The Road Ahead: Steps to a New Beginning

In our work, we've found many firms using strategies of disaggregation and reaggregation to create new business models. Based on this work, we've identified six steps that the processes of disaggregation and reaggregation follow with systematic logic. The steps are the same for any business organization—whether a start-up, a visionary firm, or a mature company. Each step involves understanding and interpreting a question and its answer to fit your firm's unique circumstance.

1. *What is the new industry structure?* It's a configuration that challenges traditional definitions of value.

2. *What does the digital customer want?* Customers want value defined in terms of the whole customer experience and accompanying expectations.

3. *What are the new economics? How to convert value creation into revenue? How do you engineer the end-to-end value stream?*

4. *How do we reorganize our business?* We do so by creating the right partnerships.

5. *Where is the value?* Value is in integration. Value is also in creating a new technoenterprise foundation supportive of customer needs.

6. *How do we implement change?* Change is implemented by developing a new generation of leaders who understand how to create the digital future by design and intent, not by accident.

Established companies need the most help in transforming themselves to meet the requirements of the new e-business era. To ensure their future success, it is critical for those companies to understand that e-commerce is transitioning from a *fringe market phenomenon,* dominated by innovators and early adopters, to a fixture of the *mainstream market,* dominated by pragmatic customers seeking new forms of value.

Why is it so difficult for established companies to see the writing on the wall? Primarily because most of them want to "stick to the knitting," that is, to continue to do what has made them successful. They don't want to cannibalize existing product lines in which they've succeeded for years. Established companies tend to fall back on the simple formulas of the traditional business models: lower cost, operational efficiency, increased product variety. Technology has historically been viewed as part of the support process, not as the core driver or competency of the business. But as we've seen, technological advances are changing the definition of value. Established firms must learn to take advantage of emerging new technologies to create and provide the new forms of value customers will increasingly demand.

Challenging Traditional Definitions of Value

Customers require the companies with which they do business to continuously improve, particularly in the following areas:

- *Speed of service.* Service can never be too fast. In the real-time world, a premium is placed on instant, accurate, and adaptive responsiveness to customer needs. Visionary companies embrace the continual need for change and consistently deconstruct and reconstruct their products and processes to provide faster service.

- *Convenience.* Customers value the convenience of one-stop shopping. In addition, they want better integration of the order entry, fulfillment, and delivery cycles. In other words, customers demand better integration along the supply chain.

- *Personalization.* Customers want firms to treat them as individuals. Little or no choice in the products offered is being replaced. Today's technology gives companies the ability to provide precisely what customers want, made to their specifications.

- *Price.* "Too affordable" is meaningless. Companies that offer unique services for a reasonable price are flourishing, benefiting from a flood of new buyers.

In every business, managers should ask how they could use the new technology to create a new value proposition for the customer. This is the key to successful entry into the e-commerce world. Many firms, such as Domino's Pizza, Dell, and Amazon.com, have already succeeded. These visionary companies meet new customer expectations by improving products, cutting prices, and enhancing service quality on a continuous basis.

In 1960, Thomas S. Monaghan founded Domino's Pizza with a lofty mission. Monaghan wanted to be the leader in off-premise pizza convenience to consumers around the world. Domino's owes its success to a few simple precepts. The company offers a limited menu through carryout and delivery, and every pizza is delivered with a Total Satisfaction Guarantee. In other words, customers not completely satisfied with their pizza experience will be given a replacement pizza or a refund. By raising the quality of service and the level of innovation that customers expect, market leaders like Domino's are continually pushing the competitive frontiers into uncharted territories and are driving their slower-moving competitors back to the drawing board.

The ability to view the world from the customer's perspective often prevents visionary companies from starting in the wrong place and ending up at the wrong destination. Innovators look for what new things customers value rather than focusing on differences among customers. Often, companies, new and old, rely too much on market-segment analysis and forget that segmentation techniques work well only in stable settings. Market-segment analyses are difficult to execute in today's turbulent environment, in which the value proposition continually changes.

Changing the Notion of Value: e-Commerce

In subtle ways, e-commerce is fundamentally changing the customer value proposition. In recent years, technological innovations, such as the Web and e-commerce, have accelerated value innovation in the service dimensions of speed, convenience, personalization, and price, thereby substantially changing the underlying value proposition. These technological innovations and resulting new forms of customer value mean that companies must either develop or acquire the talent and competencies on which the value-creating technology depends.

What do we mean by value innovation? Faced with similar products, too many options, and lack of time, the customer's natural reaction is to simplify the effort by looking for the cheapest, the most familiar, or the best-quality product. Obviously, companies target one of these niches. A product or service that is 98 percent as good, unfamiliar, or costs 50 cents more is lost in a no-man's land against a competitor whose product or service leads in one of these categories. Companies that follow such middle-of-the-road strategies will underperform, leading us to the fourth rule of e-business:

> *Using e-commerce, companies can listen to their customers and become "the cheapest," "the most familiar," or "the best."*

"The cheapest" isn't synonymous with inferior quality. Today, the cheapest product or service provides a value-oriented format, with many of the inventory and distribution costs taken out or drastically reduced, such as Southwest's "No Frills Flying" and Wal-Mart's "Every Day Low Prices." The best example of such a value-oriented format is Wal-Mart, which helped define a revolution in American retailing with its discount superstore format. This format, combined with friendly customer service, superb inventory management, and an entrepreneurial corporate atmosphere, helped the company steamroll competition. Recently, Wal-Mart has taken "the cheapest" model and applied it to the grocery business. The company is experimenting with 40,000-square-foot Wal-Mart Neighborhood Markets that will compete head-on with grocers.

When buying "the most familiar," customers know what they're getting. McDonald's is a great example of a familiar brand. Visitors to foreign countries often seek local McDonald's just because they know what to expect. It took the brand giants of the past, such as McDonald's and Coca-Cola, decades to make their products household names. By contrast, it's taken so-called Internet megabrands, such as America Online and Yahoo!, only a few years to carve out strong identities using today's superb communications technology.

Being "the best" involves reinventing service processes to enhance quality, being able to turn the company on a dime to move in more profitable directions, and raising relationships with customers and suppliers to unprecedented levels of cooperation and trust. The most obvious example of the best in exceptional service is American Express, exemplified in its Return Protection Plan. This customer benefit refunds card members for items purchased with an Amex card within 90 days from the date of purchase, if the store won't accept returns. Amex will refund the card member's account for the purchase price, up to $300 per item, up to $1,000 per year. By continuously generating innovative improvements to customer service and benefits, Amex retains high customer loyalty.

Wherever firms are in the value continuum—from cheapest to most familiar to the best—customers want continuous innovation. Bill Gates calls it the "What-have-you-done-for-me-lately?" syndrome. Faced with the burden of increasing time pressure and decreasing customer service levels, customers are no longer content with the status quo. They want companies to innovate customer service and benefits, pushing their service to new levels that make the customer's life easier in a specific way. Clearly, companies are caught in the midst of a tornado of increasing customer demands and spiraling business transformation.

Learning about Value Innovation: The Book Retailing Industry

The story of the Internet book retailing war between market leader Barnes & Noble (B&N) and Amazon.com is one of the most written about in recent years. At stake is a significant share of the worldwide book market, estimated to be more than $75 billion, with international sales some 30 percent of the several players' online business. Given the high stakes, Amazon.com forced entrenched leader B&N—and to a lesser extent Borders—to respond to its challenge.

Conventional logic dictated that Amazon.com would be dominated by B&N on the Internet because of its high name recognition, already advanced fulfillment process—it can leverage its catalog experience—and low prices. (In contrast to smaller players, B&N has volume purchase agreements with publishers.) One would also assume that online customers fit the same profile as those who shop in stores, that their needs are the same, right?

Wrong! The needs and demographics of the online customer are different. In preliminary research, B&N found that online book shoppers buy five to ten times as many books as do traditional book buyers. Online book customers have an interesting profile. They live in remote or international locations. They're interested in incremental price savings (an estimated "all-in" savings of around 15 percent), they're pressed for time, and they don't mind waiting up to three days for delivery. The demographics of online shoppers clearly distinguish what they value from their off-line counterparts.[6]

Identifying new sources of customer value is an important step, but it's not enough. Firms need to invigorate the complete customer experience. For example, Amazon.com makes the mundane process of comparing, buying, and receiving books interesting, convenient, and easy to use. The ability to streamline the end-to-end experience provides a complete solution to customer needs and sets visionary companies apart. This focus on enhanced customer experience leads to the fifth rule of e-business:

Don't use technology just to create the product. Use technology to innovate, entertain, and enhance the entire experience surrounding the product: from selecting and ordering to receiving and service.

Amazon.com has competed by continuously innovating the customer experience. Amazon.com bundled experience innovation with elements of brand building: Layout and linkages are logical, intuitive, and, just as important, entertaining. To create a satisfying shopping experience, the company created an e-retail infrastructure that meets the needs of customers. For example, titles that are difficult to find, relatively unpopular, or out of print can be traced through a special-orders department. When a customer inquires about an out-of-print book, that department contacts suppliers to check availability and, if a copy is located, notifies the customer by e-mail for approval of the price and condition prior to shipping the book. This level of service for a national and international audience is unprecedented in the book retailing business.

Amazon.com also provides third-party content, a valuable part of the book purchase process: author interviews and prepublishing information, which build a sense of urgency and also help cement the relationship with heavy users (bibliophiles, in particular); instant order confirmation; customized search engines; editorial analyses; and carefully managed delivery expectations, which set up the user for a positive surprise. These elements combine to create a rich customer experience and have resulted in a high customer loyalty rate of more than 60 percent.

At this stage, it's too early to declare the winner in the online book wars. At least 200 Web sites let you buy books, music CDs, and videos. It's fair to say, however, that the winners will need to provide value by finding the most interesting and simple way for customers to use the Web. The winners will also provide the best level of service in terms of price, speed, and control. They have to do all this because it's so easy to point and click on the competition's Web site.

As the business environment becomes more digital, established firms need to think like Amazon.com. These firms need to assess what they need to do to reset consumer expectations and experiences. Why reset experiences? Traditional customer experiences have temporal and geographic bounds: Customers must go to a specific store at a specific location between certain hours. But the online experience is quite different—largely virtual and nonspatial—and it needs to become familiar, informative, and usable.

However, implementing an effective customer experience means more than having an attractive, interactive front end. In the first phase of e-commerce, many firms got carried away by the interactive front end so easily generated on the Web. They ignored the importance of the integrated business back end, which drives the enterprise to success. Effective experiences through front-end to back-end integration is the central theme of e-business.

What does the Amazon.com example mean for executives? Amazon.com has identified and innovated one component of value—user experience—to a level of excellence that puts its competitors on the defensive. Amazon's dominance in feature innovation forces competitors to continually play catch-up and to juggle the challenges of their brick-and-mortar enterprises. Jeff Bezos isn't unique. He's following the footsteps of others who took advantage of technology to build giant businesses from scratch: Sam Walton, Bill Gates, Philip Anschutz, and Charles Schwab, to name only a few.

The role of the new-age CEO is to help the company understand the threat posed by value migration, the shifting of what customers desire in products and services, and in the experiences involved with these products and services. Some industries will be profoundly affected by this migration, whereas others will feel little impact. It's vital that executives monitor the impact of digitizing processes in their industries. To do that, executives should answer the following questions.

- *Is there an Amazon.com that can squeeze margins in your business? If not, can you create one?*

- *Are any new entrants in your industry leveraging the Web to rewire the customer experience and change service expectations?*

Cautious executives need to watch out for a new generation of players attempting to harness the potential efficiencies of the Web. Don't take your industry's conditions as a given—as a static environment not subject to change. You must understand that the technological advances can rapidly create conditions in which companies that once were king of the mountain can wake up one day to find no mountain at all.

Creating New Experiences: The Case of Microsoft

Microsoft anticipated changing customer experiences by reengineering several value chains, including travel (Expedia), automotive sales (CarPoint), real estate (HomeAdvisor), and finance (Investor). The foundation of these new value chains is the Microsoft Network (MSN) infrastructure. Let's meet these new infomediaries.

- Expedia provides travelers with a large number of resources and tools, including an interactive travel agent, a fare tracker, a hotel directory with maps, travel reviews and tips, weather information, and even a currency converter.

- CarPoint provides a wealth of automotive information, such as news, reviews, dealer invoice information, complete model listings, and a dealer locator.

- Investor is designed to help individual investors research, plan, execute, and monitor their investments. Investor supplies news, commentary, quotes, portfolio tracking, historical information, and market information, as well as direct links to online trading with Charles Schwab, E*TRADE, Fidelity Investments, and AmeriTrade.

- HomeAdvisor facilitates the home-buying process by arranging mortgage sales over the Web and offering information useful to potential home buyers, including real estate agent referrals, home sale listings, and a property valuation estimator.

According to a Microsoft strategy memo, the target markets of these online services are vast. Microsoft plans to win a major share of the sales and distribution charges in the markets for airline tickets ($100 billion), automobile sales ($334 billion), and retail goods ($1.2 trillion).[7]

Expedia illustrates how Microsoft is reshaping the economics of the markets it's entering. Expedia is selling more than $35 million in tickets and travel services every week, making it one of the largest online travel agencies. Expedia has established itself as a travel agency and negotiated deals with American Express and major airlines to sell tickets for a fraction of the standard travel agency commission rate.[8]

What is the value provided to the Expedia customer? As mentioned earlier, superior end-to-end integration differentiates winners from those that are second best. Today, travelers find reams of badly organized information that is often difficult to find or time consuming to gather. Expedia engineered the customer experience by looking at the customer's needs and then working back along the fulfillment chain, changing it based on the customer's requirements. Such an outside-in strategy requires engaging the customer's perspective and reworking inward into the company's capabilities and direction. The Expedia strategy is simple. By focusing on selection, ease of use, and aggressive pricing, Expedia builds customer traffic. Integrated, personalized service keeps customers coming back. However, profits remain elusive.

Microsoft is creating an entirely new set of service dynamics in a variety of industries. The company stands as a great example of a market leader that survived a competitive attack from upstart Netscape and came out of the fray leaner, meaner, and stronger. *Is there a lesson to be learned from Microsoft about how to manage in a fast-moving environment?*

Microsoft appears to have mastered the art of driving in turbulent weather. It's not difficult to drive a car fast on a crowded freeway in good weather; you do so without giving it much thought. But the worse the weather and heavier the traffic, the more frequently you have to change direction and speed. Therefore, few of us are capable of driving well at high speeds in inclement weather. Similarly, few companies are capable of thriving in demanding, changing conditions.

Engineering the End-to-End Value Stream: e-Business Webs

As discussed earlier, a company must be capable of engineering the entire end-to-end value stream to ensure future success. This concept is neither radical nor new. Experienced managers know to redefine business designs and processes when implementing new forms of value. What distinguishes reengineering efforts in the new era is the emergence of more intricate and committed relationships among business entities. As a result, we see the widespread use of synergistic clusters, business ecosystems, coalitions, cooperative networks, or outsourcing to create end-to-end value streams in the new environment. Business webs (BW),[9] as these networks of relationships are known, link businesses, customers, and suppliers to create a unique business organism. This trend leads to the sixth rule of e-business:

> *The business design of the future increasingly uses reconfigurable e-business models to best meet customers' needs.*

For example, Amazon.com, CarPoint, Travelocity, and other e-commerce start-ups are essentially complex e-business webs built for the sole purpose of organizing and energizing cross-enterprise relationships to create end-to-end value for the customer. Competition is no longer between companies but between BWs.

BW strategists see companies as part of an extended business family that pools the resources and benefits of each company's expertise. A BW can play a powerful role in attacking market leaders, and new entrants are using BWs to gain access to resources, customers, technology, and products. BWs are not restricted to just e-commerce start-ups but rather are everywhere. Large established companies too are moving to the BW model. But the transition is at a slower pace because BWs are difficult to integrate on a large scale, and coordination among partners can prove troublesome. Therefore, large companies are taking an incremental approach to BW implementation by first concentrating on creating flexible supplier communities vis-à-vis supply chain management.

The following strategic problem in the automobile retailing industry helps illustrate the challenge posed by e-business Webs for car manufacturers worldwide. Buying a new vehicle is the second-largest purchase the average consumer makes.[10] Consequently, the new-vehicle retailing business is fiercely competitive. A significant number of dealers in the same geographic area compete not only with dealers franchised by other manufacturers but also with dealers affiliated with the same manufacturer. These factors have fostered industry consolidation, considerably reducing the number of dealerships.

Although vehicle purchases attract significant consumer dollars ($534 billion in 1999 sales), the sales process has not changed substantially in the last 25 years. The major source of consumer irritation with car buying is the inconsistency of prices. For example, Bill goes to a dealership and buys a Lexus. As often happens, the price he gets is substantially different from that Beverly gets on the same day at the same dealer.

But the presence of the Web is changing how automobiles will be purchased in the future. With its interactive capabilities and easy access to automotive information, the Web has spawned Internet-based vehicle marketing services, such as Auto-By-Tel, an online/telephone sales intermediary.

Using primarily Web-based technology Auto-By-Tel has attempted to change car buying and selling. The business proposition is simple. For customers, Auto-By-Tel offers a painless, straightforward, money-saving alternative for purchasing and financing cars. For participating auto dealers, Auto-By-Tel provides a cost-efficient, volume-enhancing sales system.

What does the new purchasing process look like? Customers research—free of charge—the car they want at Edmunds.com, where they obtain the factory-to-dealer price. The increasing consumer use of the Web has encouraged information providers to post automotive information online and to let consumers do the research. By researching car purchases on Edmund's site, consumers can quickly determine a fair price for the model they want. They then fill out a form on Auto-By-Tel's Web site, specifying make and model, options, description of the trade-in vehicle if appropriate, need for loan financing, and so forth. Auto-By-Tel then forwards the information to a dealer in the purchaser's area; that dealer then offers the shopper a quote on the vehicle. Armed with the accurate information needed to bargain for the best price, trade-in value, and loan interest rate, consumers can cut favorable deals.

The information service is free to customers. But dealers pay annual and monthly fees to be marketed by Auto-By-Tel and for exclusive territorial rights. Auto-By-Tel's business model illustrates the power of the business web. Its model features partnerships with an information site, an insurance company, a warranty company, and a car accessories company. Also, Auto-By-Tel makes money from Web customer referrals.

What does this new trend mean for traditional car companies? Worrisome: In a speech at the National Automobile Dealers Association's annual meeting, Robert Eaton, then Chrysler chairman, urged dealers to acknowledge that the Internet is changing car-buying behavior forever by giving car buyers more information and choices. As Eaton said, "The customer is going to grab control of the process, and we're all going to salute smartly and do exactly what the customer tells us if we want to stay in business."[11] Eaton's blunt statement succinctly expresses the power of customer-centric buying processes.

This change in customer buying behavior is forcing the Big Three automakers to rethink the future of car dealerships. Today, automakers must ask the following fundamental questions about the nature of customer value, questions that shake the very foundation of their industry.

- Is online car buying a fad or a new consumer trend? If customers increasingly seek to purchase cars online, what kind of business model is needed to support this process?

- If the current business model for car dealerships doesn't provide customer value, what will the dealership of the future look like?

- If customers want to do business online, what kind of e-business applications and technology architecture are needed to support it?

How the automobile industry answers these strategic questions will shape the future of dealer networks. The industry stands today as a great example of the rapid evolution of e-commerce from an untested novelty into a mainstream information and transaction channel. If these manufacturers want to continue to control their destiny, they must understand how their industry is being transformed in this new era. As they ponder the e-revolution's implications, automobile leaders are rapidly gaining the insight required for them to shape their future strategy and for determining the skills and competencies needed for building the new value stream.

Harvesting the Partnerships: e-Business Core Competencies

The e-business environment is one of intricate and dynamic change. New business environments require finding or developing personnel with critical skills required to get the job done. For many organizations, outsourcing their need for core competencies has been the answer.

The argument for outsourcing is simple: Individual companies cannot do everything well. True enough. In the first generation of outsourcing, the focus was on gaining efficiency and reducing costs, primarily in business processes and support functions, which weren't the company's primary-line work. Administration, human resources, accounting, and often IT (information technology) functions were the targets for outsourcing. For example, with the increasing complexity of computers and networks, more and more firms began outsourcing their technology management. In the 1990s, the biggest beneficiaries of this trend were computer service firms, such as IBM, Andersen Consulting, and EDS.[12] In the first generation, the business's core competence—its line of work—was never outsourced, for the reason that turning it over to "outsiders" who didn't understand the firm's customers and their needs would be extremely risky.

In the second generation, the outsourcing boom extends well beyond data center management. In recent years, outsourcing in the form of contract manufacturing has caught on considerably as companies search for ways to cut costs. Examples of contract manufacturing abound in the high-tech industry: Solectron, Flextronics, and SCI Systems. As a result, outsourcing is changing the nature of the relationship between contract manufacturers and the original equipment manufacturers (OEMs). In the past, these two groups danced like detached partners, but now they're dancing cheek to cheek. Why? With the shared objective of pleasing customers, the best relationship for both parties is to act as a single company in a truly cooperative and integrated manner. Commitment and above all trust are critical to the success of these relationships. The participating firms must share sensitive design information, link internal applications systems, and provide shared services with partners throughout the supply chain. In a growing number of cases, outsourcers finish the product, slap on the logo, and ship it to the user or distributor. It's the wave of the future, and it's happening now. As they face complex business challenges, companies are increasingly farming out critical tasks to cut time to market. In today's world, successfully facing these complex challenges means building trusting, long-term partnerships. It is difficult for businesses today to succeed by "going it alone."

Increasingly, new e-business entrants use a strategy of GBF, or get big fast. This strategy uses outsourcing alliances as a business model for gaining a stronger market position against a proven industry leader. The experience gained from the successful e-business conversions of recent years has made implementing manufacturing outsourcing alliances less painful, especially if both sides are using similar business application software. This GBF trend makes every market leader vulnerable, but especially distributors, because new online intermediaries can replicate their business model. These distribution start-ups differentiate themselves in two key ways: (1) They're easy to do business with, which they make a top priority; and (2) they add value through innovative services, such as inventory management. Ease of doing business is critical to their success as costs go down, even if the new entrant does not lower prices.

In the third generation, companies outsource in the form of investment partnerships. As traditional brick-and-mortar companies wake up to the impact of the Internet on their industries, they're turning to venture capitalists (VC) for help with funding their online strategies. Staples has taken the VC route to obtain both funding and Web acumen for its new e-commerce division. According to Staples.com President Jeanne Lewis, the major reason for turning to venture capital firms rather than relying on resources from its parent company was access to "advice, contacts, and Web savvy" such firms command.[13]

Staples is not the first retailer to launch an e-commerce company outside the mother ship. More and more Fortune 500 companies are aligning with venture capital firms to create stand-alone Web businesses. After two homegrown efforts to build a Wal-Mart Web presence fizzled, Wal-Mart is spinning out Walmart.com with Accel Partners. In another example, Procter and Gamble (P&G) combined with Institutional Venture Partners (IVP) to invest $50 million in Reflect.com. Reflect.com is the first personalized line of beauty products and services created for and available exclusively through the Internet. IVP will invest $15 million for a 15 percent equity stake in Reflect.com, with P&G retaining a controlling interest. However, Reflect.com will be managed like a start-up, on an Internet timetable and with the possibility of an IPO.[14]

This third generation of outsourcing alliances has a variety of names, including the previously mentioned e-business webs, venture *kieretsu*, clusters, and coalitions. Although successful outsourcing strategies differ widely from industry to industry, all share a common purpose. Each strategy seeks to nullify the advantages of the industry leader by using outsourcing to quickly create a reputation, powerful economies of scale, cumulative learning, and preferred access to suppliers or channels. Amazon.com successfully attacked Barnes & Noble by using this strategy, and Yahoo! used it to overtake Microsoft Network in the portal business.

Complex outsourcing arrangements are not optional anymore. They represent the only way for companies to fill the voids in their arsenals of talent. However, few guidelines exist for managers to follow when creating new business designs that leverage outsourcing. This brings us to the seventh rule of e-business:

 The goal of new e-business designs is for companies to create flexible alliances that not only off-load costs but also make customers ecstatic.

Creating the New Technoenterprise: Integrate, Integrate, Integrate

Application integration is the key to e-business. If a sale comes into the company from its Web site, the Web application must trigger the appropriate responses in the company's sales, accounting, inventory management, and distribution applications.

End-to-end process and application integration is not as easy as it sounds. Successful process integration requires a major application overhaul in order to develop an integrated front-end/back-end infrastructure. So far, most firms don't have fully integrated infrastructures, and the resulting process inefficiencies, inaccuracies, and application inflexibility can be seen everywhere.

This absence of an integrated application architecture, although not new, becomes more critical with the advent of e-commerce. In the old business model, when customers were given little choice and all competitors were equally "bad," a company had incentive to do a better job. In the new e-business era, new entrants are flooding an already competitive marketplace, presenting customers with more choices. As a result, customers are no longer willing to tolerate the inefficient service stemming largely from a company's unwillingness to enhance the quality of its systems and processes.

Faced with the threat of losing customers, integrated infrastructure problems rocket to the top of the business agenda. The rise of e-commerce is forcing a redefinition of enterprise architecture. Managers are becoming increasingly aware of the enterprise-wide nature of e-commerce's business requirements. These managers are realizing how short the road is to e-commerce failure if they attempt to apply piecemeal solutions to supply chain process problems encountered by their customers and suppliers.

Forward-thinking companies are beginning to understand the enormity of the task ahead and realize that a number of barriers must be eliminated before they're ready to use e-commerce to their competitive advantage. Managers also realize how much more difficult it is to try and turn an old infrastructure around than to build a new one from scratch. This is "the transformation paradox."

However, a powerful catalyst for e-business is the fact that many firms have reached the limits of automating isolated functional processes. Although these firms have improved cost, quality, speed, and service, differentiation on the basis of these isolated variables is more difficult to come by. To maintain future profitability, these companies must look to the benefits attained from addressing enterprise-wide process improvements, which support increased organizational agility through integrated business applications.[15] From an enterprise perspective, corporate agility is a company's ability to meet the needs of the market without excessive costs, time, organizational disruption, or loss of performance.

Is this simply old wine in a new bottle? No. Today's business climate demands that companies live and breathe flexibility, agility, and integration when dealing with customers. For the e-business architecture to succeed, its elements must be aligned with the customers' most important priorities, which include variety, quality, competitive price, and fast delivery. An isolated functional model satisfies none of these needs. Consequently, the love affair with silo-oriented IT infrastructure is being replaced with a new passion: integrated customer-centric models capable of supporting complex business designs.

To facilitate change, companies need an effective business design that allows them to take on new strategic imperatives more quickly, and more comfortably. Such a business design would require companies to design their application architectures to be flexible enough to accommodate the continual changes the emerging e-business world presents. A number of barriers prevent businesses from developing this business design. These barriers include process inefficiencies owing to legacy applications, lack of leadership, and fragmented and distributed information.

Removing these barriers isn't easy. But there is little choice. The functional model of the past can't deliver for today's world. As technological integration problems continue to create potholes in the smooth road of business function, managers eventually run out of asphalt and ideas. Enter e-business.

Are You Ready for e-Business Integration?

Stories about start-ups and established companies that hit a wall because their e-business architectures couldn't accommodate rapid and drastic change are legion. Fast-growing companies are likely to stumble when their architectures fail to expand quickly enough to serve new customers cost-efficiently. Established companies can lose market share if their application infrastructures lack the flexibility to service customers in new channels as effortlessly as do those of their competitors.

Today, many senior managers struggle with the question, What kind of e-business architecture—vision, strategy, cross-functional processes, integrated applications, and IT infrastructure—is needed to support our new way of doing business? Most executives are clueless about emerging technologies at a time when it's necessary—even critical—to adopt them. Generally, these executives rely on their IT people to advise them. But executives who delegate responsibility for relating technology to overall business strategy to IT management do so at their own peril. Executives can eliminate their strategic blind spots by taking responsibility for understanding the implications of up-and-coming technologies and anticipating when they'll affect business strategy. *The decision to develop an e-business architecture is a business, not a technical, decision.*

Some companies are quite adept at creating business value from technology. For example, Federal Express sees itself at the crossroads of e-business. The company, now known as FDX Corporation after merging with Caliber Logistics, spends about $1 billion a year on information technology, which buys not just a system to track packages but also something much more valuable. The company can position itself to be the warehouse, fulfillment, and shipping departments for any company.

The FDX partnership with National Semiconductor is another good example.[16] Orders from the chip maker's home office in Santa Clara, California, went directly to an FDX computer in Memphis, Tennessee. That's the last time National had anything to do with the order until it received confirmation from FDX. The order was sent to FDX's warehouse in Singapore, picked and packed, and then shipped by FDX. This system cut the average customer-delivery cycle from 4 weeks to 7 days and reduced distribution costs at National from 2.9 percent of sales to 1.2 percent.

FDX makes money by both managing inventory and shipping product. According to FDX, the global express market, which was $35 billion in 1996, is projected to grow to $250 billion in the next 20 years. The percentage of product shipped to meet the requirements of just-in-time manufacturing is expected to grow to more than 40 percent in 2000, up from about 25 percent in 1996. This places FDX at the convergence of two powerful market trends, which it leverages by investing in e-architecture to manage the customer's supply chain.

Smart firms like FDX and their archrival UPS have transformed themselves proactively, improving their technology infrastructure to gain advantage in the changing market. The fortunate firms scramble and adapt. Companies that cannot or will not adopt technological and process innovation to address new customer trends will either suffer significant losses or become history.[17]

In the heat of competition, e-business execution takes on new meaning and importance. As we've seen, the task of creating an effective e-business strategy and infrastructure can be daunting. Few guidelines exist to support managers in creating new business designs that leverage the application infrastructure. This brings us to the eighth rule of e-business:

For urgent e-business projects, it's easy to minimize application infrastructure needs and to focus on the glitzy front-end apps. The oversight can be costly in more ways than one.

The tough part of e-business is getting your strategy implemented. In our experience, less than 10 percent of strategies formulated are effectively executed. With a one-in-ten chance of success in the implementation of strategy, failures litter the landscape. Add to the mix the fact that upstart, innovative competitors are streaming out of the woodwork, and the plot thickens.

The New Priority: e-Business Execution Framework

Most e-business strategies are in dire straits before they are even started. Why? Because managers fail to understand the complexity of converting an e-business strategy into a working architecture. More often than not, the e-business infrastructure is a costly and aging maze of legacy applications, hardware systems, and networks. Far from making it possible to achieve strategic goals, that infrastructure can make a mockery of them.

To implement any e-business strategy, managers need to understand the elements of the e-business execution framework. This framework must

- Provide a structure for defining, communicating, and monitoring new realities

- Redesign core business processes to align with the new organizational vision

- Enable the IT infrastructure to support change, innovation, and business goals

Our goal in this book is to develop an execution framework that will help managers convert the 50,000-foot strategy into a 10,000-foot application infrastructure design. This infrastructure design is crucial for scoping the feasibility and for communicating the project's goals and objectives.

Why is this critical? The first mistake many businesses make is the failure to accurately assess the true scope of their e-business projects. IT teams are often forced to define business requirements, design the system, and build it simultaneously, without a clear definition of project scope.

This is like fighting the battle without a plan. One of the greatest strategists of all time, Sun Tzu, wrote: *"Victorious warriors win first and then go to war, while defeated warriors go to war first and then seek to win."* This quote serves as a wonderful reminder of the importance of planning.

Second, no one person is held accountable for the e-business project's success or failure. Consequently, when it becomes apparent that the project has fundamental design flaws, the finger-pointing and sidetracking begin, and CYA ("Cover Your Ass") really kicks in. Minimizing this lack of accountability is absolutely job #1 for successful projects.

A vast majority of technology investments fail to deliver the expected returns because they were poorly linked to long-term plans, the strategies and tactics used were flawed, or the organization failed to understand everything needed to support its objective. This failure is clearly a management problem, not a technology issue. And this fact leads us to the ninth rule of e-business:

The ability to plan an e-business infrastructure course swiftly and to implement it ruthlessly are key to success. Ruthless execution is the norm.

Engineering an integrated yet agile infrastructure requires a number of critical choices. Chief executive, information, and financial officers (CEOs, CIOs, and CFOs) in mature firms are acutely aware that the business systems they are mandated to implement are often extremely difficult to create. It's not that the technology isn't good; it's that somewhere between the problem and the execution, the objective was lost or changed, or it wasn't there to begin with. The same attention given to understanding a customer's needs is required by management when identifying the business's infrastructure needs. If the business requirements are well defined and are not changed every quarter, implementation should not fail.

Changing strategy direction and scope frequently causes even the best architecture to fail. Companies must change the way they approach planning and execution in the e-world. The link between planning and infrastructure must be tighter. Traditional planning assumes that many variables, such as technology, are static in the marketplace, that competitive boundaries are fixed, and that customers are rational. As a result, traditional planning assumes that the end goal is a fixed target, not a moving one. Given the dynamic nature of strategy in e-business, new approaches to managing application infrastructure have become the focus of executive attention.

Needed: A New Generation of e-Business Leaders

Peter Drucker once described strategy as a commodity and execution as an art. In the fast-paced and often mystifying world of e-business, executives can't afford to be passive participants. Managers need to look past the hype and to realize how e-business is reshaping the structure of entire industries, creating niches for new sets of infomediaries, and enabling businesses with well-executed business designs to take quantum leaps forward while those without them suffer and lag behind. Who is responsible for developing these e-business capabilities? Everyone and no one. This responsibility vacuum is senior management's opportunity to play a leadership role.

Continued innovation in processes is one of the best tools a corporation has for adding value to its web of suppliers and customers. However, the radical change inherent when implementing new processes intimidates some CEOs and senior managers. Often, they have a can't-teach-an-old-dog-new-tricks mentality. Although spending on technology has reached record levels, these executives continue to put their businesses at risk by not aligning their business processes with the technology. In other words, e-business implementation is where the rubber hits the road.

Leadership is especially important when the future is uncertain. e-Business execution is by far the toughest thing a manager has to do. Many managers are good at planning strategy and looking at things strategically but not at implementing a strategy. Implementation takes leadership, commitment, and backbone. Almost always, the commitment to change happens at the top. For your e-business strategy to succeed, you must have a champion, and your e-business champion has to be your senior management team. Without its sponsorship, the implementation will fail. It is that team's responsibility to lead the firm into the e-business era, using your strategy—and senior management had better be committed to it.

Process innovation has to be coupled with infrastructure innovation. The rapid pace of high-tech innovation is forcing senior managers to assess the application infrastructures' ability to meet the firm's future business needs. The ongoing assessment of technological readiness is crucial to reducing business risk. The problem with readiness is that there's a lot to do and not much time to do it, given the short life span of new applications. Yet a clear understanding, from top to bottom, of how applications can support growth is critical to the future of any large organization. Keeping ahead of the competitive pack means developing a superior understanding within your management team in order to construct the right strategy. This leads us to the tenth rule of e-business:

> ▶ *The tough task for management is to align business strategies, processes, and applications quickly, correctly, and all at once. Strong leadership is imperative.*

As business flexibility drives the evolution of e-business, one of a leader's greatest challenges is gaining an intimate understanding of the products and service delivery channels in which his or her business participates. This understanding is crucial for answering the following question: *Do we stay with the status quo of how we do business, seek a challenge in the relatively safe haven of improving the existing product mix, or return to the chaos, risk, and uncertainty of new products and services?*

Tough choice, right? Not really. Meeting new customer needs does demand a new mindset. But it is the mindset on which the company was founded. The task facing managers today is how to recapture their firms' entrepreneurial spirit. Joseph Schumpeter, a professor of economics at Harvard in the early twentieth century, spoke of "creative destruction" that exists at the heart of entrepreneurial activity. By "destruction" he meant breaking free from the habits of the past and the inertia of the tried and true. Nearly a century later, Schumpeter's words are still valuable. They can help managers realize that much of the conventional management wisdom to which they adhere might work very well in stable environments but is not always appropriate when attempting to create new business models in an age of volatility.

Memo to the CEO

Whether in Berlin or Bombay, Kuala Lumpur or Kansas City, or San Francisco or Seoul, companies are developing new models to operate competitively in a digital economy. These models are structured yet agile, global yet local; they concentrate on maximizing the risk-adjusted return from both knowledge and technology assets.

Many leading companies are aggressively pursuing e-business. Arthur Ryan, CEO of Prudential Insurance, has publicly stated that his company will spend more than $1 billion updating its IT infrastructure. The spending will target development of an e-business architecture that can deliver diverse sources of competitive advantage to the company and enhanced value to its customers. Smart CEOs realize that innovation in information technology may be the single most important tool they have to advance their organizations.

However, CEOs must be aware that the real threat to the firm's future success comes not just from outside in the form a changing competitive landscape but from inside the company as well. The internal threat to future success is the reluctance of management to take ownership of technological change through understanding the technologies involved and the impact their implementation will have on the firm's operations. In order to swim the unknown and often treacherous waters of technology, true leaders will plunge into them; true leaders know that they cannot manage e-business conversion at a distance by hiring consultants or other so-called experts and giving them adequate resources. e-Business methods and its supporting technology must not be a black box to managers. If it remains so, they will lose their ability to position the company, respond to market changes, and guide the internal innovations required for success.

Today, the executive committee must see around corners, anticipate competitors coming from left field, and execute strategy at breakneck speed. Unfortunately, the classic economic "theory of the firm" provides little insight into the dynamics of the new digital economy. Yesterday's successful companies or Harvard Business School case studies are of limited help in a fluid marketplace.

Today's business leaders must also understand that the e-business concept encompasses the entire business model for how a company functions. Although it's not critically important for CEOs or senior managers to have in-depth knowledge about specific technologies, it is important for them to *understand these technologies conceptually* to enable their close involvement in shaping and directing how the firm's e-business architecture is developed and used. To fight the new war, CEOs must *listen, understand, respond, and learn.* Although they know what strategies to use to achieve their goals, CEOs need help figuring out how to support their efforts with emerging technology. By working hard to create an integrated business/technology plan and championing it through implementation, the CEO and senior management can have a significant impact on the company's bottom line and prospects for future growth.

All we can say is that you ain't seen nothing yet! Even the most far-sighted person 5 years ago would have been wrong about today's business landscape. Technological and process innovation are causing today's businesses to change more rapidly than ever before.[18] The next decade will be even more suspenseful and action packed than the past decade. Not since the industrial changes accompanying the emergence of electric power or the first assembly line has there been such profound change in business and markets.

To truly appreciate the journey that lies ahead, businesses must view e-commerce not as an interesting side aspect to their operations but as their vital tool for successfully engaging the future. Welcome to the new era! Welcome to e-business!

CHAPTER TWO

Spotting
e-Business Trends

What to Expect

Never mind what did or didn't work in the past. The landscape has changed. Managers need to concentrate on the new trends that anchor profitable business strategies in the future.

Managers can no longer afford to believe that today looks like yesterday and that tomorrow will be more of the same. They must learn to separate the few worthwhile kernels— trends—from bushels of chaff—fads. Separating fads from trends is critical for e-business strategy. The essential difference is that trends are global, tend to last approximately 5 to 10 years, and may evolve dramatically.

In this chapter, we present 20 trends—in technology, consumer buying habits, service and processes, organizations, and enterprise technology—that will shape the future of business. We identified these trends by analyzing present-day social, economic, and technological transformations that hold the greatest potential for success in the future.

Trend spotting helps you seize tomorrow's opportunities before the competition does and to capitalize on them before the landscape shifts again. It's an art and skill you can learn. Analyze how these trends impact your e-business efforts.

Things change. They always have and always will. And although there's no simple way to deal with change, the consequence of pretending that change won't happen is always the same: disaster.

To create effective strategies, companies must spot trends quickly. Trend spotting requires managers to learn to identify and to take advantage of discontinuous change the future inevitably brings and the resulting unsettling tectonic shifts arriving on an uncertain schedule. This provides an entirely new landscape for managers to navigate, and only the trend spotters can hope to conquer it.

The Achilles' heel of large corporations is often their inability to spot trends and to act on them quickly. Warren Buffett, the legendary investor, has a knack for articulating such conundrums: "The rearview mirror is always clearer than the windshield." Michael Eisner, CEO of Disney, said that if Disney does not discern consumer trends, Tomorrowland could become Yesterdayland before they know it.[1] Benjamin Franklin said it even more succinctly: "Look before, or you'll find yourself behind."

Accurately identifying trends helps businesses analyze and synthesize consumer behavior, eliminate uncertainty, and identify new opportunities. For example, Sam Walton, the founder of Wal-Mart, saw the rise of self-service in the 1960s and capitalized on it before anyone else did. Consumers were willing to accept self-help in return for lower prices. As a result, forward-looking Kmart and Wal-Mart seized the trend long before department stores did and so were rewarded with significant market share. At the same time, labor shortages in the low-wage service industry made it difficult for retailers to hire and retain good employees. The resulting poor service and lack of product knowledge among retail employees further accelerated the trend toward consumer self-service.

Trends that transform the business world are not new. The technological revolution of the late nineteenth and early twentieth centuries is a classic example. During this period, the world economy underwent a turbulent process of shifting labor and capital from a slow-growth agricultural economy to one dominated by new technologies, such as the internal combustion engine and electrification. More recently, during the 1970s and 1980s, the most significant trends included increasing global competition, greater demand for quality and process improvement, shorter product life cycles, and the need for a more flexible work force. Many of these trends are now considered boilerplate, and experienced managers understand them well.

In the 1990s, the most impactful trend was the rapid emergence of the Internet. With 50 million people connected in only 5 years, the Internet has become the most rapidly accepted communications medium ever.[2] It took the telephone 70 years, radio 40 years, and television 15 years to reach that milestone. Initially, the Internet's potential seemed limited to its function as a data network, but that is no longer the case. The Internet is a sales and distribution channel and is facilitating e-commerce, the ability to do business over the Web. e-Commerce is further enabling the integration of previously isolated information industry components. This integration of data, content, storage, networks, business applications, and consumer devices is facilitating the convergence of consumer electronics, television, publishing, telecommunications, and computer business sectors. New forms of value are being created. The Internet tsunami will soon impact every facet of our lives, personal and business.

Technology is shifting power to buyers. e-Commerce is changing the channels through which consumers and businesses have traditionally bought and sold goods and services. What are the benefits to this change? The e-channel provides sellers with access to a global audience, the ability to operate with minimal infrastructure, reduced overhead, and greater economies of scale; consumers, with a broad selection, convenience, and competitive pricing. Consequently, a growing number of consumers are embracing the Web, buying products, trading securities, paying bills, and purchasing airline tickets. But remember: e-Commerce is in its infancy. Consumers encounter such problems as browsers crashing and call-waiting features interrupting their dial-up connections. For e-commerce to realize its full potential, it must offer overwhelming value to compensate for the short-term technological deficiencies.

As buyers embrace new channels, new organizational structures are being designed around customers or market segments. Managers must ask

- What are the implications of e-commerce on the form and function of twenty-first-century organizations?

- In the race to please customers, how will existing brick-and-mortar companies transition into e-commerce companies? Can they?

- Can existing brick-and-click or e-commerce firms ward off the threat posed by new entrants?

The tension between the old guard and rival upstarts is palpable. Consider, for example, the $21 billion U.S. toy industry, which is well suited to online sales. Toys usually are small and easy to ship, and kids don't need to try them to know they love them. The convenience factor for busy parents boosts this retail category even more. Imagine traveling mothers or fathers being able to shop for and order toys from their hotel rooms for home delivery at 9 A.M. the following Saturday. This type of convenience is invaluable for working parents. At the forefront of firms providing this level of service are Amazon.com, FAO Schwartz, and eToys. Opposing the trend and protecting the status quo are the old guard, big retailers, such as Toys "R" Us, and manufacturers of brand names, such as Mattel, Hasbro, and Parker Brothers. The traditionalists are worried that selling to customers directly will wreak havoc on their finely tuned retail channels, pricing structures, and channel distribution.

The toy industry is not unique. As we enter the new millennium, we are also entering the new age of retail. The successful retailers will be those offering the right products in the right location or channel at the right time at a reasonable price with the right incentives to the right customer. This is a tough standard for which to aim but failure to satisfy any one of these variables can result in lost customers or declining market share. Increasingly, the tussle between Newco and Oldco centers on which firms will provide better, more efficient distribution channels and enhanced shopping experiences.

Trends Driving e-Business

The business world is transitioning from a physical reality based on atoms to a digital one of bits. As this transition from a focus on material to information occurs, the opportunities for revolution are many and largely unexplored. How should an entrepreneurial manager begin this exploration? By looking for ways to anticipate consumer and technological trends and envisioning new organizational forms that optimally serve consumer needs. A lot of what we find surprising and unpredictable is in fact a series of events played out in pretty much the same way in industry after industry. Once we see such a pattern, we can understand and predict change. From this understanding, we can build a new set of operating assumptions to build the strategy.

The savvy entrepreneurial manager must learn to distinguish true social, economic, or technical trends from "flavor-of-the-month" fads. Fads catch on quickly, spread, and then die a fast death. Eileen Shapiro defines fad surfing as "the practice of riding the crest of the latest management panacea and then paddling out again just in time to ride the next one; always absorbing for managers and lucrative for consultants; frequently disastrous for organizations."[3] With fad surfing, managers and consultants have a difficult time focusing on the proper opportunities and instead tend to approach e-business initiatives chaotically.

In contrast, trends often start slowly but spread like wildfire as consumers and companies fan the flames with their demands. As mentioned earlier, trends may evolve dramatically. For instance, consumers are changing their buying habits and embracing e-commerce faster than anyone's wildest prediction. Did you see online buying as a major trend in 1996? Consider the Web. It started slowly in 1989 in a remote lab in Switzerland, but with the advent of the Mosaic browser, the Web burst onto the mass market, taking everyone by surprise. Did you identify the Web as a major trend in 1994?

Trend spotting isn't just for entrepreneurs looking to start new companies or for marketers attempting to sell old products in new packages. It is useful for identifying new business opportunities as well. Consider the growing emphasis on well-being.[4] This trend encompasses several mini-trends: a yearning for stress relief, a desire for greater balance in one's life, a revitalized interest in family and home, and a new focus on the environment. The business response? Grocery stores now stock natural and organic foods, medicinal herbs, and ready-to-eat meals. Insurance companies are beginning to cover alternative medicine. Travel agencies increasingly sell spiritual-vacation packages. Hardware stores carry air and water purifiers and nontoxic paints.

The smart manager stands at the forefront of trends, such as the wireless, before they become mainstream. Because it takes years to steer large organizations in new directions, company captains must be aware of what lies ahead, or their companies will sink as quickly as the *Titanic*. Trend spotting has fast become "plan or be planned for."

In this chapter, we describe 20 major trends that are driving organizations to become e-business enterprises (see Table 2.1). As a manager, your ability to comprehend core trends will improve your chances of better grasping the opportunities facing your company. As you read through this chapter, ask yourself, *What is the common thread running through these major trends?* We address this question in the final section.

Table 2.1: Major Trends Driving e-Business

Trend Category	Trend
Customer	1. Faster service 2. Self-service 3. More product choices 4. Integrated solutions
e-Service	5. Integrated sales and service 6. Seamless support 7. Flexible fulfillment and convenient service delivery 8. Increased process visibility
Organizational	9. Outsourcing 10. Contract manufacturing 11. Virtual distribution
Employee	12. Hiring the best and brightest 13. Keeping talented employees
Enterprise technology	14. Integrated enterprise applications 15. Multichannel integration 16. Middleware
General technology	17. Wireless Web applications 18. Handheld computing and information appliances 19. Infrastructure convergence 20. Application service providers

Customer-Oriented Trends

Faster Service: For the Customer, Time Is Money

Customers count speed of service as a key reason for doing business with certain companies. Therefore, compress the number of steps it takes to serve customers. Customers hate delays; moreover, they hate waiting for service. Just look at the success of drive-through oil changes, drive-through fast food, and other quick-turnaround businesses. As their time quotas shrink, customers look for companies that provide faster service. Look at new trends in online and offline retailing. The message to the marketplace is clear: To succeed, companies must reduce the processing time of search, selection, order entry, and order fulfillment. Delays at any step of the process are unacceptable!

Why do delays occur? Often, they're caused by poorly designed processes that have excessive hand-offs. Consider the case of a specialty stainless steel producer that wanted to improve its unacceptable 40 percent on-time delivery record. The company identified unnecessary hand-offs as delaying the production process. For example, each order was entered into the system three times. First, customer service entered the information after writing down the buyer's specifications and used printed lists to check whether the order could be produced. Customer service then checked printed schedules to determine a ship date. Second, operations verified whether a particular grade of steel could be produced; information was then entered into operations' system. Third, production control used its own files to verify the scheduling and then reentered the information as well. This repetition caused significant delays and errors.

To solve the hand-off problem, companies are investing billions of dollars in integrated systems, which is exactly what the stainless steel producer did. After taking a close look at its problem, the company decided that one possible solution was an integrated system for most of its business operations: accepting orders, triggering receivables, sending orders to production, sending requisitions to the warehouse, updating inventory, updating accounting, and replenishing stock with suppliers. This scenario is not an isolated example but rather a common "hand-off-itis" ailment afflicting many companies.

What does this trend mean for e-business? When you consider the challenge of meeting the demands of busy, time-starved, dissatisfied consumers in an environment of hostile competition, low margins, and countless sales outlets selling similar products, it becomes clear that changing the entire business model is the only plausible strategy. e-Business applications must cut the time customers wait for service. Business processes, regardless of the applications supporting them, must also be reoriented to expedite customer service. Customers now penalize companies that infringe on their time through delays, mistakes, or inconveniences. If a company doesn't expedite its processes, customers will go to one that does. If a company doesn't make it easy for the customer to do business, another one will.

It's very important that managers understand and diagnose the cause behind service delays. Managers need to analyze whether an integrated system can speed service, and if so, they need to strategize, design, and implement it as soon as possible. Unfortunately, some managers wake up too late to heed the sound of customers' fists pounding on the counters for faster service, and their companies won't be in business for long.

Self-Service: Empowered Customers

Today, millions of people no longer reach for the car keys when they need to purchase clothes, gifts, or computer products but instead reach for their keyboards.

Customers are looking for self-service solutions that not only save them time but also empower them. They're embracing 24 × 7 × 365 (24 hours a day, 7 days a week, 365 days a year) self-service solutions as they look for information and merchandise without the aid of sales personnel.

The drivers of the self-service wave are obvious. Consumers are able to shop anytime, anywhere, as long as they're connected to the Internet. Trips to the mall are eliminated, along with parking hassles and long checkout lines. In the United States, a nation of families with two full-time workers, consumers generally have too much to do and too little time in which to do it. Therefore, any technology or service that helps reduce shopping time has enormous economic value. This convenience, or "time saver," megatrend—best evidenced in the tremendous increase in fast-food consumption in the past 30 years—has been growing for the majority of the post–World War II period. Online shopping fits this megatrend perfectly and extends the convenience factor to a new plateau.

Self-service has impacted a huge sector of the business work force: the intermediary, or middlemen.[5] From real estate, insurance, travel, and car purchases to auctions, parts sourcing, and retailing, very few intermediaries are left standing when buyers and sellers realize that they can meet directly online. For some, extinction is almost certain. Others are finding fresh opportunities on the Web, although virtually all will have to change how they do business.

e-Commerce takes self-service to a quantum level unforeseen by Sam Walton and the originators of retail self-service. Market leaders are giving customers the means to serve themselves whenever possible. For example, customers of Gateway Computer can assess their own software and hardware needs and then configure, order, and pay for new systems—in addition to getting limited technical support—without ever having to talk to a person.

Online trading companies, such as eSchwab, are setting the pace by making it easy for customers to trade without the help of a broker. Around-the-clock availability gives customers access to their accounts anywhere, anytime. In fact, the business model is predicated on the disintermediation of the broker.

The growing acceptance of self-service can be seen in the online travel industries, too. Leisure and business travelers increasingly make reservations over the Internet; as a result, Internet travel agencies, such as Expedia, Travelocity, and TheTrip.com, have emerged as attractive options. Using these services, customers access a central reservation service via the Web for faster, more convenient flight booking. The online medium enables companies to automate the processing and confirmation of reservations, thus lowering the cost and reducing the need for expensive physical facilities.

The lessons that first movers have learned in successfully empowering customers is that e-business should be user-centric, not technology-centric. Companies with technology-driven instead of consumer-driven e-strategies often have Web sites so confusing that customers can't figure out how to complete online purchases, resulting in lost customers and sales. To improve their focus on consumers' needs, managers must pay attention to the "total experience." In constructing their solutions, managers should

- Emphasize simplicity by focusing each interaction on one goal and removing distracting clutter

- Eliminate experience inhibitors, such as Web pages that load slowly, error messages during the buying process that confuse rather than enlighten, or product listings that are not available or in stock

What does the trend toward self-service mean for e-business? The benefits of self-service are clear and proven. Before a company can realize these benefits, it must first build a new infrastructure and design new protocols to streamline the self-service process. Enterprise-wide integration of business processes will be essential for serving the customer well. The inflexibility of mature companies puts them at a severe disadvantage. The emergence of self-service as a core customer requirement means that companies need to act quickly to transform and integrate existing applications, processes, and systems to enable self-service: no small task.

More Product Choices: More Personalization

As buyer power increases and customer attention span dwindles, companies are scrambling to increase the number of products and services offered and to customize them. Online retailers triumph over brick-and-mortar companies in one area: breathtaking product selection. Consumers, especially in the United States, seem to love one-stop locations that offer everything under one roof. Examples of such big-box retailers are Wal-Mart, Costco, Home Depot, and Garden Ridge.

These brick-and-mortar retailers are now being challenged by online players, which have unlimited shelf space. For instance, Amazon.com is able to offer all 1.5 million in-print books, as well as access to an additional 9 million hard-to-find or out-of-print books, by leveraging its relationships with book publishers, distributors, and used-book dealers. Compare this to a typical brick-and-mortar bookstore, which carries 40,000 titles, or a Barnes & Noble superstore, which has shelf space for approximately 150,000 titles. Compare Beyond.com, which offers more than 50,000 software application titles, to a CompUSA that offers just 2,000. Or CDnow, which offers consumers 325,000 titles, compared with 9,000 in a typical traditional music store or 60,000 in a music superstore.

No traditional retailer could offer as vast an array of merchandise as online companies can, because of limited shelf space and inventory constraints. For example, shelf space in national grocery store chains is so precious that food manufacturers will often pay exorbitant "stocking fees" in order to get their products displayed on the shelves. Because physical stores are capital-intensive to build or expand, it is not possible to add new products to the mix without displacing others, once the shelves are fully stocked. Yet the incremental cost of additional products is minimal for an online retailer, particularly if the inventory is carried by the manufacturer or distributor of the product.

What does the trend toward more personalized product choices mean for e-business? Customers are gravitating toward solutions that have large product selections presented in an easy-to-use manner. The most successful online portals are amassing a tremendous amount of product information and making it available to consumers on an easy-to-access, as-needed basis. When broadband access to the Internet becomes widespread, video content will be available for many products and services, visually enhancing the trend toward information at the point of purchase.

At the same time, navigating a vast selection requires personalization: knowing and tracking a buyer's unique purchasing habits. In contrast to the traditional brick-and-mortar firms, e-business companies will eventually be in a position to personalize the shopping experience for every consumer. By inducing consumers to leave profile information, tracking consumer click-stream movement, and segmenting shopper preferences, online retailers have access to far more customer data than traditional retailers do. This data can be used to personalize each shopper's experience, such as e-mail alerts for new merchandise they'll be interested in, or tailored storefronts that meet the tastes and preferences of individual consumers.

Integrated Solutions, Not Piecemeal Products

The past decade has seen an interesting shift toward integrated solutions. A good example of an integrated solution is the Microsoft Office Suite. When was the last time you shopped individually for word processing, spreadsheet, and presentation packages? The Office Suite product is one of the biggest moneymakers Microsoft has because customers love its integrated functionality. Microsoft is betting that this demand for integrated products will continue. In fact, a core design objective in many of its products is seamless integration.

It is quite extraordinary how quickly consumers have moved away from point, or best-of-breed, solutions toward integrated solutions. This trend can be observed in retailing. In today's time-strapped society, shopping is a low priority on people's to-do lists. Increasingly, customers are demanding one-stop, all-under-one-roof solutions. In response, the retail industry has created various models: one-stop life-needs providers (Wal-Mart), one-stop lifestyle providers (the Gap), and one-stop life-path providers (Toys "R" Us).

The life-needs integration trend can be observed in the success of the Wal-Mart superstore, an integrated retailer for the busy, price-sensitive shopper. Wal-Mart's execution of one-stop shopping has increased customer loyalty, the number of items sold per transaction, and the average transaction size. Other retailers, such as Target, have noted this successful formula and are pursuing strategies that include selling more to the same customer out of the same store or Web site and making shopping more convenient.

For an example of the lifestyle integration trend, look at the Gap in the apparel retailing business. The Gap has effectively marketed an image to its customers. A Gap mannequin is outfitted with three or four layers of shirts, blue jeans, a belt, baseball cap, sunglasses, socks, shoes, gloves, and a knapsack. Customers are drawn to the hip image. Other apparel megabrands, such as Polo, Tommy Hilfiger, and Donna Karan, have improved their brand loyalty by adopting "collections," a form of lifestyle merchandising whereby one brand/concept shop can outfit a customer from head to toe. During a time when customers demand fewer shopping trips, apparel retailers must move toward becoming one-stop lifestyle providers.

Toys are a model of life-path integration. Life-path businesses grow with us. Consider the strategy of a life-path retailer for kids, Toys "R" Us, that sells to parents. The Toys "R" Us marketing strategy is three-pronged: Baby goods are sold at Babies "R" Us, kids' clothes are sold at Kids "R" Us, and toys are sold at Toys "R" Us. However, although Toys "R" Us has leveraged its core customer through each of its three concepts, it faces one key challenge: The products are sold from three separate types of stores, each of which requires its own infrastructure, buildings, management, and associates.

What does the trend toward integrated solutions mean for e-business? Consumers don't need another retailer or another electronic distribution channel. They want integrated-service businesses that solve their one-stop shopping needs. There are too many choices, products, and stores. To solve the "choice" problem, customers increasingly seek integrated solutions because they make the decision process easier.

e-Service Trends

Integrated Sales and Service: Customization and Integration

The need to attract, acquire, leverage, and retain customers is still of primary concern to most businesses. Revenue growth through customer acquisition and retention remains a major requirement for competing successfully. Several studies document that the average company loses half its customers every 5 years and that it costs five to ten times as much to obtain a new customer as to keep an existing one.

To improve customer retention, companies are developing and managing customer relationships via better sales/service integration and new technology. The concept of maximizing customer relationships as a competitive differentiator gained attention in the late 1980s. Managers realized that customers do not exist in a featureless aggregate any more than do products. A one-size-fits-all philosophy, therefore, doesn't work. Sales and service messages need to be tailored to each customer. Therein, of course, lies the problem. *How do you market to a diverse customer base? How can any organization effectively and efficiently address the opportunity? How can technology help bring about better customer relationships?*

Customer relationships are the key to business growth. Firms must take absolute responsibility for a customer's satisfaction throughout the "want-it-buy-it-and-use-it" experience. This requires learning and tracking customers' needs, behaviors, and lifestyles and using this information to create a specific value proposition. This strategy is the path to consumer loyalty, and it's called "relationship selling."

Of course, the purpose for implementing technology is not just about customer acquisition or retention. Its use extends to generating revenue by selling more to existing customers through cross-selling and up-selling, as detailed information about customer preferences and buying habits is readily captured and available at the point of service or sales interaction. This strategy dictates selling to customers while serving them. You can see it at your local bank when the teller tries to sell you a new product while you're making a deposit. Service becomes a sales-prospecting activity. In other words, the bank is attempting to become an integrated sales and service environment. However, most companies view sales and service as separate functions. A sale occurs during the sales cycle, and service is an after-sale activity. Where a prospect or customer is in this cycle determines which department in the company he or she must contact. However, cross-selling and up-selling are closing the gap between sales and service.

What does the trend toward integrated sales and service mean for e-business? New organizational models need to be developed to further narrow the gap between sales and service. For instance, service centers must blur the lines between sales and service. Look at Home Depot, which services the do-it-yourself customer. Home Depot blurs the lines between sales and service by being in perpetual service mode. This, in turn, attracts prospective customers by giving them easy access to information about products and services before they buy. After the sale, the same level of service builds the kind of loyalty that turns customers into company advocates, which leads to better up-selling and cross-selling opportunities, as well as new customer referrals.

How do we design Home Depot–like enterprises online? The success of Home Depot illustrates that consumers want fast, accurate, consistent information and that they want service before *and* after the sale. Today, service must start before the sale and be inherent in every interaction customers and prospective customers have with the company.

Seamless Support: Consistent and Reliable Customer Service

The following story is true; it happened to us. We received a letter from AT&T, our long-distance telephone carrier. The letter informed us that we owed $0.00 dollars (yes! zero dollars) and that payment was past due. According to the letter, if we didn't pay the $0.00 balance, our account would be turned over to a collection agency. Naturally, we immediately called AT&T. The AT&T service representative at the call center was no help and referred us to our local service provider, BellSouth. We then called BellSouth. We were told that it was an AT&T problem. After several minutes of explaining our dilemma, the BellSouth service representative agreed to assist us and called AT&T with us on the line. Having described the problem and our account information for the third time, we were elated to be making progress.

Boy, were we wrong! After AT&T assured us that it would handle the situation, the BellSouth representative got off the line and, in the process, disconnected us. We were right back where we had started. It took us more than a year to resolve this $0.00 billing problem and resulting delinquency of payment. It left an indelible impression on us that AT&T cares very little for its customers. *Has something similar ever happened to you?*

Making customer service easy and solution oriented is one of the most important trends in business today. In this new era of customer-focused business, managers must understand that as customers value their time more, they are less tolerant of screwups in customer service. As the speed of service increases, the expectations for quality customer service grow higher. Companies that implement friendly and easy-to-use customer service processes present customers with single points of contact rather than shuffling them from one department to another so they have to start anew each time. Ask yourself, *How often have you called a company only to suffer a hand-off to partners or outside vendors? How often have you been satisfied with the hand-off?* It's likely that you were dissatisfied.

Increasingly, customer service is no longer one customer dealing with one enterprise. With outsourcing of business functionality and the increasing complexity of products, many service calls require coordinating two or more firms. To provide the kind of service that guarantees customer loyalty, companies need to better coordinate their partners and vendors. It's best to consider partners and vendors part of the company's extended enterprise; only then can customer service issues be seamlessly addressed. It also makes it easier to share customer information, which is vitally important as companies increasingly depend on third-party support.

Managers need to take a close look at their customer service processes on a regular basis and ask, Are they easy to use? Too often, a disconnect occurs as a consequence of the way business processes, including customer service, have been established over the past few decades, even if the firm has worked toward continuous improvement. Customers today must be able to call or log into any area of a company, enjoy immediate recognition, and have their requests or purchases processed smoothly. If not, customers are left with an uneasy sense of company apathy and will probably think twice before calling again.

What does the trend toward more consistent and reliable customer service mean for e-business? To achieve their business objectives, companies need to adopt integrated customer service applications that address the entire customer relationship rather than focus on departmental solutions that address only one part of the customer account relationship. Implementing integrated applications and the business practices they support will become increasingly critical for ensuring quality processes not only within a company but also in the firm's relationship with its partners. As a result, organizations should develop customer relationship solutions that go beyond the boundaries of the company to encompass the entire extended enterprise.

Flexible Fulfillment and Convenient Service Delivery

Customers want everything more quickly. The multiple responsibilities and hectic schedules of today's consumers are forcing retailers to produce innovative products and services. Home delivery and other unique fulfillment services continue to gain importance as consumer-direct sales explode.

Today, the old model of companies waiting for the customer to come to them is giving way to a new business model whereby companies bring their services to the customer. For example, Gevalia Kaffe, an importer with the largest share in the home-delivery coffee market, provides its customers with reliable service and quick delivery at unbeatable prices. Gevalia processes some 200,000 transactions a week in its customer-direct niche. However, in order to stay ahead of the competition, Gevalia knew that it had to increase sales volume and service while simultaneously reducing shipping costs.

How? Gevalia developed and implemented an e-business infrastructure. In the past, receiving, sorting, and shipping orders to customers were often manual tasks performed with few automated procedures. The old order-fulfillment process involved a paper trail of communications between distant offices and Gevalia's New York headquarters, the customer service center in Des Moines, and a fulfillment and shipping complex in Phoenix. Time consuming? Definitely. Moreover, the entire order process was plagued by inefficiencies, data entry, and rekeying errors.

Gevalia's e-business infrastructure automates the order process. When a customer makes a purchase, the network first looks for the least-cost routing by determining the warehouse closest to the customer's location. If the product is not available at the first, best-choice location, the system locates the next-best warehouse location where the product is available. Finally, the system automatically splits the order for the shippers, so they know which items go to which customer locations. By thus streamlining its distribution system and by improving communications with its outsourcing partners, Gevalia also improved access to order processing data, enabling more flexible reporting.

Gevalia's automation of the order process, and the subsequent reduction in order processing inefficiency, enabled the coffee importer to focus on marketing to the consumer rather than troubleshooting order-fulfillment problems. Benefits to the company's implementation include

- Enhanced speed of service by reducing errors

- Reduced outbound shipping costs to consumers by about 20 percent through better pick-and-pack practices at the point of distribution

- Reduced lead times even though one outsourcing agent handles customer service while another physically fills orders

- Handling the demand efficiently and cost-effectively even during peak and promotional seasons

To deliver the right product to the customer, companies must streamline their supply chain as Gevalia has. The core components of the integrated supply chain are quite simple: Take an order, give an accurate promise date, manufacture the right goods, allocate inventory properly, ship efficiently, and do this all while maintaining a minimal finished-goods inventory.

The development of integrated supply chains is by far one of the most important business trends. Whatever bells and whistles you add to the basic foundation are wonderful. But remember: If you can't do the simple stuff, there's no way you can support the newer supply chain applications or leading-edge technology. Quality business processes can be enhanced by the implementation of new technology; however, there is no technofix for poor business practices.

The popularity of e-commerce-enabled supply chain management has grown in recent years. Software companies are gearing up to support it. Consulting firms are preaching it. The trade press is eating it up. So what is it? And does it affect you? Yes, it does. Supply chain management is a combination of inevitable and ongoing trends in manufacturing and distribution: moving closer to the consumer; reducing waste (time, inventory, and so on) in the supply chain; ensuring technology-enabled, real-time information access between customers and suppliers; and building closer partnerships with virtual coordination.

Increased Process Visibility

Process visibility means providing business customers with access to accurate, timely information about order status, product pricing, and product availability. Providing visibility to products and services helps create additional demand. An excellent example of providing process visibility is the United Parcel Service (UPS) tracking system. Customers can use the Internet to track air and ground parcels anytime, anywhere, anyplace. UPS and FedEx have changed customers' expectations so that flawless delivery is now considered the norm, not the exception. Part of the change in attitude comes from how customers now view the overnight package-delivery business. Sophisticated information systems allow shippers to call any time of the day or night and to find out exactly where their packages are. Within minutes of delivery, couriers can tell customers not only when but also to whom packages were delivered.

Process visibility is an essential business feature as package-delivery companies compete with one another. What began with a promise to deliver "absolutely, positively overnight" escalated to promises of delivery the next morning, then before the morning coffee, and now "same day, next city." Customers now expect deliveries between specific hours, not just on certain days. Clearly, changes in business operations, based on accurate delivery times, serve to increase delivery expectations and, therefore, also increase the consequences of service failures.

Interenterprise process visibility is especially important in outsourced manufacturing. For example, Solectron Corporation is a major supplier of circuit boards and electronic assemblies for such companies as IBM, Hewlett-Packard, and Intel. The company has manufacturing facilities in California, Washington, Malaysia, France, and Scotland. When Solectron first planned to automate its business processes, it decided to permit each facility to act independently, primarily because of the technical difficulty in providing data access to such diverse geographical locales. There was simply no way to pull process information into a common database or to track circuit board assemblies across Solectron's divisions. As a result, managers weren't getting the information needed to monitor the shop floor; nor were customers getting the order information they needed in a timely manner.

To provide more insight into the manufacturing process for its business customers, Solectron developed the Shop-Floor Tracking and Recording System (STARS), which enables workers to record the movement of circuit boards through the assembly and testing processes. Bar code readers capture and enter the circuit board's subassembly information, test results, and quality information directly into the STARS application. Customers can access this information remotely to inquire about the status of their job orders and exactly where in the manufacturing process the order is. Solectron's ability to publish real-time information and to permit interaction with the system gives customers new methods for monitoring, controlling, and regulating outsourced processes.

What does the trend toward process visibility mean for e-business? As customer-focused companies strive to build internal applications and processes that open the black box and make transparent internal operations, they better serve both their internal and external customers. For instance, why can't customers know exactly what's happening with the mortgage or car loan applications they filed with the bank? Access to such information would enable them to better plan and manage their lives and would increase corporate accountability. Increasing visibility can have a significant impact on creating demand, as well as on retaining customers. Through close customer contact and high-quality service, a company's competitive edge and long-term relationships with its customers are maintained and strengthened.

Organizational Trends

Outsourcing Management: Flatten the Organization

The modern business climate demands that companies live and breathe flexibility in order to survive. Such flexibility is often reflected in a firm's decision to outsource specific business processes. Business process outsourcing (BPO) is the delegation of one or more business processes to an external provider to improve overall business performance in a particular area. For example, utility companies are outsourcing their cost centers (human resources and purchasing functions) in order to concentrate on their core competence: making and selling energy.

BPO offers businesses innovative ways to save money and to enter or create new markets rapidly, without a significant up-front investment. BPO provides a modular environment in which it is possible to scale up and ramp down, depending on seasonal cycles and production needs. The market trends driving the adoption of BPO strategies include pressure to increase earnings and reduce costs and an increased need to create and maintain a competitive edge.

Often, the processes being outsourced are considered support functions—accounting, IT, administration—that are the core competencies on which the company is based. This flattening of organizations is inverting operations from vertical strategic business units into horizontal business processes.

Traditionally, outsourcing has been used as a cost-control technique. However, as globalization spreads and networking technology becomes more widespread, companies see outsourcing as a way to create a virtual enterprise, change corporate culture, gain access to premium thinkers, and implement world-class capabilities and technologies. Process owners are outsourcing entire processes for business performance rather than IT efficiency.

What does the trend toward outsourcing mean for e-business? Outsourcing strategies herald the beginning of a new era. Outsourcing lays the foundation for creating the virtual enterprise, the core of the e-business concept. The complexity of operations; the regulation and deregulation of markets; the steady, rapid advance of technology; and the need for continual growth are conditions that require core competency in too many areas for any one company. A single organization working alone is no longer a justifiable business model.

Contract Manufacturing: Become Brand Intensive

Is your company asset intensive? If the answer is yes, you are probably heading toward using e-commerce to become a virtual manufacturer. Many old-line manufacturers are attempting to copy the success of companies in the computer industry and others that contract out much of their manufacturing.

For example, Sun Microsystems decided to focus exclusively on designing hardware and software and to subcontract or purchase virtually all its workstations' components. Sun limited its own manufacturing efforts to prototyping, final assembly, and testing. By relying on outside suppliers for its workstation components, Sun was able to introduce four major new product generations in its first 5 years of operation, doubling the price-performance ratio with each successive year.[6] The decision to subcontract supported Sun's key production objectives: achieve better quality, dependability, speed, flexibility, and cost advantage.

Contract manufacturing worked so well in the high-tech industry that it spread to other industries. Chicago-based consumer-goods company Sara Lee disclosed "a fundamental reshaping" of the company that would move it away from manufacturing the brand-name goods it sells. Sara Lee aims to outsource its manufacturing, much like shoemaker Nike does. Sara Lee is selling its own factories in order to concentrate on managing its stable of famous brand names: L'eggs hosiery, frozen desserts, Wonderbras, Coach briefcases, and Kiwi shoe polish, to name a few.

The trend toward specialization—marketing versus manufacturing—means that companies are focusing on what they do best. The goal of these firms is to move from a capital/asset-intensive focus—manufacturing—to a knowledge- and marketing-intensive one. John Bryan, Sara Lee's CEO, said, "It's imperative for companies to focus on new products, managing brands and building market share."[7] Contract manufacturing is also used in the relentless drive to derive profits from fewer assets, owing largely to pressure from Wall Street investors' constantly demanding higher returns. To achieve better asset utilization, companies use technology to segregate marketing from manufacturing by quickly developing contract partnerships and distributing manufacturing globally. The key components of the management trend are: Be innovative through technology, change product offerings continually, and keep overhead as low as possible.

Virtual Distribution: Become Customer-Centric

New intermediaries, called virtual distributors, are emerging in many multi-seller/multibuyer markets. Ventro, SciQuest, and hsupply.com are firms that aggregate buyers and sellers by using Web technology. These firms aggregate marketing and product information content and establish efficient markets in previously fragmented places. By combining information with transaction and distribution mechanisms to dominate a particular market, virtual distributors take advantage of the Web's ability to create efficient marketplaces by aggregating not just buyers and sellers but also technology, content, and commerce.

Many Web entrepreneurs have identified potential virtual-distributor opportunities in various industries and quickly established Web sites. For example, in the chemical industry, e-commerce is changing the principles governing aspects of production planning, strategic thinking, and sales and marketing. The industry has long made a sharp distinction between commodity and specialty chemicals. But e-commerce blurs the line because it makes all products a specialty by allowing other attributes to be layered onto the basic offering. Similarly, the chemical industry has, throughout its history, experienced boom-and-bust cycles, but now e-commerce provides the potential for matching supply more closely to demand.[8] Furthermore, large producers now find it easy to build direct relationships with smaller customers traditionally served by distributors.

New, virtual distributors can make chemical markets more efficient. It's estimated that anywhere from 10 percent to 90 percent of a chemical's cost occurs after it leaves the production plant. Significant cost cuts will result from companies' moving to e-commerce for buying and selling chemicals.

For example, e-chemicals is a virtual distributor offering 1,000 products from 20 manufacturers. e-Chemicals not merely takes orders and passes them on to the manufacturer but also provides a credit-financial settlement service through a tie-up with a financial services company and distribution through a third-party logistics company. Another example is ChemConnect, an online exchange connecting buyers and sellers. It features the World Chemical Exchange, a commodity transaction service tailored to the needs of large-scale chemical transactions. Companies listed with the service can place notices for the chemicals they need or want to sell. Qualified suppliers or buyers then submit bids and offers, including details on delivery, production, and letters of credit and other essentials of big-ticket transactions. ChemConnect says that its goal is to bring the market efficiencies of the bid-and-offer process to large-scale chemical trading.

e-Commerce comes to the chemical industry just in time to provide a solution, allowing suppliers to deal directly and cost-effectively with even the smallest customer. One of the reasons the chemical industry has been slow to move to electronic trading is the interwoven nature of trading links. The automotive and retail sectors have honed their supply chains by progressively reducing the number of suppliers and sharing product and sales information with them. But chemical companies have avoided building such close and codependent relationships, because a supplier in one product area is often a competitor in another. Now these dated industrial age business practices are being challenged by new Internet-based companies unencumbered by high fixed costs.

Employee Megatrends

Hiring the Best and Brightest

e-Business roadmap: vision, planning, execution. In order to follow this map, you must have motivated employees. In the tight labor market, it's become very difficult to hire people with e-commerce skills. e-Commerce demands that companies continually grow, deliver better service, or reduce prices. Meeting these demands requires answering the following questions.

- How do you hire the right employees and motivate them?

- How do you create the right incentives for employees?

- How do you develop an organization that is capable of innovating continually and learning continuously?

Large companies moving into e-business are finding that recruiting talented employees is next to impossible. Many of the best and brightest executives, developers, and support staff are choosing the high-risk, high-reward route of Internet start-ups over stable corporate careers. Owing to the long-running bull market, many top executives are trading in corporate perks for stock options, resulting in fewer qualified candidates available and intense competition for them. In this "snooze-you-lose" environment, companies with slow, cumbersome selection procedures don't stand a chance at hiring the best employees. But beefing up their recruitment and selection processes isn't enough. Companies have to make better use of technology to attract and select the best candidates. Remember, many new-era companies are based on innovation, speed, and creativity—goals that established companies must adopt.

Keeping Talented Employees

How does an enterprise become a learning organization that prospers in a fast-paced, demanding business climate? Upscale retailer Nordstrom is an excellent example. Long considered the bellwether in retail service standards, Nordstrom has a legendary policy of bending over backward to please the customer. Nordstrom's gold-plated service and no-questions-asked return policy make for strong repeat business. In fact, the company figures that about 90 percent of its sales come from 10 percent of its loyal shoppers. A key element of Nordstrom's success is its employees. Nordstrom uses exceptional incentives to motivate its staff, including paying high commissions and using undercover shoppers to evaluate service, with cash rewards given to employees who score a perfect 100. Nordstrom also gives workers a great deal of autonomy in decision making, telling them to use their best judgment. This practice gives an entrepreneurial zest to the store's service.

The Nordstrom example illustrates that sustainable innovation depends on motivated and empowered employees. With changing technology and business trends, management worries about employee retention are understandable; nothing is more critical to long-term success. Retaining talented employees depends on

- *Better incentives and compensation.* Pay and bonuses should be tied to continuous improvement for both employees and the organization.

- *Earned advancement.* Promotions must be based on the proven ability to lead and manage a strong group of people. If employees are given the hope that they can move up in the company, they will stay longer and work harder.

- *Better motivation.* Real, tangible commitments must be made to employees. If people believe that they're working so that senior management can get a bigger bonus, change will not happen. The work force has to be self-motivated to continuously improve processes and themselves.

What does the trend toward improved employee retention strategies mean for e-business? Supporting and sustaining a culture that can succeed and innovate is not only a requirement but also a prerequisite for doing e-business. The old ways of command and control over knowledge workers no longer work well. Technology is a key weapon in employee recruiting and motivation. New opportunities await employee-friendly companies.

Enterprise Technology Trends

Integrated Enterprise Applications: Connect the Corporation

Traditionally, most companies separated their business applications, creating specialized functional areas: accounting, finance, manufacturing, distribution, and customer service. It's a matter of divide and conquer: If a job can be defined specifically enough, a specialized application can optimize functions in that particular area. And if all functional links in a company are optimized, the company as a whole will function optimally. In recent years, however, business theorists have challenged this best-of-breed strategy. They recognize that if a chain of processes is to perform at a high level, the individual business functions and the applications supporting them must be tightly linked with other processes around them.

However, integration is difficult. Over the past decade, the notion of a corporation whose optimized business processes rested on a backbone of well-integrated application software has had great appeal. It will continue to do so far into the future. Enterprise applications offered by packaged software vendors, such as SAP and PeopleSoft, help companies connect disparate systems, provide greater access to information, and more closely link employees, partners, and customers.

Packaged software has fueled a growing debate within organizations about build versus buy. Why buy an outside vendor's packaged software rather than build one internally? The combination of more data, users, systems, and applications, compounded by a lack of time and resources, has contributed to a complex crisis for IT organizations. Internal IT departments are under increasing pressure to quickly deliver bottom-line benefits to their customers. And building complex applications under severe time-to-market pressure isn't easy, even if the customer is a user organization within your own firm. As with software developers, if an internal IT department fails, it risks alienating customers—its users—losing money—it may be overlooked for future projects—and reducing competitive advantage against outside vendors.

Buying packaged software can help IT organizations relieve some of the time-to-market pressure. But how well an off-the-shelf package meets a company's unique business requirements is often an issue. Occasionally, companies attempt to resolve these difficulties by purchasing customized off-the-shelf (COTS) software, a hybrid of buy and build. The question of build versus buy has no black-and-white answer. Identifying the benefits and drawbacks of either approach to software development or selection makes the decision complicated and build versus buy a major gray area of IT decision making.

However, a company that buys packaged software must be careful to differentiate between packaged application support and takeover. In Stanley Kubrick's 1968 film *2001: A Space Odyssey,* the spaceship computer, HAL, takes over the ship, killing several crew members in the process. HAL's role was to support the ship, not control it. In the same vein, an enterprise application must support company operations, not completely take over how the business is run. A company that considers adapting its business processes to the software's requirements as opposed to selecting or building a package that fits its needs may have HAL in the executive suite. Regardless of whether it builds or buys software, a firm should first define, develop, and document the processes it seeks to automate independent of the software to be developed or selected. These software-independent procedures become the firm's statement of how it goes about its work, regardless of the software tools used to support its work.

If managers allow enterprise applications to define and run the company rather than support it in delivering value to the customer, jobs can be lost, as was the case at FoxMeyer Drugs, a large distributor. FoxMeyer not only miscalculated the difficulty in implementing an enterprise resource planning (ERP) solution but also didn't understand the consequences to its business processes and practices. The result was bankruptcy: a cautionary tale about the perils of poorly implemented applications.

Multichannel Integration: Look at the Big Picture

The brick-and-mortar office was for a long time the only service channel available to customers for conducting business. Then came the telephone. Today, access alternatives and capabilities are exploding: the Web, direct dial-up, interactive voice response (IVR), and wireless. With all these service channels proliferating, customers are demanding multichannel service integration.

Service integration means providing standardized high-quality customer service across all the firm's service channel media. Multichannel integration is critical because customers expect consistent service when they interact with a company, no matter which channel they use. For example, suppose that Judy walks into a bank, deposits $50,000 into her account, goes home, and logs onto the Internet site of the same bank branch to pay her utility bills. Unless her account is overdrawn, she should not get a message that her account has insufficient funds. If she gets this message in error, the reason is that the channels—the physical branch and the Internet site—are not integrated. This is unacceptable customer service.

Multichannel service integration is not a technical issue but rather a management issue. It is management's responsibility to review the entire scope of the firm's service channels. The success of each individual channel part must be defined in sync with the overall system. Otherwise, each delivery channel may be successful on its own, but the delivery system as a whole will not be. Most businesses have a number of managers responsible for monitoring each channel, but few are assigned responsibility for looking at the overall picture.

A huge level of technical investment is needed to create integrated services. A number of emerging technologies, such as middleware, could make it less expensive. But many of these technologies are untested and not yet ready for 24 × 7 mission-critical applications. Thus, multichannel integration is a long-term trend worth the effort but requiring more work than most people realize.

Multichannel integration is a critical issue for any business striving to maintain its competitive advantage. Multichannel integration holds the key to unlocking information about the business and its transactions and making it available to any user, anywhere, anytime. It is the key to e-business success.

Middleware: Support the Integration Mandate

Here's the buzz in boardrooms and at company water coolers around the world: "We have to become more customer-centric." Customer information must be available across the board, spanning several departmental domains and stovepipe legacy applications. As we have seen with multichannel integration, this is easier said than done. An isolated department, no matter how efficient on its own, no longer provides the speed of service that companies need to stay competitive. To become truly customer-centric, firms must integrate legacy applications developed in the 1970s with more modern applications, providing seamless business process integration.

A business has not had compelling reasons to endure the cost, complexity, and risk of integrating stovepipe applications—until now. The heat of competition is forcing organizations to broaden their views on application integration, just as many *customer-care* initiatives are forcing companies to present a single view of the customer relationship. In addition to business trends, such as globalization, several technology minitrends—Internet/intranet architectures, quick and inexpensive data access, multimedia capabilities, open standards, the increasing demand for distributed applications—are driving the need for robust, distributed applications scalable and reliable enough to run mission-critical business applications.

To meet business and technology integration needs, a new class of technology, called *middleware*, is emerging. Integration based on middleware makes financial sense. Customers are reluctant to throw away their existing legacy investments, because the old systems cannot be easily replaced. Most major mission-critical operations still run on mainframe-based systems, owing to concerns about security, reliability, and speed. Therefore, companies are looking for robust connectivity and seamless interoperability between their mainframe and Internet applications. As they respond to these demands, corporations and vendors are discovering that middleware provides the essential glue that enables large, complex business software, such as multichannel service applications, to run effectively and reliably. However, this is difficult to do, as the available technology is not yet mature.

The middleware problem is bound to get more management attention as spending on technology spirals out of control. According to *Information Week,* the 500 largest corporate users of IT in the United States will spend a total of nearly $97 billion on IT products and services worldwide in 2000.[9] A large part of e-business integration is the middleware plumbing essential for combating the chaos inherent in a hodgepodge of unrelated systems trying to communicate by linking, or making interoperable, mainframe, client/server, and Internet environments. By leveraging existing legacy systems and skills within organizations, middleware prolongs their useful life, which can save costs. Although the technology is still immature, the middleware trend is significant and must be monitored, because it plays an integral role in creating customer-centric, distributed, and virtual organizations.

General Technology Trends

Wireless Web Applications: m-Commerce

Business of the future will be mobile, integrated, and personal. With the widespread rollout of a wireless infrastructure, a new wave of consumer and business applications will begin using airwaves for much more than just phone calls. These powerful, convenient wireless applications and the decreasing cost of wireless use will increase the efficiency of performing everyday tasks, such as organizing business and personal affairs, sending e-mail, making phone calls, and even finding the best restaurant within walking distance.

The following trends are paving the way for m-commerce.

• *More applications and higher access speed.* In 1999, for instance, NTT DoCoMo, Japan's leading wireless service provider, released its new I-mode phone, which allowed users to both make phone calls and surf the Internet. DoCoMo sold more than 1 million of these phones in the first 6 months and is taking steps to become a preeminent player in the m-commerce revolution. The company's objective is to provide consumer-friendly devices with easy access to information.

• *Integrated devices.* The first-generation devices that deliver these services will vary from cell phones to handheld devices, such as the Nokia 9000 Communicator, which consists of a phone, a Web browser, and a personal-messaging and data-organizing system bundled into a single unit. New consumer applications will help these devices gain market share, unshackling technology users from their desktops in the process. For instance, Handspring's Visor, which provides instant two-way personal communication in a text format, offers flight schedules, news headlines, and online transactions, such as movie ticket purchases or stock trades. Integrated devices are gaining momentum in the marketplace.

- *Wireless personal-area networks.* Also gaining momentum are products that incorporate Bluetooth, which delivers network access anywhere. Bluetooth is radio technology that enables various devices to talk and send messages to one another without cables, making computing-on-the-move a reality. Ericsson's earbud Bluetooth gadget is designed to eliminate cell phone shoulder crunch by beaming a call directly to your ear. In addition, Bluetooth works on an unlicensed wireless band, so it's free. When you use Bluetooth, you therefore aren't beholden to any ISP or wireless service provider.

However, the true potential for m-commerce lies in enterprise applications. As information proliferates, managers are under greater pressure to make more informed decisions—all while on the move. Much of the information on which managers depend is being sent to them via wireless network. We're on the cusp of a whole new way of working. The demand for being more mobile and productive, supported by this emerging wireless technology, will create tremendous demand for m-commerce applications.

Handheld Computing and Information Appliances

Technological innovation has enabled the e-business revolution. The traditional workspace image—with its PC-centric "box with monitor" interactive platform—is shattering. With the emergence of a multitude of access device options, from advanced digital cable set-top boxes (WebTV) and handheld mobile devices to auto PCs and netphones, consumers will be able to access the information content they need when they need it.

The handheld computing and information appliance industry is growing rapidly. Mobile users increasingly demand easier access to critical personal and professional information, interaction with Internet-based information resources, and mobile voice and data communications. This increased need for productivity and connectivity "anywhere, anytime" has led to a wide array of handheld devices.

The first generation of handheld devices focused on functions, such as calendar and contact management; the new generation focuses on communications functions, including paging, e-mail and Internet access. Although demand for these devices has grown rapidly, product evolution in this sector is still in its early stage. The emergence of more powerful, flexible devices with increased functionality and broad consumer applications will further expand the market for handheld computing and communications devices.

The following are key factors driving widespread consumer adoption of handheld computing and communications devices:

- *Demands of a mobile society.* Consumers are demanding the same productivity and communications capability on the road as they get at their desks. This demand is at the heart of a powerful trend: New devices enable new applications, which in turn enable greater mobility, which only increases the demand for more functional devices. Reductions in device size and cost and improvements in functionality, storage capacity, and reliability are all fostering these trends.

- *Need for mobile Internet and intranet access.* The growing prominence of the Internet and corporate intranets in users' everyday lives is increasing demand for access "anywhere, anytime." Demand for mobile data Internet applications, such as e-mail, stock quotes and trading, news, content, and location-based services, continues to increase. In addition, employees are demanding mobile access to corporate intranets to obtain critical business information, such as inventory levels and customer profiles.

- *Improvement in wireless communications enable compelling applications.* Digital wireless communications have become widely adopted owing to declining consumer costs, expanding network coverage, and the availability of extended service features, such as voice and text messaging. Widespread deployment of wireless networks will increasingly enable the delivery of higher-bandwidth applications, such as streaming video and audio, to handheld communications devices.

- *Growing developer community.* As the handheld computing and communications device market has grown to millions of units, a large community of independent developers is driving new application development functionality. Developers are creating software applications and complementary hardware peripherals and accessories that address new markets. This innovation is in turn creating new market opportunities and is stimulating increased demand for handheld devices.

What does the trend toward handheld computing mean for e-business? Although all this is good news for consumers, it's not necessarily good news for enterprises wishing to engage and retain customers. The handheld products disrupt our view of what computing and e-business is and means. A multitude of bandwidth options, screen sizes, and end user environments will confound the strategic planning of interactive initiatives and will drive up their cost as well.

To identify the next wave of opportunities in this mobile wave, established companies have to listen, watch, and act quickly. By thoroughly monitoring consumer demand for interactive services and devices, enterprises will be better positioned to exploit the oncoming wave and to enjoy first-to-market benefits. Furthermore, such firms will be uniquely positioned to deploy the emerging consumer technologies in the workplace, delivering a host of workplace-efficiency options.

Infrastructure Convergence: Voice, Data, and Video

It's time for IP everywhere. A major trend in the infrastructure for e-business is the convergence of various data and voice networks. Worldwide telephone, cable TV, wireless, and computer data networks are ceasing to be separate, isolated systems. Instead, they're converging into a powerful, unified network based on the Internet Protocol (IP), the packet-switching network layer that has proved to be a versatile workhorse that can transmit any kind of information quickly and cheaply.

Infrastructure convergence encompasses the following minitrends happening simultaneously:

- *The race to provide optical networking in the backbone.* Imagine that a Chicago–New York road has the entire lane blocked off for each traveler, even one going only a short distance. Meanwhile, traffic cops, or routers, stop travelers frequently to ask where they are going and whether they need directions. The resulting mess would be similar to today's backbone networks. And as more and more bursts of data traffic clog networks designed for voice connections, the problem will only get worse. The resulting trend: the movement toward optical networks, whereby traffic enters as an electrical signal but gets converted to optical data for the trip.

- *The race to provide quality of service.* Dependability and predictability of service in the network are increasing. Imagine trying to talk to someone but hearing only static, a few words, and more static. Frustrating, right? The resulting trend: companies competing with solutions that provide a guaranteed quality of service.

- *The race to provide integrated services.* Major long-distance carriers, such as AT&T, Sprint, and MCI/WorldCom, have announced plans to set up unified networks that will carry voice and data over the same line, thus saving the huge expense of maintaining separate networks. These companies join newer service providers, such as Qwest Communications and Global Crossing, that are founded on the premise of providing integrated voice and data services. The resulting trend: the dial tone of today evolving into the Web tone of tomorrow.

- *The race to dominate the customer home contact point.* Today, the customer contact point is the browser and modem. As technology improves, the consumer will use cable set-top boxes, or WebTV, to access content and services. The resulting trend: multiple customer contact points in the home, resulting in a proliferation of network appliances.

The business driver behind infrastructure convergence is service convenience. An example is EnergyOne, a venture that jointly markets phone, security, gas, and electric services to homeowners. Telecommunications companies want to offer customers the convenience of bundled packages of services that include local and long-distance phone service, online services, high-speed Internet connections, wireless phone, paging, pay TV, and tailored billing.

Another emerging user convenience is the ability to have telephone conversations over the Internet. New systems enable data networks to simultaneously handle voice calls by translating the analog sound into digital data. Venture capitalists and phone, cable, and Internet service provider companies are spending billions of dollars to realize the needed infrastructure convergence. Beneath the hype lies a very real long-term trend.

What does the trend toward infrastructure convergence mean for corporations? Like railroads in the 1830s, electricity in the 1870s, and the interstate road system in the 1950s, the infrastructure for e-commerce is in its infancy and is evolving quite rapidly. Understanding how the trend toward infrastructure convergence is playing out is critical for long-term strategic planning. If left unchanged, investments based on outdated telecommunications and networking technology will have a serious negative impact on the future competitiveness of your company.

Application Service Providers (ASPs): Software as Rentable Services

The decision to make versus buy has become that of make versus buy versus rent. Until recently, companies wanting to implement Internet applications had to develop their own software applications or customize existing packages, making each implementation unique and costly. This approach also made implementation time frames and costs unpredictable. Recently, customers have forced software vendors to lower the cost of implementation by offering standardized packages accessible via the Internet.

What does an ASP do? The simple answer: An ASP is a company that hosts and manages business applications on behalf of a client. These applications can range from basic e-mail to groupware and data mart applications to extremely complex and demanding applications, such as enterprise resource planning (ERP) and customer relationship management (CRM). Recently, major packaged solution providers, such as Oracle, J. D. Edwards, Siebel, PeopleSoft, and SAP, have released versions of their software that can be accessed and used over the Internet.

Why buy software when you can rent it? ASP-hosted software is becoming common in such areas as e-commerce, ERP, and sales force automation, where the increasing ubiquity of the Internet makes it a cost-efficient mechanism for implementing distributed functions. Some of the companies providing these rentable apps are: US Internetworking, Intel, and Curio. With these ASPs, you can have top-tier business systems right away for a predictable monthly fee.

Reasons for the growth in ASPs include

- The scarcity of IT professionals

- Companies' desire to focus on their core business processes

- The difficulties that nontechnical businesses experience in hiring, motivating, and retaining qualified engineers and IT employees

- The fast pace of technical change that shortens time to obsolescence and forces increases in capital spending as companies attempt to stay on the cutting edge

Traditionally, most enterprises faced with these problems have sought solutions from a variety of information technology providers—system integrators, ISPs, hardware and software vendors, telecommunication companies—and at least three independent suppliers: software applications providers, systems integrators, and site hosting providers. But this approach has inherent conflicts and difficulties. Each supplier is obviously knowledgeable about its specific product or service but is very limited in what it knows about the bundle of products and services required to provide the enterprise with the complete business solution.

What does the trend toward using ASP applications mean for e-business? The ASP trend creates a substantial market opportunity for those who can provide a single-source solution combining multiple-vendor software hardware, systems integration, and Internet-based communications in an integrated service. The value proposition of the ASP is very compelling: Take advantage of the ASP's expertise and economies of scale in managing applications, and avoid the pain and expense of hiring your own specialists and continually installing, maintaining, and upgrading packaged software.

What These 20 Trends Have in Common

In the e-business world, innovation means spotting a trend and capitalizing on it first. Innovation also means using information and technology to create value. In the future, senior managers will be called on to lead the innovation charge and to sponsor innovation in their organizations. Today, managers everywhere are wondering how the Internet can remake their businesses. In order to grow, corporations are using the art of trend spotting to discover new products and services, design new business processes and structures, even even create new businesses.

The 20 trends described in this chapter contain four common threads:

- *Convenience.* These trends directly impact consumer self-service and ease of use.

- *Effectiveness.* The trends directly impact the relationship between the enterprise's customers and its environment.

- *Efficiency.* These trends impact the internal structure and operating activities of the enterprise.

- *Integration.* These trends push for one-stop-shopping consolidation.

Most of these trends will push the formation of many new companies. *Why?* The long-term goal of any business is greater effectiveness in meeting the needs of its customers. Unfortunately, most of management's time and attention is spent on internal efforts designed to make day-to-day operations as efficient as possible. Therein lies the paradox. The companies best qualified in terms of resources to take advantage of new trends are often the least structurally capable of taking advantage of them. As a result, the door is open for new start-ups to fill the void.

Memo to the CEO

Learn the difference between fads and trends. In the good old days, there was plenty of time to notice fads, some of which unfolded into trends that then became mainstream practices. But today, we think in terms of nanoseconds and instant industries because the speed of change has increased tremendously. This increase is mirrored in the blisteringly fast-paced trends, including: technological innovation, rapid new-product introductions, changes in customer requirements, declining prices, evolving industry standards. Today, new products and technology often render existing services or value propositions obsolete, excessively costly, or otherwise unprofitable.

Your company's success depends on the ability to innovate and integrate new technologies into service offerings. Executives must become proficient trend spotters; if they don't, their companies will fail. Businesses have spent the past decade scaling mountainous change created by colliding technology, consumer, and quality trends. But despite how high each company manages to climb, they all reach the same chasm: the digital revolution, which affects every business equally, regardless of industry, size, or principles. Can your company ascend the peak of change, or will you watch a young, energetic upstart reach it first?

What is your company doing to be a trend leader instead of a trend follower? The new generation of e-business leaders must be imaginative in order to radically change the value proposition within and across industries. Freud once wrote, "What a distressing contrast there is between the radiant curiosity of the child and the feeble mentality of the average adult." Unleashing imagination is vitally important if large industrial age companies are to transform themselves into nimble digital enterprises.

Structural trends in industry are driven by many forces, including deregulation, a predominance of information, and ever-changing customer demands, including end-to-end process integration. And as customers increasingly practice self-service and enter their own orders digitally, their service expectations are bound to increase. To satisfy them, companies must invent new processes that compress order-to-delivery time.

In the years ahead, be prepared for consolidation to accelerate at breakneck speed as companies exploit evolving national and global economies of scale. After all, with e-commerce technology, any local industry, such as retail banking, can become national, and any national industry, such as book retailing, can become international. In the face of such unprecedented chaos, firms must be flexible when implementing new business models and strategy, their product mix, and easy-to-use customer experiences. In the past, firms dealt with these management responsibilities differently. All that's changed with e-commerce. You must now be agile in a holistic way, continuously addressing all three responsibilities at once.

Successful companies know that pleasing customers means capitalizing on new trends. These firms understand that customer and technology trends evolve unpredictably and create opportunities that often catch established firms off guard. In the face of innovation, established companies behave like ostriches, hiding their heads in the sand. Having reached their zones of comfort, these companies resist change. They make their operating models rigid, thereby opening the door for innovative upstarts that can satisfy customers' demands. Thus begins a new era.

CHAPTER THREE

Digitizing the Business:
e-Business Patterns

What to Expect

e-Business is changing businesses, jobs, and lives. The tricky part is figuring out which changes matter. Successful managers anticipate the impact of recent economic and technical trends on their current business models and accompanying business practices. These managers act before the economic ground shifts beneath them. By staking out opportunity and capitalizing, they beat out their competitors, whose superficial focus keeps them unaware of the changing business patterns beneath the world of business-as-usual.

As a result, many CEOs are asking themselves, Under what business models does my company and industry operate? How do we conceive a new model to ensure our future success? Many of the CEOs we have met over the years are overwhelmed by these questions. To answer them, CEOs enlist the help of strategy-consulting firms, academics, and other business gurus—advisers who seem to generate new theories every few months, often creating their own form of chaos. For the practicing manager, cutting through this cacophony of advice can be daunting. What's to be done? What are the first steps toward creating and implementing an e-business model that meets the company's future needs?

The journey toward creating new digital strategies starts by answering the following questions.

- *Which business models are taking hold in my industry and why? Do I clearly see the business model changes behind the apparent chaos in my industry?*

- *Which set of strategic moves puts me in the best position? Is my organization capable of adapting to the required business model changes?*

In this chapter, we highlight several emerging e-business patterns: e-channels, click and brick, e-portals, e-market makers, and pure-e. As you read the chapter, ask yourself with which of these emerging business patterns your company is attempting to compete. Reflect on the pattern's business requirements and whether it is a good fit for your firm. Answering these questions will help you get started with assessing your company's digital strategy.

- Could America Online have become more powerful as an independent service provider? What made AOL want to merge with Time Warner? Did AOL see before anyone else the potential impact of high-speed cable modems and broadband DSL connections on the business dynamics of online entertainment and competition?

- Would Amazon.com have been more profitable if it had remained a pure-play e-company selling books? Why did it have to transform into a click-and-brick firm by building warehouses? Did Amazon realize before others that successful e-retailers need to have both an online portal and a physical fulfillment infrastructure to distribute and warehouse their products? However, does Amazon have the management skills to manage bricks?

- Would Yahoo! have been more successful as just a search engine? Why did Yahoo! choose to acquire other firms and transform itself into an online media network? Did Yahoo! realize that in order for its advertising-based business model to succeed it needed more sticky portals, such as GeoCities and Broadcast.com? Is the next move for Yahoo! to merge with CBS or Disney?

- Could Disney have become a top online brand with the same durability, versatility, and magic that its offline brand carries? Is this why Disney created the infamous Go.com portal with the InfoSeek acquisition? Does Disney have the integration skills to fuse click-and-brick brands?

- Could Chemdex have become more successful if it had remained a pure business-to-business (B2B) exchange in the life sciences market? Why did it become Ventro, a holding company servicing multiple vertical markets? Did Chemdex realize that the size of the initial market was too small and the margins too tight? Would it have been better off merging with an old-line distributor?

e-Business Patterns: The Structural Foundation

Market turbulence makes understanding, let alone predicting, strategic movements very difficult. Practicing managers, consultants, investors, and students all face the problems associated with analyzing a dynamic market environment. For the manager, market volatility makes it more difficult to see the forest from the trees. As the environment changes, managers need to ask the following questions.

- Are we investing in the right business opportunities?

- Are these opportunities ever going to be profitable?

- Are we using the right business model to attack these opportunities?

In today's environment, more than ever, managers of old-economy companies need the right tools to support and to improve their effectiveness when making major strategic moves, allocating scarce resources, and managing risk. Why? Because the large old-economy companies—from consumer products to industrial manufacturing—have begun to see relatively small pieces of their markets taken away by new, Web-enabled firms. As a result, those companies are waking up to the e-business threat and have started to push toward more efficient digital strategies based on optimizing the customer's experiences, integrating their value chains, and accelerating information flow.

But choosing a target strategy is complex. For instance, as large brick-and-mortar corporations move online, they often choose one of two options: (1) swallow a start-up and take advantage of its domain knowledge, brand awareness, experienced staff, and established fulfillment services; or (2) go it alone. But what is the right approach? Take, for instance, Kodak, which is adopting a hybrid approach, both competing and collaborating with digital companies. Kodak made an equity investment in Snapfish, an online photo-processing company but also launched its own photo-finishing service: PrintAtKodak. Simultaneously, Kodak unveiled a vendor-supplier relationship with Shutterfly, whereby Kodak will process prints for Shutterfly. Kodak is clearly hedging and attempting to reduce risk by pursuing multiple strategies at the same time.[1] *Is your company adopting a strategy similar to Kodak's?*

As the focus shifts from physical assets to digital assets, managers should monitor macroeconomic and customer trends to trigger new e-business structural designs. The resulting new business models, in turn, are the genesis for the next generation of corporate strategic planning. However, many companies still don't take the digital world seriously. As America Online president Bob Pittman noted, some of the retailers he meets have "500 people devoted to new store openings and two college kids working on the Web site."[2]

Clearly, we are in the early stages of a revolution that is changing the business landscape. As with any revolution, there will be moments of extreme optimism, when the potential reveals itself; there will also be moments of extreme pessimism, when skepticism rules. However, one thing is certain: e-Business is creating new opportunities for companies willing to adapt. For other companies, this same revolution represents a destabilizing threat to the status quo of business-as-usual. When all is said and done, we'll find a few big corporate winners joining the ranks of the premier companies in the world. In this chapter, we help identify these winners, discussing the characteristics leading to their success. We also analyze several discernable e-business patterns in hopes of bringing a better understanding at a time when the revolution is loud and the din of shifting paradigms is everywhere.

Going Digital

e-Business is tricky business. The first step in identifying an e-business leader is looking at which companies are asking the innovative questions that are transforming the rules of today's business game. When innovative companies change the types of strategic questions they ask themselves, the result is a revolution in business. By changing the questions asked, the innovators changed the rules of the game for everybody else.

For example, the auto industry changed radically when the Japanese changed the rules in the 1970s by asking a series of powerful questions: Instead of manufacturing gas-guzzlers, how do we create a fuel-efficient car? Instead of cars that break down frequently, how can we create a high-quality car with few manufacturing defects? Instead of creating huge stockpiles of "just-in-case" inventory, how can we create a just-in-time inventory process?

Prior to the 1970s, the auto business pattern of the 1950s and 1960s was relatively simple. The large auto companies would design and produce what you, the consumer, were going to buy next year; they would build it and you would buy it. As the car aged, the same companies would sell you the parts and service needed to maintain it. By questioning the industry's most basic assumptions, the Japanese automakers changed the rules of the game worldwide.

The old auto industry business pattern—you buy what we produce—became unsustainable because the new entrants to the market focused on "quality." The Japanese quality program revolutionized manufacturing by defining quality largely in terms of customer, not industry, requirements. The result was smaller, more fuel-efficient, reliable automobiles radically different from those manufactured by the Big Three automakers, which stood transfixed by a tidal wave of imports from the Japanese and whose failure to react quickly resulted in a 30 percent loss in market share. The entire U.S. auto industry had to change from a business model based on low-cost mass production and standardization to one focused on quality and greater product differentiation. It took the industry two decades to adjust to this change in the rules of the game. It was not until the 1990s that the quality of U.S. auto companies' products could stand up against the best produced by Asian and European firms.

However, another major auto industry change has taken place in the past few years. The emergence of e-commerce technology, customer choice, and product and service customization is threatening the industry again. People can access more information and choose from more options than ever before. Automobile consumers expect automakers to "build to order," delivering custom vehicles to their doorsteps within a few days of order placement. Clearly, the automakers are about to be blindsided again by another change brought on by process and technological innovation. This time, the U.S. auto industry doesn't have two decades to respond.

During the mid 1980s, many businesses reevaluated their operations for key processes by asking the basic question: What business are we in? The leadership at Wal-Mart asked a different question: What business should we be in? In answering it, Wal-Mart changed the rules of the game by digitizing its logistics network. By installing sophisticated satellite networks to provide real-time sales and ordering information, Wal-Mart moved from being a retailer into being a supply chain expert. As a result, the company outperformed its competitors by offering the right product mix at the right store, cutting costs, integrating its operations with its suppliers, and capturing valuable information about its customers. Over the past few years, innovations in logistics technology have led to Wal-Mart's implementing scan-based trading (SBT), a supply chain innovation gaining momentum in the distribution industry. SBT sounds like the answer to every retailer's prayers: to pay for product only when it is sold at the point of sale. No more inventory management headaches and carrying costs: that's the supplier's problem!

In the early 1990s, with the process revolution booming, managers and consultants focused on reengineering processes asked, What are our core competencies, those activities critical to the nature and success of our business? What cross-functional processes support these competencies? Every noncore process or activity was considered fair game for elimination or outsourcing. Business process reengineering (BPR) was driven by the simple awareness that overlaying newly improved or best-practice processes on the existing processes does not work. Enterprise-wide, not function-specific, change initiatives offer the greatest benefit to firms seeking to revolutionize how they do business.

In the mid 1990s, the focus shifted from process analysis and reengineering toward assessing the business model and a more precise understanding of customer needs and characteristics. The emergence of widespread entrepreneurial risk taking, coupled with a free flow of venture capital funds and the blurring of boundaries between companies and industries, prompted this change. Business analysts raised new questions: What is our company's business model? Who is our customer? Who is our competitor?

Using business models based on recent technological, marketing, and organizational innovations, new entrants have risen to challenge almost every leading company. America Online reinvented the business model for interactive services—to the dismay of CompuServe and Prodigy. Dell reinvented the personal computer build-to-order model—to the dismay of Compaq and IBM. EMC reinvented the business model for terabyte data storage—to the dismay of IBM and StorageTek. Sun Microsystems reinvented the business model for dot-com servers—to the dismay of Hewlett-Packard and Silicon Graphics. New players raised the standards for bold and innovative strategy. In almost every instance, new models produced cost advantages of 15 percent to 20 percent for the innovators.

In the 2000s, the focus of change will be the speed with which a firm implements the e-business solutions powered by recent innovations. The questions for today's business leader will be: How fully digital can you make your customers' experience? Your supply chain? Your internal operations and processes? Take, for instance, Intuit, whose business model responsible for the company's success in the stand-alone PC era was starting to drag it down with the emergence of the Internet. The market share and profit margins for the company's flagship products—Quicken, TurboTax, and QuickBooks—began to shrink, and it appeared that their growth potential would be limited. To survive, Intuit transformed itself into an online financial services portal. By taking advantage of e-business,

Intuit found new ways to retain customers. Intuit started with a terrific strategic position, charted an economically logical next opportunity, and then moved laterally into a new market space significantly larger in both size and opportunity.

Start-up firms continue to shape the direction of today's business by taking advantage of recent technological innovations, such as Web commerce or mobile e-commerce, to create new digital processes. Conceived correctly and done well, digitizing your business processes can change the way your company interacts with its customers, communicates, sells, purchases, manufactures, and even how it develops products. Whether it's the reengineering movement of the early 1990s or the customer-first mantra of recent years, asking a new question not only produces new answers but also reinvents the game. The result is a cost advantage that's not 10 percent better than your competitor's but rather many times better.

Analyzing the Environment

"Going digital" is not a luxury but a necessity. It's not a means of ensuring subtle increments in operating margin. At such companies as GE, learning to become digital and at the same time ensuring high levels of quality are matters of survival for managers. However, digitizing the business requires systematic actions.

The first step is to analyze this changing environment, looking beneath its surface activity and chaos for the emerging e-business patterns, models, and designs on which the companies of the future will be built. Figure 3.1 captures the distinction among e-business patterns, models, and designs. Patterns set the rules of the game. In chess, for example, the object is to checkmate your opponent's king: the game's basic rule and strategic objective. The other rules in chess govern how this basic rule, or end goal, is achieved. In business, the object is to establish a dominant position that is highly profitable.

The first step in identifying a pattern is finding either disruptive technologies or recurring inefficiencies in existing models. Finding disruptive technology can be a tricky endeavor. High-tech industries continuously create new market patterns. These new market sectors achieve varying degrees of legitimacy; the products and services they offer range from the truly beneficial, such as the browser and the Web, to good prospects, such as wireless Web and digital products, to the flashes in the high-tech pan, such as pen computing or push technology. But the basic rule underlining the high-tech industry's quest is finding and then exploiting the right technology, like checkmating the king, creates new game patterns.

Once a pattern is understood, it is time to drill deeper. The e-business model determines how you achieve your end goal. Models set the tactical framework of

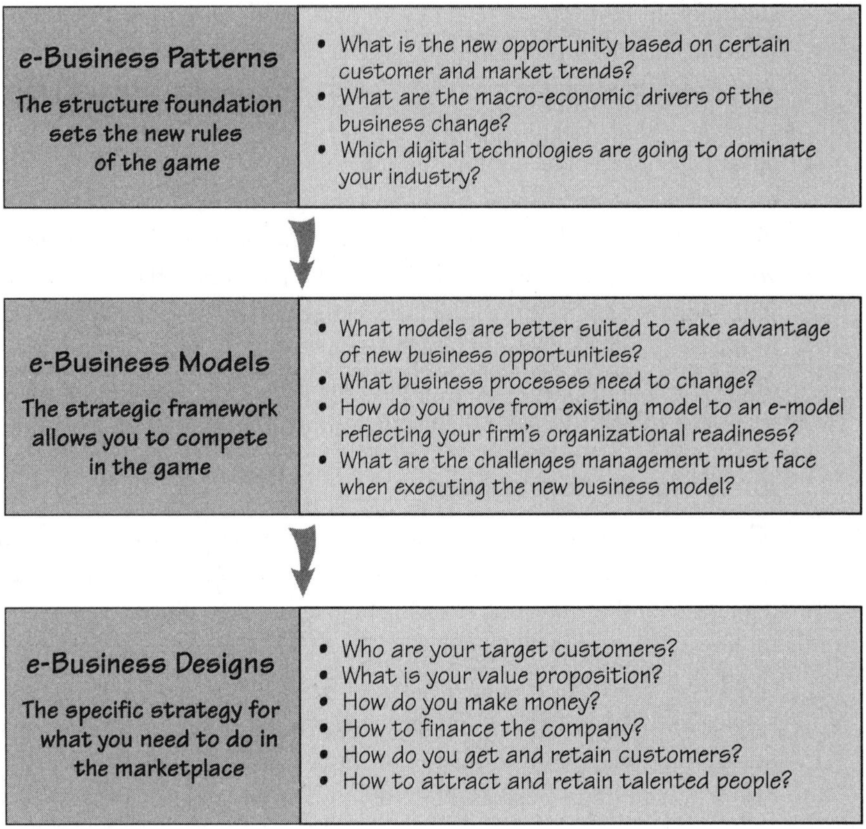

e-Business Patterns The structure foundation sets the new rules of the game	• What is the new opportunity based on certain customer and market trends? • What are the macro-economic drivers of the business change? • Which digital technologies are going to dominate your industry?

e-Business Models The strategic framework allows you to compete in the game	• What models are better suited to take advantage of new business opportunities? • What business processes need to change? • How do you move from existing model to an e-model reflecting your firm's organizational readiness? • What are the challenges management must face when executing the new business model?

e-Business Designs The specific strategy for what you need to do in the marketplace	• Who are your target customers? • What is your value proposition? • How do you make money? • How to finance the company? • How do you get and retain customers? • How to attract and retain talented people?

Figure 3.1: Digitize Your Business

action—of both competitive and customer behavior—under which the game is played. In chess, these models for action are called openings, tactics, and end games. There are many types of generic openings, such as moving the king's pawn or the queen's pawn. The goal of the opening move is to position a piece, highlighting its significance, preferably in a way threatening to your opponent. Perhaps the opening move threatens an opponent's piece or takes firm control over the center. In business, models are analogous to the tactics used in chess. Models help us focus on those customer, supplier, and internal actions leading to the profitable exploitation of an opportunity.

Once the model is set, it is time to take it to market. e-Business designs represent your operational go-to-market strategy for playing the game. You must motivate your company to act appropriately and to initiate the organizational changes required for its success. You begin the e-business design by answering the questions in Figure 3.1. The answers to these and other questions give you a knowledge base from which to approach the market. You make this knowledge base operational and context-specific when you apply it to your daily marketplace activity, based on your customer's needs and on your competition's moves, positioning, and experience.

All managers interested in the new economy should master the art of identifying, understanding, and exploiting the knowledge gained from analyzing their business, using the pattern/model/design approach. In this chapter, we discuss the various emerging e-business patterns. We then develop these further by drilling down into the pattern's implications for a given business model. The specifics of how to make your chosen model operational and apply your e-business design are discussed in Chapters 4, 12, 13, and 14.

Focusing on the Whole Picture

Thanks to the Internet, industry landscapes have undergone major upheavals, allowing previously unrelated industries to clash. A seemingly endless number of innovators are bringing their creative ideas to the market. Visionary entrepreneurs see boundless opportunities in today's world and act with lightning speed to capitalize on them. No company is unassailable. No longer do huge corporations have sole access to the capital markets. Today, it's possible for relatively unknown but talented people to raise huge sums of money.

How should management respond in these turbulent times? Begin by asking the right questions. e-Business is teaching the same historical lesson we've seen before: Change the competitive question, and you change the rules of the game. By focusing on the right question, companies can proactively alter the nature of competition.

Businesses must change behavior in order to remain competitive, shifting from old market channels to new, from production-centric to customer-centric processes, from old business models to new, from old intermediaries to new, and from physical products to digital products. Before you jump into the deep end of e-business change and begin shifting your operation toward the future, it's important to stop and consider the emerging structural patterns that characterize the e-economy (see Figure 3.2). In the following sections of this chapter, we discuss each of these e-business patterns to help you better understand which one best addresses your firm's needs. Understanding the e-business pattern

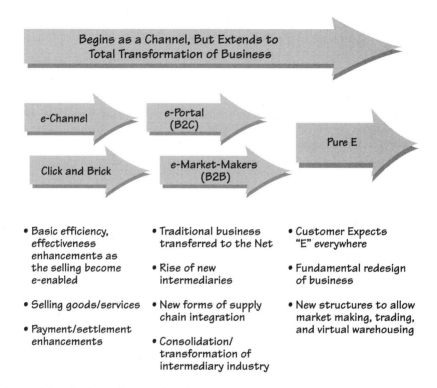

Figure 3.2: e-Business Structural Patterns

that best meets your requirements helps you answer the following fundamental questions.

- How do you segment and serve your customers in the best and most cost-effective way?

- Which of the digital technologies can help with this goal?

- When is it the right time to make the investment to digitize your company?

- How do you make the most of the competitive advantages digitalization brings to all your business operations, including increased process speed, enhanced quality, and personalized customer service?

The e-Channel Pattern

An e-channel is the chain of relationships between companies and customers and between companies and their partners/resellers. These chains, also called marketing channels, are interdependent organizations linked to deliver a product or a service to the marketplace.

For example, should McDonald's use the Internet in its selling process? Should Ford Motors? Disney? Nucor Steel? The answer is yes. Today, the customer's cry for new products and improved service—better, faster, more—is reaching a cacophonous roar. And the big firms are listening. Firms are using technology to alter the marketing channels in which they participate. Either certain links in the chain are being removed, or new links are being added to improve the marketing channel's effectiveness. Business leaders are eager to understand the types of channel structure changes that firms can make as a result of e-commerce and what customers expect from these new e-channels.

The requirement to provide continuously improving service makes the competition for customers fiercer than ever. The new ways for linking businesses and customers vastly change the dynamics of channel management. With products and services only a mouse click away, customers have more choice than ever before, and the rules governing customer loyalty have changed as a result. This new technological environment gives firms the opportunity to enhance how they do business in ways undreamed of a decade ago.

Which e-commerce channel strategy is the right choice for a firm to adopt? The answer depends on which business model is appropriate for the business. e-Channels operate on the following business models:

- *Transaction enhancement.* This approach uses the current marketing channel differently through the enhanced functionality technology provides.

- *e-Channel compression.* This approach uses technology to reduce, through disintermediation, the number of steps in the channel.

- *e-Channel expansion.* This approach lengthens the channel by adding brokering functionality.

- *e-Channel innovation.* This approach uses technology to develop new channels to satisfy unmet customer needs.

Transaction Enhancement

The simplest form of transaction enhancement is providing information in a presale format. This means making marketing information from the manufacturer or the distributor available electronically. The Web presence is used solely for information sharing. One could argue that this does not constitute e-commerce, as the transaction still takes place offline. This is technically true, but the counterargument is that the transaction may not have occurred without the supporting Web marketing. Therefore, although such sales are not considered e-commerce sales, creating a new information source does qualify as an e-commerce channel strategy.

In another form of transaction enhancement, the transaction is done online. Take, for instance, Home Depot, whose first Web site was informational, providing do-it-yourself (DIY) information and enabling customers to easily locate the nearest store. The site was relaunched with an updated design and e-commerce capabilities. The company's strategy appears to dovetail quite nicely with the company's decision to implement professional customer "Pro Initiatives" company wide. Internet ordering capabilities give customers the option to place an order either for delivery or for in-store pickup, thus saving customers time and effort.

However, Home Depot expects DIY customers to use the e-channel as an information tool but to visit the stores for additional advice or information, such as to check out a paint color in person and to complete the purchases. To Pro customers, however, the Web could become an important sales venue. In total, the Pro business represents a $200-billion opportunity, but it is the $70 billion in sales to the smaller Pro customers that Home Depot has the best chance of capturing. Home Depot's Pro sales are roughly $10 billion annually.

Transaction enhancement augments or replaces the old transaction method but in most cases does not alter other aspects of the process. In some instances, more technically savvy companies may gain business from other firms, thereby altering the identity of players in the channel. To continue the "chain" analogy, the links may be reshaped, or even replaced, but the same number of links exists. Computer manufacturer Dell and apparel provider Gap are in this category, as they are encouraging customers to replace 1–800 orders with Web orders. The companies' marketing channels have not changed except to permit online transactions (see Figure 3.3).

e-Channel Compression

e-Channel compression eliminates redundant steps in the channel. When the value added by the channel is less than it costs to operate, a compression, or direct-to-consumer disintermediation, strategy becomes appropriate. Shortening the legacy channel via disintermediation results in a closed, more direct relationship between the customer and the supplier (see Figure 3.4).

For example, partner/reseller e-channels, such as Cisco, enhance channel efficiency by managing inquiries, resolving technical configuration issues, providing

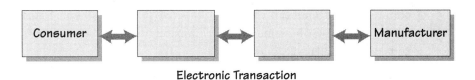

Electronic Transaction

Figure 3.3: Transaction Enhancement

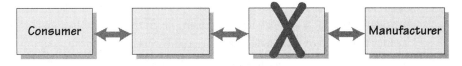

Electronic Transaction with Disintermediation

Figure 3.4: e-Channel Compression

quotes, and monitoring sales transactions for products over the Web. Rather than having to rely on dated product information, time-consuming fax orders, and calls to customer service organization, e-channels help customers help themselves directly. This "always-on" support not only increases the speed at which channels operate, thus enhancing customer satisfaction, but also drives down the cost of sales. In addition, using e-channels to process and manage orders directly over the Web enables companies to focus on helping channel partners devise better ways to sell their products.

The airline ticketing process provides another example of the benefits e-channel compression can bring. Southwest Airlines, the seventh-largest U.S airline, made its name by flying short routes between such cities as Austin and Dallas, Texas, and Birmingham, Alabama. Today, Southwest is the biggest airline on the Web. Almost 20 percent of its ticket sales in 1999—$846 million—came from purchases made over the Net. By comparison, United, the world's largest airline, sold $500 million in tickets online in 1999, even though its total revenue—$18 billion—was almost four times that of Southwest. In this case, the ticketing agent link in the chain is removed because it no longer adds enough value to the process. Moving the information sharing and transaction processing online undermined the value of the existing intermediary.

Channel compression is a strategy that is being practiced everywhere. Online stock trading provides another example of the power of channel compression and its socioeconomic impact. For example, some companies, such as E*TRADE, have recognized that by permitting the customer to make the stock trade via online services, they can eliminate the need for the traditional stockbroker. Amazon.com uses the same model, eliminating the need for traditional brick-and-mortar retail bookstores.

e-Channel Expansion

e-Channel expansion lengthens the legacy channel. On the surface, this seems counterintuitive, but because of inefficiencies in the marketplace, this approach may be needed. In a number of markets, customers desire many disjointed or unrelated products and services. For example, in the automotive market, the customer may need or want a new car, a used car, parts, car insurance, or any number of products or services. Finding information on each of these market components is difficult, especially from a single information source. Thus, the role of the infomediary, or information broker, is of critical importance to such markets.

Infomediaries, such as CarPoint for the automotive industry and Intuit for financial services, consolidate information about the various market components, making it available to potential customers, often with implicit or explicit purchasing recommendations. The infomediary steps into the existing market channel, thus lengthening the chain. Although they may never directly handle the product/service sought by the customer, they do so indirectly by providing access to it (see Figure 3.5).

An interesting variation of channel expansion is Vstore.com, which is leading the way in the newly defined e-business category of "affiliate e-commerce." Personal e-commerce enables anyone to sell online. However, unlike traditional affiliate programs, store-building tools, or online auctions, personal e-commerce empowers users to leverage existing relationships and to sell a personal selection of brand-name products through their own individually branded online stores. In other words, Jean can create her own petstore, bookstore, and electronics store

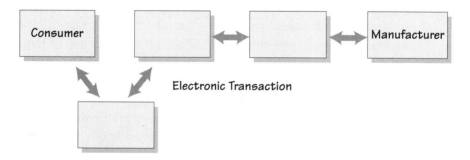

Figure 3.5: e-Channel Expansion

at Vstore.com. She can obtain the URL jean.vstore.com
friends to buy from this customized e-channel. Vstore.com ha
and customer service infrastructure that delivers products from
pliers to Jean's customized, personalized storefronts.

e-Channel Innovation

Channel innovation occurs when companies successfully attract customers by
neering new channels to satisfy and to anticipate unmet and potential custom
desires. For example, E-Stamp is attempting to transform postage stamp distribution channels. The company is the producer of the first computer-generated
postage downloadable from the Internet. At E-Stamp, customers buy postage
online by credit card, by an electronic transfer of funds, or by check. E-Stamp then
downloads the postage into its secured hardware, which is about the size of a ciga-
rette pack. This "pack" plugs into a computer port and acts as an electronic vault.
When it is time to put postage on an envelope, the customer draws the amount of
postage from the vault and uses a laser printer to print the postage, in the form of a
bar code, onto the envelope. E-Stamp's bar code includes not only the postage
amount but also the ID of the user and device, the address where the mail is going,
the date the postage was printed, the postal-rate category, and a digital pattern that
makes it difficult to counterfeit.

E-Stamp's target market—the 20-million home and small-business PC users
in the United States—is growing at close to 20 percent a year. According to Pitney
Bowes, the market for online postage is extremely broad, as anyone who generates
mail by PC would be a prime candidate. Some large firms are betting on E-Stamp's
success. AT&T Ventures and Microsoft invested several million dollars each in
1999 for a 10 percent stake in the company. E-Stamp has also worked closely with
Hewlett-Packard, to make sure that the electronic stamps are scanned and printed
correctly.[3] Meanwhile, other companies are testing similar products with the
Postal Service but are awaiting approval before proceeding with consumer testing.
Pitney Bowes, which revolutionized the industry with the postal meter in 1920,
has developed the Personal Post Office for the PC.

Clearly, the stakes are high. Companies everywhere want to make it easier and
more enjoyable for their customers to do business with them. Companies want to
provide their customers with a variety of choices. In literally every industry, the
customer base has fragmented into demographic segments, each with its own
unique behaviors and needs. This increasing diversity of customer tastes and
needs has led to a revolution in where, when, and how customers buy the products

and persuade all her
s built a fulfillment
hundreds of sup-

pio-
er

ɔany that is able to impose its solution as the dom-
the customers and the profits.

·der = Click and Brick (C&B). So-called brick-
e looking increasingly like new-economy firms
nieve greater productivity. A growing number
ll Lynch, Circuit City, Toys "R" Us, Wal-Mart,
1g to transform their operations to support a
e time, several Internet-based companies are
physical channel, in addition to their virtual
...... The nottest trends in e-tail probably won't be pure-play companies selling strictly through the Net. The most likely trend is toward the click-and-brick pattern, a hybrid online/offline business model incorporating both physical and online business practices.

The C&B pattern allows an existing offline business to profit from partnering with an emerging online presence (Figure 3.6). A great example of C&B is discount stock brokerage Charles Schwab, whose success has proved that storefronts can drive traffic to the Web sites. The firm continues to open new storefront offices every year, because that's where customers feel most comfortable signing up for their accounts. But once the relationship is established, the majority of customers use Schwab's Web site to monitor and to manage their accounts, where the customer costs less to serve. This lesson has not been lost on other retailers, which are finally starting to see benefits of combining e-commerce with old-fashioned department store service. An established retailer's name has tangible advantages in cyberspace, a world in which consumers are swamped with too many choices.

Established retailers are creating new C&B patterns. One example is Lands' End (LE), a $1.2 billion direct marketer of apparel, domestics, luggage, and other products, which is combining catalog retailing with the Web. In 1995, LE saw the Web as the next step in the evolution of a merchant-direct model providing convenience, selection, and security. The Web enables LE to respond quickly to changes in consumer lifestyle, attitudes, and buying trends; costs considerably less than print media; saves on postage expenses; and provides dynamic product assortments easily updated to take advantage of current fashion trends. LE has worked hard to lessen the impact on the customer's Web experience of online retail's shortcomings, including image quality and the absence of dialogue with a phone representative. To deliver a richer experience, LE has integrated core retailing best

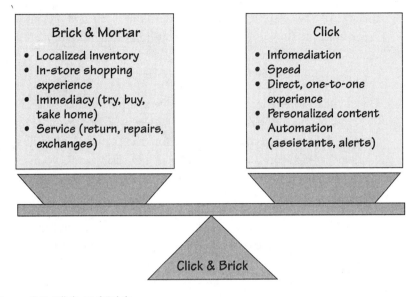

Figure 3.6: Click and Brick

practices with Web site design elements, including an intuitive user interface and personalization options.

A new variation in C&B strategy unfolded when Amazon.com revealed a 10-year partnership with Toys "R" Us. Under the terms of the deal, Toys "R" Us will provide the product, and Amazon will sell and deliver it through a new cobranded toy and video games Web site. Visitors to Toysrus.com will be redirected to Amazon.com. Amazon will receive periodic fixed payments, per unit payments, and a single-digit percentage of revenue. Many analysts see this strategic move as an acknowledgment by Amazon that it can't compete outside its core markets without significant help selling such things as hardware, lawn and garden supplies, and furniture. Also, it is an admission by Toys "R" Us that it is better off sticking to its knitting.

Why the Click-and-Brick Pattern?

At the dawn of an era in which the consensus business wisdom is that everyone will soon order everything—from books and furniture to clothing and food—over the Web, many strategists are realizing that one of the best assets for online selling is an offline store. The key to maximizing the potential of both channels is to weave them seamlessly together, allowing the consumer to buy any time and anywhere. C&B places the customer at the center of the purchasing process.

Using C&B, the customer can either order from home and pick up at the store or order from the store and take delivery at home. Any questions or problems the customer has can be resolved at either place.

C&B is built on the following key concepts.

- Physical stores can offer convenience and personal service unlike anything available on the Web. In the C&B pattern, you order online and can return the product to the company's store for an exchange. And while you're there, a good salesperson—who should be able to easily access your on- and offline purchasing history—might tempt you with something else to go with your online purchase.

- An established retailer's vendor clout should procure higher-quality merchandise for its Web sites than a start-up site with no vendor track record or ongoing relationship can get for the same money. The exceptions are commodity items, such as books, CDs, and software.

- Branding matters more than ever in a crowded world of more than 2 million Web sites. Established retailers' storefronts are living, three-dimensional billboards. They introduce consumers to a brand experience more vivid than anything available on the Web. Although Amazon.com or eToys might be well known to early Web adopters, the average shopper, who does the bulk of purchasing, probably doesn't know about them, much less trust them. For the company that cracks the code, brick-and-mortar store fronts provide a great opportunity to drive traffic to the Web outlets.

- From an expense perspective, traditional retailers have serious advantages. For example, traditional retailers spend half as much to acquire each new customer as do Web-only retailers. Williams-Sonoma can tap its database of 19 million catalog shoppers and encourage them to move their buying online. In addition to giving a carton of eggs to anyone who offers an e-mail address, Costco sends the e-mail recipients a coupon worth $5 off their online purchases.

The basis for an established firm's successfully executing a C&B strategy is the speed and momentum with which it gets its online operation up and running. One example of this is Nordstrom, which combined its store presence with a powerful Web presence. However, C&B strategies are not easy. They require flexibility, resources, recruitment skills, and political skills for making a hybrid online venture successful.

A C&B Example: Webvan

In 1913, *McCall's* magazine published "Dinners by Parcel Post," an article detailing a grand new idea: shipping food by mail to arrive directly at the doors of consumers.[4] Sound familiar? It should. Most recently, online grocers are using C&B to figure out how to sell food directly to households.

Until now, most e-commerce strategies were based on national distribution. For example, the PC you purchase online is typically shipped from a warehouse to a regional transport hub, then to a local distribution center, and finally to you via parcel service within a few days. But merging grocery megaportals with personal-courier services, take a radically different approach. These companies guarantee prompt delivery of locally stored, frequently requested items, such as groceries, dry cleaning, video rentals, or beer.

Two distinct online approaches to servicing the personal-courier market have emerged. The companies using the first approach offer convenience-oriented services. For a modest delivery charge, such companies as Kozmo.com and Urban Fetch satisfy consumers' midnight cravings for ice cream, a video, or a six-pack of beer. Companies using the second approach include the higher-end, mega-grocery sites, such as Webvan, Streamline, Peapod, and HomeGrocer, and deliver at no charge for a minimum $50 order. The firms deliver prepared meals, flowers, meats, vegetables, packaged goods, and just about everything else the major grocery chains offer. These sites rely on higher average orders to make their margins. (A typical Webvan order is $80.)[5]

Webvan's goal is to reinvent the grocery business and to expand the boundaries of home delivery. Succeeding in the grocery-delivery business takes more than cash, a savvy advertising campaign, and a cool Web site. It requires fast and error-free order fulfillment, the basis of quality customer service. Once the order is placed, automated carousels and conveyors at Webvan's distribution center bring the purchased goods directly to an employee who then prepares the shipment for delivery. With this automated warehouse system, Webvan expects to achieve better profit margins than its brick-and-mortar relatives, eventually enabling it to sell groceries at lower prices than traditional supermarkets do.

Webvan's edge is its well-designed business processes. To meet its service levels, Webvan must keep an enormous number of items on hand, many of which are perishable, and store them in the proper conditions. Continuous replenishment from distributors—Fleming Companies and SUPERVALU—which supply Webvan with merchandise, is key. However, the real key to Webvan's success will be whether it can deliver groceries and other products by using half as many employees as a large supermarket chain store. Webvan's lower labor costs per order suggest that it may enjoy higher operating margins than the supermarket chains. Webvan says that it's aiming for 12 percent margin per order, compared with the industry standard of 8 percent.

The jury is still out on the future of Webvan's business model. Can Webvan ever make money? That depends on the number of stops on a route and number of dollars per stop. In the personal-courier service, inventory location is a major success factor, along with pricing, service, and selection, and Webvan's $35 million local distribution centers are one of its major points of differentiation. Webvan is spending nearly $1 billion on warehouses and state-of-the-art Bechtel-built distribution centers. The company claims these centers can dispatch as many products in 1 day as shoppers could cart away from 18 supermarkets in a metropolitan area. Webvan plans to roll out distribution centers in 26 markets by the end of 2002. Can the company spend this much cash and yet survive in a low-margin business? Only time will tell.

Management Challenges

Weaving e-commerce into an existing operation takes a lot more effort and commitment than constructing a pure-play Web brand from scratch. The successful companies use the basics of traditional retailing while leveraging the Web to transform interactions with consumers and suppliers and, at the same time, reducing supply chain costs, broadening existing markets, and opening new ones.

Multichannel synchronization presents the following management challenges:

- *Lack of merchandise selection on the site.* Many retailers hold back their best-selling wares for fear of cannibalizing offline sales and cutting price margins. Failure to clarify ownership and strategy issues between the IT and marketing departments is one major reason for this problem.

- *Lack of communication and management collaboration between the Web site and store staffs and separate channels for fulfilling orders and resolving customer and process problems.* Failing to integrate the Web channel into the existing supply chain means that neither the Web site nor the store staff places the interests of the customer first.

- *Hiring second-tier talent to staff the Web sites.* The top IT talent has been attracted to start-up companies modeled after Amazon.com, where stock options could make employees millionaires. A modest salary from a big-name retailer offers little incentive when the alternative is a chance at independent wealth.

- *Continuing to invest millions of dollars on Web commerce initiatives without generating a positive ROI (return on investment).* The capital expense accounting rules used by existing brick-and-mortar companies have limited applicability to Web start-up investment. The Web commerce investment—$15 million to $20 million per year—required to build out, market, and run the Internet site comprises immediate expenses requiring a big charge against earnings. In the traditional retail investment, you capitalize the expenses, and they depreciate over time.

Implementing a C&B strategy as a division within the parent company is very difficult. Toysmart was one of the fatalities of e-commerce. A flawed partnership with Disney took only 9 months to doom an online business that seemed to have everything going for it. ToySmart's e-commerce infrastructure was state-of-the-art. Its 270 employees were attentive to customers, and the site reflected the company's overall quality. So what were ToySmart's biggest mistakes? Picking the wrong partner and hobbling itself by tying its fate to a slow-moving, hierarchical behemoth. Decisions that took a day to make began to take a month or more. Disney's Internet strategy was in a state of flux, and Toysmart was left out of the loop. With too little revenue and too few customers, the tiny retailer was outgunned in its own competitive market. So an impatient corporate parent shut it down. Big ideas are often crushed by larger companies that own and benefit from the status quo.

Finally, the entrepreneurial character of start-up culture is often at odds with the conservative cultures of established firms. For this reason, Nordstrom spun off its dot-com as a separate division. Dan Nordstrom, CEO of Nordstrom.com, states it clearly: "You need to have a physically separate environment. You can't have people running into each other, where everyone knows that one person's doing better than the other."[6] The spin-off can also help ease the talent problem by attracting skilled staff and giving stock options as part of its compensation package. For old-line retailers, giving new hires the stock packages common in the Web world is a foreign concept. Clearly, the old dogs have to learn new tricks as they migrate, kicking and screaming, from pure brick to click and brick.

The e-Portal Pattern

Portals are the so-called "killer" applications of e-business. The term "portal" has a variety of meanings in today's business world. For our purposes, we define a portal as any intermediary or middleman offering an aggregated set of services for a specific well-defined group of users. For example, Yahoo! and Lycos are portals that organize collections of news, search, and communication services consumers want to use. Users of the eBay, E-LOAN, and E*TRADE portals conduct the business activities associated with auctioning, loan financing, and stock trading, respectively.

A portal occurs when new players succeed in positioning themselves between customers and suppliers. Usually, these extremely customer-focused new players enter the chain to address a specific customer dissatisfaction with the current way of doing business. New portals offer either value-added services to the market channel or decrease the transaction costs associated with the customer/supplier relationship. Portals operate on several business models: eyeball aggregaters, such as Yahoo!; auctions, such as eBay; and megatransaction portals, such as Expedia.

Eyeball Aggregaters, or Superportals

Eyeball aggregaters, such as AOL, Yahoo!, Amazon.com, and Microsoft, are superportals, using the powerful attraction of their free content and service offerings to aggregate and to direct consumer traffic on the Internet. This ability to direct Internet traffic places superportals in a unique position for delivering potential customers to online retailers, in return for a fee. To date, superportal fees have been mostly in the form of advertising charges; however, the trend is toward pay-for-performance, whereby the superportal takes a percentage of each transaction, further integrating its services with those of the value chain.

Whether the superportals will experience continued success with such value chain integration remains to be seen. Prominent online retailers are leery of ceding too much power to these portals, which practice their own form of disintermediation by trying to get consumers, and particularly repeat buyers, to visit their sites directly. On the other hand, the mass buying power wielded by these large consumer aggregaters is considerable. This may force online retailers, particularly late entrants to the market or those unable to attract consumers directly, to bid for the business of the superportal's members.

Figure 3.7 captures the evolution of Yahoo! from a search engine into a media network—all in the span of 5 years. We believe that AOL, Yahoo!, MSN, and perhaps other superportals, will most likely continue to position themselves in the value chain, in one form or another. The conventional business perspective is that competition is only one click away on the Internet. In truth, time-constrained shoppers are not likely to shift online allegiances once established, unless the competitor provides significantly superior value, service, or both.

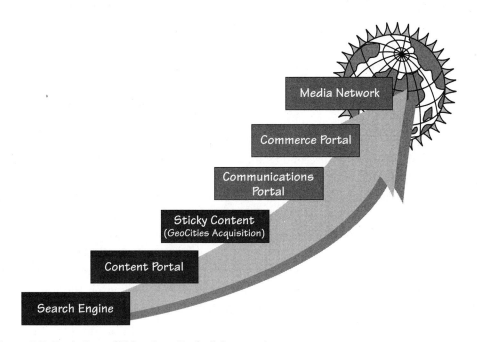

Figure 3.7: Evolution of Yahoo!, an Eyeball Aggregater

Auction Portals

If you're looking for a hot collectible or simply a good deal, online auctions may appeal to you. Auction portals enable buyers and sellers to engage in transactions across geographic and demographic boundaries, with optimal results for both parties. Through these seamless interactions, the buyer enjoys the pleasure of the hunt and finds what he or she is looking for, and the seller obtains the best price from the largest possible market. Auction portals are more than just market-places. They are a unique community of collectors, hobbyists, and enthusiasts who spend much of their Internet time on auction portals, such as eBay, uBid, Onsale/Egghead.com, Amazon.com, and Yahoo! Auctions.

In general, online auction houses work like traditional auctions, where the highest bidder "wins." But that's where the similarity ends. Because an online auc-tion house doesn't have the physical merchandise of its offline counterpart, the highest online bidder deals directly with the seller to complete the sale. If you're the highest bidder, the seller typically contacts you by e-mail to arrange for payment and delivery. Most sellers accept credit cards or use a third-party escrow agent to collect payment, obtain the product you're buying, and process the delivery of each.

The auction portal eBay is the leading person-to-person online marketplace for any form of secondhand merchandise. Items up for auction range from antiques and collectibles to cars and computers. This portal has transformed the traditionally inefficient and expensive activity of auction trading into an easy, "friction-free" online marketplace. With its global, online, person-to-person marketplace, eBay has revolutionized the way people buy and sell secondhand merchandise. The estimated value of this worldwide marketplace—more than $180 billion—comprises secondhand transaction forums, including not only auctions but also swap meets, garage sales, and classifieds.

How does eBay work? At eBay, merchandise is placed for sale by the selling individual and is openly bid for within the time limit set by the seller. Sellers have the right to place a reserve price on their property, below which the seller will refuse to sell. Sellers list items for a fee ranging from $0.25 to $2.00 per item. The sellers are charged a commission ranging from 1.25 percent to 5 percent of the transaction amount, which is scaled inversely, depending on the transaction's value. The firm estimates that more than 75 percent of all first-time property listings are successfully sold.

With more than 1.2 million online accounts and averaging more than 800,000 daily auctions in 1,100 categories, eBay captures about 90 percent of total consumer-to-consumer transactions in a "winner-take-all" marketplace, winning by having a critical mass of buyers and sellers in each consumer-to-consumer category. The company's market dynamic illustrates how Internet "cluster" economics naturally turn in a virtual cycle, with market leaders extending their ownership of a category and enjoying accelerating cash flow at the same time.

Megatransaction Portals

Several megatransaction one-stop shops are emerging as dominant, such as Travelocity in online travel and Hoovers for financial news. Some e-commerce analysts argue that the economic barriers to entry will remain low for aspiring online retail entrants. We disagree. In our view, barriers to market entry will become higher and more difficult to overcome. The emerging mega e-tailers will function as category killers, locking up portal real estate and creating a critical mass of satisfied customers. Their power to attract and to retain a large consumer aggregate will make it far more difficult, and expensive, for competitors to attract customers.

In the travel industry, for instance, megatransaction portals are taking dominant positions. The travel industry began its online offerings in 1995, with such isolated products as online booking. The industry market value is estimated at

$2.4 trillion, with the travel expenditures in the United States alone representing $500 billion annually.

What economic trends drove online travel? Reduced agent commissions, consumers' growing acceptance of paperless transactions, and the ease of completing such transactions online are the key factors in the growth of online travel. From the seller side, airlines' desire to cut travel agency commissions was a big driver. The first salvo was fired by Delta Airlines, which limited domestic ticket commissions to 10 percent with a maximum commission of $50. United Airlines then followed suit, cutting commissions further, from 10 percent to 5 percent. As a result, most travel agencies are less and less involved with routine flight ticketing, instituting service charges for ticketing transactions.

In the online travel industry, expect to see a significant amount of consolidation. As customers experience online shopping as a more complete, end-to-end experience rich with options rather than as purchasing an isolated product, they will expect integration to be the norm. The megatransaction portals will respond to this customer demand. For example, Expedia offers airline tickets, hotel rooms, and air/hotel packages over the Internet through agreements with the major airlines and hotel chains. The travel services portals are likely to consolidate along two market segments: the full-service online agency sector and the off-price discount segment. However, success for a portal means that a business must accomplish the goals of automating the look-to-book process and achieving channel synchronization, offering the 24×7 customer service regardless of the channel the customer contacts.

The e-Market Maker Pattern

An e-market maker, or Net market, is an online intermediary that connects disparate buyers and sellers within a common vertical industry, such as chemicals or steel. Net markets provide the opportunity for eliminating channel inefficiencies by aggregating offerings from many sellers or by matching buyers and sellers in an exchange or an auction. As we have seen, the online market facilitates the real-time transfer of information, money, and goods.

e-Markets are proliferating at an astounding rate because of the benefits they offer buyers and sellers. For buyers, e-markets lower purchasing costs while reaching new suppliers. For suppliers, e-markets lower sales cost and help the supplier reach new customers. An e-market functions as trusted intermediary whose well-integrated business procedures and technology save costs and streamline the purchasing and sales process.

Table 3.1 lists the various types of e-market makers. These e-market makers derive their revenue from using a transaction, subscription, or mark-up business model. Using the transaction model, the market maker takes a percentage of the overall transaction amount. This percentage is normally between 0.5 percent to 10 percent, and the fee is often divided between the buyer and the seller. Market

Table 3.1: e-Market Maker Business Models

Concept	e-Market Business Models	Examples
Exchanges	Two-sided marketplaces where buyers and suppliers negotiate prices, usually with a bid-and-ask system, and where prices move both up and down. Work best with easily definable products without complicated attributes: commodities; perishable items, such as food; or intangibles, such as electric power. Particularly appropriate if a true market price is difficult to discover. Also work where brokers make high margins by buying low and selling high to purchasers who don't know the original sellers.	Altra (energy), Paper Exchange (paper products), (GoFish.com frozen fish)
Virtual Distributors	The market maker takes control of the accounts receivable but does not take control of the physical inventory. Typically, marketplaces in which intermediaries focus on reintegration of the value chain. In many industries, small changes in economics, technology, or customer relevance can lead to huge variations in profitability along the chain.	VerticalNet, hsupply.com, Chemdex
Lead generation	Typically seller-driven, they derive revenue from ads, commissions on sales, or fees for delivering qualified leads to suppliers. Also may generate RFPs (requests for proposals) and RFQs (requests for quotes) for buyers. Provide value by understanding information needs of their users and integrating and aggregating content, information, and transactions for buyers and sellers. Most lead-generation markets seek to migrate to a transaction-oriented catalog aggregation model.	PhotonicsOnline (lasers), SolidwasteOnline.com (sewage treatment systems), Questlink (electronic components)

Concept	e-Market Business Models	Examples
Catalog aggregaters	Catalog aggregaters help normalize information coming from diverse sources to ensure like comparisons of similar products and services. They function as virtual distributors but don't take possession of goods themselves. They collect transaction fees on purchases but can generate additional revenue via credit checks, logistics management, fulfillment, insurance, or other functions that support the transaction process.	PlasticsNet, SciQuest, Testmart
Auctions	Auctions permit multiple buyers to bid competitively for products from individual suppliers and are best suited for hard-to-move goods, such as used capital equipment (forklifts) and surplus or excess inventory. Auction prices move only up. However, buyers can buy below list price, and the seller sells for more than a liquidator pays.	AdAuction, TradeOut.com
Reverse Auctions	Buyers post their need for a product or a service; then suppliers bid to fulfill that need. Unlike an auction, reverse auction prices move only down.	FreeMarkets, DoveBid

makers using the subscription model charge a flat fee/fixed cost, based on the number of transactions completed. Under the mark-up, or virtual distributor, model, the market maker buys from the supplier and resells to the buyer. The markup can vary from 2 percent to 10 percent, depending on the product purchased or the auxiliary services provided.

e-Market makers play a major role in industries that have the following characteristics:

- *Large market size.* An industry that supports a large dollar volume of transactions is likely to support a Net market. Although the dollar volume varies by industry, a reasonable rule of thumb is $10 billion in underlying transactions. A Net market focusing on a $10 billion industry in which sales and distribution costs make up 30 percent of total costs can potentially be a bigger business than a Net market focusing on a $30 billion market in which sales and distribution account for only 5 percent of total spending.

- *Fragmented supply chain.* With a large number of buyers and sellers, search costs to find vendors run high. With only a small number of buyers or sellers, they probably don't have trouble finding each other.

- *Unrecognized vendor or product differentiation.* Fragmented buyers and sellers often result in unrecognized vendor or product differentiation not merely on price but also on product availability, support, delivery, or other dimensions. In commodity markets, a Net market offers value by allowing new buyers and sellers to find each other.

- *High information-search costs.* Rapidly changing product information can result in high information-search costs, even if vendor-search costs are low. Even if a search finds no vendor or product differentiation, the cost to determine that can be high. Rapid product introductions, rapid inventory changes, or rapid price changes can produce high information-search costs.

- *High product-comparison costs.* Often, buyers have difficulty comparing similar products from multiple vendors because the products are not clearly differentiated, typically because they have many features and characteristics, not all of which are easy to find or to clearly define.

- *High work flow costs.* Internal procurement processes, credit verification, or logistics tracking can create high work flow costs for purchases.

Like technotermites, new e-markets are experimenting with new business models that are gnawing at the foundations of the old-economy companies.

The Pure-E "Digital Products" Pattern

For anyone who stays abreast of the technological changes we are witnessing today, it's easy to feel that we have seen nothing yet. New innovations in software, hardware, and communications are revolutionizing our economy and placing digital content—software, music, video, and news—at the center of business. The emerging digital-goods business will provide software, music, photos, video, and documents that can be produced, delivered, consumed, and licensed electronically.

How digital goods will be delivered is already changing. In the future, delivery will come, in many cases, as a service across the Internet instead of as a packaged product. Even the means for creating digital content is changing. Contributing to the growth of digital products are the proliferation of Internet-access devices—such as set-top boxes, TiVo, and video game consoles—the cheap and abundant availability of bandwidth, inexpensive PCs, more free PC programs, and industry standardization of application programming interfaces (APIs). More recently, eXtensible Markup Language (XML)—a programming language that provides a means of describing and exchanging data in an open format—permits digital content to be written so that it interfaces with speech and other systems, which means that such content will appear in a new, different form.

We are entering the pure-e decade, during which digital media will define how business is done. Digital products and software will define how you share and find information, even the way you think of music, software, books, and photos.

Three types of entrepreneurial activity characterize the digital-goods market.

- High-quality end user technologies, services, and products provide consumers and businesses with the interactive experiences they demand.

- Software and hardware platforms support expanded and sustainable business models for the digital products industry.

- A distribution infrastructure enables digital products to be delivered quickly, easily, and at lower cost to anywhere and on any device.

High-Quality, High-Speed Content to Consumers: Digital Music

A wide variety of companies—from old-line record labels to new upstarts—hope to make money by making music available over the Web. Recent events in the digital-music industry have illustrated a classic distribution pattern. This pattern—the collapse of the middle—is characterized by the elimination of intermediaries in the market channel and first appeared in retailing, financial services, and computing.

As Figure 3.8 shows, in the old distribution model, multiple intermediaries touched the music product on its way from the artist to the customer. Consequently, the product cost steadily increased as each participant added its margin to the product. The Internet has altered how music will be distributed. Consumers are now able to bypass the traditional distribution network, threatening entertainment industry status quo.

New companies are emerging to meet the needs of the digital-music download business. These new players are positioning themselves in the artist, retail, and fulfillment sectors of the business. For example, MP3, a San Diego–based

Old Music Industry

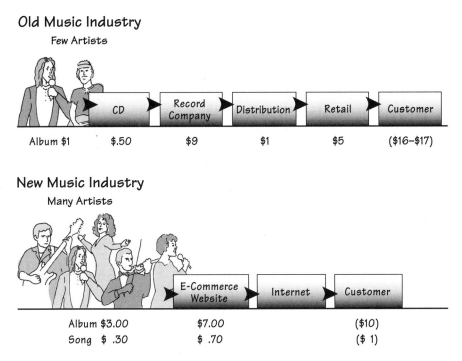

Figure 3.8: Digital-Music Industry

company, offers about 250,000 songs from 40,000 artists—mostly regional and lesser-known acts—for free downloading at its Web site.[7]

With free-download business models, artists can bypass the major labels and reach their audiences directly. Without having to sign a record contract, artists have an incentive to provide MP3.com with the free tunes in exchange for exposure. However, the greatest incentive for the musicians is freedom. They no longer have to conform to studio requirements or compromise their artistic vision just to have their music heard. In fact, the musicians can cater directly to their customers—the music listeners—without relying on all the intermediaries: from record studios to radio stations to music stores. Industry analysts estimate that the major labels sign only 7 percent of all artists. The other 93 percent are left to wallow in obscurity. In all likelihood, great talent is being lost as a result of an arbitrary selection process.

Most of MP3.com's revenues come from three primary sources. The first source is e-commerce through sales of CDs by specific artists and sales of compilation CDs. The second source is offline sponsorships involving concert sponsorships and other promotional agreements. The third source of MP3 revenues is online advertising in the form of Web site advertisements and sponsorship of free CD samplers.

The digital-music arena is burgeoning with creative activity, and new peer-to-peer technologies are continually emerging. Programs that allow new ways of locating, accessing, and distributing content are cropping up on the Internet. Napster allows users to find music files through a centralized index on the company's servers and to then download those files directly from other users' computers. Gnutella skips the centralized index and allows users to find and to download content in a variety of file types, including music, videos, and documents, directly from other users who are also using the Gnutella software. Pointera skips the downloading process by allowing users to play content, such as music or videos, directly from other users' computers without downloading the file. These new "distribution" models are creating quite a stir in the music industry because they lack the means for content originators to collect royalties and to protect copyrights on music. But the implications for the world at large are also significant. These programs represent the emergence of new distributed and decentralized models for searching for and accessing data of all kinds.

What does this all mean? The traditional intermediaries involved with the music industry supply chain are in for an interesting ride. Sure, the major record labels, music stores, and radio stations will continue to be around in one form or another, but do expect more industry consolidation and a much smaller major-label presence. The era of the major labels is over. The Internet is transforming the music business and is placing greater power in the hands of new digital-music industry players, individual artists, and fans. Business-as-usual will soon mean no business at all for many of the industry's middlemen.

New Platforms for Digital-Media Delivery

Seemingly overnight, the wireless revolution exploded, intensifying the movement toward mobile commerce. New programming languages, platforms, and protocols are embraced almost with abandon or little consideration, and new partnerships and wireless portals are announced daily. The market for the delivery of Internet services through handheld devices is new and is evolving rapidly. The introduction of Palm Computing's first handheld device ushered in a new generation of handheld products that offered users a combination of simplicity and powerful functionality. Innovations in design, synchronization technology, user interface, programmability, functionality, and battery power management transformed these devices into convenient personal productivity tools. These enhancements significantly accelerated user acceptance.

Three companies are racing to take the pole position in the pocket PC market: Handspring, Palm Computing, and Microsoft. The business strategy behind these players is straightforward. If you take control of the operating system infrastructure, you will also control the software applications developed to run on it. As handheld devices are adopted in greater numbers and as handheld device applications become integrated into other information appliances, an opportunity exists for these operating system developers to extend their platforms for use on other handheld devices.

One such example is Handspring's Visor handheld computer. Handspring was established in July 1998 by Jeff Hawkins to develop innovative handheld computers that are fun, smart, approachable, compelling, and personal. Visor is a personal organizer that is enhanced by an open expansion slot, called the Springboard platform. Examples of the Springboard-ready modules are content items, such as books and games; consumer applications, such as an MP3 player, a digital camera, and a global positioning system receiver; and communications applications, such as wireless modems and two-way pagers offering Internet and intranet connectivity. Handspring's goal is to be an innovator in designing expandable handheld devices that enable new mobile computing and communications applications.

The wireless revolution isn't only about handheld devices. It is also about the new generation of mass-market wireless phones, which will soon enable the convergence of the Internet and mobile telephony. Phone.com, which developed its initial technology in 1995, pioneered the delivery of Internet-based services to wireless telephones. In 1996, Phone.com introduced and deployed its first products based on this technology. To provide a worldwide open standard enabling the delivery of Internet-based services to mass-market wireless telephones, Phone.com, Ericsson, Motorola, and Nokia formed the Wireless Application Protocol (WAP) Forum.[8]

By complying with WAP specifications, wireless telephone manufacturers, network operators, content providers, and application developers can provide interoperable Internet-based products and services. In 1998, the WAP Forum published the Wireless Markup Language, or WML, which is designed to be an industry standard that will encourage the development of Internet applications and content for wireless telephones. Content providers and application developers use WML to optimize the display of, and interaction with, Web-based data on wireless telephones. WML is optimized for the delivery of Internet content to mass-market wireless telephones, which have numeric keypads instead of full keyboards, small screens, and limited memory capacity, processing power, battery life, and bandwidth. WML is compliant with the XML specification published by the World Wide Web Consortium.

The next-generation mobile delivery systems include voice browsers and telephony-based speech-recognition systems. Now telephony-based speech recognition is extending to the Web. Many companies, such as TellMe and HearMe, are racing to make telephone access to e-commerce and Web information ubiquitous. The type of content that would benefit the most from these types of efforts is real-time high-value information, such as flight information, weather information, and stock quotes. A number of companies, including Motorola, Nuance, AT&T, IBM, and Lucent, have introduced initiatives and technologies that will allow users to access time-sensitive Internet content using their voices over a wireless phone. Recent advances in speech-recognition technology, including natural-language and interactive-dialogue processing, speaker-independent speech recognition, speaker verification, multilingual text-to-speech synthesis, barge-in options, and keyword and phrase spotting, have made it possible to use the telephone to search the Web. The business models in this area are in their infancy.

Given the dynamic and still unfolding nature of the mobility's business patterns, it is too soon to declare a dominant platform. But the wireless revolution and its implications for mobility will be fascinating to watch for the next several years.

New Infrastructure Services for Digital-Content Delivery

As digital media become more widely used, new infrastructure services are required to support faster content distribution. For example, the ability of a Web site to attract users is based in part on the richness of its content. Increasingly, Web site owners want to enhance their content by adding more graphics, such as photographs, images and logos, and digital music and by deploying newer technologies, such as secure video, audio streaming, animation, and software downloads.

To solve the problem of Internet bottlenecks—access, routing, congestion, and rich content distribution—new infrastructure services are emerging. Among them are

- *Content delivery.* Content delivery, or congestion management, services help popular Web sites, such as AOL, maintain protection against peak crowds, perform at optimal speed, and support the ability to serve engaging, rich content. Digital Island and Akamai Technologies are two companies that are providing congestion management services.

- *Caching services.* Caching services vendors, such as Inktomi and CacheFlow, deliver to users content from high-speed storage spaces called caches. Caching is a hardware and/or software solution sold to Internet service providers (ISPs) to help them improve network performance by placing electronic copies of selected Internet content on geographically distributed servers on their own network. For instance, AOL might buy from Inktomi a caching product that keeps in memory the most frequently requested pages. These functions are similar to the Internet browser's cache that stores the pages you visit most frequently. Unlike content delivery services, caching is not designed to address the needs of Web site owners that need to deliver their content with high performance and reliability across the multiple networks that comprise the Internet.

- *Outsourcing services.* Outsourcing, or colocation services, permit Web sites to increase their capacity by using an outside hosting service. Outsourcing Web server management to hosting companies, such as Exodus or Level 3, enables Web sites to add server capacity as needed and to increase server reliability. However, transmission disruption problems can arise as data leaves the hosting company's servers and traverses the public network to the user.

Each of these services has a different business model. For example, the caching model differs from that of content delivery services. Whereas content delivery vendors are paid by their customers—the Web site owners—caching suppliers are paid by the ISPs, which seek faster response time for their customers, the individuals sitting at Web browsers. Will one business model win out over the other? Given the large size of the market and the different needs of the players, the answer is probably no.

For instance, the premise behind Akamai, one of the leaders in digital-content distribution, is simple: The Internet was not designed to provide a rich multimedia environment for users. Since its origin as a research project, the Internet has evolved into an aggregate comprising many networks, each developed and managed by different service providers. The Internet was never designed to manage traffic between these disparate networks and to find the optimal route to deliver information content. Congestion or transmission blockages significantly delay the information reaching the user. As the volume of information requested on a Web site increases, large quantities of repetitive data traverse the Internet from that location. The storage of Web site information in central nodes further complicates Internet content delivery.

Here is how Akamai's services work. A typical commercial Web page includes a number of objects, such as logos, photos, ads, and even audio or video files and executable programs. Most of these objects are stored on the Web site's home server and must be transmitted across the network every time a user requests the page. But when a site is "Akamaized," the page a user downloads consists of only a basic outline, within which are embedded instructions for fetching the various objects from the Akamai network rather than from the home site. Web sites hand content to Akamai for guaranteed delivery—sort of a digital version of FedEx or UPS. The model is based on the widespread deployment of Akamai servers across the Internet locating them as close as possible to end users. Working together and using sophisticated algorithms and continuous monitoring of Internet conditions, the servers retrieve and deliver the requested objects to the user in the shortest time possible and also deliver video streams quickly and reliably. To provide optimal delivery, Akamai rebuilds an Internet congestion map—similar to a weather map—every 7 minutes.[9]

Digital content requires new delivery services to serve the increasing volumes of online traffic and to enhance the user experience with increased graphic, video, and audio content. These new services must deliver content to users, enhance Web site response times, and avoid delays and outages caused by peak demand and public network congestion. These services must be fast, reliable, and easy to implement and also capable of delivering rich content that is continually updated. In addition, these services may be cost-effective for the customer only if they do not require significant capital or labor expenditures but can be implemented at a cost based on customer use.

Memo to the CEO

Good managers must think not only like CEOs—vision, team building, and profits—but also like venture capitalists—new opportunities and speed—and must do so at the same time. Managers need to evaluate opportunities quickly and to set a path of action decisively. This boils down to the question, How do we select the right business model, one that will be a winner? Even with the uncertainty surrounding the early stages of e-business, it is possible to identify those companies that are building a solid foundation for their future success. From within this group will come the rule makers of the new millennium.

Digital strategy is becoming a game played at breathtaking speed. Whereas a successful strategy could once give a company a sustainable edge over its competition for decades, a successful strategy today might be out of date a few years after it is implemented. Following are some of the traits we believe will characterize the long-term winners in the race to e-business success.

- *Winners go after very large market opportunities.* Once a company meets the basic criteria for driving traffic, converting buyers, and making profitable sales, it is important to understand the company's addressable market opportunity. When it comes to market opportunity, bigger is obviously better.

- *Winners select a business model to suit the market opportunity.* Winners pick large, addressable market opportunities and then create business models suited to the opportunity. For example, retailing has multiple business models. At one end are well-informed customers who want basic products and services at the best price possible. At the other end are customers who prefer high-end, tailored solutions to their needs. In retailing, one-size-fits-all companies, such as J.C. Penney and Montgomery Ward, have stagnated over the past decade. The lion's share of retail growth has come at the extremes, with Wal-Mart epitomizing the low end and Nordstrom and other upscale retailers locking up the high end.

- *Winners change the economics of the supply chain.* Technology, combined with improved processes, can eliminate inefficiencies in the supply chain and distribution channels. When the product value chain becomes more efficient, consumers benefit in the form of lower prices. Online retailers are often able to complete transactions at lower costs than their traditional retail counterparts because of improved technological and process efficiency. As we have seen, the travel industry provides an excellent example of the benefits accruing from technology. Online travel agency transaction costs are 68 percent lower than the average brick-and-mortar travel agency. Eventually, once critical mass of customers is achieved, online travel agency transaction costs will be 80 percent lower than traditional travel agency costs.

- *Winners enjoy economies of scale.* The rule makers often invest in up-front fixed costs, minimize variable cost, and allow for a continuously improving business model as the company grows. Rule-maker investments tend to be focused on technology and distribution center facilities. Currently, online retailers that outsource key functions, such as site operations or product distribution, tend to have reduced costs at low-volume levels. However, we believe that these same retailers will be at a significant competitive disadvantage at higher-volume levels. In addition, online retailers using outsourcing may face quality-control issues from poor process management in the out-sourcing firm.

- *Winners build a strong consumer brand.* Today, brand equity encompasses much more than just consumer recognition of a brand name, which can be achieved through heavily-funded ad campaigns. Brand equity includes all-in product price, the product delivery time, excellent customer service, word-of-mouth advertising, site "buzz," and entertainment value—everything comprising the consumer's total shopping experience. Although the strength of a brand is difficult to measure, we view customer acquisition costs and repeat customer purchases as proxies for brand equity. A great consumer shopping experience drives word-of-mouth advertising, which is far more cost-effective than paid media advertising, and a loyal customer base is far more profitable for retailers than one that is churning.

- *Winners have management teams that are focused on execution.* When the pace of change is as fast and furious as it is today, managers must be able to "turn on a dime," altering strategies when the market requires it. Managers who are incapable of such flexibility will fail. At the same time, they must practice the fiscal discipline necessary to bring the company to profitability. Fluidity and discipline are an unusual combination, and most managers tend to be more of one than of the other. However, we all recognize the rare manager in whom the blend is seamless and balanced, resulting in powerful leadership.

The pressure to rethink how we do business is analogous to the gut-wrenching changes companies underwent during the quality wave, when many U.S. industries were threatened by competition from Japan and other Pacific Rim countries. The auto, steel, and textile industries lost market share to a wave of imports. U.S. TV, camera, and other consumer electronic companies were almost wiped out. After the prosperous 1950s and 1960s, U.S. companies had grown fat and happy, leaving themselves vulnerable to nimble competition from abroad. To survive, many corporations went through a painful period of restructuring, reorganizing, downsizing, and reengineering. Many old-line companies could not compete with companies that had implemented more effective business processes and better technology. However, out of the 1980s economic upheaval emerged leaner, more nimble, and more competitive U.S. companies. Sound familiar?

CHAPTER FOUR

Thinking
e-Business Design:
More than Technology

What to Expect

First movers—the dot.com companies that reached the market first—appeared to win the war for e-market leadership. But in reality, the war has just begun. Although these early entrants have won many battles, we are in the early stages of the conflict between the challengers and the established firms against which they compete. The battlefield is shaped by three dominant factors driving the new economic revolution: the shift from supply chains to demand chains, the emergence of Web and mobile commerce, and the escalating pace of technological innovation. These are just three reasons why business-as-usual has changed forever.

In order to thrive in this dynamic environment, companies must consciously choose the next phase in their growth and evolution: the age of continuously innovating e-business design. In this new era, competition is not primarily between one product versus another or between one technology versus another. The true competition is between the viability of traditional business design in a business environment increasingly dominated by e-business design.

The challenge confronting today's manager is in the creation, execution, and ongoing evolution of a successful e-business design. How do you craft an e-business design? How do you transform a traditional business design into an e-business design? In this chapter, you'll learn e-business design secrets from three successful market leaders. You'll learn the right questions to ask and the right answers to seek.

e-Business can be a blessing or a curse, depending on your perspective. When asked the main issue they lose sleep over, the majority of winning e-business executives we questioned expressed the following concern. They fear not being proactive and farsighted enough to make smart decisions about where their companies should focus their attention. The reason for this is simple. A CEO can think of many interesting ideas and directions to improve company performance, but the company has the time, resources, and people to implement only the best ones. What if the CEO chooses the wrong cutting-edge concept or strategic path? In a fast-moving environment, every mistake made gets magnified, and few companies, much less their managers, get second chances. We call this architecting e-business.

e-Business success depends on how well company executives make such decisions while crafting an e-business path that was not preordained but that is of their own choosing. When crafting its e-business direction, management must pay careful attention to three interlocking layers: e-business design, e-business application infrastructure, and e-business infostructure (see Figure 4.1).

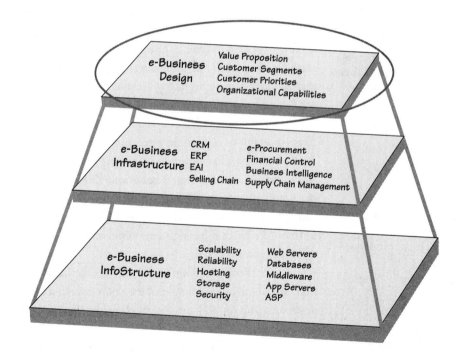

Figure 4.1: e-Business Interlocking Layers

e-Business designs are the first-level strategic weapons in the new digital economy. In an environment in which multiple variables—technology, customer requirements, supply chains—are changing simultaneously, the old weapons of differentiation—low cost, quality, and incremental process improvement—are playing a lesser role in sustaining growth. Business design is no longer an optional part of corporate strategy; rather, it's the very core. To create an innovative e-business design, you must first answer the following questions.

- *What business design can make your customers' shopping and service experiences unique and memorable?* Although it's not easy, a good way to outperform competition is to render it passé by pleasing customers in novel ways. Essentially, that's what e-business is all about. e-Business uses technology and processes to keep the finger on the pulse of the customer. Over and over, we see examples of innovators leapfrogging over competition by delivering better end-to-end service. Total and complete service is important because it's what a customer experiences and, moreover, truly cherishes. *When assessing a business design's value, ask yourself whether it meets your customers' priorities not only today but also in the future.*

- *What capabilities and competencies create rich customer experiences?* This question helps define the capabilities required to match your customers' most important priorities. These decisions determine what your customer sees and encounters when interacting with your e-business design. For example, at Dell, value is defined as the convenience of purchasing a high-quality product at a low cost. Making the purchase process convenient has resulted in an explosive growth of Dell's Web-based sales. *In the quest for customer-centricity, are you product or process oriented? How do you sell to the customer—through a sales force, reseller channels, or a call center (direct)?*

- *In the quest for efficiency, how do you structure your organization for efficiency?* Dell is innovative in how it not only sells but also manufactures computers. The company uses a build-to-order (BTO) business model. Dell doesn't start building a machine until an order is received. This helps keep computer components and finished-computer inventory levels low, which in turn controls costs. Understandably, competitors Compaq and IBM are working overtime to replicate Dell's BTO e-business design. *In the quest for cycle-time reduction, how much does your company manufacture internally, and how much does it outsource? How do you distribute your product?*

Each of these e-business design elements must be in alignment for your company to excel at providing exactly what customers wish to experience when doing business with you. Once this design is in place, you are ready to move to the next level: creating the application infrastructure.

The *e-business application infrastructure* supports the e-business design by providing the software functionality required for the business design to work. Early in the e-business revolution, many businesses raced onto the Web only to discover—often quite painfully—that having a URL doesn't spell automatic success. If you attempt to win the business of the e-customer without rock-solid, bullet-proof e-commerce applications and back-office integrated systems, you will succeed only in alienating that customer. In order to ensure their e-business success, companies must create a strong application infrastructure foundation from which they can deploy their e-business applications. Addressing enterprise-wide infrastructure needs first means avoiding the integration issues resulting from disparate systems, data formats, and legacy applications.

The *e-business infostructure* is the structural foundation supporting the application layer. Building a reliable infostructure ensures that applications are working and that online operations are accessible and available. A well-built e-business infostructure

- Is a balance of structure and flexibility

- Harnesses, safeguards, manages, and permits use of information in ways that are fast, safe, and simple

- Comprises the technology, utilities (tools), and services needed to enable an uninterrupted flow of commerce

In this chapter, we discuss the why, what, and how of e-business design. We use case studies to illustrate the various aspects of successful e-business designs.

The Race to Create Novel e-Business Designs

Jack Welch, CEO of General Electric, once said, "When the rate of change in the marketplace exceeds the rate of change in the organization, the end is in sight."[1] The demands that corporations place on their managers in charge of corporate strategy have never been greater. CEOs are asking their managements to invent the next generation of breakthrough products, find innovative ways to cut costs and manage channels, and develop a strategy for getting products to market faster—all while achieving quality throughout. More than ever before, corporate strategists responsible for new product and service offerings are held accountable for getting it right the first time, in terms of cost, time to market, and quality. Aside from the obvious competitive pressures, huge dollar amounts are at stake if any of these factors is misread. Choosing the right strategy accelerates market penetration and minimizes cost. Choosing the wrong strategy can cause years of repercussions in cost, quality, customer satisfaction, and supply chain issues—serious problems no amount of tinkering will fix.

The business world provides us with a number of exemplary firms whose management teams discern and implement new strategies with consistent success. Why do some companies always seem to be in the right place at the right time with the right strategy? How does American Express continually improve service in the competitive charge card and business travel markets? How was Dell able to operationally outmaneuver Compaq, IBM, HP, and others in the cutthroat computer industry? Why are Cisco's competitors losing market share to this innovative supplier of networking gear?

What sets the truly great organizations apart is their ability to use state-of-the-art e-commerce processes to transform themselves. They do the following three things well.

1. They redefine value for their customers.

2. They build powerful e-business designs that outperform the competitions.

3. They understand customer priorities and consistently raise customer expectations to new heights.

In other words, these companies change the rules of the game with their new business designs. They use business designs to leverage emerging trends before the rest of the world—and their competitors—catch on. For example, the giant car warehouses CarMax and AutoNation recognized that customers are looking for a more friendly experience in buying a car. Customers want no-hassle treatment, cars at low prices, and a wide selection of new and used vehicles. CarMax and AutoNation have reshaped the car dealer network by consciously selling an experience as much as a product.

When transforming a business today, the focus is no longer limited to process improvement. Improvements in isolated company processes bring only incremental benefits in a new business environment requiring enterprise-wide change at a minimum. Today, the focus of change initiatives has shifted to business redesign. Innovation in business design is gathering momentum with the rise of e-commerce. The retail drug industry provides an excellent example. Drug retailers, such as CVS, Walgreen, and Rite Aid, suddenly faced competition from Internet start-ups, such as Drugstore.com and PlanetRx, which sell over-the-counter medicines, medical supplies, and prescription drugs (an $87.8 billion market).[2] The established drug distributors are responding to the e-commerce threat by revamping their business models. Walgreen customers can also order prescription refills over the Web. Rite Aid not only offers online refills but also uses the Web to remind its customers when their prescriptions are due to be refilled. Today, members of Merck-Medco Managed Care network, which handles prescriptions for more than 60 million consumers, can refill their orders electronically. Also, Medco is clobbering the online competition. Every week, it processes 80,000 online prescriptions, raking in $10 million in revenues—about what PlanetRx.com sells in a quarter.[3]

So, what's the single best *next* opportunity for your organization to pursue? Business success depends on how quickly a company can formulate novel business designs and adapt them to its markets. Incremental process improvements won't work. If you're pressed for time, would you take a horse-drawn carriage if you had the option of taking a car or, better still, an airplane? Today's business environment is driving the switch to e-business design by demanding not only enterprise-wide change at the individual company level but also total supply chain and marketing channel transformation.

Step 1: Self-Diagnosis

Before embarking on your journey to create an e-business design, you must first assess the impact of recent customer, business, and technological trends on your company by asking the following questions.

- *Has the recent wave of technological innovation created new ways of doing business and reorganizing priorities within your firm?*

- *Is your company responding to changing customer expectations? Is it aware of the dimensions of value that your customers care about?*

- *Is your company willing to question and to change countless industry assumptions to take advantage of new opportunities while also preserving existing investments in people, applications, and data?*

- *Is your company successful at lowering operating costs while making complex business applications adaptive and flexible to change under the relentless pressure of time to market?*

If *all* your answers are yes, you and your firm are in the *innovator,* or *market leader,* category in today's business environment. You and your firm are indeed lucky and rare. Savor the moment.

If *most* of your answers are yes, you and your company are in the *early adopter,* or *visionary,* category of today's environment. You too are rare. Your company is among the first to exploit new technological innovations to achieve a competitive advantage over its rivals. Let's take a look at an example of another early adopter, Charles Schwab. In an industry in which the fast pace of innovation is not for the faint of heart, Schwab has built a discount brokerage colossus of more than 5 million customers placing more than $931 billion worth of total assets into Schwab accounts. Schwab is building its entire business model around an e-business infrastructure. This includes eSchwab, the largest online brokerage service in the world, with more than 1.5 million customers. In 1998, eSchwab customers moved more than $100 billion worth of assets through online connections. What can we learn from Charles Schwab? *Even large, established firms can be early adopters and compete successfully with small, fast-moving innovators.*

If *few* of your answers to the preceding questions are yes, your firm belongs in the *silent majority* category. Interestingly, as Geoffrey Moore points out in *Crossing the Chasm,* the silent majority is often made up of three types of people: pragmatists, old-guard conservatives, and die-hard skeptics.[4] We believe that these three categories represent not only individual but also company behavior. They vary in the degree of risk they are willing to take. In all three categories, the company management chooses to believe that e-commerce is a fad never to become a key facet of mainstream business. In the process, their belief in e-commerce's "faddishness" causes these managers to miss one of the biggest stories of modern times: nothing less than the transformation of our society and its economy. As we analyze and discuss each of these categories, you'll no doubt recognize them in people you've known and in places where you've worked.

Managers in pragmatic firms see the world changing around them, but they want proof that the changes are long term before they commit their companies to action. Pragmatists often stay very close to their current customer base in order to keep focused on delivering superior customer value. Pragmatists, who often find it difficult to be creative in the day-to-day grind of business activity, should read the opening lines of A. A. Milne's classic, *Winnie-the-Pooh:* "Here is Edward Bear, coming downstairs now, bump, bump, bump, on the back of his head, behind Christopher Robin. It is, as far as he knows, the only way of coming downstairs, but sometimes he feels that there really is another way, if only he could stop bumping for a moment and think of it."[5] Too many demands often keep managers bumping along, unable to concentrate on their changing business designs to adapt to the coming new world.

The management at old-guard conservative companies is in a state of denial. Conservative companies avoid growth prospects that do not align with their distinctive core competencies. Old-guard management remains pessimistic about the ability to gain any new form of value from its technology investments and undertakes them only under duress. Only the threat of impending bankruptcy can convince this risk-averse type of management that its business model is changing.

Robert Galvin of Motorola is reported to have said that in the 1940s, his father viewed 14 firms as key competitors but that today, most of them don't exist.[6] Why? Each stuck to its knitting too long. Since the 1920s, Motorola has routinely abandoned existing markets, even though it meant relinquishing considerable equity. The company jumped from car radios to two-way radios, to televisions, to microprocessors, to cellular pagers and wireless systems. Each transition was full of risk, but had Motorola not taken those risks, it wouldn't be here today. What can we learn from Motorola? In the face of continuous product innovation wrought by technological change, sticking to your knitting leads to business failure.

Die-hard skeptic companies are destined to fade away. These companies are like the nineteenth-century British Luddites, reactionaries who feared competition from machinery and its potential for the disintermediation of labor. They smashed machines with sledgehammers in a futile attempt to arrest the march of industrial progress fueled by science and technology. The stubbornly obsolescent management of the die-hard skeptic firm is convinced that technological change will never affect its firm or its industry. In this view, almost everything—including news of technological innovation—is media hype. In its heyday, for example, the railroad industry refused to believe that consumers would prefer air travel to rail travel. A more up-to-date example is the mainframe computer industry, which refused to believe that personal computers would ever amount to much. What can we learn from these two industries? By not taking technological change seriously, your company risks failure or, worse, extinction.

Companies today can be classified as market leader, early adopter/visionary, or silent majority (pragmatist, old-guard conservative, and die-hard skeptic) types of firms. If you see where you and your firm are in the picture we've painted and don't like it, you must make a path to get to where you'd rather be. This requires you to better understand how customer needs are changing, by making customer priorities your priorities and by developing and adopting an e-business design. As you pursue this path, you'll find that the e-business model represents a complete reversal of the value chain strategy model taught in MBA programs and preached by consultants everywhere! So, where does this leave you? Read on.

Step 2: Reverse the Value Chain

The greatest challenge in e-business is linking emerging technology to a company's new business design. Were it just a matter of linking emerging technologies to existing markets or vice versa, management's challenge would be relatively easy. But when both current technology and markets are changing and are doing so dynamically, this linking becomes a delicate process indeed. As new technologies emerge, they affect customer needs by raising expectations of the possible, and these changing customer needs influence a company's business design, requiring it to change as well. As a new business design is implemented, it alters the way a company's processes work. As a result, process requirements change, influencing the next generation of technology.

Technology alone cannot make a business design dynamic, but it can make a dynamic design a real dynamo. As new technologies and customer needs emerge, managers find creating new business designs difficult, for two reasons. First, most have been trained to concentrate on improving products, increasing market share, and growing revenues. Second, in the e-business world, the distinction between products and services often blurs. Therefore, success depends on creating new "product offerings" in which customers see the additional value.

Successful companies no longer just add value; they invent it. To invent value, managers must reverse the traditional value chain thinking characteristic of the inside-out model in which businesses define themselves in terms of the products they produce (see Figure 4.2). In this traditional model, managers concentrate on being effective and competitive by putting well-understood products on the market. In the new world we're entering, however, the business design must be outside in.

In an outside-in approach, the strategy revolves around the customer's requirements, not the company's. Why is this so crucial? A recurring pattern throughout the history of business is one of business conditions suddenly changing direction, causing entire industries to completely rethink the way they do business. Often, the stimulus for such change in the market is a new entrant that does not play the game by the understood rules. More important, the new entrant perceives customer needs not met by the product offerings of the game's current players. The challenger reconfigures the offering and suddenly starts running away with the business. A customer-centric business design places customer priorities and requirements first and know that these continuously change.

Traditional coffee companies, such as Folgers and Maxwell House, experienced the competitive impact of a customer-centric business design firsthand when they failed to see the shifting consumer trend toward gourmet coffee. Starbucks saw it and created its business around the gourmet-coffee drinker. If management at the established coffee companies had stayed focused on changing customer tastes, they would have migrated toward the gourmet-coffee market, changed their delivery systems, and restructured their pricing. In the process, they would have made it much more difficult for Starbucks and other upstarts to break into the market and steal their customers.

The need for an outside-in, customer-centric approach becomes essential in times of great structural transition in the economy, when old categories and concepts suddenly become obsolete. Businesses must redefine themselves in times of flux, a danger for companies married to a business definition that's fixed to specific products. How do you navigate today's dangerous waters? By defining new product and service offerings, based on a continuous sensitivity to customer needs (see Figure 4.2). Dell, American Express, Charles Schwab, Microsoft, and Wal-Mart are shining examples of firms that understand what the customer wants.

How does one create the most effective, enjoyable purchasing experience for one's customers? A well-crafted business design results from reconfiguring and integrating your company's competencies, its market channels, application infrastructure, and employee talent to address this question. New e-companies, such as Ariba, Yahoo!, and E*TRADE, have been quite effective at this reinvention process. How can established companies follow suit?

Traditional Business Design

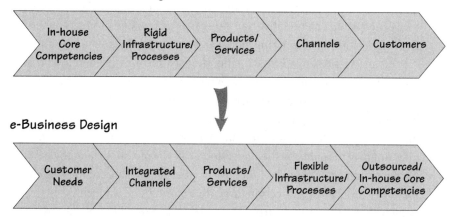

e-Business Design

Figure 4.2: Reversing the Value Chain

The creation of an e-business design is inextricably linked to the management of change. Change begins when the organizational mind thinks in new ways that later translate into and are shaped by new ways of behaving. However, change is not necessarily an uncontrolled activity. The boundaries of change and the terms of its successful management are set by choosing a specific business focus at which you want to excel. In the next section, we discuss three types of focus excellence—service, operational, and continuous improvement—winning companies use to narrow their creative thinking and to orient their business direction.

Step 3: Choose a Focus

Although adopting new technology can enable firms to excel, it can also disable firms that don't concentrate on its best use. Market leaders use three types of e-business designs to narrow their focus and to retain market leadership, knowing that few organizations can do many things well. No visionary company shines in every dimension of business cost, quality, price, convenience, and ease of use. Amazon.com, for instance, doesn't ship books any faster or more conveniently than anyone else does. Dell is not the cheapest computer online. Charles Schwab doesn't offer better online trading than its competitors. Rather, these companies thrive because they provide intrinsic, narrowly focused value that their customers care about.

In order to narrow its circle of competence, a successful firm chooses one of the following types of focused excellence:

- *Service excellence:* Delivering what customers want with hassle-free service and superior value

- *Operational excellence:* Delivering high-quality products quickly, error free, and for a reasonable price

- *Continuous-innovation excellence:* Delivering products and services that push performance boundaries and delight customers.

The objective is straightforward. To succeed, a company's e-business design must be focused. Once this focus has been decided, commit the resources required for its implementation.

Service Excellence

Imagine that you frequently fly between Atlanta and London. Now imagine what your trip would be like if every airline employee with whom you came in contact—

at the ticket counter, at the gate, and as you take your seat—knew you by name and knew all your travel preferences. For example, they would know that you prefer evening flights and an aisle seat, that you're on a low-fat diet, and that you don't watch movies. As a customer, you would feel both important and valued. It would certainly strengthen your bond with that airline, and you'd probably tell your friends about it.

Service excellence involves selecting a few high-value customer niches and then making a concerted effort to serve them well. If you're focused on service excellence, your company will be responsive to and in tune with your customers' desires (see Figure 4.3). This strategy requires a commitment to customer relationship management (CRM). CRM means anticipating the customers' needs and sharing relevant information with your customers to provide expedient self-service, if that's what the customers expect.

The operating principles of service excellence are as follows.

- *Prepare your company for the unforeseen.* For example, imagine that your top competitor just dropped its price by 10 percent. A customer calls your call center to see how you'll respond to the drop in price. Are you prepared to quickly rearrange your company's priorities, people, and processes to head off such competitive threats and to take advantage of sudden opportunities?

- *Gather and maintain all the up-to-date, accurate business and economic information you need, where you need it, and when you need it.* Your company must be able to blend intelligence and information in order to make wise decisions quickly.

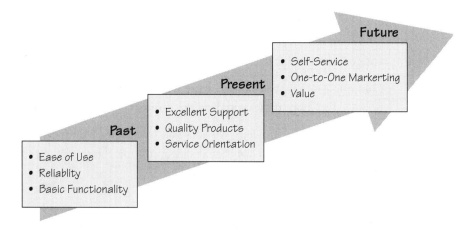

Figure 4.3: Shifting Customer Service Expectations

- *Use customer contact management.* You must know when a customer's last encounter with your company was, which channel he or she used to contact you, the nature of the encounter, and the outcome. Few companies have this level of sophistication in tracking their key assets—their customers.

- *Develop a corporate philosophy about customer service.* Business practices that result from a company-wide attitude provide insights into breakthrough customer service about how to improve the value proposition.

Operational Excellence

Imagine if you could break down the process barriers between your organization and others so you could work better with your vendors and suppliers. Imagine how much simpler it would be if you could let your vendors access the information they need to service your company. If they could see your inventory levels, production plans, and product designs, your suppliers could be much more responsive in meeting your needs. You'd spend a lot less time on the phone or at the fax machine coordinating routine purchasing. Likewise, imagine how much easier life would be if you had access to your vendors' shipping schedules, materials availability, and production plans. You could work together as a single, virtual organization rather than as separate entities. Think of the edge such operational excellence would give you in producing and delivering products.

Operational excellence means providing the lowest-cost goods and services possible while simultaneously minimizing problems for the customer. A business focused on operational excellence finds working with customers and partners to be a lot like working with departments within its own company. Knowing their customers intimately and working closely with their partners gives such companies a clear advantage in today's business world (see Figure 4.4).

The success of operational excellence depends on several key principles:

- *Efficient leveraging of assets.* Resources are allocated in the most efficient manner and at the lowest cost possible.

- *Management of efficient transactions.* For greater efficiency and speed, business processes between suppliers and the organization are often integrated.

- *Management of sales intelligence.* Imagine that you're a PC manufacturer. You need to know what's selling, where it's selling, and when it's selling. And you need to convert all these facts, details, and insights into information you can use.

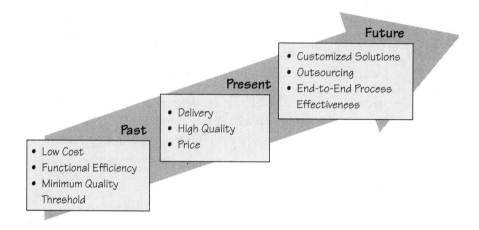

Figure 4.4: Shifting Operational Expectations

- *Dedication to measurement systems.* Businesses dedicated to operational excellence monitor and measure all business processes, continually searching for ways to reduce cost and to improve both service and quality.

- *Management of customer expectations.* Under the principle that variety kills efficiency, operationally excellent companies provide a manageable set of product or service options and manage customer expectations accordingly.

Continuous-Innovation Excellence

Change, change, change: Create it or die from it. Continuous innovation demands dedication not only to providing the best-possible products and services but also to offering the customer more exciting features and benefits than does your competitor (see Figure 4.5). Why is continuous innovation critical? The marketplace is a dynamic playground. Continuous innovation results in product leadership, as several examples illustrate. Microsoft is expert in continuous innovation in several markets it serves, including operating systems, productivity packages, and online services. Sun Microsystems excels in the enterprise server market, and Nike eclipses competition in the sports shoe market. A company's failure to adapt to the increased business-process speed and economic turbulence resulting from technological change can cause even the best to lose ground. For example, lack of technological innovation has pulled down such mighty corporate giants as AT&T, Eastman Kodak, Sears, and General Motors.

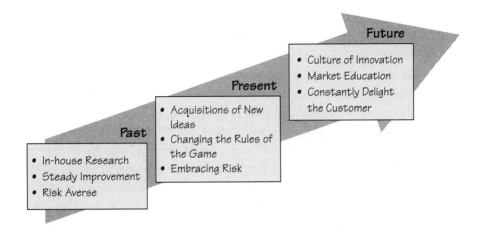

Figure 4.5: Shifting Innovation Expectations

Continuous innovation is based on the following principles:

- *Risk-oriented management style.* Product-leadership companies are innovators, and innovation requires recognition that the risks, as well as rewards, are inherent in new ventures.

- *Growth by mergers and acquisitions.* A company's current success and future prospects lie in its acquisition of new products and those that design them.

- *A market-education style.* Recognize that your company must lead the market in educating your customers about how to use and benefit from new products.

- *Encouraging innovation.* If you develop a mindset of experimentation is good and create compensation systems that reward success, continual product innovation will be encouraged.

Step 4: Execute Flawlessly

Once you've made the tough decisions required to coordinate these business processes, you must then figure out how to change your company and how to implement the decisions you've made. *How can you move from where you are today to where you want to be? How do you integrate and tailor your legacy infrastructure to meet new e-business requirements?*

Like a battlefield commander who assumes great losses in order to ensure future success, executives must be willing to cut their losses and abandon important current projects that do not support the goals of the e-business design. Resources from these noncritical projects must be reallocated to support the business design effort so critical to the survival of the company. Although it's risky to abandon old directions representing millions of dollars and countless work-hours of effort, time to formulate new plans is running out.

Everyone, including your competition, faces the same tough reassessment of company direction and the proper application of its assets. To preserve their businesses, corporate executives must vigilantly prioritize new projects, based on their congruence with the newly emerging e-business design. Managers must do so in a continually changing, dynamic business environment. *Are you ready?* Let's examine three companies that have been executing flawlessly: American Express, Dell, and Cisco.

Case Study: Service Excellence at American Express

For a century and a half, American Express (Amex) has been successfully developing new, innovative products and services. The company began as a cargo agent forwarding freight on the railroads. While the freight business was still growing, Amex made a transition to issuing money orders, primarily as a service to the immigrant community. Later, the company branched out into retail travel services, credit cards, and traveler's checks.

In the 1980s, the company expanded into the integrated financial services sector, including banking and financial planning. In essence, the business shifted from money transfer to money storage. Amex acquired investment banks and brokerage companies to ensure financial product diversification, in hopes of countering the inherently cyclical nature of the financial services industry. However, the strategy backfired, and Amex had to divest itself of several noncore businesses in the early 1990s.[7] Why did Amex's diversification strategy fail? It failed because of the absence of a customer focus. Amex's business model was classic management by the numbers. Senior management knew little about the company's diverse businesses and had no idea what was going on in the company's divisions, resulting in chaos and poor performance.

In the 1990s, Amex's CEO, Harvey Golub, transformed the firm from its global financial services one-stop-shopping model to a more narrowly focused service model. This latest transition has resulted in a new e-business design that concentrates on the profitable management of customer relationships.[8]

Amex Business Overview

Amex provides services in travel, financial advisement, and international banking in more than 160 countries. The business is organized around three segments: Travel Related Services (TRS), Amex Financial Advisors (AEFA), and the American Express Bank.

TRS issues the Amex charge card, the Optima card, Traveler's Cheques, and other stored-value products, targeted mostly at the high-end customer. The strategy: The more customers spend, the more perks they get. Depending on the type of card, Amex encourages member loyalty through MembershipRewards, benefits that include savings on airline tickets and other purchases. TRS is also the leading provider of travel services to large and small businesses. Amex's corporate cards are integrated with business travel services as a means to help businesses manage their travel and entertainment budgets. Services include trip planning, reservations, and ticketing. TRS also has more than 1,700 locations in more than 200 countries and publishes food- and travel-related magazines. It also operates an online bank, Membership Banking, which is the nation's second-largest operator, behind Bank of America, of ATMs, many of which are located in 7-Eleven stores.

AEFA provides financial services and products to both individuals and businesses. Products include financial planning, sales of insurance and annuities, mutual funds, limited partnerships, retail brokerage services, trust services, and tax preparation. AEFA provides financial planning that addresses financial protection, investment, income taxes, retirement, estate planning, and asset allocation for a fee.

Amex Bank is a subsidiary focused on providing financial services for corporations and affluent individuals, primarily outside the United States. Commercial banking is provided to corporations with trade finance and risk management services in emerging markets. Wealthy entrepreneurs are targeted by the bank for investment and trust management services.

Amex faces new challenges, as depicted in Figure 4.6. Amex's latest projects include revamping its online brokerage service; launching Blue, a chip-embedded secure card for Internet buying; and some new online tools for customers of its financial planning business. The cost of these ventures would be $250 million a year. Clearly, the business environment is changing, and many products are transforming as a result of new customer priorities. Also, the company's profits and margins are under pressure. Like all credit card companies, Amex needs to

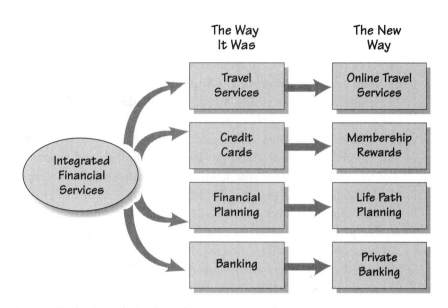

The Way It Was → The New Way

Integrated Financial Services

The Way It Was	The New Way
Travel Services	Online Travel Services
Credit Cards	Membership Rewards
Financial Planning	Life Path Planning
Banking	Private Banking

Figure 4.6: The Transformation of American Express

acquire and to retain more customers to compensate for its shrinking margins. Thus, its superior service provides a much-needed competitive edge.

Service Strategy Shall Lead the Way

As Table 4.1 shows, Amex's business design is changing from a traditional model to an e-business model based on customer relationship management, or segmenting customers and tailoring offerings to create value. Although the word *value* is mentioned quite frequently in business, just what is it? Value consists of price, quality, intrinsic product features, brand, service, and a pleasurable buying experience and relationship with the company over time. Often, value means different things to different people. For example, service may be of utmost value to many customers, in part because product quality and pricing in many industries are close to parity. *Put another way, in an era of limited personal time, customers appear to be more concerned about quality service, especially its simplicity, flexibility, and consistency.*

Amex understands this concern and plans to excel at CRM by combining detailed customer knowledge with service flexibility. For example, Amex's CustomExtras, built on strategic use of technology to cull information from its extensive databases, enables the company to offer custom discounts and other deals directly on card members' bills. This provides customers with great service

Table 4.1: Evolution of Business Design at American Express

	Traditional Business Design	e-Business Design
Key Trends	• Product focused • Rigid, functionality-oriented systems	• Customer focused • Flexible, integrated service applications
Key Assumptions	• Cost reduction as key to success • Task oriented	• Customer relationship as key to success • Solution oriented

at no extra charge, a smart way to add value. Amex hopes that the program will engender tremendous customer loyalty.

At Amex, creating Customer Relationship Statements (CRSs), also known as monthly bills, is a technology-intensive task. Convincing customers to spend more means presenting the right customers with exactly the right offer at the right time. By extracting spending patterns from the company's mainframe databases, which are jam-packed with customer transactions, the system comes up with a custom set of promotions for each customer. The result is printed right on the cardholder's monthly statement. Thus, customers who frequently purchase jewelry are likely to find an offer for a $100 discount on their next purchase of jewelry at their favorite store. The program is a powerful incentive for customers to use their Amex cards and for merchants to accept them.

The CRS is a great place to entice customers with discounts because bills are required reading, unlike most promotional mail, which goes straight from the mailbox to the trashcan. The message inserted with a bill has close to a 100 percent readership rate and costs zero in extra postage. The goal is to transform the monthly billing statement into a communications channel and a vehicle for delivering added value. Amex intends to encourage merchants to grant discounts displayed on favorite customers' CRSs.

The focus on value has forced Amex to rethink its definition of service to include offering service before a sale to help customers make better choices. To build the base for service excellence, Amex is investing roughly $1 billion annually in the construction of a sophisticated service infrastructure. The scale and scope of service is quite incredible. Amex handles 215 million customer service inquiries a year. Within the financial services industry, these expenditures can provide Amex with a means to develop a competitive advantage and also raise competitive barriers to entry.

Service Excellence and Application Infrastructure

In the financial services industry, technology is not a luxury but an absolute necessity. Amex illustrates how enhancing the Amex brand is contingent on a technologically dependent service-excellence strategy.

Several e-business initiatives are under way at the company. The Amex Corporate Services Group (CSG) has launched several new e-business initiatives. American Express @Work is a corporate desktop portal that provides for online management of corporate card and corporate purchasing card programs. AXI TRAVEL is an online corporate travel portal with more than 500,000 registered users. In addition, CSG further enhanced its interactive business travel portal through a strategic alliance with GetThere.com to give its customers a choice of online travel reservation systems.

Amex customers can use the purchasing card to order directly from manufacturers and suppliers rather than the traditional system of requisitions, purchase orders and invoices, and retail store purchasing. TRS pays the suppliers and submits a single monthly billing statement to the company. To expand its online purchasing capabilities, TRS is teaming up with Ventro to build a new online marketplace where companies will buy and sell everyday business products and services. The new company, MarketMile, will target the buying needs of midsized companies, offering everything from office and industrial supplies to computers and temporary labor.

Amex is trying to bring customer-targeting capabilities to the Internet. Already, card members can check their balances, view their statements, and look up offers from merchants on Amex's Web site. Nearly 1.6 million customers are registered with Amex Online Services. This service enables customers to review and to pay their Amex bills electronically, view their MembershipRewards accounts, and conduct various other functions quickly and securely online. In addition, the company redesigned its Web site and launched My American Express, enabling customers to tailor the site to their needs, and established online hubs to provide integrated financial, travel, and entertainment services to customers. Amex has also made progress in developing additional interactive utilities, such as a common framework for Web site design, to facilitate implementation of new Internet initiatives across its businesses in a more timely and cost-effective manner.

Continuous enrichment of the Amex brand is a critical element of its future growth. The firm's goal is to integrate all Amex products into a cohesive service framework further enhancing the brand.

Case Study: Operational Excellence at Dell Computer

Dell Computer is the number-two computer systems company in the world, with revenues over $27 billion. As one of the first major companies to move its sales channel onto the Internet, Dell generates more than $40 million a day in Internet sales: roughly 40 percent of its revenues.

Dell Computer's roots are interesting. At age 13, Michael Dell ran a mail-order stamp-trading business from his home in Houston. Dell started college as a premed student but found time to establish a business selling memory chips and disk drives for IBM PCs from his dorm room. Dell bought his products at cost from IBM dealers, which at the time were required by IBM to order large monthly quotas of PCs, which frequently exceeded demand. Dell resold his inventory through newspapers and computer magazines at 10 percent to 15 percent below retail.

Dell's computer business was grossing about $80,000 a month in early 1984, enough to persuade him to drop out of college. At that time, he started making and selling his own IBM clones under the brand name PC's Limited. Dell sold his machines directly to end users rather than through retail computer outlets as most manufacturers did. By eliminating the retail markup, Dell could sell his PCs at about 40 percent of the price of an IBM. Dell's strategy was relatively simple: Beat competition on price and performance by using standard components and software and pull down the profit margins of competition in the process.

Company Overview

In 1988, Dell raised $34.2 million in an initial public offering on NASDAQ. Dell tripped in 1990, reporting a 64 percent drop in profits. Sales were growing, but so were costs, mostly from efforts to design a PC using proprietary components. Also, the company's warehouses were oversupplied. Within a year, Dell turned itself around by cutting inventories and coming out with new products. It added international sales offices and started to focus on selling to government agencies and Fortune 1,000 customers.

Dell entered the retail arena in 1990 by allowing Soft Warehouse Superstores (now CompUSA) to sell its PCs at mail-order prices. In 1991, the company made the same agreement with the office supply chain store Staples. In 1992, Xerox agreed to sell Dell machines in 19 Latin American countries. That year, Dell sold a new line of PCs through Price Club (now Price/Costco). In 1994, Dell abandoned the retail stores to go back to its mail-order and telephone-order origins.

Today, Dell is growing rapidly in the European and Asian markets. How does Dell sell overseas? Just as it does at home—customer-direct. Dell has things arranged so that customers all over the world can dial toll-free to one of six call centers in Europe and Asia. A customer in Lisbon, for instance, places a local call that is automatically forwarded to Dell's center in Montpellier, France. There, the customer is connected to a Portuguese-speaking rep. Dell ramped up its efforts in Asia with new mail-order service in Hong Kong, Japan, and Singapore; a new Asia/Pacific customer center in Malaysia; and direct-sales operations in South Korea and Taiwan.

Build-to-Order e-Business Design

Our generation is studying the Dell build-to-order model—e-commerce driven by a fine-tuned supply chain—like our parents' generation studied Henry Ford's assembly line. Dell's direct-sales model illustrates how close you want to get to your customer and yet be operationally efficient.

What is the key to Dell's success? The company offers superb low-cost manufacturing and fast-cycle product development. In other words, Dell's focus is end-to-end operational excellence. The company adopted this focus at a time when the PC business was changing and old-line companies, such as IBM and Compaq, seemed ill suited to meet the needs of rapid change. The integration of customer demand from the direct-sales channel with the back-end supply chain is reshaping the PC industry. This integration enables the cost-effective selling of build-to-order computers directly to customers, thus bypassing the resellers and their markups.[9]

As a result, Dell has reengineered the $76 billion computer-distribution business. Computer distributors once controlled the PC business. Now, a number of them are bankrupt. The cause: Dell's direct-sales model. The direct-sales model squeezed the margins of the middlemen, like CompuCon, which were traditionally between the PC makers and customers. To survive, distributors automated and speeded up their inventory cycle—cutting warehouse time from 12 weeks in 1997 to 5 weeks in 2000—but they still couldn't keep up with Dell's 6-day average: not when shelved PCs lose 1 percent of their retail value every week.[10]

To compete with Dell, Compaq, HP, and IBM started to cut out the middleman wherever they could. In May 1999, Compaq dropped all but 4 of its 39 distributors. At that time, only 20 percent of sales were direct; today, it's aiming for 60 percent. The few distributors left standing absorbed another blow: a major cutback in rebates and advertising support from PC makers. In a short period, three giants—CHS Electronics, MicroAge, and InaCom—have all declared bankrupcy. The corpses will continue to pile up.

Dell's Build-to-Order Operation

Dell assembles its U.S. PCs in Austin, Texas; its European PCs, in Limerick, Ireland; and its Asian PCs, in Penang, Malaysia. All the plants are located close to supplier plants, such as Intel; Maxtor, which makes hard drives; and Selectron, a motherboard manufacturer with just-in-time shipping of parts. An order form follows each PC across the factory floor, starting when the machine is nothing more than a metal chassis. Drives, chips, and boards are added according to the customer's request. At one spot, partly assembled PCs roll up to an operator standing in front of a tall steel rack with drawers full of components. Little red and green lights flash next to the drawers containing the parts the worker must install. When the operator is done, the machine glides on down the line.

To compete in the cutthroat PC and desktop server market, Dell needs a supply chain that is very flexible and agile, for the following reasons.

- When products become noncompetitive, Dell must be agile enough to move to a line of new products that are compatible with existing capital and human resources.

- As their incomes rise, customers demand better selection and higher-quality products. Therefore, customized, build-to-order products and services become more commonplace.

- As competitors introduce new models, Dell must make design changes quickly by switching supply sources. Also, when competitors start offering multiple quality and price levels, Dell needs more flexible product mixes.

- When customers want fast delivery and are willing to pay premium prices or when competitors start offering expedient deliveries, Dell's supply chain needs to be more flexible in its transportation and delivery approach.

- Because new microprocessors and other innovations prompt changes in customer demand, Dell needs to respond quickly to these changes by supplying new products in a short time.

Dell's build-to-order approach gives it several advantages.

- Dell has no finished-goods inventory. The company manufactures the central processing unit but purchases monitors and keyboards from others. When it receives an order from Dell, UPS Worldwide merges the shipments of the processor, monitor, and keyboard from various origin points at one of its facilities in Reno, Nevada; Louisville, Kentucky; or Austin, Texas. The entire system is delivered intact.

- Dell's tailor-made computer systems contain the latest high-margin components. This is important because inventoried components depreciate quite rapidly.

- Unlike manufacturers that use resellers, Dell has direct contact with its customers. If a trend pops up and customers request 40GB drives, Dell knows immediately.

- Selling directly means that Dell isn't getting paid by resellers. It gets paid directly by companies, such as Boeing. Dell receivables have a very high credit rating.

- Consumers and small businesses pay for their orders by credit card, which means that Dell has its money in the bank before the motherboard meets the chassis. Dell has a cash-conversion cycle—the difference between the time it pays its creditors and the time it takes to get paid—of 8 days.

A key element of Dell's operational excellence is the interface to the supply chain. In the build-to-order model, the link with the customer is extremely critical. The business design model of operational excellence for delivering the highest customer satisfaction is built on an e-business infrastructure with four characteristics: ease of use, rich functionality, reliability, and delivery of integrated performance. These characteristics imply a need for supply chain excellence in anticipating and responding to changing customer requirements. In Dell's case, this link is its Web site.

Operational Excellence and Application Infrastructure

Dell was the first major PC manufacturer to implement a Web-based business model by integrating all its operations on the Internet. Originally, during phase 1 of the site's development, the site presented customers with simple product and price descriptions, rather like an online catalog. Now, in phase 2, visitors can take advantage of more sophisticated services, such as the ability to enter specifications of the hardware or software they require. Visitors then receive information only on the machines and prices that match these criteria.

Also during phase 2, customers can take advantage of a more sophisticated online customer support system, including an order-tracking system complete with courier-tracking technology. Customers can find out exactly where their orders are, from the time they enter their purchase to the moment the goods arrive. To enable more customization, Dell introduced Premier Pages service to provide more than 27,000 corporate, institutional, and government customers with the ability to readily access company-specific pricing, use a paperless purchase order system, and seek advanced help desk support and asset management information.

The objective of the Premier Pages service was to increase Dell's business-to-business (B2B) direct sales significantly and thus turn inventory more quickly. Dell has for some time maintained customized procurement pages, with specific rates for each customer. Customers would shop through their specific page, select products, and deposit them directly into a shopping cart. Once a purchase was completed, though, the customers would have to manually rekey each order into their own ERP, procurement, or other Web purchasing system. The customers' inability to access Dell's applications directly has made procurement a difficult and time-consuming task.

This direct, Web-based model has worked well for Dell. In the minds of its management, however, it's not enough. What's the next competitive step? Dell is focusing on further tightening of its ties with its top customers. To accomplish this, Dell is now upping the ante with a phase 3 model based on B2B integration. B2B integration is the exchange of information between applications across corporate boundaries. Dell's model, called B2B Direct, is creating a business community in which its operational systems are directly integrated for real-time data exchange with the operational systems of its customers. This seamless integration speeds up the business, production, order, fulfillment, shipping, and payment cycles. With B2B Direct, Dell wants to streamline e-procurement for its customers, thus reducing operation costs, shortening transaction and fulfillment cycles, and increasing productivity. Dell is using open standards, such as XML, to achieve B2B integration. XML makes it easier to exchange data and to translate from various data formats, thus shortening cycle times and cutting costs. Based on early research, Dell estimates that several of its largest customers will save $4 million annually through reduced procurement costs and improved productivity.[11]

In phase 4, a Dell customer will enter a tag code located on the back of the machine and will be able to view pages of technical support that correspond to that particular computer's hardware and software. Increasingly, the service side of Dell's business will be the differentiator in operational excellence.

What can we learn from Dell? The company's major goal is to make the internal operations of the company agile enough to respond to the ever-increasing and ever-changing needs of its customers. Operational excellence implies that successful companies succeed by developing flexible business designs built on solid technical foundations.

Case Study: Continuous Innovation at Cisco Systems

Cisco is the leader in the rapidly growing market for internetworking equipment, enabling its customers to build large-scale integrated computer networks. Companies worldwide are demanding increased hardware and networking capability in order to move ever-increasing amounts of digital information within and across their sites. This surge in data traffic is driving the exponential growth of the internetworking industry.

Cisco's story best depicts the new model of continuous-innovation management. At Cisco, the business design centers on its core belief in what continuous innovation demands from the organizations attempting it. Continuous innovation means that organizations must

- Build on change, not stability

- Organize around networks, not a rigid hierarchy based on interdependencies of partners—not self-sufficiency

- Construct their operations on technological advantage, not on old-fashioned bricks and mortar

Cisco's application foundation aids and abets this business design.

Company Overview

Cisco was founded in 1984 by Stanford University husband-and-wife team Leonard Bosack and Sandra Lerner and three colleagues. Bosack developed technology to link his computer lab's network with his wife's network in the business school. Deciding that there could be a market for internetworking devices, Bosack and Lerner mortgaged their house, bought a used mainframe, installed it in their garage, and got friends and relatives to work for deferred pay. They sold their first router in 1986.

In the beginning, Cisco targeted universities, the aerospace industry, and government facilities, relying on word-of-mouth advertising and contacts made via the Internet. In 1988, the company decided to expand its marketing to include large corporations. Short on cash, Cisco turned to venture capitalist Donald Valentine of Sequoia Capital. Valentine bought a controlling stake in the company and became its chairman.

As the market for network routers opened up in the late 1980s, Cisco, whose products already had a proven track record, had a head start on competitors. In addition, the company was the first to offer reasonably priced, high-performance routers. Cisco's sales exploded, jumping from $1.5 million in 1987 to $28 million in 1989. Cisco went public in 1990.

With the explosion of the Internet, Cisco's products became the foundation for the networked business model. Today, the company's products are at the heart of nearly every large network worldwide, and Cisco intends to keep it that way. By using acquisitions to broaden its product line, Cisco can offer customers one-stop shopping for networking gear. Cisco Systems is emerging as the strategic internetworking vendor of choice, a powerhouse equal in stature to such household names as Microsoft and Intel.

Exponential Growth: Playing the Acquisitions Game

Most companies struggle to absorb one or two acquisitions. Cisco is considered a master at the acquisitions game, having accomplished more than 50 in the past 5 years. Increasingly surrounded by larger competitors, Cisco eventually made acquisitions the cornerstone of its business strategy. For example, by 1991 Cisco's sales had reached $183 million, but the company faced increased competition from both start-ups and computer giants IBM and DEC.

In order to survive, Cisco began a program of rapid expansion via acquisition in 1993, swapping about $95 million in stock for Crescendo Communications, another California-based networking company. Cisco also debuted products for the lower end of the router market. The following year, Cisco bought Kalpana, the leading maker of Ethernet switches. In 1995, Cisco pumped up its position in the fast-growing ATM (asynchronous transfer mode) switching markets when it bought LightStream.

In 1996, Cisco acquired Statacom in order to enter into the Frame relay marketplace. That same year, the company increased its presence in the Internet connectivity market with purchases of MultiNet software maker TGV Software and Internet Junction, makers of software connecting Novell NetWare users with the World Wide Web. In 1997, Cisco acquired Granite Systems, which manufactures Gigabit Ethernet switching capable of moving data at rates up to 1 billion bits per second. In 2000, Cisco bought Cerent, developers of a device to deliver high-bandwidth, multiservice transport

Cisco's earnings growth, stemming from its acquisitions, has made Cisco among the best performers on the NASDAQ. A $10,000 investment in Cisco stock in 1990 was worth well over $2.5 million by 2000. Cisco's market capitalization has also passed the $500-billion milestone, a landmark feat for a company just in its teen years. A rising stock price is a critical element in making a modern business strategy successful. A rising stock price provides currency for companies like Cisco to use stock to buy other companies.

As voice and data networks increasingly merge into one, Cisco faces competition from Lucent Technologies and Northern Telecom. This unfolding battle of networking giants will be interesting to watch over the next decade.

Continuous Innovation via Acquisitions

Cisco's acquisitions are managed and carried out by an acquisitions group that fulfills two functions: strategic and tactical execution. On the *strategic* level, the acquisitions group is responsible for identifying companies that help Cisco enhance its product line and keep up with the changing marketplace. Based on what customers are saying and what competitors are doing, Cisco might perceive a potential missed market opportunity because it hasn't moved quickly enough or in the right strategic direction. Acquiring a company with the necessary technology already in place provides a quick fix.

On the *tactical* level, the acquisitions teams must make sure that Cisco's culture absorbs each acquisition without skipping a beat. From the day the transaction closes—a window of between 1 and 3 months after the acquisition is announced—Cisco begins integrating the target company into its operations, ensuring that the new product line quickly adds to Cisco's revenues.

Cisco's tactical integration strategy is not unique. Other market leaders follow similar strategies. For example, Newell Corporation, which merged with RubberMaid, is a gigantic maker of housewares, hardware, and office products—everything from Levolor blinds to Mirro cookware and Rolodexes—that has devoured more than 40 companies in the past decade. Newell's dynamism comes from its ability to readily assimilate the acquired entities. How? Through integrated application infrastructure, of course. All 47 of its disparate manufacturing plants use the same processing and purchasing applications from American Software. All payroll processing is handled by Cyborg, and all financial transactions are handled by Global AP & GL. Oracle's IRI Express runs Newell's data warehouse, tracking point-of-sale information on each and every Newell product. Newell says that because of standard application usage, it realizes significant cost savings when integrating its acquisitions.[12]

Cisco's e-business architecture must be flexible enough to support the organizational structure imposed by its acquisition strategy. An acquisition strategy creates an innovative business structure, one characterized by a strong center surrounded by freewheeling satellites, or business units. The challenge is to manage this type of loosely coupled structure while continuing to provide the customer with seamless product integration. This degree of business unit harmony is often difficult to achieve, and if Cisco isn't careful, this strategy could be its undoing.

Continuous-Innovation Excellence and Application Infrastructure

To support its innovation-excellence business model, Cisco began by building its Extended Enterprise model in 1992. Cisco, growing at the spectacular pace of 100 percent a year at the time, believed that traditional business processes couldn't provide the level of communication integration necessary to maintain and to increase customer satisfaction. Cisco needed a new approach, one that hadn't been taken before.

Cisco's strategy was to focus on its core competencies—the design and selling of innovative networking solutions—and to form partnerships with suppliers that could provide other key capabilities. Cisco's decision to partner was based on its belief that suppliers add more value than Cisco can in such areas as manufacturing. This decision—to focus on its core abilities and to hand off those functions to which it added less value than its suppliers could—has contributed to Cisco's growing revenues and the creation of shareholder value. Suppliers—typically, low-margin businesses—benefit by improving asset turns. Cisco benefits by managing costs down and improving responsiveness.

Cisco Connection Online (CCO) is a key component of Cisco's e-business strategy. Through CCO, users are linked to Cisco's internal operational systems and databases and can access a wide variety of support materials and applications. Product and technical information, assistance from technical support engineers, software downloads, order tracking, and e-commerce are available from anywhere in the world.

CCO has demonstrated the following benefits:

- *The ability to scale for growth.* More than 73 percent of orders are now placed through CCO. Sales quadrupled while call center staff grew only 10 percent.

- *Self-service technical support.* Eighty percent of routine calls by customers to technical support are now solved online. The estimated savings is $83 million.

- *Increased speed and accuracy in order processing, shipping, and deployment.* Order rework decreased from 15 percent to 2 percent. Lead time was reduced by 2 to 3 days.

- *Minimized software upgrade distribution costs.* More than 90 percent of software upgrades are distributed electronically, for an estimated annual savings of $250 million.

To achieve such positive results, Cisco designed and implemented initiatives in several areas of the supply chain. Rather than attacking these areas all at once, Cisco began small, with its automated product quality testing system, to support suppliers. Over time, these successful initial efforts were expanded to incorporate more of the supply process, and other initiatives were added. Collectively, these initiatives have transformed how Cisco does business and has allowed the company to grow very rapidly while simultaneously building customer satisfaction, responsiveness, product quality, and keeping cost much lower than its competitors'. In short, Cisco's Extended Enterprise is a tremendous competitive advantage.

Lessons from e-Business Design

The successful businesses of the next decade will not be found among those companies fighting today's battles with yesterday's tactics and tools. The objective is not to catch up with the competition but to outperform it by quantum leaps. What today's market leaders are really good at doing is finding new ways to delight their customers.

Effective business design and execution depend on how managers use technology to deliver services faster, cheaper, and with better quality than their competitors can. Technology is the only theme common to the three case studies discussed in this chapter. However, their *management of technology*—to reconfigure underlying business infrastructures and to deliver outstanding value—provides important lessons to be learned.

Be customer focused. Of the many business imperatives to which organizations must respond, none is more difficult, more perilous, or more vital than being customer focused across multiple business units. To accomplish this, innovative companies are using the Web and the Internet to build interactive relationships with prospects, customers, resellers, employees, and suppliers.

Value creation is a continuous process. Even the best business designs have short life spans. Today's rising stars can become complacent, move too slowly, incorrectly anticipate competitors' moves, or miss strategic opportunities. Then they may face the unsettling question of whether value is beginning to migrate toward start-ups with better business designs.

Transform business processes into digital form. A fundamental premise of an e-business enterprise is that all information must be available in digital form. In other words, nothing is available on paper that isn't also available electronically. This may sound obvious, but it's an essential concept. Digital information is more efficient to create and to maintain. Rather than entering the same information multiple times, each item is entered only once. That's significant. Even more important is that words and numbers on paper are dead—you can't work with them. In digital form, information comes alive. It can be analyzed creatively, searched quickly, updated easily, and shared broadly.

Decentralize management but centralize coordination. Taking an enterprise perspective brings with it both challenges and opportunities. Corporate integration efforts seeking to coordinate complementary but independent departments or business enterprises must find ways of dealing with the inability to control a decentralized organization from a single, centralized authority. This approach calls for breaking up large entities into smaller units, each with its own defined responsibilities and each capable of communicating with the others by using a common language. Decentralized management with centralized coordination means designing the business and the technology around the information flow.

Create an e-business application architecture. The American Express, Dell, and Cisco case studies repeatedly emphasize the power of having a forward-thinking application architecture that addresses the following three critical requirements:

- *Interface.* Business innovators do not want new technology just for its own sake. They want new systems to support the key business practices within their industry and the interfaces they have with their suppliers and customers, without losing a step.

- *Integration.* Business innovators want to streamline and to integrate their business processes, using their new information systems.

- *Innovation.* Business innovators demand new and more advanced applications to help them grow quickly.

The foremost objectives of the e-business application architecture are to improve customer satisfaction and to reduce operating cost. Process integration allows innovators to gain operating efficiencies, improve information flow among various departments, and build predictability and repeatability within their business processes.

Integrate, but plan for continuous growth and change. Keep in mind the following maxims.

- *Start small.* Pick a project that can be addressed in less than 4 months but that has potentially high impact for the business. For example, create a Web page and make it available to your key suppliers for them to acess key business information, such as inventory levels.

- *Build on success.* Undertake and complete follow-on projects that build on your company's initial efforts. Add more features to the supplier Web page, allowing suppliers to download a bill of materials, for example.

- *Build, launch, and learn.* Be willing to scrap a system. Initial efforts may need to be reworked later as you expand your capabilities. Choosing simple initial projects that can be completed quickly and with minimal investment leads to a faster ROI and easier replacement, when necessary.

Integration efforts over a very large scope must work with the prospect of continuous change. Nothing is permanent. However, managers may find that in conquering the vexing problems associated with large-scale integration efforts, they will have acquired the ability to exploit change and to maximize the value they derive from their technology investment. The solution to the e-business design problem means organizing a firm's application software the same way the firm organizes its business units.

Memo to the CEO

If you are reading this book, you are probably responsible for steering your company or business unit through the stormy waters of e-business: continuous growth, cost reduction, and customer retention. As you witness the emergence of the electronic enterprise, you will notice more opportunities than ever before for adding value to your company and for making money. But it is tough to figure out how deep the business impact of this emerging technology will be, where to invest, and what changes to make. So here you are at the beginning of the twenty-first century, searching for a place to start, a path to follow, a destination to reach.

Creating an e-business design is only the first step. The most difficult part of the e-business journey comes next: the execution of your e-business design. In recent years, many best-selling management books have exhorted managers to be innovative and to develop a vision for the future. Also, the "strategic" consulting industry is making a killing by guiding executives in how to render their business strategy intelligible, develop strategic vision, make choices about product and service offerings, develop better competitive timing, segment and target customers, and outsource noncore competencies. Analyzing core competencies, planning strategy at the 50,000-foot level, and developing mission statements make great reports that, unfortunately, few read. Almost all firms these days have great visions and strategies, but relatively few execute them, and even fewer execute them well.

Execution of the e-business design is the name of the game. *e-Commerce technology must be embedded in an effective business design, or an e-commerce technology investment alone will not generate differentiated or sustainable value.* This seems obvious, but it's amazing how many firms fall prey to the lure of the technology silver bullet. The source of differentiation between you and your competition lies not only in how well you plan but also in how well you execute your plan using technology.

With e-commerce, we have entered a new phase in the history of business: the age of e-business design. The challenge facing today's companies is in the creation and execution of an effective e-business design. For example, American Express aims to improve the quality of customer interaction while cutting costs and increasing market share. But these opportunities can be realized only if organizations take advantage of emerging electronic business designs and overcome the organizational, cultural, and philosophical obstacles standing in the way.

In order to successfully execute a company's e-business design, management must focus its time and the company's resources. Realistically, a firm can choose only one of three business design disciplines—service excellence, operational excellence, or continuous-innovation excellence—in which to specialize. Some exceptional companies are able to do all three well. Unfortunately, most companies do not specialize in any of these and therefore realize only mediocre or average levels of achievement in each area. In no sense can these companies be viewed as market leaders; nor will they ever be. In today's increasingly competitive business environment, the need for competitive differentiation is greater than ever. Refusing to create and to implement a focused business design, and the complacency this attitude reflects, will not lead to increased market share, sales, or profits but rather could, in fact, lead to bankruptcy or extinction.

CHAPTER FIVE

Constructing the e-Business Architecture: Enterprise Apps

What to Expect

Many businesses raced onto the Net only to discover—quite painfully—that a Web presence doesn't spell automatic success. If you attempt to win e-customers' business with a less than rock-solid and bullet-proof application architecture, you will succeed only in alienating them. Clearly, the business logic and knowledge contained in enterprise software applications provide the foundation on which leading companies build their e-business designs.

The e-business design built on an application architecture has become a boardroom topic as more companies than ever integrate applications to streamline operations and compete in the e-commerce arena. But disparate applications are like modular building blocks—they have to be put together systematically to create an e-business enterprise.

In this chapter, we'll show you what application integration is, why it's important, and what business and technology megatrends are driving application integration. We present case studies of companies that have embraced application frameworks and explain how they did it. We then show how you can integrate various applications to create an e-business architecture.

Imagine running your office with computers designed 30 years ago or taking orders by hand and using runners to get them from one place to another or shipping merchandise with a fleet of Model T cars. Ludicrous? Of course. But this is exactly what many corporations do in the e-business world with their outdated applications.

As a result, CIOs face an overarching challenge from their CEOs: "Give us next-generation enterprise applications that make us more competitive and deliver benefits quickly, so we can improve our business performance today, not years from now." CIOs increasingly recognize that the fastest and most effective way to deliver business benefits is to bridge the chasm separating customers, back-office operations, and the supply chain. The cost of this chasm? Tens to hundreds of millions of dollars in higher service costs and longer order-fulfillment cycles.

The modern CIO's job is to develop an e-business architecture, which means turning abstract e-business design concepts into working solutions on time, within budget. The rubric of e-business architecture includes three best practices: (1) to create a clear map of the company's strategy for the next 2 years and to use it to manage all aspects of the company's application development activities; (2) to generate a seamless application strategy, one that leaves no holes for customers to complain; (3) to collect, interpret, and assimilate good information about the technical and marketplace uncertainties.

Application design and business design are now irrevocably linked. According to Bill Gates, "Virtually everything in business today is an undifferentiated commodity, except how a company manages its information. How you manage information determines whether you win or lose. How you use information may be the one factor that determines its failure or success—or runaway success."[1]

That brings us to the question, How does a company manage its information? The simple answer is, through its business applications (apps): order and inventory management, financials, and customer service. Linking isolated apps into a cohesive architecture is the central theme in e-business execution.

Modern business designs are constructed from well-integrated modular building blocks called *enterprise applications,* which provide a common platform for apps in a given functionality, such as enterprise resource planning (ERP), customer relationship management (CRM), and supply chain management (SCM). These enterprise apps form the backbone of the modern enterprise. Although the Web may have grabbed most of the media attention recently, the business world's steady deployment of enterprise apps is one of the most important developments in the corporate use of information technology in the 1990s. Emphasis on enterprise apps increased significantly in the mid 1990s as companies scrambled to find ways to root out old legacy apps incapable of meeting the stresses of the global economy. Today, as companies race toward the information economy, their structures are increasingly made up of interlocking business apps. Isolated, stand-alone applications are history.

So, in reality, a large part of e-business is about how to integrate an intricate set of apps so they work together like a well-oiled machine to manage, organize, route, and transform information. This vision is not easy to achieve, and failures are more frequent than successes. It is estimated that one of three e-business projects fails and that more than half come in over budget.[2] Also, the bigger the company, the bigger the problems. Large companies suffer from projects that are too large and that have too many requirements to fulfill on a timely basis.

For instance, TCI attempted to create a massive computerized customer billing service called Summitrak to handle customer service and billing functions. But three years and $132 million later, the system barely ran. TCI extricated itself from the mess and sold the system to CSG Systems International, a cable billing services company.

What happened to TCI can happen to any company, any time. In summer 1999, Hershey Foods, the $4.4-billion candy maker, suffered a glitch in a $112 million new enterprise system built to automate and track every step of the candy-selling business. Just days before Halloween, the problem manifested itself as lost orders, missed shipments, and disgruntled customers. Although Hershey would not reveal its losses from the glitch, third-quarter revenues were down $151 million from 1998.[3]

As these examples illustrate, creating and deploying large-scale applications is not easy. The reason is simple. As the rate of change increases, the complexity of problems increases. The more complex these problems are, the more time it takes to solve them. The more the rate of change increases, the more the problems change, and the shorter the lifetime of the solutions. Therefore, by the time one finds solutions to many of the problems being faced, the problems have morphed so much that the solutions are no longer effective. In other words, many of the solutions are dead-on-arrival. As a result, companies that attempt massive application projects in fast-changing markets are digging themselves into a deeper hole.

The actual cost of creating and deploying large applications, such as SAP, is much greater than most firms anticipate. Little wonder, then, that making application investment decisions is rising to the top of the management agenda. As businesses apply technology to address new opportunities, the bond between the business design and its application architecture inevitably grows closer, and the question of how to steer this relationship becomes more and more urgent. How well you manage and use information depends on the e-business design that your company's "C"-level executives—CEO, COO, CIO, and CFO—are contemplating.

Senior managers must play the role of corporate architects in order to shape the application infrastructure so that they can meet the demands of customers and build lasting value by connecting business strategy with operational reality. Top management cannot afford to leave this task to developers or lower-level managers who don't see the big picture. The challenge facing management is evident: Create and deliver customer value through integrated business apps. That brings us to the questions managers must ask.

- What key trends will drive new e-business application investments over the next 5 years?

- What is the realistic e-business application architecture needed to satisfy business and technical objectives?

- Will business requirements like mobile computing change priorities massively once the specifications are done?

- What is the role of packaged apps in creating the architecture? Is the focus on infrastructure or a point solution?

- What management structure will help my organization manage and deploy business apps despite ever-increasing complexity and volatility?

Clearly, unique customer experiences based on integrated business apps are becoming catalysts for the corporate change. However, with firms banking on visions of an e-commerce-enabled, "wired" enterprise, separating market hype from technology reality demands new levels of insight and shrewd decision making. Taking a multiyear planning perspective, this chapter focuses on the most important business and technology megatrends driving application architecture, as well as key areas of investment necessary to harness and exploit business apps effectively.

Trends Driving e-Business Architecture

The following three business trends are driving e-business architecture decisions.

- *The velocity of business is increasing.* Speed to market is essential for seizing opportunities.

- *Enterprise boundaries are disappearing.* The new business paradigm requires that nonemployees have controlled access to internal systems.

- *Expectations for technology solutions are rising.* Customers, employees, managers, and partners expect more in a short period of time.

At the same time, other internal IT events are happening: integrating applications from mergers and acquisitions (M&A) companies into the portfolio of systems, moving applications to the Internet, moving applications from legacy systems to new platforms, upgrading the network infrastructure to handle high-bandwidth traffic, building an integrated data model. Every layer added to a business's application environment increases its complexity and creates more potential points of failure.

Unfortunately, there are no quick fixes. Application architecture and the underlying information infrastructure are quite complex in the face of the e-business requirement to integrate your front-end and back-end systems to provide accurate, real-time information to your customers. With all the changes happening in the marketplace, an organization is not safe with an outdated, ineffective application infrastructure. To deploy a workable e-business design, management must be on top of which application architecture will best meet the company's needs. This takes work and a lot of vision.

Whether you like it or not, your company may be forced to undertake application integration for a variety of reasons, including better customer care, new competitive conditions, or the need to offer more integrated services. Let's take a look at each of these in detail.

New Customer-Care Objectives

Needless to say, an integrated application architecture is key to serving the customer seamlessly, especially in e-commerce. This strategy is exemplified by Amazon.com, whose goal is to create a seamless buying experience for the mainstream customer. Seamless buying and fulfillment is important because as the novelty of e-tailing fades and customer expectations increase, rapid, error-free fulfillment will increasingly play a major role in retaining customer loyalty. Realizing this, Amazon.com's business goal is to significantly improve order fulfillment and shipment speeds.[4]

How does its integrated fulfillment work? Once an order is placed on the Web site, Amazon.com uses an integrated packing and shipping system via an online connection to the order management system. This system monitors the in-stock status of each item ordered, processes the order, and generates warehouse selection tickets and packing slips. Once picking and packing are done, the package is sent via Airborne or UPS to the customer. The high level of integration in order fulfillment can, potentially, enable Amazon.com to turn its own inventory more frequently than do traditional competitors, which average two to three times longer. Frequent inventory turns is critical to keeping warehousing costs down.

The Amazon.com example shows that to achieve the business goal of creating a richer customer experience, firms need to integrate their Web sites with their back-office systems, the heart of their operations: inventory management, order processing, financials, and customer service. Again, easier said than done. Companies spend billions of dollars on application software every year and still do not have the ability to process customer transactions seamlessly. Why? Because companies lack integration across apps. This happens because most application software automates some tasks but not entire processes. Clearly, the challenge facing large companies, not start-ups, is how to integrate enterprise apps for seamless flow of orders and customer information that e-business designs demand.

Managers understand that the Web is a powerful tool for slicing margins and increasing interactivity with customers and prospects, but if companies don't practice the fundamentals of fast, error-free service, they will fail miserably. In the same vein, as customers become more Internet savvy, their tolerance for wasted time and lack of integrated processes diminishes. To survive, companies must refine their business processes if they hope to win the hearts of fickle consumers and reap the benefits of integrated front-office and back-office apps.

New Competitive Conditions

The changing competitive environment is driving the need for integrated apps. Consider the case of New Brunswick Power (NB Power), which has provided electricity to customers throughout the Canadian province of New Brunswick since 1920. With 2,500 employees and assets of $4.3 billion, NB Power has developed one of the most diverse power-generating systems in the world, with a mix of hydro-, nuclear-, coal-, oil-, and diesel-generating units.[5]

Deregulation and the growing demand for better customer service began to strain the limits of its existing apps. Pending regulatory changes leading to a far more deregulated and competitive environment forced the company to reevaluate its business processes, especially its customer service functions. NB Power anticipated that the existing software and system infrastructure would soon lack the functionality and flexibility needed to meet changing business requirements.

As the power industry deregulates, NB Power and other utilities are quickly realizing that integrating internal apps is merely a down payment on a competitive advantage. In order to remain a player in the new century, firms better start thinking about ways to tie their various apps together tightly and smoothly. Another important goal for NB Power is to improve the quality of services it provides. This requires improving the quality, timeliness, and types of information available to the corporation and increasing control over resources through improved process integration.

Unfortunately, business objectives are in conflict with existing apps. NB Power's previous application infrastructure included both purchased apps and in-house apps running on IBM mainframes. Within that mainframe environment, access to information was cumbersome, software and hardware had become obsolete, and maintenance, support, operation, and integration of the systems were becoming difficult and expensive.

To achieve better alignment between business needs and application capabilities, NB Power decided to migrate to a more flexible environment. After exhaustive research and a thorough comparison of various application solutions, NB Power decided that its demands would be met best by customizing a packaged application infrastructure provided by SAP. But the game is far from over after choosing a packaged application architecture.

The challenge for managers is to make sense and good use of what packaged apps offer. Not all purchased apps add value. In the coming years, managers will need to figure out how to make an integrated application architecture a viable, productive part of the work setting. They will need to stay ahead of the information curve and learn to leverage information for business results. Otherwise, those managers risk being swallowed by a tidal wave of data, which is not a business advantage.

Fast-Moving Competitors

Established companies are forced to scrutinize their existing application architectures after an M&A transaction. At the same time, they have to determine whether they are capable of competing with new entrants that enter their turf with new products and services. This is the question facing Norwest Mortgage, a leading residential mortgage lender.[6] Norwest is going through a very complex series of M&A transactions and at the same time faces challenges from new online players, such as E-LOAN and HomeAdvisor. These upstarts offer mortgage marketplaces, where consumers can shop easily for home loans from a number of companies.

Norwest presents a good case study because it's in a traditional, non-automated industry caught in the midst of an e-business transition. To understand the application challenges facing Norwest, we must first understand their business. Norwest provides funding for 1 of every 15 homes in the United States and serves more than 2 million customers. Norwest has grown rapidly, with more than 11,000 employees and more than 750 branches in all 50 states. Growth has come from both internal expansion and aggressive acquisition, most recently the 1996 purchase of Prudential Home Mortgage. Along with Prudential's $45-billion portfolio, Norwest acquired an added complement of legacy computing systems.

Postacquisition Norwest faced many challenges, including how to take advantage of new economies of scale, leverage existing technology assets, and use new Web and Internet technologies in the best way to provide real-time quotes to agents, telemarketers, and other online users. The issue is not how much information exists or how to store it but rather the speed and agility with which the "right" information can be transmitted to solve a particular customer problem. The idea is simple: Put information at the customers' and employees' fingertips so they can act more quickly and make better decisions.

Norwest's strategy is to enable customer convenience. In the old days, customer convenience in the mortgage business was defined by three simple words: location, location, location. Web access, however, makes geographical proximity an obsolete virtue. Today, consumers define convenience as access to any information, in any form, anytime, anywhere. To meet their customers' needs, Norwest must offer a range of delivery and access options to customers, insurance agents, and employees and provide customer convenience.

Norwest's first task is to simplify the application infrastructure by evaluating and selecting the best systems in each of the newly merged firms. Next, it has to find a way to integrate all business systems into a single, unified platform that will support an expanded user base and a growing revenue stream. The most difficult task is integrating various apps, as most rely on proprietary solutions.

Norwest realizes that in the rapidly changing and fiercely competitive financial services industry, the firms that flourish are those that offer the best service and deliver it ahead of the competition (see Figure 5.1). With this understanding, Norwest quickly recognized the necessity for a completely flexible and scalable e-business architecture that allows it to

- Enhance customer service and quality of operations through enterprise-wide apps

- More closely link technology to business objectives

- Develop apps more quickly, reliably and cost-effectively, with minimum training or cultural change

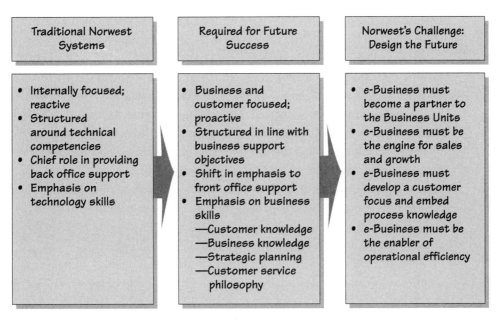

Figure 5.1: e-Business Architecture Challenges

• Meet the standards for performance, reliability, and security of mission-critical systems

The case of Norwest may sound familiar because many large companies are going through similar experiences. Today's e-business architecture must enable companies to analyze their businesses like chessboards, on which they seek to be two, three, or four moves ahead of the competition.

Problems Caused by Lack of Integration

The lack of integrated application architecture can bring companies down rather quickly. Consider the case of Oxford Health Plans, a $4-billion health maintenance organization (HMO) whose motto is "The health and healing company." Oxford Health operates in New York, New Jersey, Pennsylvania, and Connecticut, offering traditional HMO service, point-of-service plans, Medicare/Medicaid plans, employer-funded plans, and dental plans. Oxford has been a juggernaut in the managed-care arena, buoyed by strong membership growth and keen marketing.

Beyond this, Oxford has been praised for use of the Web, giving members access to lists of providers and allowing physicians to check the status of claims.

At the end of 1997, Oxford Health announced that a computer problem in the accounting and billing system had caused the company to underestimate medical costs and to overestimate revenue. The announcement that it was poised to post its first-ever loss stunned investors, and the stock fell more than 80 percent. Who is to blame? Initially, Oxford Health blamed computer conversion for rendering it unable to bill customers and to make payments to doctors and hospitals. However, Oxford later discovered that the problems stemmed from the fact that the company's internal financial controls were virtually nonexistent. A chastened—and now former—Chairman Stephen Wiggins didn't duck culpability, conceding, "At the end of the day a computer problem is probably a business problem, and somewhere along the line I obviously made a mistake."[7] No kidding.

The example of Oxford Health illustrates that careful design of application architecture is essential for business survival. Oxford is not alone. W. L. Gore & Associates—the maker of weather-resistant Gore-Tex fabric—sued PeopleSoft for failing to properly install its human resources management system, resulting in damage to Gore's business.[8]

Getting the integration right is even more important. However, there are many minefields. Some of them are system related (see Figure 5.2), whereas others

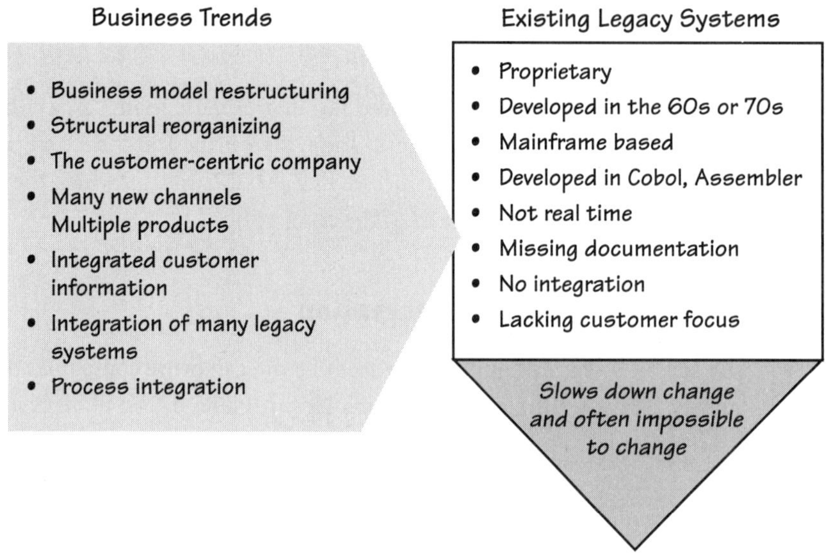

Business Trends

- Business model restructuring
- Structural reorganizing
- The customer-centric company
- Many new channels Multiple products
- Integrated customer information
- Integration of many legacy systems
- Process integration

Existing Legacy Systems

- Proprietary
- Developed in the 60s or 70s
- Mainframe based
- Developed in Cobol, Assembler
- Not real time
- Missing documentation
- No integration
- Lacking customer focus

Slows down change and often impossible to change

Figure 5.2: Application Challenges Facing Large Organizations

are related to the organization. The typical organizational barriers to be dealt with are

- Focusing too much on efficiency and cost cutting. This often leads to myopia and the inability to take advantage of opportunities for revenue growth in new lines of business.

- Getting the business units to understand why they need to use the software. Listen to the customer's perspective and use it as the best arbiter of success.

- Rehashing competitors' ideas (often positioned as "industry best practices"), resulting in diminished returns. Businesses need fresh ideas.

- Pursuing drawn-out, enterprise-wide projects in search of a "perfect" answer, thus failing to address today's need for faster response.

- Frequently reorganizing, which often leads to weak executive involvement and support. Consistently, this is one of the top five causes for the failure of e-business initiatives. An effective transition strategy must be in place before executives are shuffled around.

- Placing too much emphasis on outside consultants for execution. Often, consulting firms focus their change efforts exclusively on bleeding-edge technology, which may achieve nothing more than incremental benefits.

Businesses today need to automate a much broader process, cover a bigger chunk of the organization, and pull together more information from more places than in the past. By "bigger chunk of the organization," we mean the cross-functional business processes, such as customer management, that often cut across many departments and are bigger in scope than any one existing application.

The New Era of Cross-Functional Integrated Apps

The success of e-business strategies depends on management's proficiency in creating next-generation services on a software foundation. So getting such e-services out the door on schedule must be routine for companies, right? Not quite. For most managers, software development still resembles witchcraft: Product requirements are provided, magic happens, and software is produced. This type of thinking needs to change if e-business designs, which are built primarily on software, are to ever see the light of the day.

What sets the adept minority of successful e-business companies apart from the rest? The successful companies have all learned to deal with the technical and marketplace uncertainties. That is, they have learned how to overcome the chaos in their e-product-development processes by embracing application frameworks. That is, various companies can independently design and produce application modules, such as ERP or CRM, and those modules will be molded to fit together into a complex, smoothly functioning product.

Clearly, we have entered an era of complex, cross-functional integrated apps, called *application frameworks,* which represent the foundation of e-business. At the heart of this remarkable advance is application modularity: building a complex service process from smaller subsystems that can be designed independently yet function together as a whole. To understand how we got here, however, it's important to understand the evolution of business apps. It has been a process of stages, as illustrated in Figure 5.3.

Stage 1 was one of simplification and segmentation. Historically, business apps were narrowly focused and task oriented, simplifying such processes as order entry. Although task specialization improved productivity dramatically, it also fragmented processes beyond recognition. In a task-centric world, processes tend to fall between the cracks, becoming slow, inflexible, error prone, and replete with the costs of the managerial overhead needed to hold them together.

Stage 2 was one of reintegration and transformation. In the 1980s, the task-oriented nature of apps evolved to become more functionally integrated. Fortunately, information technology is allowing us to reintegrate tasks into connected processes. For instance, order entry was transformed into sales apps. But in the reality of today's global economy, functional specialization can be crippling. What is needed is the ability to provide solutions, which requires that everyone comprehend the big picture and remain flexible in the face of new or complex situations. This requirement has created the need for cross-functional application integration.

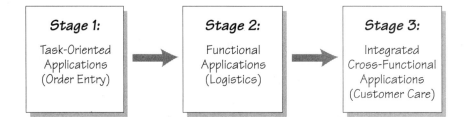

Figure 5.3: Evolution of Business Apps

With the early 1990s came the advent of business process reengineering, and organizations began focusing on managing and optimizing cross-functional business processes. A process perspective transforms a group of ad hoc and fragmented functional activities into a system that is organized, repeatable, and reliable. The shift from task-oriented to process-oriented organization may not sound very dramatic. In fact, it is the kind of discontinuous change that occurs only rarely.

Clearly, the trend in business is toward software-enabled process support, which is accomplished by deploying business apps that fuse multiple functions into a collection of well-orchestrated frameworks. For instance, sales apps are increasingly being integrated with customer service and marketing apps to form customer relationship management solutions. Why is this fusion of disparate apps necessary? Price wars, market-share wars, and quality wars are forcing companies to streamline and to integrate processes at unprecedented levels to become solution oriented and more effectively serve the needs of customers.

Stage 3 is one of cross-functional integration and fluid adaptability. Most of the activity in an organization does not follow the functional model. As change becomes continuous, cross-functional processes become the principal means for coordinating activities spread out across different functions. This gave rise to application frameworks, emphasizing coordination across departments. Application frameworks are of different types, each representing a related cluster of functionality. The implementation of application frameworks represents a total overhaul of enterprise systems. These application frameworks are designed to integrate an array of lateral functions, including

- Customer relationship management

- Enterprise resource planning

- Supply chain management

- Selling-chain management

- e-Procurement

- Enterprise application integration

- Business intelligence, knowledge management, and decision support

Companies are pursuing the application cluster route by buying and deploying packaged apps developed by business application vendors, such as Siebel, SAP, Baan, PeopleSoft, J. D. Edwards, Vantive, and Clarify. The logic behind buying packaged apps is simplified by using an analogy of a car. Companies should buy cars instead of building them from scratch if the objective is to get the customer from point A to point B. It's better to focus on driving than on building the car.

The same logic applies to application cluster development. Companies should focus on buying the applications rather than spending precious dollars on developing complex applications. These packaged apps have helped some organizations adapt significantly to shifting conditions, improved the competitive standing of others, and even have positioned a few for a far better future. The following sections describe each of these application frameworks with a detailed example.

Customer Relationship Management (CRM) Apps: Charles Schwab

Consider application integration at Charles Schwab. Millions of do-it-yourself investors rely on Schwab for its wide range of brokerage services and mutual fund products. As executing stock market trades becomes a commodity, Charles Schwab has successfully made customer service the core of its strategy. Still, there was a slight problem: Most of Schwab's business is done over the phone or in person. This means that sales reps and service people need to have easy access to the most current information on the company's clients and products. A few years ago, Schwab realized that its salespeople weren't getting enough information to best serve their customers. The existing systems were fragmented, and it would be too expensive to integrate them.

Thus began an exhaustive evaluation process to buy an integrated sales and service application. Schwab selected Siebel's Sales Enterprise system, which has a wide array of CRM functionality. Sales Enterprise allows Schwab's sales reps, who handle more than 10 million telephone calls every month, to gain real-time access to customer profiles and histories and to improve responsiveness to the needs of its nearly 3.5 million active customer accounts and prospects. The integrated apps also enable service reps to market new products while talking to the customer. Now service reps are able to develop a big-picture view of their customers and the company's relationship with them, which shapes how they communicate with and sell to them.[9]

What does Charles Schwab's example tell us? Schwab no longer manages customer service as an isolated function. In order to address the needs of its customers, the company has linked all its sales and customer service organizations with one another and with all the customer-interfacing parts of the company. Key to the implementation of this initiative has been a new information infrastructure to capture information about customers and their behavior. And the company is still trying to better integrate its back-office systems and data marts to give workers a more complete view of individual customers.

Integrated CRM apps (see Figure 5.4) provide immediate value to the Fortune 500. Even large, resource-rich companies are resorting to purchasing and implementing packaged apps over custom-built solutions. For most organizations, selecting a packaged CRM application is more economical than building one with a set of low-level tools. No longer do they have to wait through long development cycles to realize the benefits of a CRM application.

Does the Charles Schwab example sound familiar? Is your organization going through similar sales and service integration issues? Is your company facing a build-versus-buy decision for integrated customer relationship management solutions?

Enterprise Resource Planning (ERP) Apps: Nestlé

Nestlé, an international company operating in 69 countries, sells products that range from drinks, sweets, and foods to pharmaceuticals and has 210,000 employees and 500 factories in 80 countries. Nestlé technology consists of nearly 900 IBM AS/400 midrange computers, 15 mainframes, and 200 UNIX systems that run operations worldwide. The business challenge facing Nestlé is how to integrate systems and business activities while gaining high quality, consistent, and efficient management of information.[10]

Nestlé realized that to compete in e-business, the company had to standardize its business processes. Nestlé's worldwide operations—which let each factory conduct business according to rules that fit the local business culture—are costly

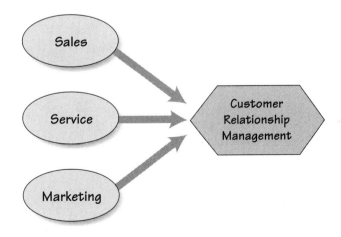

Figure 5.4: The Trend toward Integrated Customer-Centric Apps

and inefficient. For example, Nestlé can't leverage its worldwide buying power for the raw materials used in its products, even though each factory uses the same global suppliers, because each facility negotiates its own deals and its own prices.

Sustained optimization of business processes throughout the entire logistical chain, together with closer linking of international locations, were among the goals Nestlé set for itself before selecting an integrated application suite. Ineffective integration of information is an issue of great concern to Nestlé's managers, who are charged with increasing market share, reducing costs, and improving service. Management also wanted software that was able to speed up information flow and to standardize reporting to improve international comparability of results.

Nestlé selected an ERP application suite from SAP to run its order entry, purchasing, invoicing, and inventory control. Figure 5.5 captures the various functions that form the ERP integrated suite. The key benefits that materialized after implementing the ERP suite were optimized service, integration of worldwide logistics, an improved ability to meet deadlines, shorter turnaround times from customer inquiries to delivery, and a shift away from stock-oriented to demand-driven production.

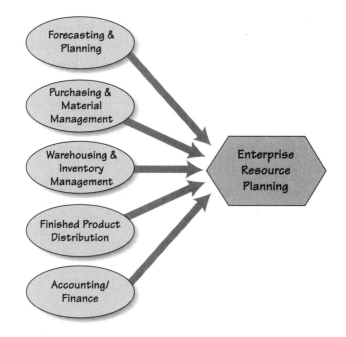

Figure 5.5: The Trend toward Integrated Enterprise Resource Planning Apps

Is your organization going through similar application integration issues? Is your organization attempting to integrate diverse functional areas in order to align your business and application strategies?

Supply Chain Management (SCM) Apps: Visteon

Visteon Corporation, a spin-off of the Ford Motor Company, manufactures chassis components: axle and drive shaft assemblies designed for the Mustang and Crown Victoria, as well as for limousines, pickup trucks, and sport utility vehicles. Visteon already is a large global company with about 82,000 employees in 21 countries; 81 plants, including 32 joint ventures; and 36 sales offices and engineering and technical centers.

The $17 billion Dearborn, Michigan–based Visteon is banking on the estimated $100 million makeover to streamline its business and to power its recent entry into the fiercely competitive auto parts market. The key goals of the IT overhaul are to cut product development times from an average of 30 months to 10 months, to reduce manufacturing time for parts from an average of 5 days to 1 day, and to have 20 percent of its business come from non-Ford sources by 2003.[11]

Balancing production capacity with market demand is one of the Visteon's biggest challenges. In the automotive industry, missing scheduled delivery-due dates is not an option, as delay of a key assembly can cost millions of dollars in lost productivity. To help balance demand, planners are responsible for scheduling various sections of the plant. The planners used unconnected Excel spreadsheets for production scheduling, a process that was difficult and time consuming. Efficiency and throughput were not optimal, and inventory was higher than it needed to be.

Reengineering Visteon's business organization is equal to designing and engineering a space shuttle. Visteon has to develop people's skills, product procedures, and documentation on top of setting up links with customers and suppliers on a global basis.

To solve the problem, Visteon chose an integrated SCM application. The scheduling application was integrated with the company's market demand database and legacy systems that stored resource and capacity constraints. The integrated functionality enabled planners to perform scheduling independently over ten sequential production departments, standardize and link reports, and integrate scheduling with supplier functions. Visteon calculated that, with an advanced scheduling solution, its total inventory was reduced by 15 percent—significant savings.

As businesses increasingly move toward real-time reaction to demand fluctuations, multicompany supply chain management apps are becoming a way of life. SCM apps are designed to help streamline production schedules, slash inventories, find bottlenecks, and respond quickly to orders (see Figure 5.6). Used properly, the software removes logistical barriers by creating a seamless flow of supplies and finished products, but the technical challenge of integrating the supply chain is awesome.

Supply chain management is getting a lot of attention in e-business. Why? Existing supply chains are mostly outdated for the e-business era, in which inventories and costs must be eliminated wherever they are found. Traditional supply chains were designed in a time of modest competition and slow response time. To succeed in today's customer-driven environment, firms must streamline intercompany processes just as they do with processes that reside within a company's boundaries. By reengineering the intercompany supply chain, corporate boundaries are becoming meaningless. The result: enormous payoffs for all partners in the chain.

Selling-Chain Management Apps: Whirlpool

Whirlpool is the world's second-largest producer of major home appliances. The company makes washers, dryers, dishwashers, dehumidifiers, microwave ovens, ranges, refrigerators, freezers, and air conditioners. Whirlpool suffered from a labyrinthine pricing process that stifled its profitability and frustrated customers.

To reduce operating costs, Whirlpool is taking a hard look at streamlining its sales processes. Whirlpool's selling organization consists of hundreds of account

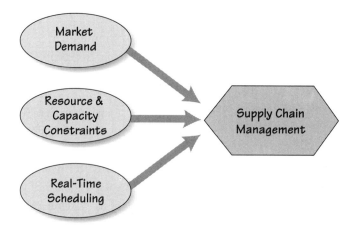

Figure 5.6: The Trend toward Integrated Supply Chain Apps

managers and field marketing representatives who promote and sell products. The company also implements thousands of promotional programs per year, but because of the lack of analysis tools, many of these programs have been launched without anyone's understanding how they affect the overall business.

Whirlpool's paper-based pricing system consisted of multiple price sheets that were updated several times a year. The pricing calculations were modeled in an 180,000-cell Excel spreadsheet that took about 110 days to update. Manual reentry, continual repetition, and 15-day pricing blackouts for price book printing were standard procedures.[12]

To manage its pricing and promotions, as well as to provide its channel partners with the tools to facilitate the sales process, Whirlpool decided to overhaul its sales processes. What did it require? An integrated set of apps that makes it easy for customers to do business with Whirlpool. Whirlpool bought an enterprise software suite to integrate each function in its sales and marketing operation, including pricing management, product management, sales, commissions, promotions, contract management, and channel management. The goal was to allow Whirlpool to sell products more quickly and profitably at reduced overall costs.

What pressures is your company facing from the mass-customization trend? As firms move increasingly toward a mass-customization world, the contemporary business environment puts extraordinary demands on sales and marketing organizations. Facing sophisticated customers and intense competition, salespeople must configure custom solutions from an enormous range of complex, changing products and then price them appropriately. Traditional sales and pricing processes are unprepared for this challenge. This situation gives rise to a new cross-functional application cluster (see Figure 5.7) called selling-chain management apps.

e-Procurement Systems Apps: CIBC

Business-to-employee (B2E) apps have exploded in the last couple of years. Delta and Ford are two companies providing a heavily subsidized computer with Internet connectivity to all their employees—not just white-collar employees but *all* employees. Connectivity is a vehicle that allows companies to self-source human resource, benefits management, and procurement functions.

Let's focus on e-procurement: the procurement of the goods and services it takes to operate a business—anything from industrial supplies, office supplies, and capital equipment to services, travel, and entertainment. Figure 5.8 shows the various categories of procurement that come under this class of integrated apps.

Consider the case of Canadian Imperial Bank of Commerce (CIBC), which is looking to slash more than $100 million a year by implementing e-procurement

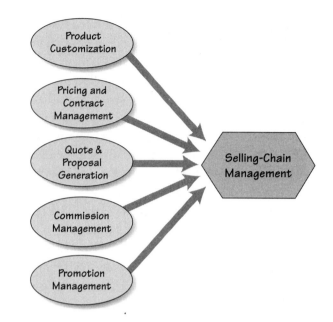

Figure 5.7: The Trend toward Integrated Selling-Chain Apps

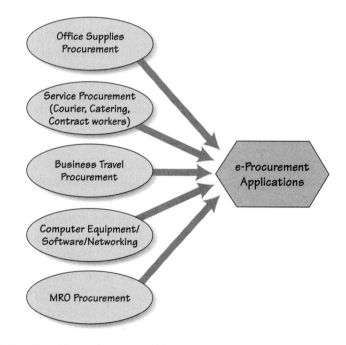

Figure 5.8: The Trend toward Integrated Procurement Apps

apps. Although plans are to start slowly, the purchasing system aims to support more than 1,400 branch offices and 40,000 employees. CIBC projects a savings of up to $130 million annually, or 10 percent of the bank's annual $1.3 billion in purchases. The e-procurement solution will include software to manage employee travel and expense reports, as well as high-volume transactions conducted with the top several hundred of CIBC's 14,000 suppliers.[13]

The goal of CIBC is to create an e-procurement application cluster that enables employees to buy online from designated suppliers, while maintaining approval routing and purchasing consistency. By hooking up employees to preferred suppliers, e-procurement apps route employee purchase requests internally before turning them into orders. The potential cost savings from e-procurement is quite high because it's estimated that close to 95 percent of the procurement process is paper based.

Procurement is one of the last nonautomated processes in large companies. In fact, the overhead of processing a purchase order runs from $70 to $300. The goal of e-procurement apps is to empower blue-collar and white-collar employees by automating the procurement process, thereby cutting purchasing costs. By automating the purchase process, organizations are looking to cut the overhead by at least 50 percent. For low-cost, frequently used items, allowing employees to act as purchasing agents makes a lot of sense. Another advantage is control. e-Procurement apps enable companies to consolidate information and to negotiate better with suppliers. These apps also permit companies to track expenses by category: employee, department, month, and so forth. e-Procurement represents a new wave of employee self-service apps.

Does the CIBC example sound familiar? What challenges is your company facing? Is your organization going through procurement automation decisions?

Enterprise Application Integration (EAI) Apps: Nortel Networks

Nortel Networks provides a complete line of products that meet the connectivity requirements of corporate enterprises, service providers, and telecommunications carriers. Nortel sells its products through multiple channels: resellers, field sales, and support personnel. Among Nortel resellers are network and systems integrators, value-added resellers (VARs), distributors, and original equipment manufacturers (OEMs). Nortel leverages sales channels to provide appropriate coverage, integration services, and specialized vertical-market support.

In support of its global customer service operations, Nortel built a custom interface between its CRM application (Clarify) and ERP application (SAP). This interface ensured that product deliveries to customers recorded in SAP were recorded in the installed product base information that resides in Clarify for contract and warranty validation. This custom interface processes more than 10,000 new delivery records per day.[14]

This example highlights a new breed of apps called *connectors,* enterprise application integration apps that unite front-office CRM apps with back-office, core-operation ERP apps (see Figure 5.9). Why are EAI apps essential? These apps become important in companies that have different vendors for their front-office and back-office apps. For instance, a purchase order or a purchase requisition can be generated in the ERP application, and a repair order or a restock request can be created in the CRM call center application. If the two application frameworks are not integrated, customers will not be able to get prompt replenishment of their spare parts inventory. How do you get disparate front-office and back-office apps to work as well together as they do independently? In other words, how can you coax your independent enterprise apps to collaborate as a seamless, integrated suite? This issue is central to the emergence of EAI frameworks.

In a multivendor setting, EAI is critical. Most large companies run dozens of different applications that weren't designed to talk to other systems. So do their suppliers and buyers. EAI software closes the gap by pulling information from applications—often stored on rigid ERP systems—and sending it to a server that "brokers" the data as a message that can be understood by the receiver.

For example, an order comes in via the Web. Customer information captured in the order process is sent by an EAI broker, such as WebLogic, to a new-customer process, which distributes the new-customer information to multiple back-office applications and databases. Once the order is validated (customer, credit, items), relevant details are sent by WebLogic to order fulfillment, which

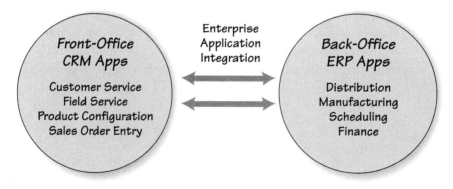

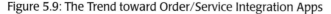

Figure 5.9: The Trend toward Order/Service Integration Apps

may pick the requested items from inventory, schedule them for manufacture, or simply forward them. Fulfillment returns status and shipment info to WebLogic server, which then forwards the information to the order-entry system and to the Web front end, where the customer may want to know about outstanding orders.

Without EAI apps in a multivendor environment, your sales force cannot immediately respond to customers' order-status requests, your customer service reps cannot initiate stop orders or process returns online, and you can't bill your customers as you provide service. EAI apps

- Streamline sales order processing, allowing organizations to deliver products and services more quickly

- Improve the customer experience by helping companies become more responsive to customer demands

Tibco, Vitria, WebMethods, BEA, and CrossWorlds Software are examples of vendors providing this functionality. Another marketing term for this class of enterprise application software is "processware." *What is your company doing to resolve EAI issues?*

Business Intelligence (BI), Decision Support Systems (DSS), and Knowledge Management (KM) Apps

BI, DSS, and KM apps enable both active and passive delivery of information from large-scale databases, providing enterprises and managers with timely answers to mission-critical questions. The objective of these apps is to turn the enormous amounts of available data into knowledge that companies can use.

The growth of this class of apps has been driven by the demand for more competitive business intelligence and increases in electronic data capture and storage. In addition, the emergence of the Internet and other communications technologies has enabled cost-effective access to and delivery of information to remote users throughout the world. Because of these factors, the overall market for BI, DSS, and KM is projected to grow substantially.

The following scenarios illustrate the importance of this class of apps.

- Someone is trying to use your Sprint phone card to make a call to Pakistan. Because this usage is unprecedented and potentially fraudulent, Sprint forwards a notification to your two-way pager, along with a request for permission to place the call. A detailed breakdown of every call made in the previous 2 weeks will be on your fax machine by the end of the day.

- It's Monday morning and your PC at work is creating a report detailing all significant week-to-date customer transactions in your territory. Your PC automatically computes comparisons with previous months and years. When budgeting time arrives, a spreadsheet model is automatically populated with last quarter's performance statistics. You tweak some growth and cost parameters and e-mail it to the CFO.

- A customer sends inventory replenishment requests and purchase order codes directly to your mobile phone, taking advantage of the digital messaging capabilities of the new PCS digital phones. In the event of a stock-out situation, you will know within minutes. When things are running smoothly, your phone remains silent.

What's new with these apps? For the first time, we are seeing the integration of data capture, analysis, and delivery into comprehensive solutions (see Figure 5.10). This class of apps enables users to query and to analyze the most detailed, transaction-level databases, turning data into business intelligence any time and distributing it anywhere through a broad range of pull-and-push technologies, such as e-mail, telephones, pagers, and other wireless communications devices.

Figure 5.10: The Trend toward Integrated Knowledge Management

e-Business Architecture = Integrated Application Frameworks

Business executives increasingly are understanding the power of integrated architecture in servicing customers. As these managers transform their companies from isolated fiefdoms to process-centered organizations, every aspect of the organization is being transformed by integration of disparate processes. This thinking, first applied to manufacturing and order fulfillment, is now found in sales, employee self-service, and customer service. An integrated-process view infuses support areas, such as finance and human resources, with a strong customer orientation.

Figure 5.11 shows how all the various application frameworks are integrated to form the model of an e-business enterprise. This blueprint is useful because it assists managers in identifying near-term and long-term integration opportunities, based on predefined strategies. Most of all, it helps managers grasp the big picture, so they can set priorities.

Figure 5.11 also illustrates the underlying premise of e-business design: Companies run on interdependent application frameworks. If one application framework of the company does not function well, the entire customer value delivery system is affected. The world-class enterprise of tomorrow is built on the foundation of world-class application frameworks implemented today.

The notion of integrated application frameworks has been around for a long time in new-product development. In 1925, for instance, Henry Ford wrote a very detailed description of a specific, systematic approach to new-product development. Rather than view the automobile as a monolithic entity, Ford focused on the major subsystems comprising the automobile and on his approaches to innovate and to measure performance for these subsystems. Then, Ford described the integration of these subsystems into the final product—the car—and how its performance and cost might be measured as a total system.[15]

The concept of modular subsystems is beginning to take root in e-business software development. Designing and developing every application from scratch and in-house was the norm in software development for a long time. The invent-everything-from-scratch syndrome of software development has been overthrown by the packaged-software revolution. Companies that don't recognize this trend will be in trouble.

Unfortunately, the road to an integrated picture has a lot of twists and turns. Unlike the old days, when you could not go wrong for buying IBM, no one vendor in the e-business world can provide every modular piece of the puzzle. Hence, customers purchase multiple apps from multiple vendors. As a result, large companies run the risk of having multiple applications that are not designed to work

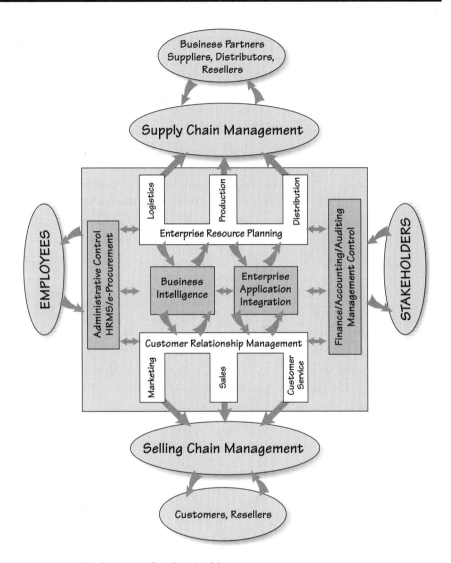

Figure 5.11: e-Business Application Architecture

together and find themselves having to integrate business solutions. This situation sets the stage for understanding how disparate functional frameworks can be integrated into an e-business architecture.

To get around the problem of deciphering each vendor's pros and cons, managers should focus on the end-to-end process. Can the integrated picture service all the processes that you want to digitize? Only by focusing on end-to-end processes and business apps can organizations achieve the levels of performance that the market demands. A clear roadmap of the various cross-functional apps and how they integrate to form the backbone of the enterprise becomes essential. Without such a roadmap, managers cannot have a clear idea of what steps to take and what decisions to make.

The complete enterprise, including customers and suppliers, cannot be integrated in one fell swoop. A staged approach is often useful in aligning software with business requirements. Consider the case of Wal-Mart, consumer products retailer. Legendary founder Sam Walton maintained a view of business that has long been one of end-to-end integration, from store systems to merchandising systems to distribution systems. Like many companies, Wal-Mart started down the road to total integration by first linking its internal systems. Then, the focus shifted toward an emphasis on integrating Wal-Mart's systems with those of its suppliers. More recently, Wal-Mart has initiated efforts to bring processes and systems from the customer side of its business into the loop.[16] What's left is a customer-to-supplier architecture that allows Wal-Mart to follow its customers' shopping habits so closely as to know their likes and dislikes and to parlay that information into pinpoint promotions.

Wal-Mart has stumbled a bit only in selling to consumers via the Internet. Wal-Mart in 1996 was one of the first retailers to set up a Web site but has yet to become a major online presence. That contributed to a decision to turn Walmart.com into a separate company based in Silicon Valley and funded by venture capital. Given its size, market clout, and profitability, Wal-Mart can afford to deliberate about the Web and get it right. But soon the company will have to figure out a way to resolve the channel conflict between brick-and-mortar stores and the Web channel.[17]

The Wal-Mart example illustrates that creating the e-business application architecture is a continuous process of integration, encompassing the enterprise's entire operating base—apps, information, communications, and infrastructure—to support the business. To achieve this goal, Wal-Mart managers took a very high-level view of the overall apps landscape: stepping back, looking at the entire system as a whole, then considering how integration should be initiated to support its strategic goals.

Unfortunately, such cases are rare. Integration in established companies is often easier said than done, owing to infighting, turf issues, and lack of strong leadership. A high level of mergers and acquisitions within large organizations further exacerbates the problem. Also, large-scale integration of customer-facing apps, supplier-facing apps, and internal apps requires business transformation and reengineering of legacy apps.

Clearly, creating an integrated application architecture like the one in Figure 5.11 is a top-management issue. Unfortunately, senior management in many companies is not paying attention to the critical issue that seems to be just over the horizon. While management is overwhelmed with such issues as mergers and acquisitions or is busy implementing solutions for isolated apps, the challenge of creating an integrated infrastructure or initiating major mission-critical application development efforts around the e-business paradigm falls through the cracks.

Memo to the CEO

Business as usual. Let's be realistic and not fool ourselves about the difficulty of the task that lies ahead. To succeed in the digital economy, we must design our business soundly for the long term to take on competitive challenges, bring in new customers, and keep old customers happy, while maintaining a smooth operation.

Organizations have to eliminate a number of barriers before they are ready to use e-business for competitive advantage. One barrier is that old ways of doing business powered by legacy applications seem to live on forever within companies, leaving not so much an efficient business architecture as a graveyard of computing. The problems posed by legacy infrastructure are clearly illustrated by the Y2K problem.

The accelerating rate of change in business cycles and the difficulty in maintaining an equivalent rate of innovation within an enterprise's application architecture are causing many organizations to lose their edge and to suffer dire consequences, such as missed opportunities, inflexible processes, and poor customer satisfaction. We anticipate that many companies will either suffer huge losses or go bankrupt because of bad application development. Unexpected changes in management or business direction or the loss of key staff members can send high-profile e-business projects into a tailspin. Many problems are preventable, and yet the same nasty ones seem to crop up time and again. CIOs can minimize the risk by clearly defining leadership roles, getting commitment of sponsors from the business, and securing executive support and participation. Other steps are less obvious.

Unfortunately, engineering change in enterprise apps is very difficult, and a high percentage of change efforts fail. A proportion of this failure occurs because, although the business environment has changed radically in the past ten years, the approach of big firms has changed little. To create value via e-business design, managers need to address serious structural questions.

- *How do you structure your company on an e-business apps architecture to assimilate ever-increasing rates of business change?*

- *How do you structure a robust application architecture that can not only survive but also thrive in a business environment characterized by rapid technological change, frequent introduction of new products, changes in customer demands, and evolving industry standards and practices?*

- *How do you deploy an application architecture quickly, in a matter of months rather than years?*

The e-business architecture must be very well thought out in order to survive an introduction of products embodying new technologies and functionality that can and will render existing business apps obsolete. As a result, any organization's future success will depend, in part, on its ability to continually enhance its existing apps and to develop and introduce new apps that keep pace with technological developments, satisfy customer requirements, and achieve operational objectives.

e-Business integration is a far cry from data processing. Forty years ago, data processing was wrestling with relatively simple challenges, such as how best to relieve the tedium of such daily tasks as typing checks. Today, the cutting edge for line-of-business apps lies in integrating and leveraging an enterprise's relationships across the entire business chain.

Only with relentlessly integrated systems does a firm stand a chance of keeping up. The acceptance of packaged software, however, leads many managers to wonder how they can differentiate their businesses if everybody is running the same systems. How can they achieve differentiation from their huge financial investments in software? We will address that question in the next few chapters.

Finally, although success depends on a flexible and forward-thinking application architecture, companies must be smart enough to understand that success doesn't come simply from choosing the right apps, Web-enabling the right process, or forging the right links to legacy systems. Instead, success requires fundamental changes in organizations, corporate behavior, and business thinking—inside and outside corporate boundaries. Technology is often the easy part. Changing organizations to align with the technology is more difficult.

CHAPTER SIX

Integrating Processes to Build Relationships: Customer Relationship Management

What to Expect

Today, customers are in charge. It is easier than ever for customers to comparison shop and, with a click of the mouse, to switch companies. As a result, customer relationships have become a company's most valued asset. These relationships are worth more than the company's products, stores, factories, Web addresses, and even employees. Every company's strategy should address how to find and retain the most profitable customers possible.

Today's customers make the rules; if organizations are to survive, they must do business in any way the customer wants. However, this is easier said than done. Most companies consider themselves customer focused, but in reality, they're product-centric. Meanwhile, e-commerce has increased customer expectations, which have raised the bar on service levels. If they fail to leap over this hurdle of ever-rising service standards, companies are out of the game.

Creating a customer-focused company starts with a customer relationship management (CRM) strategy, which must include process reengineering, organizational change, incentive-program change, and a totally revamped corporate culture. In this chapter, we'll take the often vague notion of customer focus and put it in a concrete application framework. We'll dissect customer relationship management and show you how to add it to your arsenal. We'll present the tools you'll need to build an excellent customer relationship infrastructure.

Customer dissatisfaction with service is widespread, and the expectations of customers interacting with companies are higher than ever. When you consider what's possible in customer service, it's easy to understand why customers expect more. For example, you call your insurance company with a question about your homeowner's policy. The agency's telephone system identifies you and greets you by name. The agent knows your policy, answers your question, and asks whether you would like information on a new line of auto insurance that could save you money. You say yes and begin to rattle off your address, but the agent already has it and says that the information will be in the mail to you that day.

Your customers and prospects are continually asking, Does your company deserve my patronage and loyalty? Customers are taking what used to be exceptional service as a baseline, or starting point. As competition intensifies, they are expecting more from companies they have ongoing relationships with. Customers are continually raising the bar for customer service to a higher level. As they attempt to meet new customer expectations, organizations with long-standing customer bases often find that they lack the information and data enabling them to make good service decisions and therefore make less than optimal decisions. As a result, companies are unable to satisfy customers.

For ongoing customer relationships to remain strong, companies must view the service encounter through their customers' eyes. Firms must take a customer-focused view and move away from the more traditional account- or product-centric perspective. Old paradigms for interacting with customers are becoming less successful, and failure to move toward a CRM environment will result in suboptimal business practices. Ask yourself, *Has my company taken an outside-in view in creating a service experience?*

When developing your company's CRM approach, remember these facts.[1]

- It costs six times more to sell to a new customer than to sell to an existing one.

- A typical dissatisfied customer will tell eight to ten people about his or her experience. The primary reason for dissatisfaction: lack of customer service. Of the 15 most-cited complaints, 12 were related to poor customer service, from busy phone lines to unanswered e-mail queries.[2]

- The odds of selling a product to a new customer are 15 percent, whereas the odds of selling a product to an existing customer are 50 percent.

- Seventy percent of complaining customers will do business with the company again if the complaint is quickly addressed.

• More than 90 percent of existing companies don't have the necessary sales and service integration to support e-commerce.

The Basics of Customer Relationship Management

Customers don't care how a company stores information or how data from various sources must be combined to give them what they want. They don't even care if they've called the wrong location. All customers know is that they want excellent service and want it now. The timely delivery of excellent service is customer relationship management.[3]

CRM, a combination of business process and technology, seeks to understand a company's customers from a multifaceted perspective: Who are they, what do they do, and what do they like? Is CRM critical to the survival of companies in the age of the never-satisfied customer? Industry leaders believe so. Increased competition, globalization, the growing cost of customer acquisition, and high customer turnover are major issues in such disparate industries as financial services, telecommunications, and retail.

Research shows that effective management of customer relationships is a source of competitive differentiation. Statistics such as those cited earlier are driving an enormous investment in CRM.

When competition is fierce, the best companies go back to basics: creating value for the customer. Many company executives now find themselves contemplating new value creation issues. In the 1980s, cost cutting and downsizing led to record corporate earnings and stock price performance. But by the early 1990s, executives realized that this success was a house built on sand. As their focus shifted from cutbacks to growth, many senior managers saw how their zeal to run lean had caused them to lose touch with their customers, who were slipping away. To complicate matters, those customers remaining had grown—and continue to grow—more sophisticated and discerning. Today, any advantage based on a company's product or service innovation is short-lived; instead, continuously creating new value propositions for customers is key to survival in an increasingly dynamic market. Executives must ask whether their *companies' infrastructures allow such value creation.*

Technology, in the form of the Web, has definitely acted as a catalyst for CRM. Customer service and support tools often need to be jolted out of an inertial state. Web technology functions as a major catalyst, as companies fear disintermediation and losing touch with their customers. Established channels of distribution are in question, and several could be eliminated. New competitors, such as Yahoo! and AOL, can establish brand names quickly, with a first mover's advantage. CEOs are reading about hot Web start-ups taking away a significant portion of market share from established companies, and no one wants to be another well-documented victim in a business school case study. Executives must ask whether their companies' *existing CRM infrastructures support doing business in the e-world.*

For these reasons, CRM has more visibility than ever before, moving from a sales productivity tool to a technology-enabled e-relationship strategy. Companies are racing to use technology to tie themselves more closely to their customers. At the same time, competitors are using technology to break this link. As a result, the market for CRM systems is expanding at more than 40 percent.

It's nearly a cliché, but in the contemporary world of sophisticated customers and intensifying competition, the only way for an organization to succeed is by focusing diligently on customer needs. To keep the best customers, management must concentrate on quick and efficient creation of new delivery channels, capturing massive amounts of customer data, and integrating the data to create a unique customer experience. Customer incentives, such as frequent flyer loyalty programs and buy-*x*-amount-and-get-one-free punch cards, no longer go far enough. Only by integrating their sales and service infrastructure with all aspects of operations can a company's management expect to see a change in customer relationships. Yet few companies succeed in making customer focus a business reality, for three primary reasons. Past business models didn't require a customer focus, today's technology wasn't available, and organizational resistance to changing business models remains quite high.

The goal of this chapter is to clarify the concept of the multichannel organization. In addition, we discuss the applications that support a customer-focused business model and how marketing practices and systems must be reworked in order to support the e-commerce environment.

Defining CRM

Anyone can keep one ball in the air; some can even juggle two or three. But CRM requires the whole company to work together to keep the flaming sticks, bowling pins, and razor-sharp knives of customer demands in the air. CRM is defined as an integrated sales, marketing, and service strategy that precludes lone showmanship and that depends on coordinated enterprise-wide actions. CRM software helps organizations better manage customer relationships by tracking customer interactions of all types. The suite of products spans all the steps of the selling and customer service cycle to help automate direct-mail marketing campaigns, telemarketing, telesales, lead qualification, response management, lead tracking, opportunity management, quotes, and order configuration.

Becoming customer focused doesn't necessarily mean improving customer service. It means having consistent, dependable, and convenient interactions with customers in every encounter. The goals of the CRM business framework include

- *Using existing relationships to grow revenue.* This means preparing a comprehensive view of the customer to maximize his or her relationship with the company through up-selling and cross-selling and, at the same time, enhancing profitability by identifying, attracting, and retaining the best customers.

- *Using integrated information for excellent service.* By using a customer's information to better serve his or her needs, you save the customer time and ease any frustration. For example, customers shouldn't have to repeat information to various departments again and again. Customers should be surprised by how well you know them.

- *Introducing consistent, replicable channel processes and procedures.* With the proliferation of customer contact channels, many more employees are involved in sales transactions. Regardless of size or complexity, companies must improve process and procedural consistency in account management and selling.

As these business goals illustrate, CRM is an integration framework and a business strategy, not a product. Putting CRM into practice requires developing a set of integrated applications to address all aspects of your front-office needs, including automating customer service, field service, sales, and marketing. Companies look to application software vendors to support this integration. In doing so, these same firms must remember that technology is only one aspect of successful CRM practice. Implementing CRM also means redesigning functional roles, reengineering work processes, motivating people in the company to support the new approach, and then—and only then—implementing CRM technology.

By investing in CRM applications, companies hope to build better customer retention programs to maximize customer lifetime revenue. For many industries, customer retention is a driver of profitability. It's no wonder that business strategies for achieving close relationships between companies and their customers—while containing costs—have taken center stage in most industries.

In addition, new technologies are increasing demands on customer service. As customers assimilate new technology, their expectations change about service, support, and how they make purchases. Enterprises choosing not to use application software to tie their customers on the outside with their line-of-business systems on the inside will be at a competitive disadvantage.

CRM applications are also gaining a foothold in small and midsized companies. The technology enables these organizations to enjoy the customer relationship capabilities that, until a couple of years ago, only the largest enterprises with deep pockets could afford. Integrated applications providing a comprehensive view of customer information to such business functions as sales, marketing, customer service, and accounting are now available to organizations with fewer than 100 employees.

As a result, CRM is driving the next major wave of investment in information technology. Spending on this strategy will continue to grow by 25 percent to 30 percent over the next 5 years. Given the importance of CRM both today and in the future, we turn now to the three phases comprising a CRM solution.

Managing the Customer Life Cycle: The Three Phases of CRM

In a personal relationship, the level of understanding and intimacy grows over time, as long as both parties are committed to making the relationship work. The same is true in the world of business. In today's competitive environment, this is a critical lesson to learn. Consumers are realizing that in today's marketplace, they have a wide selection of dance partners from which to choose.

CRM comprises three phases: acquiring, enhancing, and retaining. Each phase supports increased intimacy and understanding between a company and its customers. Each impacts the customer relationship differently (see Figure 6.1), and each ties your company more closely to your customer's life and dance card. These three phases are

1. *Acquiring new customers.* You acquire new customers by promoting your company's product and service leadership. You demonstrate how your firm redefines the industry's performance boundaries with respect to convenience and innovation. The value proposition to the customer is the offer of a superior product backed by excellent service.

2. *Enhancing the profitability of existing customers.* You enhance the relationship by encouraging excellence in cross-selling and up-selling, thereby deepening and broadening the relationship. The value proposition to the customer is an offer of greater convenience at low cost (one-stop shopping).

3. *Retaining profitable customers for life.* Retention focuses on service adaptability—delivering not what the market wants but what customers want. The

value proposition to the customer is an offer of a proactive relationship that works in his or her best interest. Today, leading companies focus on retention much more than on attracting new customers. The reasoning behind this strategy is simple: if you want to make money, hold onto your good customers. This is not as easy as it seems.

All phases of CRM interrelate. Let's review each phase in detail and examine its business implications more closely.

Acquiring New Relationships

Beginning a new business relationship is similar to going on a first date. Both participants feel varying degrees of insecurity, hesitancy, fear, and anticipation. Only a determined suitor acts despite these feelings. Acquiring new customers demands a similar level of determination. Strategies for successful customer acquisition require a great deal of planning in order to orchestrate a rich, highly integrated purchasing and support experience for the customer. For example, imagine that you're surfing the Web, looking for a new laptop computer. You land

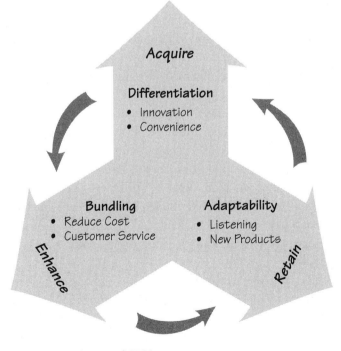

Figure 6.1: The Three Phases of CRM

on IBM's site. Interesting stuff, you say! The IBM ThinkPad looks like just what you need. You go to the product information page, fill out the online request form, press the Enter key, and submit the form. Then you hang around the Web site to read some more. All of a sudden, your phone rings. "Hello, this is Patti from IBM. I just received your request for information about our products." She asks about your requirements, walks you through an online demo of the product, and before you know it, you're on your way to acquiring the system you need.

Such an instantaneous response is not magical, though it can feel like it. It's the result of an intricate, well-planned, and finely tuned strategy of sales and service integration. Potential customers, or prospects, are impressed when companies call them while they're still browsing their Web site. Preliminary market research shows that the probability of sales goes up when prospects receive a response to their request within 1 to 3 minutes. A well-executed sales-and-service strategy eases those first-date jitters and creates a smooth transition from prospect to customer.

Enhancing Existing Relationships

In an established, committed personal relationship, most people do not break off the relationship when problems arise or at least not until they have discussed the issue. A healthy couple takes the time to listen to each other's concerns and to work through the problems. The result is a richer, more solid relationship. Similarly, companies prove their commitment on a daily basis when they take time to hear a customer's concerns and by developing a service focus.

For example, Best Buy, a specialty electronics retailer with more than 300 stores in 32 states, realizes the importance of committed relationships with its customers. The Best Buy Consumer Relations Call Center receives about 3,000 calls a day, with each call averaging 15 minutes. More than 50 percent of the calls are computer-related inquiries. These calls cover a wide variety of topics, as well as specific questions about Best Buy's products. Customers request assistance for many reasons, including determining whether a computer repair issue is a hardware or a software problem, challenging the returns policy, taking advantage of manufacturer rebates, and checking on coupons, gift certificates, or delivery schedules.

The call center's primary concern is customer satisfaction through the effective resolution of issues and concerns. As competition increases, companies such as Best Buy realize how CRM-capable call center applications are necessary for attaining and maintaining customer relationships. When a customer calls about a product, CRM applications let the agent automatically suggest a complementary item, a practice known as "cross-selling." For example, a buyer who has selected a camera can be offered a tripod. Or an agent can suggest a similar product of better quality, known as "up-selling." By using technology to access and to use customer information more effectively, Best Buy can offer superior service, differentiating itself from its competitors.

Retaining Customer Relationships

Of course, no one said that relationships are easy. On the contrary, they take a lot of work, but the rewards are usually worth the effort. Just as personal commitments need patience and understanding, so do business relationships. Retaining customers requires as complete an understanding of the needs of the customer as possible and the determination to stay in the relationship regardless of its ups and downs.

State Farm has chosen to make retaining customers its primary objective. State Farm is highly selective when choosing its new customers. Someone who has had an automobile accident in the past 5 years cannot become a State Farm customer, because the company has decided that it wants a different kind of customer. The company attempts to identify and to recruit the "best" customers, with whom they seek lifetime relationships through a complete life-cycle product line.

Several State Farm practices exemplify the importance the company places on customer retention. The company's pricing policy rewards customers who continue their coverage with the firm. For example, policyholders who have been with the company for 2 or more years receive price breaks on their insurance rates. In addition, rather than monetarily rewarding agents for attracting new customers, as most insurance companies do, State Farm gives higher commissions to those agents who retain existing customers. The company measures customer retention and defection rates and distributes the results throughout the company. These financial and competitive incentives encourage agents to work harder at keeping customers satisfied. State Farm also involves its agents in decisions affecting themselves and their customers. Such practices form the basis for State Farm's close-to-the-customer business objective.

As this example shows, the work of growing a company can focus on getting customers and keeping them. Customer retention is increasingly the strategy for companies operating in competitive environments and is likely to become a core strategy for companies everywhere as customer buying options increase and the cost of switching vendors lowers.

The New CRM Architecture: Organizing around the Customer

How does application technology work together with a CRM strategy? Technology is a critical tool for supporting a CRM implementation and the strategy's ongoing success. By answering the following questions, you can determine how CRM and its supporting technology would work together at your firm.

- Are most of the company's applications designed simply to automate existing departmental processes?

- Are these applications capable of identifying and targeting the best customers, those who are the most profitable for the organization?

- Are these applications capable of real-time customization/personalization of products and services, based on detailed knowledge of customers' wants, needs, and buying habits?

- Do these applications keep track of when the customer contacts the company, regardless of the contact point?

- Are these applications capable of creating a consistent user experience across all the contact points the customer chooses?

If the answers to each of these questions is no, you should seriously consider implementing a CRM architecture in the near future. The timing for such an implementation couldn't be better. Corporate demand is rising for integrated applications built around customer life cycles and customer interactions. The IT industry is answering this demand with a smart new-generation CRM architecture capable of seamlessly integrating a company's customer-serving processes (see Figure 6.2).

Features of the New CRM Architecture

The new CRM architecture differs from the old in the customer-centered nature of its software applications. The new CRM organizes business processes around the customers' needs. Older CRM architecture focused on internal processes in functional areas, such as marketing and sales. Measurements and feedback from the customer drive improvements in the new CRM process. The customer's viewpoint becomes integral to the sales and service process, allowing it to change and adapt with the customer's needs. In other words, companies base their actions not on the priorities set by the company's functional fiefdoms but on the overall corporate objective of providing customer satisfaction.

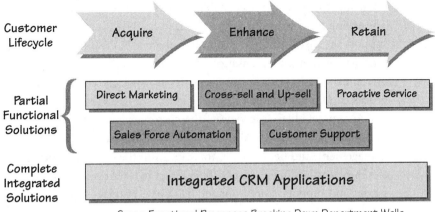

Figure 6.2: Integrated CRM

However, before aggressively deploying a suite of CRM applications, managers must determine whether customer-interaction processes need restructuring. In older business models, functional and organizational structures tend to compartmentalize the various activities that contribute to serving the customer. Such fragmentation prevents customer information from being distributed broadly enough within the organization to be useful. Functional fragmentation often stands in the way of building a rich, more solid customer relationship. As a result, customized service is difficult; consequently, organizations end up treating all customers the same—a damning impediment to building closer relationships based on personalized service.

To counter functional fragmentation, leading-edge companies take a more customer-centered approach to CRM. More and more leading-edge firms coordinate all the activities associated with identifying, attracting, and retaining customers. This integrated approach manages these activities as processes cutting across all functional departments. By so doing, organizations create end-to-end, cross-functional communications and performance accountability for all CRM-related activities. In short, a CRM infrastructure is a portfolio of the cross-functional process competencies required for creating successful customer relationships.

Portfolio of CRM Process Competencies

The CRM application area is more complex than it initially appears. When implemented properly, CRM software applications support more effective marketing, sales, and customer service, enabling a customer experience that builds loyalty. The selling process means more than lead tracking. It also requires the ability to support the distribution of promotion materials, customer presentations, territory management, compensation incentives, target account selling, multiple sales cycles, expense reporting, quota analysis, real-time coaching during the sales process, and order configuration.

A complete life-cycle view of the customer is attained by tying these functions into the broader CRM product portfolio for service and support, call center management, and field service. You can distill the core CRM process competencies into cross-selling and up-selling, direct marketing and fulfillment, customer service and support, store front and field service, and retention management (see Figure 6.3).

Identifying the CRM core process competencies with your firm is critical to the strategy's success. A company cannot manage and develop its CRM infrastructure if its managers disagree about the company's areas of competence. A company's managers must realize that these competencies form the soul of CRM

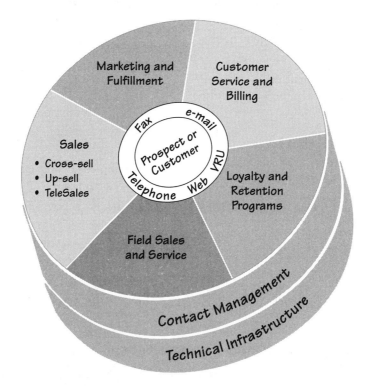

Figure 6.3: Core CRM Process Competencies

and are distinct from the underlying technical infrastructure. Managers must also be able to identify which competencies are missing from their business processes and to set goals for their development.

Sales: TeleSales, Cross-selling and Up-selling

Consider the following scenario. Gail Brown is on the phone with her insurance agent, discussing an auto claim she has made. While they are talking, the agent accesses an online synopsis of Gail's insurance information and notices that she has no life insurance policy. The agent takes the opportunity to ask Gail whether she has ever considered buying life insurance. What began as a service situation has now become a sales opportunity.

Telesales, cross-selling and up-selling applications typically include the capability to qualify prospects, track contacts, and refer them to salespersons when appropriate. More and more companies view cross-selling and event-driven marketing as tools that provide a strategic advantage for their marketing departments. By implementing a cross-sell strategy, including the applications necessary to track customer contacts, event triggers can be established identifying prospects for additional sales. For example, in a bank transaction, an event, such as a large deposit, triggers a salesperson to call a customer and ask whether he or she is interested in investment options.

Telesales, cross-sell, and up-sell software enables users to schedule sales calls, keep detailed records about sales activities, and check on the status of customer orders. The software may also be integrated with an inventory application showing what products are in stock or with a field service/external customer support application to learn how the product is working for the customer.

Telesales, cross-selling, and up-selling depend on identifying customer life-path needs. For example, in the finance industry, banks are attempting to build lasting relationships with customers by matching their life-path needs to complementary products and services. As customers approach retirement, banks could recommend investing in such assets as money markets, bonds, and annuities. If customers with young children could be identified, banks could cross-sell plans for education savings or even loan consolidation. The bottom line is that in order to prosper in today's business environment, companies must sell complementary products and services to deepen and lengthen their relationships with their customers.

In short, call center applications enable agents to manage, synchronize, and coordinate all customer interactions over multiple communication channels, such as the Web, telephone, fax, e-mail, interactive voice response (IVR) systems, and voice-over IP. These applications offer out-of-the-box computer telephony integration (CTI) and work flow management to automatically assign customers or opportunities to the right call center representative, based on language, product expertise, named account, availability, lead quality, geography, or other criteria.

Marketing and Fulfillment

Direct marketing and fulfillment work like a one-two punch in a prize fight: Sell well and deliver fast. Presale interactions, such as direct marketing and other forms of advertising, provide potential customers with the necessary information to make or influence a purchasing decision.

Automating the marketing function is critical as organizations grow larger. Why? Managing multiple simultaneous programs and tracking costs across multiple channels become increasingly difficult as firms grow. Campaign management, a direct-marketing process, allows companies to manage, integrate, and leverage marketing programs by automating such tasks as managing customer responses, qualifying leads, and arranging the logistics of events and transactions. New applications software can look up and send an e-mail reply containing the information the customer requested.

The large number of direct-marketing efforts under way is causing a huge consumer backlash. Customer e-mail boxes are being cluttered with unsolicited messages. In response, firms have developed permission marketing as an alternative to direct marketing in order to handle customer concerns. Permission marketing delivers personalized, relevant e-mail only to customers who have requested information. The business community has two schools of thought about permission marketing. Some believe that it will result in lost sales, with too few people requesting information. Others believe that sending unsolicited e-mail, giving a customer an opt-out capability, will result in more people reading and responding to the ad.

Fulfilling customer requests is another critical CRM core competency. Marketing departments today are deluged with requests for product and service information via the Web and other channels. Effective fulfillment strategies provide a myriad of information to customers and prospects quickly, easily, and efficiently. Whether it's a product or a service inquiry, a direct-mail response, a pricing or billing issue, or a request for literature, responding to customer requests in a timely manner is critical. A company must have a fulfillment infrastructure and capability in place in order to get product information, literature, collateral packages, or other correspondence into the hands of customers and prospects at a time when they are most receptive. Effective fulfillment is not a trivial pursuit; it requires a company to develop a sophisticated interface with campaign management, sales force automation, and posting systems.

Customer Service and Support

Customer support applications provide such customer-care services as service request management, account management, contact and activity management, customer surveys, return-material authorizations, and detailed service agreements. These discrete applications work together to permit customer service representatives to assign, create, and manage service requests quickly. The representative can also look up detailed information about customer service contracts, contacts, and activities.

A company's customer support capabilities assist customers with resolving a product or service problem. Help-desk applications automate the management and resolution of product support calls and improve the efficiency and effectiveness of the help-desk process. These applications typically permit help-desk staff to

- Verify the level of support the customer is entitled to receive

- Open trouble tickets

- Track specific tasks needed to resolve problems across multiple workgroups

- Monitor service-level agreements

- Maintain permanent incident histories

- Capture support costs for charge-backs

Customer service functions have benefited greatly from automating their processes. Some companies, such as eGain and Kana-Silknet, have developed packages to address all facets of customer service on multiple channels, including e-mail, Internet, chat, IP telephony, and conventional telephones. New customer service applications help companies provide superior customer service by enabling real-time interaction via text chat through a Web browser, directing the customer to a specific Web page.

e-Mail management is a critical issue for companies implementing a CRM strategy. Customer service software can help to route and track customer e-mail messages and online forms to the appropriate agents. These same applications generate reports about the efficiency of agents in answering e-mail messages and live text chat requests. When a customer's complaint comes up on a representative's screen, routine responses are rapidly assembled from a library of prescripted remarks, or blurbs. These remarks are customized with the customer's name and other relevant information and are then sent out electronically, permitting the representative to move on to the next problem to be dealt with. Such real-time Web interaction is becoming an important component for all call centers. Armed with such complete customer and product information, service professionals can resolve customer issues efficiently and effectively.

Customer Billing

Although U.S companies issue nearly 20.4 billion bills every year,[4] most CRM application frameworks don't include billing capabilities. We think that Internet billing promises a new way to build customer relationships with residential, commercial, and industrial customers.

The Internet bill will be an interactive entry point to a host of additional services, including customer self-care, automated sales, and one-to-one marketing. The Internet bill can easily become the gateway through which customers and companies have digital dialogue. Instead of interacting with customers through monolithic, undifferentiated home pages, one-to-one dialogues can be initiated through millions of individual bills. In the paper environment, bills often include teaser ads with a number to call for more information. Online, this coupon can now link to a Web page that will include all the information that would have previously required service representative interaction. By establishing a one-to-one interaction with each customer through the Internet bill, companies can establish the Web as a mission-critical channel without the need to dial a service center.

Despite the potential, very few bills are delivered online today. Even those that are—for instance, by Internet service provider EarthLink—lack any logical application of even basic CRM principles. Paper bills are now the primary channel of communication between companies and their customers. However, their potential for personalization is limited, and they are not interactive. A customer who wants to react to something in a paper bill—for example, to make a customer service inquiry or to order a new service—must pick up the telephone and call an 800 number.

Companies can use their CRM infrastructures to provide electronic bill presentment, bill payment, and inquiry management—an online, real-time balance to reduce the number of calls about how much the customer owes or whether payment has been posted. The Internet provides companies with the opportunity to significantly reduce the cost associated with maintaining customer relationships. For instance, billing related to customer support is a considerable cost to such recurring billers as telecom, utility, and credit card companies. The typical call associated with billing-related questions can last several minutes. Many companies are already using an interactive voice response (IVR) unit to reduce cost by addressing simple questions. A significant subset of services can be provided online without a real-life service representative. Providing interactive customer care via the bill and the Web site could lead to a reduction in customer-care costs of approximately 50 percent, as 40 percent of all calls are related to or stimulated by the customer's review of the bill.[5]

Field Sales and Service

Field sales applications enable account teams to seamlessly share information, manage sales pipelines, rapidly create customer quotes and proposals, easily configure products and services to meet the unique needs of each customer, and provide superior after-sales service and support. Sales teams can generate customized presentations and proposals and can easily produce customer communications, such as personalized invitations, letters, and other correspondence.

The other side of the field sales is field support. Nothing replaces on-site, hands-on support for instilling customers' faith in your company. Field service is the hands-on component of external customer support. A field service response is activated when a problem cannot be solved over the phone and requires sending someone to the customer site. Field service and dispatch applications have become mission-critical tools for delivering effective customer service and for containing costs. Field service software helps manage field service activities, preventive maintenance, break/fix service events, service inventory, dispatch and scheduling, warranties, invoicing, return-materials authorizations (RMAs), quotes and orders, shipping and receiving, and advanced parts exchange.

Field service clients are changing. Web technology promises lower total cost of ownership and access through lighter, less cumbersome machines. Web technology also opens up the opportunity for deploying field applications to new devices, including palm, pocket PC, and other handheld devices.

The emergence of mobile applications is effectively blurring the line between sales and service boundaries. Mobile devices give remote sales and service professionals real-time access to comprehensive customer and prospect information through voice recognition, Wireless Application Protocol (WAP)–enabled mobile phones, and a wide variety of handheld devices. Users can update opportunities, review account information, access calendar and contract details, order parts, and respond to service requests.

Loyalty and Retention Programs

Retention means that customers return again and again to do business with you, even if you do not have the best product, the lowest price, or the fastest delivery. Why? Because relationships deliver value above and beyond the product or service the customer pays for. The clear leader in customer loyalty is Harley-Davidson (HD), the motorcycle manufacturer. The fact that Harley-Davidson is the only corporate logo found tattooed on its customers demonstrates its model relationship with them. HD keeps tight quality control on a small line of well-known products, supports its dealers, listens to customers, and uses licensed products as advertising.[6] Ask yourself, How do we build HD-like customer loyalty?

Effective CRM is based on distinguishing customers by using their account and transaction histories. Today, few organizations are able to make these distinctions. The ability to effectively segment customers is dependent on *decision support technology providing detailed, accurate information about customers and their relationship with a company.* Most executives see decision support tools as powerful enablers of CRM and critical to understanding the drivers of customer loyalty.

CRM applications must track all customer activities in order to provide a comprehensive, integrated view of customer behavior. Ideally, CRM products track customer activities from prospect, to buyer, to customer, to prospect again. Understanding exactly which customers are the most profitable, creating their profiles, and determining their likely behavior is beyond the current technical and process capabilities of most firms. Many companies still can't tell customers how many accounts they have with the firm or what they've purchased in the past, much less predict their behavior in response to pricing changes and promotions.

Strategies for retention management depend on the ability to gather vast amounts of customer information at a significant level of detail. Specific customer knowledge allows companies to treat each customer individually and, in many cases, disengage from, or "fire," customers who are high-maintenance, low-margin prospects.

The ability to analyze large amounts of data in hopes of obtaining meaningful and useful customer information is hindered by data access issues. Much of the customer data to be analyzed resides in disparate transactional, e-commerce, and legacy applications or is delivered from third-party sources. Integrating these various data sources to provide a comprehensive view of the customer presents a significant technological challenge. For example, most companies' e-commerce systems operate independently of their traditional sales channels and fulfillment applications.

In order to successfully analyze corporate data from disparate sources, many companies have resorted to building customized analytical tools. These firms have used a combination of data extraction tools, data marts or data warehouses, data mining technologies, online analytic processing software, campaign management software, and, increasingly, e-commerce reporting tools and Web logs. Many of these internally developed solutions require substantial amounts of time to integrate, are expensive to deploy and maintain, and limit the ability to embed sales, marketing, finance, and e-commerce expertise and functionality. Finally, these solutions often have complex user interfaces and may not be accessible to all business users across the enterprise.

To enable all employees in a company to analyze and act on meaningful customer information located throughout the organization, companies are looking for a new generation of analytic solutions from such vendors as E.Phiphany, Broadbase, Broadvision, and Siebel. Addressing integration issues will be a major technical requirement when developing the next generation of CRM infrastructure tools.

Integration Requirements of the Next-Generation CRM Infrastructure

The hot topic, the buzzword, the sweeping technological trend that business will ride into the next century: integration, integration, integration. The next generation of CRM applications is no exception. Customer intimacy requires integration. For a CRM infrastructure to be effective, it must integrate

- Customer content

- Customer contact information

- End-to-end business processes

- The extended enterprise, or partners

- Systems

Integration of Customer Content

The ability to access, manage, and process all relevant customer content, including the seamless integration of structured and unstructured customer data, has emerged as a key requirement for CRM applications today. For example, customer service agents and loan officers need access to various types of structured data, such as customer and product information, and to unstructured data, such as faxes, digitized voice messages, images of applications, and credit reports.

Without a holistic view of the customer and the ability to understand his or her desires, the promise of CRM cannot be realized. Customer service will continue to be mediocre at best. In the past, companies realized the importance of customer data and vigorously began collecting customer information. But then they didn't know what to do with the volumes of data they had collected. With the levels of customer service attainable with a well-executed CRM strategy, companies are learning how to use data they've gathered, integrating it into their daily operations. Today's challenge is to make customer information easily accessible to all users in an organization, thus ensuring a clearer, more complete picture of your customers and your relationships with them. This accessible, fully integrated profile of the customer and your relationship allows for numerous service and sales opportunities, as well as level-of-service distinctions for your best customers.

Integration of Customer Contact Information

Excellence in contact management means not forcing your customers to play "hot potato" every time they call for service or support. Contact management (CM) is the electronic capture of customer information with the capability to access and share this information throughout the organization for sales and service purposes. Today's managers must pay close attention to the firm's contact management capabilities, as the number of opportunities for customer interaction has increased significantly in recent years. Today, customer inquiries and transactions can come from a variety of channels, including the call center and the Internet. Capturing and sharing these interactions within an organization should be top CM priority.

Effective CM is the cornerstone for achieving a company's goal of zero leakage of customer information. Providing CM consistency across all channels is nearly impossible unless contact data from previous interactions is stored and made accessible to all customer contact personnel. Effective CM requires information about the customer relationship to be current, regardless of when, where, or why that customer contacted the company. The same business rules and procedures must be followed in every customer contact, no matter what channel the customer uses to make contact—the Web, a call center, or a store front. This level of CM is called the *channel-independent solution.*

A well-designed CM infrastructure allows a company to centralize information by creating a virtual contact center and making the information available

24 hours a day, 7 days a week, across all service delivery channels. CM information also has a dual temporal aspect, meaning that it can be accessed in the here-and-now to provide service during interaction with a customer, and it can also be accessed offline, extracted to a decision support system for further analysis, and used in creating sales opportunities.

Integration of End-to-End Business Processes

Today's restructuring efforts must focus more on identifying solutions that anticipate and address customer needs and less on solving internal process problems. In order to make this shift in focus, a company must first integrate its business processes across functions. For example, sales and service are often viewed as separate functions: Sales occur during the sales cycle, and service is an after-sale activity. When these functions are viewed as separate, customers often get different answers, depending on whether they talk to a sales or a service representative. With so many firms breaking down the barriers between the sales and service functions, keeping them separate is no longer tenable if a company is to remain competitive.

In today's customer-driven environment, service must start before the sale and be present in every interaction a customer has with the company. Imagine the following scenario. Bill Robinson, a long-time customer of Eastwest Mortgage, realizes that the 30-year fixed mortgage rates have fallen so low that it would be to his advantage to refinance immediately. Bill remembers having received a letter about submitting a refinancing application via the Internet or phone. For Bill, a self-service access channel, such as the Internet, is the easiest choice.

Bill logs on to his mortgage company's home page and is prompted to enter his name and policy number. The details of the policy, monthly payments, and balance due are displayed on his computer screen, collected from several customer information databases. He fills out a form with the loan specifics he wants. The only information the mortgage company needs is his name, e-mail address, summary of asset and liability information, current housing expenses, the money he has for closing, the price range of the property being refinanced, and how large a down payment he expects to pay.

Bill is on a tight schedule, so he chooses a feature that says, "Please call me" and selects 7:00 P.M. At 7:00 sharp, Bill receives a call from a mortgage broker, who tells him that his loan request has been processed and that he qualifies for the full amount requested. The broker offers to bring the paperwork to Bill's house to complete the transaction. Bill is delighted with the level of service he's received.

As this scenario illustrates, the Web offers an unprecedented opportunity for businesses to achieve an end-to-end, integrated sales-and-service environment.

However, the keys to successful cross-functional integration and customer interactions are consistency and simplicity. Today's prospects and customers want access to companies through a variety of channels in order to obtain fast, accurate, consistent information. They want exceptional service both before and after the sale—not traditional service, in which they're sold a product and then handed off to a service group.

The Web continues to transform from a marketing channel to an interactive customer-care-and-fulfillment center capable of handling multiple communications channels, including faxes, e-mail, video, Internet calls, and, of course, traditional telephone contact. The Web's shift from a marketing tool to a customer support tool places a premium on highly integrated customer self-service interactions.

Integration of the Extended Enterprise: Interenterprise Customer Care

Although the benefits of having tightly integrated front-office systems were significant, they did not address the company's need to communicate with its business partners or third-party service providers. Sharing customer information with employees, customers, and partners or third-party service organizations is critical as companies increasingly depend on outside alliances. From this perspective, a company's partners are part of the firm's extended enterprise. This perspective enables your company to share leads or customer support issues with everyone who comes in contact with the your customer, regardless of whether they work for your company.

One form of this integration is partner relationship management (PRM), which focuses on channel sales functions, allowing resellers to work in real time with their vendors. The goal of PRM is to create long-term competitive differentiation by giving a company and its partners the ability to trade information and to distribute leads and data about common customers. The greatest benefit of PRM is on distribution channels, long underserved by the traditional CRM applications. The next wave of PRM applications, such as Pivotal and Asera, will use the Internet to integrate lead generation, pricing and promotions, configuration, and available to promise (ATP) functionality, providing the salesperson visibility into partner inventories and production schedules. For PRM to work, it is critical for a company to select the right partners, take responsibility for keeping them trained, manage incentive programs, and deliver the information their partners need.

Providing the kind of service customers expect guarantees customer loyalty. In order to meet these customer service expectations, companies must extend a

CRM infrastructure to their partners and vendors, via the Internet and intranets. Through this infrastructure, partners can share information, communicate, and collaborate with the enterprise, using Web-based applications, regardless of their own companies' internal network platforms and without the complexity and cost issues typically associated with current applications.

Integration of Systems: Customer Application Integration

The demand for complete relationship management is driving the need to integrate telephony, Web, and database technologies to provide a 360-degree view of customer attributes and account history. Such integration means that a company could combine information on all products and services a customer uses and share this information across all delivery channels and points of contact.

For a company's CRM infrastructure to provide the fullest possible benefit, the following four technologies must work together:

- *Legacy systems.* Many organizations have 20-year-old systems that cannot be discarded and that must be integrated into the CRM infrastructure. The primary integration tools are middleware and messaging software to increase the efficiency of extracting data from these systems.

- *Computer telephony integration (CTI).* CTI allows companies to apply consistent business logic in managing incoming calls. Real-time information about a caller is captured and linked with customer information from a company's varied data repositories. This information is then used to determine the resources needed to address the caller's needs.

- *Data warehousing.* Data warehouses extract data from transaction systems and structure the information so it can be effectively analyzed. In order to execute a CRM strategy, tremendous volumes of data must be organized or massaged in order to be used. Massaging information is no longer the repetitive, mechanical process used by traditional transaction systems.

- *Decision support technology.* This technology uses sophisticated analytical and modeling tools to assist companies with making decisions about customer needs. These decisions are based on accumulated relationship data. Once in place, these systems, such as E.Phiphany, help companies to retain their best customers.

As companies accelerate their investment in alternative delivery channels, the integration problem becomes more difficult. What is needed is a platform that hooks together all the other customer-facing apps. There is growing need for application integration packages that connect a number of front-office systems, including CRM packages, data warehouses, Web sites, and legacy applications.

How does this work? Specialized adapters collect customer information, such as transaction history and contact information, from multiple touch points, including the Web, legacy systems, and CRM apps. The adapters then reconcile that data into a customer profile so that information comes up whenever the customer contacts any part of the business. For example, if someone named Judy surfs a Web site, the system lets customer service reps know that she's the same Judy who called in or is in a marketing campaign database. Among the companies providing customer adapters are Blaze Software and YellowBrick Solutions.

Next-Generation CRM Trends

It's important to note that a CRM infrastructure alone isn't sufficient. The growth of the CRM market is also occurring at customer contact points, such as call centers and the Web, and managers should pay close attention to the customer dynamics at these contact points (see Figure 6.4). As CRM infrastructures become more widely accepted, we anticipate that customer needs and expectations will change subtly across various channels, reflecting the enhanced customer support capacity of CRM systems.

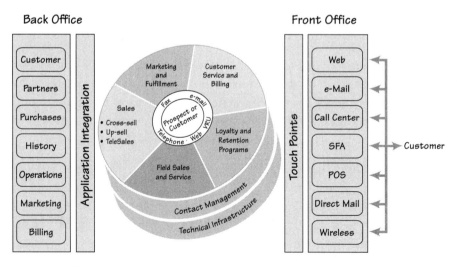

Figure 6.4: The Channel Interface to the CRM Infrastructure

Managers not only need to understand the dynamics of call center and Internet customer contact points but must also determine the impact that Internet-delivered customer service will have on traditional communication channels of support. Specifically, managers need to determine whether online customer service will really be cheaper than traditional support channels. In this section, we discuss several trends we see as relevant to the new versions of the customer contact point.

The Multichannel Integrated Experience

You are still undecided which car in the $15,000–$20,000 range you want to buy. You visit the Web home page of a car manufacturer and browse the features and options of its latest model. You click a button, and an agent from the manufacturer calls you within a minute, answering your questions and scheduling a test drive at your home on Saturday morning.

The very same technologies responsible for raising customer expectations can also be used to meet and exceed them. Integrated solutions can offer superior customer service at every contact point—the Internet, call centers, store fronts, ATMs, kiosks, and person-to-person selling. A CRM project is doomed if it fails to integrate all customer touch points. No matter how or why customers contact you or you contact them, you can offer a uniformly effective, and therefore positive, customer experience. Ask yourself, *Is my company creating an integrated, positive customer service experience?*

Your CRM solution may be made up of many elements: Internet customer service, e-mail routing, Web chat, Web collaboration, speech-enabled applications, and CTI. Trying to sort through all these elements to determine which are right for your company can be confusing. Product consolidation helps companies integrate their customer touch points, as evidenced by mergers and acquisitions, such as PeopleSoft and Vantive, Nortel and Clarify, DataSage and Vignette, Rubric and Broadbase, and Kana and Silknet. Such mergers and acquisitions will help clear up some of the clutter in the puzzling CRM market space and lead to reduced prices and enhanced features.

The Rise of the Call Center as a Multipurpose Customer Contact Point

The call center is one of the main growth areas of customer contact. Although a lot of hype surrounds Web service channels, 70 percent of all customer contact occurs at the call center. The scale and complexity of call centers are growing at an unprecedented rate. For example, British Telecom's 35 call centers across England, Scotland, Ireland, and Wales provide 24 million customers with 18,000 products and services.

A call center is a group of agents and voice response units (VRUs) that assist customers with support, inquiry, and transaction functions. As the call center evolves into a sales-and-service channel, understanding the dynamics of this channel will help us prepare for the future. Why? Because the Web is also evolving into a self-service sales-and-service channel. Although it's currently only a tiny market, we expect the Web to be one of the fastest-growing portions of the CRM software market, leveraging the rapid growth of the Internet. However, the key to success in this area will be in identifying where the changes will take place and where growth will happen in the near future.

People will continue to be a vital part of customer service, even in the online world. Many companies are extending traditional call center responsibilities to include handling online transactions. One customer touch point—Click for Help—allows customers to click a button that will immediately connect them to a live person via a real-time chat feature. The Click for Help technology gives customers immediate answers to their queries, helping the company to develop a sticky Web site and to build customer loyalty.

For service companies, the call center's focus has evolved from a customer service interaction center to a selling channel. All questions must be answered correctly and lengthy hold times and annoying call transfers eliminated. An agent answers a call from a customer and uses a sophisticated software application to obtain a detailed record of the products the customer uses and his or her spending habits. The agent also has a script to follow in selling additional products or services, which ensures company-wide consistency. The next task facing customer service and support managers is how to transfer the high-touch capabilities of the call center to the low-touch medium of the Web.

Listening Portals: Next-Generation CRM Capabilities

Most companies don't listen to their customers. The next-generation CRM applications must be transformed into listening outposts that track what customers are talking about. However, care must be taken to make sure that you listen to the right set of customers and hear what they are saying.

Most organizations fail to maximize their sales potential because they make the mistake of asking the wrong customers for feedback on how to improve their performance. One company that made this mistake, and paid heavily for it, is the now defunct Manhattan bookstore Shakespeare and Co. The bookstore was unperturbed when a larger bookstore chain opened shop across the street. Although it took some initial precautions by asking customers for feedback on, how to improve its service, this feedback didn't prepare the bookstore for the competition. The customers the company surveyed were loyal Shakespeare customers who were quite pleased with the bookstore; therefore, they failed to offer any suggestions for improvement. Because the firm limited its survey to existing customers, it didn't learn about the additional services offered by its competition.

The experience of Shakespeare and Co. underscores the fact that feedback from competitors' customers also counts.[7] Managers must identify how their companies listen to customers and understand what systems are in place for doing so effectively.

Why is listening increasingly important? Today, customers have many more choices. Once apathetic, customers are now becoming increasingly engaged, well informed, and demanding of the firms with which they interact. Customers are beginning to ask companies, What have you done for me lately? This may be the biggest challenge corporations face as they move forward into the e-business future. Like it or not, the vast changes resulting from Internet technology have made people smarter, more aware of the business landscape, and better able to find information about you and your competitors: what you sell, what you don't sell, and what people have to say about you. Understanding *how your CRM apps help you build customer loyalty is critical to your future success. For example, when your customers call your firm, do they get courteous service? Are they delighted when the call is over?* If you did not respond with a quick yes, your company needs to take steps to build better listening capabilities.

CRM Portals, Sales Force ASPs, and Hosted Applications

Regardless of their size, most companies have limited IT resources and need alternatives to deploying and maintaining CRM applications themselves. Small companies often lack the financial and personnel resources to maintain enterprise-class applications yet still desire the benefits and features of such products. Larger companies usually have greater IT resources but must support a growing number of projects in the backlog. These and other factors are converging to fuel the need for pay-as-you-use CRM portals and application hosting services.

CRM portals offer users Web-based functionality in a single personalized interface that combines marketing, sales, service, and other front-office applications and relevant Internet content. The target market is an estimated 42 million sales professionals worldwide, according to IDC and Dataquest. Some companies that offer these services are Interact Commerce, Salesforce.com, Sales.com, and Upshot.

Another segment that is growing rapidly is the hosted CRM market. For example, SiebelNet is a service that delivers Siebel's suite of sales, marketing, and customer service information systems on an outsourced basis. This new application outsourcing service will offer Siebel customers complete, network-based services that include the underlying software, hardware, and network connectivity needed to support a front-office implementation. Also offered are packaged services enabling customers to quickly implement and certify software configurations and supplement customer support operations.

What is the value to customers? Following are some of the key benefits of CRM portals and sales force application service providers (ASPs):

- *Increased speed of deployment and realization of benefits.* Even after an organization has decided to buy CRM software, additional time is still needed to acquire the resources, the product expertise, and the hardware/network infrastructure to deploy it. ASP solutions can accelerate deployment by implementing a fixed-price, subscription model. After signing up for the ASP service, a customer has access to an existing infrastructure. The customer will not lose precious time on non-value-added functions, such as acquiring hardware and assembling the infrastructure.

- *Address all project deployment risk factors.* Many CRM projects fail because teams focus solely on the technical aspects of deploying the system. These technical aspects—deploying server hardware and installing and configuring software—are more tangible during the implementation phase of a project and grab most of the project team's attention. But the human factors that contribute to an application's acceptance by end users—such as change management, training, and communications—ultimately determine the project's success. By turning to an ASP solution, customers can take advantage of ready-made infrastructure and concentrate on the human factors that will drive application acceptance within their company.

- *Level financial commitment over time.* To deploy CRM software, a company has to commit substantial resources up front to purchase license fees and annual maintenance charges; set up development, testing, and production server environments; integrate the application into the company's business processes; create a help desk; and establish other components of a support infrastructure. ASPs provide comprehensive services to satisfy these needs and allow a company to expense the monthly charges and evenly distribute them over the life of the contract.

The CRM portals and ASP solution marketplace is very young. Many issues still need to be worked. But watch this trend carefully.

A Roadmap for Managers

How to Build a CRM Infrastructure

Are start-up firms creating new value propositions for your customers? For some companies, CRM represents a radically new approach that will require them to do many things in different ways and for very different reasons. Managers looking to get started with their CRM implementation should follow these steps.

1. *Involve top management.* You need strong executive sponsorship of CRM if it is to be successful. For the customer-centric perspective to take root in the organization, the entire management team must participate in creating the CRM strategy.

2. *Define a vision of integrated CRM.* Understand what services and products you want to offer your customers and how you want to track customer interactions (see Figure 6.5). It's critical to examine the entire relationship with

Applications	No cross-channel systems	Customer information	Limited functional integration	Functional integration
Service and Support	No access to customer information	Access to customer information	Access to relationship information	Integrated sales and service information
Marketing	No marketing tools	Batch processes for marketing	Marketing Customer Information File	Closed loop integrated marketing
Decision Support	No customer analysis	Limited customer analysis	Data Warehouse Applications	Data Model Analysis

Figure 6.5: CRM Scorecard

the customer and not limit yourself to a traditional stovepipe view. The CRM vision must be clearly communicated across the organization, and it must be designed to work across functional boundaries.

3. *Establish the CRM strategy and specify its objectives.* Adopt a strategy consistent with the overall company strategy. Involve your company's marketing, sales, and service organizations, and understand how each deals with customers. Ask about current and future product and sales offerings.

4. *Understand the customer.* How does he or she use the existing products and services you offer? What is good or bad about the current process from the customer's perspective? Understand the customer life cycle value. Focus on the customers you want to keep for a lifetime.

5. *Review cultural changes that will need to occur.* Look into such issues as employee compensation and incentive structures to see whether they are supporting the new customer-centric view. Companies serious about CRM tie employee incentives to customer indicators, such as retention and satisfaction.

6. *Develop a business case.* Analyze where you currently stand and where you need to go. Do not use subpar technology as an excuse for inaction. There will always be technical weaknesses.

7. *Evaluate current readiness.* Determine your company's position relative to the competition. Assess the ability of existing sales and service infrastructures to gain and retain existing customers.

8. *Evaluate appropriate applications with an uncompromising focus on ease of doing business.* Ensure that the applications meet today's needs *and* the strategic direction of the firm. Look at the applications from an *integrated* viewpoint. Also, take the customer's view, not the product or account view. After selecting an application, ensure that the process redesign will benefit and retain the customer.

10. *Identify and target quick wins.* Set aggressive and realistic milestones. Accomplish attainable objectives early in the process to build support and ensure completion. This allows you to implement incrementally and successfully. Celebrate your successes along the way.

11. *Put the ownership of the end-to-end project in the hands of a single manager.* Partner your team members with experienced business leaders and developers who understand how to deliver and deploy integrated applications.

12. *Implement in stages.* Because of the cost and complexity of CRM, a staged approach will offer a greater chance of success and allow for continuous evaluation of strategy. Also, challenge the solution. The usefulness and benefits of a CRM strategy continually change in the real world. Be ready for it. Be proactive about change.

13. Be sure to create a closed-loop CRM environment. The goal of the CRM strategy is zero leakage of information. As customers contact the company, regardless of the channel, purpose, or outcome of the interaction, make sure that it is captured.

14. *Create concrete measurement goals.* When implementing any new strategy, it is critical to measure progress and continuously assess performance. Measurement is often overlooked in the rush to make things work. Often, the most difficult part of this process is deciding what the critical success factors are and knowing when you are successful.

Also, monitor your effort by using the scorecard in Figure 6.5 to help determine whether you are on the right path to relationship management. Although this CRM scorecard is at a high level, it shows the importance of measurement at both the organizational and project levels. Also consider setting up critical success factors, measuring such areas as scheduling, relationship agreements, costs, and customer satisfaction. Measuring results is a critical component in determining current and future success.

Anticipate Organizational Challenges

It is an unfortunate truth, but nothing is ever simple, especially when change is in the air. And change is churning the air with hurricane force these days, threatening to blow away those businesses comfortable with the status quo. However, for the storm chasers of the e-business world, CRM offers another exciting, progressive challenge.

Implementing CRM requires a high degree of political, cultural, and organizational change. Today's fragmented and departmentally stovepiped approach to managing customer relationships leaves many organizations impotent. Many organizations lack the interdepartmental cooperation, collaboration, and compensation strategies to help them move closer to CRM readiness. Many executives feel the pain and stress of fragmentation as new sales become more difficult to come by, customer complaints increase, existing customers fail to renew business, and, before long, revenue growth and even stock prices flatten or decrease. Leadership begins to realize that current operations need to change, but few firms know where to begin. Unfortunately, the response from many executives is to put pressure on employees to drive revenues or decrease costs. Often, this pressure becomes unbearable, turnover among the ranks begins, and, if left unchecked, the departure of skilled employees reduces the profit-producing muscle of the enterprise.

If CRM is the greatest thing since sliced bread, why such organizational resistance? Political resistance arises because CRM generally cuts across autonomous business or functional units that are not typically required to cooperate with one another. Corporations may bow to political pressure by allowing individual business units to set their own strategies, resulting in handling customers differently across lines of business. A good CRM framework can handle these situations, but it can't overcome cultural resistance, arising when individual business units lose the power to make decisions. In order for CRM to be adopted and accepted by a company, the CEO's backing is essential. Successful CRM always starts with the unqualified sponsorship of top management. If it does not lead the CRM implementation, it will not happen.

Organizational resistance to CRM is unfortunate but almost inevitable. The organizational issues companies must tackle to implement CRM include the following.

- Current incentive systems work against CRM because they reward performance that deals with only part of the customer's relationship to the company. Therefore, a sales manager who is evaluated on individual product sales has no vested interest in ensuring that the service organization is meeting the needs of the customer. Most companies today lack financial incentive programs that promote CRM.

- CRM requires making a careful transition from an existing silo-centric infrastructure to an integrated customer-centric infrastructure. Over the years, however, large enterprises have built, bought, or inherited a wide variety of CRM applications. Some of this software is proprietary and will be difficult to share across departments.

- Organizations with global operations must manage customer interactions in different languages, time zones, currencies, and regulatory environments. In this environment, providing consistent, customized service is difficult to accomplish using traditional technology.

CRM has a definite impact on the shape of an organization and the roles of its employees. This impact is especially evident on the corporation's front-line staff, the critical point where the CRM process and the customer make contact. The effectiveness of CRM processes depend on the close link between front-line activities and the company's internal operations, such as product development, strategic planning, and financial processes. The goal of CRM is to make it easy for the front line to relay customer requirements and issues to upstream portions of the process: in other words, to carry the voice of the customer deep into the organization and use it to guide the company's decision making.

CRM is complex, costly, and not without its challenges. However, the alternative is for a company to remain functionally fragmented, inefficient, and less than optimally productive. Refusal to implement a CRM strategy will essentially give your competition license to win customers away. Do you want that?

Memo to the CEO

Is managing the relationship between your business and your customers fundamental to your company's success? Is customer service a critical component for achieving and sustaining competitive advantage? Should the process of fulfilling your customers' requirements differentiate you from the competition?

If you answered yes to any of these questions, your company is a candidate for CRM. If you answered no to these questions, you should take this chapter to heart: CRM should be your company's lifeblood. CRM means offering the right product or service to the right customer at the right time and price via the right contact point. CRM paints a compelling picture. The changes possible through sales-and-service integration today were inconceivable a few decades ago. The service levels such integration can bring are resetting the bar on what customers have come to expect.

Why is the CRM trend important? For many companies, the focus of organizational change has shifted from internal operational efficiency toward effectiveness in external relationships. During the coming decade, businesses will focus on controlling the customer. Companies will succeed at customer management by rapidly shifting their investments in technology from internally focused process efficiency to an external customer orientation. This trend is driven by corporations' focus on improving customer satisfaction and loyalty, as well as increasing revenue from existing customers.

Why should CEOs care? Because the ability to capitalize on this new trend and to deliver new information-based services effectively rests on corporate leadership. Companies that change to a customer-centric service garner a competitive differentiation in the e-business world unlike any other.

In summary, the goals of the new CRM infrastructure are to

- Create a single, long-running customer dialogue across all business functions and customer access points

- Create an integrated approach across functional units, enabling company-wide management of customer relationships rather than departmental management of customer transactions

- Ensure that every channel your customers use is easy and consistent

- Understand customer behavior by recording all interactions with the customer and using customer data to identify segmented marketing and trigger events

- Understand when to take action by learning how and when to create appropriate marketing offers and opportunities

To remain competitive and to maximize profits, companies must align people, processes, strategy, and technology and search for innovative, cost-effective ways to build, retain, and deepen the lifetime value of customer relationships. You must understand your customers like never before and use this knowledge to serve them. A well-planned CRM infrastructure captures, stores, and analyzes customer interactions that are essential to the future of business.

CHAPTER SEVEN

Transforming Customer Contact into Revenue: Selling-Chain Management

What to Expect

Selling is both a science and an art. e-Business presents us with new sales channels, such as the self-service and mobile sales force, which are rapidly increasing in importance. We are beginning to see selling-chain software applications that integrate and streamline the sales and order cycle by moving information more rapidly between buyers and sellers, resulting in buyers' making quicker, more confident decisions.

Companies selling products and services over multiple channels require a new generation of e-business sales applications. Next-generation selling applications must support traditional direct and indirect selling channels to maximize revenue channel effectiveness and to establish a common, enterprise-wide view of the customer. These applications must allow companies to target products, services, and Web content to individual customers. Without these applications, companies will be unable to execute successful e-business strategies and instead may be forced to rely exclusively on either point solutions or traditional human-assisted sales channels for their revenue streams.

In this chapter, we examine the future implications of sales automation in an integrated, multichannel e-business environment. We discuss the business trends driving the corporate use of selling-chain solutions. In the future, success in sales will require a significant shift in strategy. The chapter also contains a roadmap for building an integrated order acquisition application framework and discusses its key features, including on-demand product availability, pricing, and interactive configuration capability.

The business of business is selling: what customers want and need when they want it and need it. Unfortunately, most B2C and B2B sales initiatives have failed to deliver on the customer-interactive promise of the Web. The first-generation B2C and B2B portal sites ignored customer goals and failed to provide even the basics of a positive buying experience.

Consider this: Your best customer walks in the door, you know how to make the sale in person, but how do you do it online? First-generation sites present customers with islands of disjointed information that provide little or no buying assistance. For example, on Sony's Vaio Notebook Web site, the product-selection area is poorly integrated with the ordering and shopping basket features, frustrating the user by making it difficult to select additional items during the checkout process. These first-generation sites also fail at gathering more complete customer profile information beyond basic demographics and buying-pattern data. Limited customer profile information restricts a company's ability to effectively manage individual customer relationships over time. To date, the main achievement of the early e-commerce sites has been the online delivery of targeted product and service content to customers/users by using niche applications or by building customized applications on top of their static e-commerce sites.

The resulting technological environments are made up of complex, loosely integrated sales systems that are difficult to maintain, customize, and extend. More important, the vast majority of current e-commerce apps that have been deployed into online sales have to be managed separately from a company's traditional sales channels. By doing so, companies have, in effect, isolated their Internet channels—and the customer and marketing information it gathers and provides—from the rest of the enterprise.

As the sales channel changes, so does the selling process itself (see Table 7.1). Companies must decide which new business practices need to be implemented in order to support real-time, one-to-one, or self-service selling. Companies must also determine what new applications they need to support the changing character of online and offline selling. In response to these needs, a new generation of application infrastructure for one-to-one relationship selling is emerging.

Table 7.1: Evolution of the Selling Process

Salesperson Titles	Selling Orientation
Drummer or peddler (1750–1900)	Negotiate price and/or barter with customer
Salesperson (1900–present)	Transaction-oriented selling: canned high-pressure selling; sales as an art form
Account executive; sales consultant; relationships marketing rep.; sales engineer (1960–1990)	Adaptive selling: building long-term
Account team; relationship managers (1990–present)	Consultative and collaborative selling: solving problems and guiding customers
Self-service online selling (1996–present); guided selling (1998–present)	Customer needs paramount; real-time visibility into the process; synergistic relations with suppliers

The Basics of Selling-Chain Management

Selling-chain management is an application framework that helps sell better—and more effectively—across all channels (see Figure 7.1) by establishing linkages between previously disconnected sales functions within a company and the firm's sales processes. Such links integrate the complete sales cycle: initial customer contact, configuration, and ordering. The strength of selling-chain management is that it can enable the creation of new revenue channels while simultaneously improving the effectiveness of a company's existing channels.

Why is this type of application framework needed? The e-business landscape has created new business and technical challenges that are straining traditional enterprise software models and presenting substantial barriers to companies pursuing multichannel sales opportunities. As a result, companies are seeking new

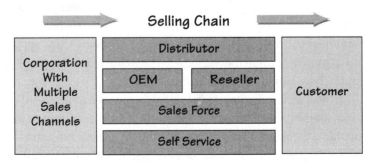

Figure 7.1: Types of Sales Channels

ways to define and to deliver integrated sales solutions. This chapter will explore the impact of the Web on the selling chain, opportunities for exploiting the Internet, and the shortcomings of traditional approaches. The chapter will then present a new approach that meets the requirements of the Internet age.

Selling-chain management has been in the making for most of the past decade. Consider this quote from *ComputerWorld* in 1994: "Having lost more than $1 billion in the past two years, Xerox is laying its hopes for future profits on the doorstep of the virtual office. The $14.2 billion company is rolling out notebook computers to its 4,000-person sales force, automating that sector of the company for the first time. Xerox hopes the move will cut costs and sharpen sales force productivity. The goal of this movement is to put salespeople, engineers and customer service reps where their customers are. Leading the charge at Xerox is the New England North District sales group, which became one of the first of the company's 62 U.S. sales districts to receive either Compaq Elite or IBM ThinkPad 755 notebooks. The notebooks give the sales force immediate access to Xerox's corporate network and provide it with software to quickly create proposals for customers."[1] Xerox's first flirtation with selling-chain innovation did not work and is credited with the company's losing market share steadily. Part of the problem is that the technology was immature, the application infrastructure was not there, and salespeople were not ready.

Xerox is a great precautionary case study for companies embarking on selling innovation. If the business goals get way ahead of the application capabilities, you will have problems. If rhetoric and reality are far apart, you will have the business equivalent of the *Titanic*. Before we proceed further, let's look at the business problem created by disconnected front-office systems.

Identifying the Problem: Disconnected Front-Office Systems

Over the past decade, companies' software investment focus shifted from automating internal back-office operations toward managing customer relationships and increasing revenue. In response to this customer-oriented, front office systems focus, many companies have invested heavily in CRM applications designed to automate administrative support for traditional corporate sales, call center, and service employees.

CRM solutions, including customer contact management, call center service and support, and marketing automation, help to eliminate cost inefficiencies within a company's sales and marketing organization by streamlining and consolidating customer information and other internal administrative tasks. Contrary to hype, CRM applications focus on the administrative aspects of a company's sales, marketing, and service efforts, they generally do not directly enhance the customer's buying experience.

Also, traditional CRM solutions don't provide value directly to a firm's customers. These older CRM applications were designed before the widespread use of the Web became commonplace and were not intended for large-scale, Internet-based customer-driven transactions. Many companies that implemented traditional CRM applications realized that their systems are not sufficiently interactive and fail to engage customers in ways that add value or enhance individual buying decisions.

To overcome the limitations of older CRM applications, a variety of niche applications have been introduced into the market, including Internet content management and personalization software, which target a specific aspect of the customer relationship or buying process. Known as point solutions, these tools provide tactical value by encouraging customer use of the Internet for the purchase of basic, consumer-oriented goods.

However, current versions of these point applications do not interact with a company's traditional sales and distribution channels, resulting in an incomplete view of an individual customer's behavior, transaction patterns, and preferences. This inability to enable a common view of individual customers across a firm's multiple selling channels limits the firm's ability to develop strategies for improving its product offerings, services, and selling processes in ways that encourage repeat business from those customers.

For example, information about a customer making a purchase online may not be available in a call center. Similarly, detail from a company's telephone orders is not reflected on the Web. Finally, information about a customer's visit to a company's Web site, where the customer created a customized product matching his or her need and then asked for a quote, is generally not available to the sales rep covering that sales territory. As these examples illustrate, implementing an integrated multichannel sales strategy that aims to please the customer faces a wide range of issues.

- When there are multiple sales channels, salespeople are often inundated with non-value-added, noncore tasks, spending 30 percent to 50 percent of their time on administrative tasks.

- Web sites may display inaccurate sales information. The information is not kept current, because the marketing information is not consistent, the printed collateral is old, and the pricing information is out of date. This is a major problem in self-service selling.

- After-order customer support is fragmented, as customers must deal with multiple company contacts who have difficulty accessing order status information.

- Current sales applications are not sufficiently responsive or flexible, because the IT staff cannot handle its current backlog of application enhancement, much less new ones.

- Because current systems are not integrated, customer orders must often be rekeyed several times.

These problems wreak havoc on a company and its customers, not only increasing costs and reducing quality but also decreasing customer satisfaction. Today, companies face a dual challenge. First, they must equip their distribution channels with systems that differentiate them from their competitors when a customer's buying decision is being made. Second, they must provide their customers with a consistent, valued sales experience across all channels, including the Internet.

Defining Selling-Chain Management

Traditional sales force automation has focused on helping salespeople track contacts and update databases remotely. But the market is undergoing a radical overhaul that focuses the technology on the buyer, not the seller. Vendors are coming out with new selling-chain management frameworks—software suites that support such customer-oriented tasks as configuration, dynamic pricing, order entry, and order management.

Selling-chain management is an integrated order acquisition strategy set in a multichannel environment. The focus is on the buying process, not the sales process, enhancing the buying process and making it faster for both customers and salespeople. Selling-chain management ensures that salespeople and customers have the information they need at their fingertips: on a single screen or window. More broadly, selling-chain management includes the application of technology to sales activities throughout an order: from the initial customer inquiry to order delivery.

The underlying premise for implementing selling-chain management is straightforward. Success in the next generation of selling will mean a significant shift in strategy. Companies will focus less on automating discrete tasks, such as lead management, configuration, and pricing, and more on developing an integrated infrastructure that views order acquisition holistically: an end-to-end process involving every department, from marketing to logistics (see Figure 7.2).

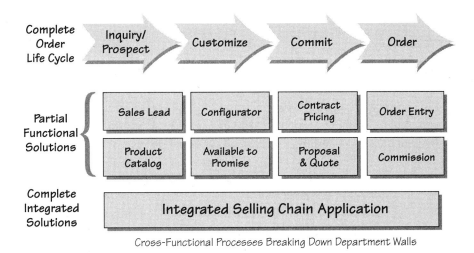

Figure 7.2: Complete Order Life Cycle

By approaching buying, or order acquisition, as a process rather than as a function, companies begin to adopt their customers' point of view, arguably the perspective from which to win a customer's loyalty, respect, and purchases. Selling-chain applications are tools for streamlining the integrated group of buying-related activities that businesses perform to acquire and to fulfill customer orders.

Selling-Chain Application Framework Goals

Companies, such as 1-800-Flowers, Dell, Schwab, and Delta Airlines, have redefined order acquisition to involve direct interaction with the customer. Direct customer interaction means providing information about products, configuration services, pricing updates, and order entry functionality. The aim of the next generation of selling-chain solutions is to help a company's direct sales force understand and focus on

- The most appropriate and profitable market opportunities

- Shortening sales cycles by keeping all members of the sales team up to speed on what tasks to perform and when

- Increasing repeat sales by learning more about customers and their interests

- Improving order pipeline visibility, leading to more accurate sales forecasting

- Delivering more timely market intelligence to company decision makers

The basic difference between traditional business and e-business is in the transition from functionally oriented sales automation to process-oriented selling-chain management. In order to be successful in the new economy, sales activities must be managed as a cross-functional, interdepartmental process. Sales processes must break down functional boundaries, focusing on customer needs and incorporating key performance indicators that support end-to-end process measurement. Focusing on interactive selling means turning your current organization on its side and rethinking every sales activity you do.

The goals of a selling-chain management business strategy are to

- *Make the ordering process easier for the customer.* Make the entire order process a seamless series of transactions. For example, Haworth, a manufacturer of office furniture, lets its customers participate directly in the office design process. Traditionally, if you needed an office system, an architect would design it for you. However, architects took several months to do this, with much time spent gathering requirements. Haworth implemented an online system that allows the customer to do more of the work. The customer and the dealer sit in front of the PC and design the customer's office system in real time. Instead of taking weeks or months, the entire design process takes only an hour. To Haworth, the value of customer-designed systems is that it processes few returns. Once an office system is delivered, customers don't send it back, because it's what they created.

- *Add value for the customer.* This involves conceiving of the order process as adding value for the customer. A Web site that functions only as an order taker isn't going to be around for long. Companies must collaborate with the customer in order to identify the customer's requirements, configure a solution to meet the customer's needs, and then deliver the solution to the customer's location. Personal computer manufacturers, such as Dell and Gateway, have mastered the art of delivering customized solutions made to customer specifications.

- *Make it easy to order customized products.* Match what customers want with what companies sell. This reduces unsold inventory, increases inventory turns, and increases sales. Companies are exploring the possibility of integrating their front-end sales configuration systems with their back-end planning engines to base delivery-date promises on material availability in the supply chain. The goal is to increase overall revenue by meeting customers' orders quickly, accurately, and, of course, profitably.

- *Increase sales force effectiveness.* Despite the tactical productivity advances made possible by technology, few innovations have focused on improving salespeople's strategic effectiveness by increasing sales volume, trimming sales-cycle times, or lowering costs per sale. The focus on sales effectiveness is increasing as companies look for ways to increase revenues while reducing the cost of operations.

- *Coordinate team selling.* Storing customer information in a common, central location for use in coordinating global sales activities becomes increasingly important as the number of multinational companies grows and their international markets increase. Coordinating activities and sharing information is especially critical in complex, team-selling environments in which team members work together to close a deal.

The order acquisition environment today is significantly different from that of only 5 to 10 years ago, and the pace of change continues to quicken. Changes in regulatory policy, shifts in reseller channels, and the expansion of product lines are increasing the pressure on a company's sales organization.

Integrated Selling Infrastructure

Multiple distribution channels, shorter product life cycles, intensified competition, and more sophisticated customers are making the salesperson's life increasingly difficult. Customers are demanding solutions designed and configured to meet their specific needs. These sales challenges are made worse by difficulty with pricing, promotion, and commission management. Sales organizations are faced with simultaneously increasing value for the customer, improving operating efficiency, and reducing costs.

For example, a sales representative meets with a prospective customer. Despite being armed with volumes of product information, the salesperson cannot answer the customer's questions: Can you deliver the product with these modifications by this date? How much will the product cost if we make these modifications? When will it be delivered? The intricacy of the company's product and service offerings, with their associated pricing combinations and discount structures, makes it difficult for the salesperson to respond easily to a customer's inquiries.

The salesperson tells the customer, "I'll get back to you in a couple of days," returns to the office and begins the time-consuming process of configuring the order. First, the salesperson develops and submits a price quote and then negotiates with manufacturing and the company's shipping department for an acceptable delivery date. Several days or even weeks later, the customer's questions are finally answered. Meanwhile, a competitor with the ability to provide timely and accurate answers to the customer's questions has walked away with the business.

Once aware of the lost sale, the salesperson complains to management, "Give me the ability to configure orders in real time, deliver a price quote, and know product's availability on the spot, at the point of sale. Also, give me software that seamlessly integrates with our company's back-office processes—manufacturing and distribution—in order to track sales orders and provide customers with accurate promise dates." *Does this scenario sound familiar? How are your salespeople spending their time? How effective are their tools? What similar obstacles do they face when trying to close a sale? Does your organization have the sales tools it needs to facilitate order acquisition?*

In traditional sales settings, getting the customer's order right has never been easy. During a typical conversation with a customer, a salesperson may need to confer with manufacturing to ensure that a product can be configured with certain features, contact engineering to verify that a solution meets the customer's needs, or check with distribution to confirm that a product is in stock or is ready to ship. Obtaining all this information can be an arduous, time-consuming task that slows down the sales cycle. But without doing the legwork needed to obtain this information, the risk of order errors, which can cause delays, annoy customers, and result in lost revenues, is high.

A salesperson has enough difficulties getting a prospect's attention, coordinating schedules, and even keeping the prospect on the telephone. Keeping a prospect's attention is even more difficult than getting it, especially if the prospect has questions or objections that can't be responded to quickly. Modern sales forces must have integrated point-of-sale applications that provide real-time access to all current product, price, and inventory availability information so that they can answer customer questions completely, handle objections skillfully, and, ideally, close the sale on the spot.

In most enterprises, the sales process has undergone little automation to date. However, recent advances now make selling-chain automation solutions feasible. In the real-time economy, sales have a profound impact on downstream decisions, as well as decisions related to outside suppliers. However, management at many firms is uncertain as to which aspects of the selling-chain life cycle should be automated and how software can be used to support it. The dynamic nature of the market and vendors, combined with the fluid scope of software capabilities, exacerbate the confusion.

In order to better understand the benefits of sales automation, it is important to first understand how the Web is changing the sales process. By examining the steps involved in originating a typical mortgage versus a mortgage online, we can truly appreciate how the Internet is changing the sales process.

Offline processing of traditional mortgages involves the following steps.

1. The potential borrower submits an application to the loan officer, who is responsible for collecting the initial paperwork necessary for originating the loan.

2. After submitting an application, the borrower receives from the lender a package containing a Truth in Lending form. The lender orders the necessary third-party services, such as a credit check, title search, and property appraisal.

3. After receiving the Truth in Lending form, the loan processor can verify the borrower's assets and income.

4. With all the information in hand, the loan processor packages the loan and sends it to the loan underwriter for a compliance review. The loan is approved, conditionally approved, suspended, or declined outright.

5. After reviewing the application, the underwriter sends the loan package back to the loan officer to inform the borrower of the loan's terms and conditions.

6. Once the loan conditions have been satisfied, the loan papers are ordered, and the loan is sent to the title company (or escrow agent or lawyer) for closing.

7. Once closed, the loan is sent back to the lender for funding.

The origination process takes approximately 30–45 days in order to accommodate the level of communication and data sharing that occur between the borrower and the loaning institution. It is also important to note that the party administering the closing does vary across the country.

In contrast, online mortgage processing can come back with an underwriting decision and a conditional rate quote in a matter of minutes instead of days. The key to this process is that the data collection and underwriting are all completed before any third-party services are ordered and before the asset/income verifications are performed. The automated underwriting system determines how much additional data is needed instead of collecting all the relevant information up front and requiring the underwriter to review it.

Processing mortgages online involves the following steps.

1. The prospective borrower fills out the application, providing the lender with the relevant income and asset information, a property description, and the type of loan.

2. After receiving the information, the lender performs a credit check and submits the loan to the underwriter. If the borrower accepts the loan rate, the loan is granted on the condition that the loan information the borrower provided is accurate.

3. A data verification person collects any additional relevant data, orders third-party services, and distributes the Truth in Lending form. A key feature is the ability of the underwriting system to inform the underwriter what information is still needed. The role of the data verifier is to confirm data accuracy, requiring considerably less skill—and cost—than traditional underwriting.

4. Once the loan is verified, the loan papers are generated and checked.

5. After the loan papers are processed, the loan is closed and funded.

The online mortgage model is faster for the borrower, provides a more efficient method of communication and data sharing, and rate shoppers do not significantly add to the online lender's cost structure. The lender benefits include lower acquisition costs, better productivity, and increased capital use.

One disadvantage to the online model is the absence of a local loan contact person, which means that the closing documents are sent overnight instead of being hand delivered by a loan officer or a broker. If there is a loan document error, the documents must be returned, reprocessed, and regenerated, which takes time. For this reason, many people believe that online lending is a valuable service in a refinance market but not in a purchasing market. The handholding needed when purchasing a home makes having a local, accessible loan agent a requirement for many borrowers.

The online mortgage industry is young, and as consumers adapt to the process and as lenders hone their product and service offerings, the following issues will be worked out.

- A low percentage of loans make it from application to close.

- A low percentage of consumers fill out the application without picking up the phone.

- As noted earlier, a high percentage of refinance-driven loans and a lower percentage of purchase-driven loans are being captured by the online lenders.

The online model reduces the number of mortgage-processing errors and time. Still, many aspects of the model can be improved or automated. First, asset and income verification can be performed online instead of over the phone or through the mail. Second, electronic property appraisals can be performed instead of the time-consuming and costly physical appraisal process. Third, title insurance can be ordered electronically. Software applications are being developed that automate these steps. How much of the process can be automated will depend on the requirements of the secondary mortgage market. If "Fannie and Freddie" approve the use of an electronic appraisal, widespread adoption of the model will ensue.

Business Forces Driving the Need for Selling-Chain Management

How do you help buyers and sales reps complete the purchase of complex products over the Internet? This question and several other market issues are driving the interest in selling-chain applications: the rise of self-service, the excessive cost of presales support, the increasing cost of order errors, changing sales channels, increasing product complexity, and the rise of mergers and acquisitions.

The Rise of the Self-Service Order

Sales process complexity is increasing as customers demand higher levels of service, faster turnaround, and more options for customized products and services. During the early 1990s, the concept of mass customization first appeared in the marketplace, giving rise to the concept of a "market of one." Consumers want what they want, when they want it, and they want it packaged uniquely to meet their individual needs. In this new market, companies must reexamine their sales procedures for ease of use. For example, for years, Citibank captured a significant share of the college student market for credit cards simply by making it easy for students to obtain credit, whereas the competitors made it difficult.

Product selection is one aspect of the selling process that has changed by self-service ordering. Having narrowed the possibilities, today's consumer is demanding a final selection process that is comfortable, convenient, and less frustrating. The online car industry provides a good example of how an e-business achieves this degree of ease. For many potential customers, the experience of choosing a used car is an ordeal. But new methods for selecting used cars are transforming the industry. Auto-By-Tel, CarPoint, CarMax Auto Superstore, and AutoNation USA are companies that have targeted the selection experience as their competitive focus. At a CarMax showroom, customers sit in front of a computer, specify what features they want in an automobile, and scroll through detailed descriptions of cars that might meet their needs. The final, no-haggle price for each vehicle is listed. A sales assistant then lets the customer inspect the autos of interest and handles all the paperwork if the customer decides to buy. The "selling" is done not by the salespeople but by the customers themselves.

Self-service ordering as an option in complex settings, such as the mortgage industry, will take time. For example, in the mortgage business, the process is complex, with human input still playing a major role. However, as consumers become more comfortable with the Internet-based origination process, adoption of the service will increase. Also, if the borrower information entered into the application is correct, the quoted rate will be used. However, if the borrower makes an entry error, the error will show during the data verification stage, and the rate will be changed accordingly. Finally, the current percentage of processed and closed online loans is lower than for loans processed by using the traditional model. However, as mentioned earlier that stems from the youth of the industry, not to problems inherent in the process itself.

The Excessive Cost of Presales Technical Support

Companies that fail to improve the quality and to reduce the turnaround time associated with preparing sales quotes and proposals are likely to lose sales and market share to more responsive competitors. Consider the supplier enrollment problem facing Ariba, the B2B procurement marketplace. Exponential growth of suppliers eager to join the Ariba Network taxed the supplier support resources. Ariba's consultants guided potential suppliers through a phone evaluation of their catalog content, catalog format, technology, ordering system, geographic location, and budget. The process took 1 to 2 hours and ended with a recommendation for implementation and next steps. Recognizing the limits of the existing process, Ariba looked to the Web to remove the processing bottleneck. Using a guided selling tool from OnLink, Ariba codified support procedures into 4 steps and 16 questions. With conversational distractions removed, Ariba streamlined the supplier enrollment process down to less than 15 minutes.[2]

The specialized product knowledge of today's technical sales specialist is critical to effectively translating a prospect's needs into clearly stated product specifications. As a result, companies will increasingly use technical sales specialists during the presale phase of a sales process. Generally, technical sales specialists have a superior grasp of the capabilities of the entire product line and a better understanding of how these capabilities may meet a prospective customer's needs than do regular sales representatives.

Although highly effective, involving the technical support staff in the sales cycle drives up the cost of selling and shifts the burden of expertise from the salesperson to the technical sales specialist. Often, an excessive amount of time is consumed preparing complex sales quotes and proposals. With consumers expecting shorter response times to their inquiries, it's imperative that companies deliver accurate and thorough sales proposals in record time.

The trend toward the market of one increases the difficulty of creating standardized proposals, as each document is as nonstandard and unique as the product it proposes to sell. Thus, the cost of preparing accurate quotes and proposals rises relative to the level of product complexity and customization required.

The Increasing Cost of Order Errors

The sophistication and complexity of customized products, services, and systems has resulted in more frequent and costly order errors. These errors occur throughout the sales-and-delivery cycle. At the point of sale, an error can be made by simply proposing a product configuration that fails to meet a customer's technical requirements or by offering a product that can't be made.

Order entry errors occur because incompatible product options have been overlooked and are not rejected or because ancillary equipment has not been included in the order. In manufacturing, an invalid product configuration can shut down the production line. If a miscalculated, multivendor product configuration is shipped to a customer, the cost of correcting the mistake in the field can be excessive, if not unrecoverable.

Order mistakes often result from the following human errors: insufficient access to product information; outdated, inaccurate back-office information; misinterpretation of a valid product configuration; misunderstanding the product line or how a product will perform; and keystroke errors when entering or processing an order. By not automating their order processes and integrating their sales functions with their back-office systems, companies will continue to experience significant order-processing error rates, resulting in increased costs.

The Proliferation of Channels

Selling is not the simple process it once was, owing to the rapid proliferation of sales and distribution channels. The numerous channel applications serving the order acquisition process include

- Field sales and in-store/branch sales providing assisted in-person selling

- Telesales providing assisted call center selling

- Self-service providing unassisted selling via the Web

- Third-party resellers, or channel selling

The direct-to-the-end-user and build-to-order business models have experienced relative success. As a result, many companies are being pressured to improve the information flow through the various sales channels they use in order to improve product time to market, reduce their costs, and compete more effectively.

In addition, many organizations are attempting to implement integrated multichannel sales strategies so they can achieve global expansion and/or market penetration more quickly. These strategies require the efficient passing of sales leads and the even tougher challenge of keeping all parties informed on the status of the sales process.

The Increasing Complexity of Products

Increasingly complex products and the rise in customer demands for time-efficient ordering processes are forcing companies to increase the productivity and responsiveness of their sales forces. Furthermore, new products are introduced at an accelerated pace, resulting in shorter product life cycles and making the salesperson's job of staying knowledgeable even more difficult.

In many industries, sales efficiency and productivity are major issues requiring seasoned professionals to compete in tight labor markets. Sales forces must learn to deal with an ever-growing, ever-changing set of products and services as companies broaden their product portfolios to sustain or to accelerate sales-growth rates.

As a result, it's difficult for sales representatives and end users to keep up with changing product and compatibility information. These difficulties underscore the need for a central repository of up-to-date product information and tools to access it, to increase sales representatives' productivity, and to enable end users to freely select, configure, and order products.

The Rise of Deregulation and Mergers and Acquisitions

Some organizations face new sales and marketing challenges arising from newly emerging distribution channels and product-line expansions; other companies face dramatic changes within their own industries. For example, the impact of deregulation on sales and marketing in both the telecommunications and utility industries has not, until now, been an issue, as these industries enjoyed a monopoly. In a competitive environment, many of these companies are rapidly adopting selling-chain applications not only to improve service but also to survive.

Along with deregulation, merger and acquisition strategies have created corporations with diverse product lines, which are often sold by a consolidated sales force formed from the companies involved in the transaction but with little experience in selling the entire range of products represented. Mergers create interesting problems for salespeople. For example, one software company habitually merges with its suitors and changes the name, function, and physical attributes of its product lines without any strong justification. Even worse, it changes its name at regular intervals, thus confusing existing and prospective customers about its product. The firm's customers have experienced great difficulty in locating the product and the firm. As a result, the company was forced to spend a substantial amount of money to retool and repackage its sales applications.[3] Not paying attention to customer needs during mergers is often the primary cause of the newly formed company's failure.

Technology Forces Driving the Need for Selling-Chain Management

The preceding business drivers highlight the importance of watching customer preferences and trends when implementing selling-chain management strategies. Equally important are the technology issues and trends that determine a company's future direction and position it for either success or failure.

A company's management should clearly understand the limits of any technological solution in which it is considering investing. Over the past decade, many sales automation software vendors overpromised when it came to the functionality their software could provide. Many of these packages could not perform as promised because

- Ease of integration was not a factor used when selecting or implementing these applications

- Many older sales automation applications were unwieldy or difficult to implement

- The breadth of the software product's functionality did not meet the company's business requirements

- The sales and marketing staff refused to use the products because they didn't increase sales effectiveness

However, since the mid 1990s, technology advances have addressed many of these problems.

The Selling-Chain Application Continuum

The limitations of existing applications in today's business environment and the emergence of innovations to improve sales technology have contributed to increased corporate investments in sales automation solutions in order to keep pace with a company's more technologically advanced competitors. In order to understand the possible future of automated sales processing, you must understand how sales applications have evolved over time and the application continuum showing the range of corporate sales technology (Figure 7.3). The selling-chain continuum shows where most companies are focusing their energies today and in which direction we need to move. It is important to understand where your firm is on the continuum.

Consider the case of Snap-on, a global manufacturer and marketer of equipment for professional tool users. The business problem: Snap-on needed to make more than 14,000 professional tools available online to its large industrial customers, such as the U.S Navy. Snap-on requirement: Ensure that it maintain its reputation for high-quality products and service over the Web. To do so, the company's virtual sales application needed to act as a sales rep guiding customers through the entire buying-decision process, complete with tool specifications, illustrations, and

	Traditional Sales Force Automation	Evolving Sales Force Automation	Customer-Centric Sales	Relationship-Oriented Order Acquisition
Integration	Task oriented	Functionally Isolated	Lines of Business and Select Integration	Enterprisewide & Highly Integrated
Sales/Service Approach	Account Centric	Account Centric	Customer Centric	Relationship Centric
Business Emphasis	Productivity	Productivity	Effectiveness— Closing the Order	Effectiveness— Revenue Growth

Figure 7.3: The Selling-Chain Application Continuum

prices. To ensure service, the application needed to include up-sells to special promotions, such as for complete tool sets, and cross-sells to complementary items, such as a tool chest. Another quality service requirement was that customers have a seamless, integrated visit: from an initial customized home page to product selection, to order, to delivery status, and, finally, to support information. For this, Snap-on's requirement was integration with its Baan enterprise resource planning system.

Today's business environment requires that even industrial companies need to offer the right product or service to the right customer for the right price via the right channel at the right time. This requirement goes beyond customer-centric sales functionality. An effective *sales function* requires a broad range of capabilities that integrate, automate, and manage sales interactions enterprise-wide. Although enterprisewide integration is a hot topic, few companies understand why it's so critical. Current integration efforts concentrate on linking isolated, independently designed systems with a specific line of business, division, or department. These approaches are insufficient for achieving an enterprise-wide order acquisition environment.

Problems with Existing Sales Force Automation (SFA)

The first generation of SFA selling-chain solutions was used to manage the entire sales process by capturing information at every step, from lead generation to contract closing. This software included stand-alone, task-oriented tools, such as personal organizers, or appointment calendars and address/telephone directories. The focus of these products was to coordinate and to manage the diverse activities of a direct sales force throughout the sales process.

Second-generation SFA software focuses on improving the administrative productivity of salespeople by automating such functions as contact management, opportunity management, sales forecasting, and commission tracking. Second-generation SFA also manages telesales, which increases the productivity and efficiency of call centers by increasing sales-closure rates. Although many companies have already invested heavily in projects to implement second-generation SFA, their success has been limited, owing to

- *Limited, task-oriented functionality.* These second-generation SFA systems have inflexible, archaic interfaces, which often require different SFA software sessions to access various core programs.

- *Functional isolation.* Often, second-generation SFA software has limited back-office integration capability and is therefore unable to check inventory availability, monitor fulfillment functions, provide real-time pricing, and manage an account, all of which are critical to any successful sales-initiated customer contact.

- *Organizational resistance.* No enterprise wants to buy an off-the-shelf sales automation solution. Almost every company views its sales processes as a unique, key part of its competitive differentiation. Although most companies realize the inefficiency of building and maintaining a custom application, they don't want a cookie-cutter approach, either.

- *Limited view of the customer.* Salespeople are mobile. They don't sit at desks. It is therefore difficult to tie them directly to the enterprise applications they need and to provide a comprehensive, 360-degree view of the customer. In addition, sales activities are most often organized by product or by account for operational efficiency. Thus, this partial understanding of the customer's perspective is characteristic of the entire customer interaction and destroys sales opportunities.

Sales professionals often view current software applications as administrative burdens rather than as productive tools. As a result, they eventually stop using them. The market is clearly ready for a new generation of sales force applications that mirror the realities of sales and order acquisition.

Limited Process Functionality

Many sales applications offer a narrow range of process capabilities, as they are designed to support a limited subset of sales process functions and requirements. For example, a banking sales application supports only the bank's credit card, mutual fund, or insurance products. The company's ability to assume the customer's perspective—an integral part of customer relationship management—is thus severely restricted. This results in lower sales force productivity, an increased volume of customer call-backs when their needs are not met with one phone call, and an increased possibility of error when data has to be entered more than once.

Sales professionals, typically mobile users who access their support applications remotely, require applications that let them operate primarily offline and occasionally connect with a network in order to synchronize their data with the company's central database. Selling-chain applications, by definition, must automate processes across multiple user types and functional areas. These issues add a significant degree of complexity to the implementation and successful use of any selling-chain application.

Selling-chain software vendors are now introducing first-generation SFA solutions that address the software issues of varying customer requirements, mobile computing, and cross-functional process integration. The selling-chain software market is poised for success, owing largely to the quality and sophistication of the applications now available, the ability of these applications to integrate with enterprise systems, and the increasing number of selling-chain software success stories. Businesses are also heavily influenced by current marketing hype for fear that if they don't take advantage of this popular technology, they will fall seriously behind their competitors.

Limited Sales Effectiveness

Salespeople can be only as effective as the systems with which they work permit. Improved sales effectiveness is critical for companies seeking to achieve market leadership. A company's global sales force must be able to sell a variety of products, from simple items, such as office supplies, to the more complex, build-to-order systems, such as a Boeing 777 aircraft.

How does application integration facilitate effective selling? Salespeople are demanding the integration of sales applications with their enterprises' back-office systems, which has far-reaching implications, as all departments will be affected. For example, with full integration, a completed sales transaction will book the sale automatically, update the demand forecasting model, affect the production and delivery schedules, update the customer relationship file, and provide input to the calculation of sales performance metrics. An example of this trend is Selectica Connectors to Siebel Sales Enterprise. The connector integrates the capabilities of Selectica's Internet Selling System with Siebel sales force automation tools. Selectica Connector to Siebel Sales Enterprise enables companies to increase sales productivity by providing salespeople with access to powerful needs analysis, configuration, pricing, and quoting capabilities, directly linked to their customer relationship management system.

To facilitate effective selling, the sales support system must place emphasis on ease of use. By assisting at every step of the selling process, selling-chain management apps make buying a complex product or service as easy as buying a simple one. Also, effective apps can take the knowledge and experience of your best salesperson and product manager to guide the customer to the right selection. Knowledge capture permits companies to quickly train and deploy new staff and to retrain existing staff to sell the company's ever-changing product lines.

The Universal Business Problem: Managing the Order Acquisition Process

The order acquisition process has become more complex and difficult to manage because of the need for customized products and services, new distribution channels, and multiple pricing options. Selling complex products requires dealing with two different types of complexity.

- *Product complexity* arises when products have many features that interact with one another to influence functionality, price, and performance, as well as the manufacturing and delivery process. Networking and telecommunications equipment, automobiles, and computers are examples of complex products.

- *Needs complexity* arises in selling even relatively simple products and services, such as home theater equipment or insurance policies. The product itself may be relatively simple, but many factors come into play when evaluating a customer's needs and matching them with the best product or service.

Figure 7.4 illustrates the tasks associated with the order acquisition process. These fall under the following categories: needs assessment, option selection, order configuration, and order quote and proposal, complete with drawings, schematics, and performance metrics.

Selling complex products requires needs analysis. In companies with no sales support applications, account managers are often responsible for performing ad hoc needs assessments. Some of the questions raised are, Which model best matches specific needs within the budget? What are the need-to-have versus optional features? How much do they cost? Are there incompatibilities among versions, or configurations? Traditionally, sales reps assisting prospects have performed this analysis. In fact, at most companies, what separates the top sales reps from the others is how well they provide this assistance.

Complex products usually represent the higher margin in any product line. So, the quality of assessment is critical for profitability. The quality of these assessments varies with the selling skill, product knowledge, and experience of the individual manager. After the account manager makes the initial customer contact, a technical sales specialist makes subsequent calls in order to properly configure the solution to fit the customer's needs. The demand for such an intensive technical sales specialist's involvement is found mainly in high-tech markets, where complex products are required.

The technical sales specialist's detailed assessment includes a description of the solution in production terms, including price and delivery schedule, or the

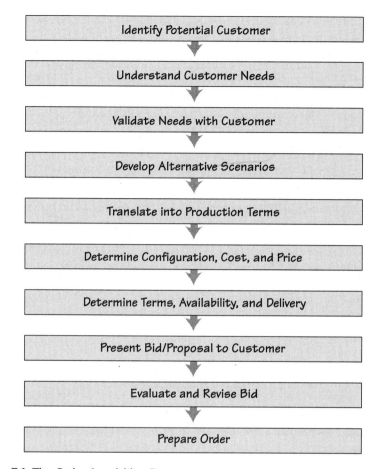

Figure 7.4: The Order Acquisition Process

technical sales specialist passes this technical information to an associate who calculates the pricing and manufacturing schedule. Once the product and delivery information is complete, it is then either returned to the salesperson or given to a proposal specialist who prepares a detailed document restating the customer's requirements and the company's proposal outlining the manufacturer's best product configuration, price, delivery date, and any other relevant terms. This manual process leaves a great deal of the engineering, pricing, and manufacturing information to individual interpretation; the likelihood of human error in the process is high, and the proposal cycle time is long.

What does the sales process at your company look like? What do you need to do to transform this current process into one that provides strategic differentiation through technological innovation? The first step toward developing an integrated sales system application is to profile the customer's current experience with your firm's sales order process. We recommend that companies perform this exercise for each major customer segment. Assemble groups from all areas of your company, particularly those groups that use marketing data and that have face-to-face or phone contact with your customers. Charge the groups with identifying, for each major market segment, all the steps through which customers pass from the time they become aware of your product to the time the order is entered into the system.

Specific industries implement selling-chain automation for a variety of reasons, but corporations everywhere are choosing selling-chain apps management to gain and use intimate, detailed customer knowledge in the context of the order acquisition process. It's simply easier for any company to sell its products and services when the sales team is equipped with comprehensive customer information and can demonstrate its ability to understand and quickly respond to a customer's possible needs or concerns. Reengineering an entire order acquisition process is a daunting task. In such cases, it makes sense to focus on reengineering only those aspects of the sales process that would benefit the most from redesign and automation.

Elements of Selling-Chain Infrastructure

How did the selling-chain infrastructure evolve historically? First, programmers developed isolated applications to automate key aspects of the order acquisition process.

- Internet relationship management, which includes order entry and management

- Sales configuration systems

- Product catalog and marketing encyclopedias

- Pricing engines

- Proposal/quote generation systems

- Sales compensation systems

As Figure 7.5 shows, these isolated sales applications were then interconnected, with true integration emerging as team and self-service selling become prevalent.

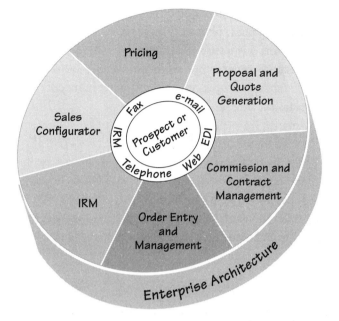

Figure 7.5: Elements of Selling-Chain Infrastructure

Self-service and team selling are driving now application integration efforts. Today, most sales opportunities in large companies occur in complex team-selling environments, in which various members of a sales team—telemarketing, the presales rep, the field sales rep, regional sales manager, VP of sales—need to coordinate activities and share information to develop and to execute an optimal sales strategy. Coordination of these activities is critical, particularly for organizations selling products with long, complex sales cycles. It is also important to coordinate sales activities when multiple companies sell jointly and when many decision makers must be kept informed.

In large companies, the need for multichannel, multiteam sales integration is growing exponentially. As the time to close the sale goes down, team members need to share information, such as pricing updates, the customer relationship history, and the status of other orders in the pipeline. Team members also need to better coordinate prospect management, including the timing of their next prospect meeting, identifying the key customer decision makers and what their current attitudes are likely to be, identifying those responsible for "working" key decision makers before and after the meeting, and outlining appropriate follow-up actions for each team member in order to close the deal. Right now in most large companies, sales managers have very limited visibility into all the elements of the sales process. This makes coordination next to impossible.

If there is one lesson e-business is teaching us, it is that each aspect of the sales process is critical to a successful order acquisition process. An integrated process with little process variation is much more effective than well-automated isolated tasks.

Online Sales: Internet Relationship Management (IRM)

Coinciding with the growth of e-commerce is an increase in consultative selling on the Web. Internet relationship management (IRM) helps deliver targeted, dynamically generated content to a company's customers. IRM is used to manage customer interaction and for deriving revenues. IRM strategies are still in their infancy and vary from BroadVision, Firepond, and Vignette Corporation's template-driven packages to the more flexible development platforms of Art Technology Group and Blue Martini Software.

What is the benefit of IRM? Sophisticated Web sites require a personalized, customizable sales platform. Research has shown how a positive customer experience results in more sales than do traditional attributes, such as product selection or price. In traditional channels, you can lose customers if they walk into a brick-and-mortar location and are disappointed with the store layout, appearance, have an unsatisfactory experience with a salesperson, or can't find what they want.

The Internet environment is no different. You must excel in the online experience your company offers and do so in a convenient, helpful, and reliable way. Your Web site must reflect this. However, current Web site development focuses primarily on generating and monetizing traffic (external functions); rationalizing inefficiencies within a business (internal functions), and creating a communication and transaction platform.

This means that the current proliferation of brochure-ware Web sites, which feature stale company background and static content, are giving way to full-featured sites offering a full range of community features, including free e-mail, discussion boards, and up-to-date, relevant content. Furthermore, these community sites are being replaced by IRM sites offering a more sophisticated, timely, and textured experience.

The goal of IRM is to translate customer contact opportunities into sales. To produce such experience-oriented sites and to use them as online business channels, companies must address a complex set of development, site production, merchandising, and customer-care issues. For example, a company must quickly develop its Web applications, develop Web work flow procedures, and establish processes for the site's editorial content and version control. In addition, a company must design one-to-one marketing schemes so the Web site can effectively target customers based on their interests and preferences. Enterprises must balance these activities in order to maximize their online revenue opportunities and their "looker-to-booker" conversion rate: all this while keeping internal labor and systems costs under control as the online business expands over time.

The golden rule of IRM is to make the online sales experience better than the sales experience in the physical world. Some sales situations will not and cannot be translated into a superior online experience. In their quest to deliver such an experience, the IRM tools industry is evolving rapidly to meet rising demand. Companies currently have a variety of choices, from tools for dynamic content generation, site analysis, profiling systems, data analytics engines, and collaborative filtering products. However, sophisticated software alone can't solve the personalization problem. Carefully assessing a customer's needs and well-developed e-business models are equally important.

Sales Configuration Systems

In many companies, the process of selling configurable or customized products is cumbersome at best. From the time a sales quote is prepared, through the product's manufacturing and shipment, customer requirements must be identified, and product configuration questions must be accurately answered. In the old model, a company's direct salespeople, or its channel partners, had to "check with the home office" because they lacked the tools and information needed to provide accurate and complete configuration quotes in the field.

Consider Hewlett-Packard's dilemma. HP is the world leader in laser printers, with more than 60 products designed to capture, fax, copy, and print digital images. With a diverse product line, HP's challenge was not determining whether it had the right printer for each customer but rather how to guide the customer to the right printer. A simple online catalog listing all the products and asking users to choose based on technical specifications was not the answer. In an effort to simplify the selection process, HP launched an effort to implement a sales configuration system. A three-step Q&A process narrows down the possibilities. When users feel that the number of printers is manageable, they click a See Your Results button to view the products that meet their criteria. Another click allows users to see a side-by-side comparison of up to three products or takes the users to the appropriate HP store to purchase the product.[4]

During the early 1970s, companies began implementing configuration-checking tools for sales, order entry, manufacturing, and support. These early tools were options within either a manufacturing resource planning (MRP) or enterprise resource planning (ERP) system or were the company's own customized, internally developed system. ERP/MRP systems guaranteed well-designed system configurations that accurately reflected the customer's requirements. However, vendors and companies in the 1970s checked the configuration's accuracy only after it was sent to manufacturing. They prevented incorrect orders from hitting the manufacturing floor but didn't catch problems until after the order had been placed. Identifying misconfigured orders early in the order process is critical to reducing rework costs and customer returns.

As a company's business and its product lines change, internally developed, customized IT solutions tend to be difficult to maintain. For example, Digital Equipment Corporation (DEC) built a custom configuration system for configuring minicomputers. The system was abandoned because it could not be maintained at a reasonable cost. Unlike off-the-shelf software, customized solutions don't benefit from the large investments in development tools, graphical user interfaces, and core technology that commercial system developers must make to stay competitive.

Modern system configurators are designed to go beyond checking to see whether a product is configured correctly. Today, they embrace the needs of the customer and enable a sales force to generate requirements-based, accurate configurations and quotes at the point of sale.

For complex order processes involving build-to-order products, configuration is a basic prerequisite for doing business. An example of a modern configurator is Concinity from Calico Systems. Concinity allows users to select a large set of features and options that must work together. The tool lets customers create custom orders from a diverse product line, especially where the number of options for each product is large. Other configurator vendors are Selectica, Firepond, and Trilogy.

Product Catalogs and Marketing Encyclopedias

Easy access to product information is an essential requirement in modern selling systems. The rapid growth of catalog sales in channels formerly dominated by retail chains can be attributed to the ease of finding product information. Consumers can obtain detailed, up-to-the-minute information about a wide range of products over the telephone or through the Internet, without having to endure the inconvenience of visiting a showroom and the frustration of interacting with an ill-informed floor sales staff.

A marketing encyclopedia is a valuable tool for online-assisted selling. A marketing encyclopedia is an intelligent electronic catalog that connects sales reps and customers to a company's most current product and service information, including brochures, pictures, and pricing and availability data. This encyclopedia provides a single point of entry for gathering and distributing product information. Product managers update product information in the database and immediately broadcast any changes throughout the enterprise.

The critical requirements for keeping a marketing encyclopedia useful include the ability to

- Easily create and maintain a repository of product information

- Create multiple search mechanisms to assist in locating information

- Alert sales representatives and customers to bundled products and services, promotions, and complementary products

Increasingly, a marketing encyclopedia uses Web technology to display product information, perform searches, and share data with other applications.

Pricing: Data Maintenance, Distribution, and Configuration

How complex are your company's pricing and discounting structures? Does your firm need flexible pricing to deal with market conditions by market area or trading/ channel partners? Does your company suffer from high customer adjustment claim rates, owing to promotional pricing and customer deductions? Does your pricing vary by customer contract or rebates? Do expensive pricing maintenance costs or untimely pricing distributions plague your company?

If the answer to any of these questions is yes, your firm suffers from "pricing complexitis." Many enterprises with extended selling channels, which include resellers and partners, have difficulty responding to changing market conditions, owing to elongated pricing update cycles, ineffective pricing strategies, and poor price distribution to their channel partners. These problems can result in lost market share, poor margins, or increased inventory.

Selling complex products requires effective pricing configuration support. Pricing is often determined by a company's sales strategy. Pricing can vary because of a company's use of tiered customer hierarchies, multiple distribution channels, various product lines, "effectivity" dates, and authorization ranges. In order to address these pricing issues, a new sales configuration tool has been developed. Pricing configuration and update management tools assist companies with developing, managing, and deploying complex pricing and discounting structures to their selling channels.

Proposal and Quote Generation

Proposal- and quote-generation systems enable companies to provide an intuitive, professional layout to customers requiring complex quotes. Proposal and quote applications include the following features:

- *Opportunity creation/tracking.* This feature enables salespeople to organize, locate, and restore versions of existing quotes and configurations by customer, session, or date.

- *Interactive needs assessment.* This feature enables salespeople and customers to articulate their buying criteria and solution requirements.

- *Automatic quote generation.* This feature generates quotes directly from the sales configuration, with the ability to add spare parts, apply custom discounting, select currency type, apply special charges or discounts based on geography, and affix special shipping and packaging charges.

- *Proposal wizard.* This tool automatically generates tailored proposals from configurations, needs assessments, and quotes, reducing the time and effort required to generate custom proposals.

Proposal- and quote-generation systems allow sales representatives to include information relevant to the individual customer on each quote, such as product promotions or company legal statements. Product details and descriptions can also be expanded or contracted to illustrate various levels of product information.

Sales Incentives and Commission Processing

Systems used to process sales incentives and commissions are potent levers for increasing sales effectiveness. These systems are used to design, process, and analyze sophisticated incentive programs for large sales organizations.

Commission systems have three core modules: incentive design, incentive processing, and incentive analysis. The incentive design module enables a company to

- Create sophisticated commission and bonus rules that reward salespersons based on various sales credit points, including booking, shipping, and payment

- Create individualized and account compensation programs, using an unlimited number of commissions, bonuses, and quotas

- Create and use customized performance measures, including profit margin, net discount, and customer satisfaction

The processing module enables companies to use nonrevenue performance metrics, such as customer satisfaction and service quality, to calculate commissions and bonuses. The incentive analysis module provides a company with an accurate view of the entire sales process. This module enables detailed account-, product-, and customer-level analysis, as well as the examination of profit margins and discount trends.

Compensation design, planning, and processing, however, comprise one of the most complex, error-prone, and time-consuming areas facing today's sales executive. Sales executives must also face the issues of how sales incentives and commissions are calculated in an online or in a self-service environment.

Case Studies in Selling-Chain Management

Custom Foot: Transforming Shoe Sales with Technology

Successfully addressing the technical issues surrounding selling-chain management does not guarantee an implementation's success. These implementations are extremely complicated. Custom Foot provides an excellent, and sobering, illustration of a company that attempted to completely reengineer its sales process by using selling-chain management technology.

The shoe industry's greatest business challenges are providing value to the customer in the form of quality, selection, and convenience at the right price while simultaneously minimizing its inventory-holding costs. Custom Foot, based in Westport, Connecticut, aimed to solve these customer value and inventory problems by implementing a selling-chain solution in which customers could have shoes made to their specifications in about 3 weeks—for prices starting at less than $100.

Custom Foot's order process worked as follows. First, the customer put his or her feet on an infrared scanner that measured foot size. The 3-D scanner translated the data of each foot's contour into one of 670 shoe sizes. Next, the customer sat at a kiosk to select the options, such as leather grade, style, color, and type of sole. Custom Foot used a sales configurator from Trilogy Software to allow its salespeople to configure orders interactively. A dynamic image of the shoes was visually displayed to the customer during option selection. Customers could also see, in real time, how their choices changed the shoe's price.

Once the customer was satisfied with the style, features, and price, the order was routed to the back-office system. The shoe specifications were sent electronically to a manufacturing plant in either Italy or Maine. Three weeks later, the shoes were either shipped to the store for pickup or delivered directly to the customer. Custom Foot hoped that this system would enable it to carry no inventory or associated stocking costs, because each pair of shoes was manufactured only after it had been specified and ordered by a customer. The goal was to eliminate 30 percent to 50 percent of the warehousing and distribution costs typically associated with retailing.

The case of Custom Foot illustrates the opportunities created by using new selling techniques coupled with new configurators. Many analysts and experts thought that Custom Foot would be an overnight success. Unfortunately, Custom Foot ceased operations and filed a bankruptcy petition on June 1, 1998.

The reasons for Custom Foot's failure vary. In attempting to reengineer its core process and implement a new business model, Custom Foot encountered a number of issues. The first problem was a conflict between shoe size and shoe-fit calculations. Initially, the company relied solely on its scanners for precise sizing. But when Custom Foot began selling its shoes, many customers complained that, although the shoe might have been the "right" size, they didn't like the fit.[5] Some people like shoes to fit snugly, whereas others prefer a looser fit. Also, many people's right and left feet are different sizes. According to James Metscher, the company's CEO, the single biggest mistake that Custom Foot made was misjudging the importance of subjectivity in shoe fitting.

As a result, Custom Foot lost money as customers returned their custom-made shoes and demanded that the company rework their orders. To solve this problem, the company replaced the infrared scanner with a new one that offered three possible sizes for each foot measurement. Before an order was finalized at one of Custom Foot's five stores, a customer tried on left and right shoes in various sizes and expressed a preference. This tactic resulted in a sharp decline in shoe returns.

Custom Foot also had a problem with forecasting demand for various kinds of leather. Forecasting errors caused the company to frequently miss its 3-week delivery guarantee. To better predict leather demand, Custom Foot modified its forecast process to capture orders in a centralized database that tallied the forecast daily.[6]

The experience of Custom Foot illustrates a basic e-business tenet: The flow of precise order information from customers to companies dealing in customized products or services is crucial to success. When such information is lacking or misleading, it undermines the success of the entire sales system.

Cisco and Selling-Chain Management

In early 1996, Cisco Systems embarked on a project to completely change the way it sells routers. Cisco's customers are resellers that sell a variety of networking products to retail outlets, businesses, and end customers. In the past, Cisco's salespeople would go to a customer's site to help fill out the order forms, or the customers would fill them out themselves. The completed order forms were then faxed to Cisco's headquarters, where they were entered into the order processing system.

Order errors, go home. Cisco realized that by automating much of the buying process, it could reduce the number of order process errors committed and the number of staff involved in the process, thus saving time and money. An automated buying process would free the salespeople from taking orders and allow them to devote more time to selling. Cisco envisioned a system that went beyond automated order taking. The system would be integrated into the company's operational planning process, allowing the company to better forecast demand, streamline planning production, and reduce the lead time between when a customer placed an order for a router and took delivery.

Cisco used a phased approach[7] to creating its selling-chain suite (see Figure 7.6). Phase 0 represented "the old way," the state in which people faxed purchase orders, called representatives for pricing, and, typically, reworked the selling and delivery terms for complex products multiple times. During phase 1, Cisco built the Information Center, which offered a one-way customer information service so customers could look up pricing and product information and inquire about an order's status.

In phase 2, Cisco built the Marketplace Product Center, which provides customers with the self-service capability to configure and order all products Cisco offers. In phase 3, Cisco further harnessed the power of technology to customize its products and services and serve each customer efficiently and uniquely. The company is now in phase 4, which involves restructuring its customer fulfillment process. During phase 4, Cisco is using the Web to build better customer relationships with special customers having unique requirements. The phase 4 plans include building a customer profile agent and custom order scheduling for this select customer segment.

Phase 4 provides competitive advantage by streamlining customer interactions and increasing the number of clean, error-free orders. In the past, resellers

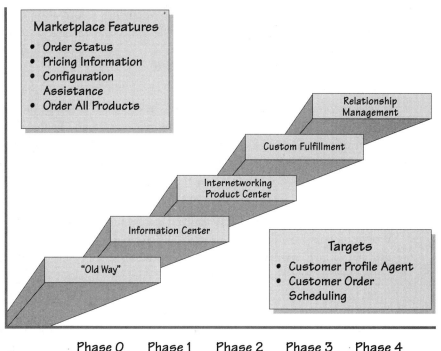

Figure 7.6: Evolution of Cisco's Architecture

would make a proposal to Cisco's end customer, which would then issue a purchase order to the reseller's customer service department. The reseller's customer service department then sent the purchase order to Cisco. If Cisco discovered a configuration or pricing problem, it informed the reseller, which told the end customer. The end customer would have to completely redo the order, causing significant delay. With electronic order entry, Cisco is able to achieve order lead-time reduction of more than 3 days. The company is also able to provide more personalized customer service and support.

Changes to a company's business architecture often have a ripple effect. As Cisco implements the phases of its e-commerce architecture, every organization conducting business with Cisco's customers, partners, or resellers is challenged to determine how it can reengineer and automate its own sales processes and accrue the same customer and corporate benefits as Cisco.

Cisco is essentially taking over the back-office system functions of its resellers, thus allowing them more time to concentrate on selling Cisco's products. For example, Cisco provides its customers with a private-label delivery service. The customer provides Cisco with copies of its corporate logo, tag lines, and water-marks. Cisco reproduces these on packing slips and shipping labels before shipping to the end customer. The company's objective is to maintain contact and trust with their customers, avoid undermining the reseller and, in the process, avoid channel conflict.

Memo to the CEO

Selling-chain management is one of the fastest-growing market opportunities in enterprise software. The demand for such software has always existed, reflecting businesses' need to make their sales organizations more productive, increase per customer revenue, and more accurately forecast future sales. These needs have only intensified in recent years, owing to the increased level of global competition, shorter product life cycles, and the use of more complex multichannel and/or team-selling strategies.

Selling-chain apps are attempting to solve problems in

- *Standardizing best selling practices.* You can model many of the best selling practices of your top salespeople and make them available to your entire sales force.

- *Closing more sales.* It is widely known that 75 percent of Web shopping carts are abandoned in process. This means that the majority of e-commerce transactions go uncompleted. A good selling application can encourage users to complete their purchases by guiding them through the sales process and providing accurate and complete information at every step.

- *Increasing average order size.* You can identify up-selling and cross-selling opportunities during the sales process and offer related products to the buyer at appropriate times.

- *Multichannel selling.* No matter what channel, the sales process is consistent. This makes your company the easiest and most accessible firm to do business with—and isn't that what your customers want?

What has changed the most in recent years, however, is the emergence of several technologies that have, for the first time, enabled the development and deployment of large-scale multichannel sales automation solutions. In particular, these new technologies address the fact that, unlike most other enterprise application users, salespeople are not desk-bound and are, therefore, not tethered to their companies' corporate infrastructures. Rather, they are located in small, remote offices and spend most of their time on the road, meeting with customers and prospects. The emergence of the Web, powerful laptops, intuitive graphical user interfaces, and mobile computing capabilities are the critical contributing factors to the intensified demand with the selling-chain market.

Selling chain, with an emphasis on the buying process, represents a new shift in enterprise computing. In the recent past, the focus was almost exclusively on reengineering legacy back-office applications. Today, companies have increased spending on front-office applications and processes. Companies operating in highly competitive markets have no choice. Such companies must develop and implement selling-chain management applications. In so doing, these companies will increase their firms' sales and the return on investment and thereby ensure a competitive advantage.

The challenges facing managers when implementing selling-chain management applications are

- Keeping up with continuous changes in vendors, applications, technologies, pricing, and tools

- Selecting the right vendors and software for your company

- Ensuring successful software implementation and deployment

The projected payback period on an investment in selling-chain software is 6 months for the early adopters. The software's strategic value for enabling businesses to increase their revenue opportunities and expand market share has led market research firms to project the selling-chain market to be in the billions of dollars.

In summary, a multichannel selling infrastructure is necessary for companies to manage all facets of the order process. In this infrastructure, prospects become customers only when they are offered and provided the best in presales service. Companies attract new prospects by providing them with easy access to product and service information before they buy. Once the sale is made, this same level of service builds the type of loyalty that turns customers into company advocates, resulting in better up-selling and cross-selling opportunities, as well as new-customer referrals.

CHAPTER EIGHT

Building the e-Business Backbone: Enterprise Resource Planning

What to Expect

When a customer buys something from a Web site, a store, or a call center, a response is automatically triggered in your sales, accounting, planning, and logistics applications. To put it simply, e-commerce is the front office, and enterprise resource planning (ERP) is the back office.

ERP apps reshape a company's back-office structure because they address a difficult IT problem: overcoming the integration challenges posed by system portfolios containing disconnected, uncoordinated back-office applications that have outlived their usefulness. Although the Web stampede and the Internet gold rush have seized most of the media spotlight, the corporate world's steady embrace of ERP apps was one of the most significant business and technological trends of the 1990s.

With the rise of e-business, ERP in its current form is rapidly approaching the end of its reign as the central focus of the business applications universe. Today's managers must assess what this change means for them by analyzing the following questions.

- *What is the role of ERP apps in the emerging click-and-brick world?*

- *How do companies leverage the investments they've already made in ERP apps?*

The change in focus from operational efficiency to customer-centricity, intimacy and innovation are causing fundamental back-office changes. In this chapter, we discuss the evolution of ERP in relationship to the e-business world. We discuss ERP's historical roots in MRP II and its evolution into as CRP and XRP. The chapter also presents real-world examples of how e-leaders are using ERP to gain operational efficiencies. However, as many firms have discovered, adopting an ERP solution significantly affects a company's architecture, processes, people, and procedures. Today's senior managers must make the right choices when creating their e-business back offices.

What do Microsoft, Coca-Cola, Cisco, Eli Lilly, Alcoa, and Nokia have in common? Unlike most businesses, which operate on 25-year-old back-office systems, these market leaders reengineered their businesses to run at breakneck speed by implementing a transactional backbone called enterprise resource planning (ERP). These companies credit their ERP systems with having helped them reduce inventories, shorten cycle times, lower costs, and improve overall operations.

Why did ERP technology suddenly become so popular? For large companies, the ERP revolution represents the Holy Grail of corporate computing.[1] The traditional corporate computing environment has been typified by a 20-year-old application running on a mainframe that is too old and slow for modern business. The old systems worked well in their day, when customers expected order fulfillment to take several weeks. Today, in the age of overnight delivery and split-second Internet speeds, customer expectations have changed. Top management realizes that its company's outmoded technological infrastructure cannot meet the demands of the new economy and must be quickly replaced.

Overhauling a company's antiquated systems is the first step in back-office transformation. ERP integrated application suites provide a framework of applications to automate a company's financial, manufacturing and distribution, human resource, and administrative functions. ERP unites a company's major business processes—production, order processing, inventory management and warehousing, accounts payable and receivable, the general ledger, and payroll—within a single family of software modules. ERP's strategy helps companies streamline their work flows in order to become more efficient organizations. For large companies, ERP speeds communications and the distribution and analysis of information, facilitating the exchange of data across corporate divisions by unifying the company's key processes.

The ERP phenomenon is not restricted to large firms. In the dot-com world, managing customer relationships is the key to success. If companies don't provide the services customers expect, they will go elsewhere. In an e-business setting, ERP offers customers a more efficient and higher-quality level of service, including the ability to order products online and to inquire about product pricing and an order's status. Smaller dot-com firms are adopting ERP solutions as their prices drop and the rented applications service provider (ASP) business model becomes more prevalent. As a result, leading ERP vendors, such as SAP,[2] Oracle, PeopleSoft, and J. D. Edwards, are reinventing themselves to focus on e-business.

ERP is the technological backbone of e-business, an enterprise-wide transaction framework with links into sales order processing, inventory management and control, production and distribution planning, and finance. In the early 1990s, only large manufacturers saw the benefits to implementing an ERP suite of applications. Today, medium-size and dot-com firms are recognizing the necessity of integrating their back-office processes if they wish to have front-office success in the e-commerce world.

Who Really Uses ERP Suites?

Has your company implemented an ERP system as the foundation for its e-business strategy? If not, your company will face serious technical and process limitations as you attempt to achieve your e-business strategy. Without an ERP solution in place, system integration is almost impossible to attain. If your front- and back-office operations are not linked, sales orders will literally have to be rekeyed. Imagine using such "sneakerware" to process 1,000 orders an hour! As the e-business economy evolves, ERP suites will continue to function as the technological backbone of the enterprise. Implementing an ERP system is at or near the top of many large corporations' IT agendas.

For example, 3Com Corporation, the data networking company, operates in an industry in which the ability to respond quickly to changing customer needs is the cornerstone of competitive advantage. The company made its business case for an integrated back-office infrastructure around gaining a strategic and operational edge over its competitors. 3Com required a technology platform that could handle hypergrowth, support expanding worldwide operations, and adapt to continuous changes in business and customer needs. 3Com's back-office integration business case also argued for an infrastructure to support its extended enterprise model. Unlike the classic vertically integrated leviathans of the past, 3Com and other high-tech organizations are often, in reality, a widely dispersed collection of subcontractors producing specific products, linked by technology to form an extended enterprise.[3]

Another example is the Chevron Products Company, the refining and marketing arm of the Chevron Corporation. Chevron Products represents about

$16 billion of Chevron's $39 billion total revenue and employs some 8,500 people who are responsible for more than 10,000 storage terminals and service stations across the United States. Chevron Products refines crude oil for sale as gasoline, jet fuel, and other petroleum-based products. The company's old information system consisted of approximately 120 disparate, mainframe-based applications. Chevron made its business case for an integrated back-office infrastructure that would radically reduce the number of software applications used to support Chevron Products' reengineering and massive cost-cutting efforts. The goal of its cost-cutting and business process efforts was to improve its procurement, accounting, and plant management functions.

General Motors (GM) developed a business case for back-office integration to standardize its financial data and its business processes worldwide. The back-office integration initiative is part of the GM's continuing effort to cut costs by updating legacy infrastructure. GM's financials form a critical backbone link connecting the corporate office with its factories, engineering, and marketing, as well as its growing international operations. In the past, business operations were so different from one division to another that the company's software systems had difficulty communicating. A major impetus for GM's ERP initiative was to reduce the cost of the computer systems the company needs as it builds a series of new auto and component plants throughout the world.[4]

What do 3Com, Chevron, and GM have in common? These companies have chosen to purchase preintegrated ERP software frameworks in order to gain control over disparate groups of core business applications. GM's back-office operation is evolving from a business operations bureaucracy to a point-and-click service-delivery network.

Although not every ERP implementation is the same, most will fall into one of three primary categories. The first category consists of organizations that sell a single product or a few products within a single industry. Among single-product companies are many e-commerce companies, such as eToys, which require fairly simple ERP capabilities. The second category, strategic business unit (SBU) firms, includes organizations that sell only a few products, largely in a single industry. Delta Airlines, Dell, Microsoft, and Nike are single SBU firms. The third group comprises large corporate conglomerates that market their products to many industries and have many SBUs. General Electric, IBM, Colgate-Palmolive, and Nabisco are multiple-SBU firms. ERP implementations in multiple-SBU companies, such as Chevron and General Motors, are extraordinarily difficult and require uncommon project management and leadership skills in order to succeed.

The Basics of Enterprise Resource Planning

Figure 8.1 illustrates the core applications that form a standard ERP framework. ERP is a phase in the increasing integration of not only technology but also all of an enterprise's internal and external constituencies. ERP is the second phase in this process, as depicted in Figure 8.2.

The multiple applications comprising an ERP system are themselves built from smaller software modules that perform specific business processes within a given functional area. For example, a manufacturing application normally includes modules that permit sales and inventory tracking, forecasting raw-material requirements, and planning plant maintenance.

The systems' integration across the various ERP modules allows managers to know what's going on in the farthest reaches of their businesses. Is it worth investing millions of dollars to obtain such operational transparency? Corporate management seems to think so. Today ERP applications in turn are evolving into sophisticated corporate portals. This new generation of portals is easy to use and more effective in providing integrated access to crucial data, applications, and processes.

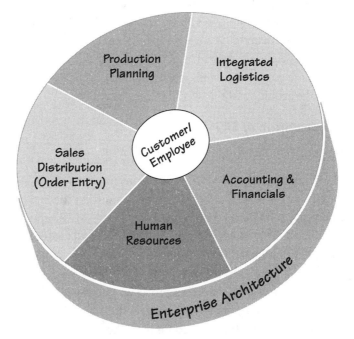

Figure 8.1: Elements of Enterprise Resource Management

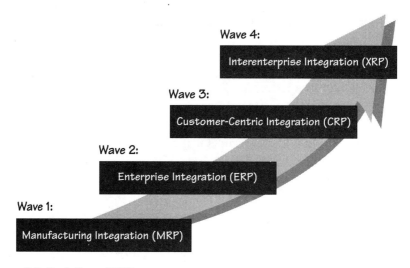

Figure 8.2: Evolution of ERP

Why enterprise portals? The portal metaphor mimics the way people work. The applications today are too convoluted requiring too many separate actions. To get things done employees have too many applications to interact with, scan through too many data sources, and manually pull information from multiple sources. The portals, such as MySAP, are designed to do this integration seamlessly.

Before going into details of each element of the ERP, it is necessary to understand the evolution of the overall framework.

The Evolution of ERP

Wave 1: Manufacturing Integration (MRP)

The historical origin of ERP is in the inventory management and control software packages that dictated system design during the 1960s. The 1970s saw the emergence of material requirements planning (MRP) and distribution resource planning (DRP), which focused on automating all aspects of production master scheduling and centralized inventory planning, respectively.

During the 1980s, the misnamed MRP II systems emerged to extend MRP's traditional focus on production processes into other business functions, including order processing, manufacturing, and distribution. MRP's integrative capabilities showed the business community how technology could link seemingly disparate business functions. As MRP's contributions became apparent, corporate executives sought to achieve similar benefits by integrating other company functions, including finance, human resources, and project management. MRP II is a misnomer, as it provided automated solutions to a wide range of business processes, not just those found within a company's manufacturing and distribution functions. As a result, MRP II was renamed ERP.

Wave 2: Enterprise Integration (ERP)

The key business drivers forcing structural migration from MRP to ERP include replacing legacy systems, gaining greater control, managing globalization, handling regulatory change, and improving integration of functions across the enterprise. These drivers vary in intensity by industry, but their combined impact is forcing managers to reevaluate the IT application's capabilities.

- *Replacing creaky legacy systems.* Too many systems and too little integration make for poor business strategy. Companies with large volumes of outdated software applications spend considerable sums on application maintenance but derive minimal benefit from their use, compared to the competitive advantages attainable using more recent technology. Core systems in businesses everywhere contain applications that need to be replaced. The replacement market for human resources apps alone represents a $30 billion installed base of software for migrating businesses' processes from legacy systems to newer e-business solutions. The goal is to deploy modern application frameworks that reflect current business practices and are capable of adapting to changes in the business environment of the future.

- *Gaining greater control.* Too many expenses and too many administrative headaches: Managers want to know how much their business has sold, what's been shipped, and a complete inventory status. Most legacy applications cannot provide such information. As one manager of a large company told us, "You can't manage what you don't know. Before our ERP implementation, it was 4 to 6 weeks after the close of the month before we had information reconciled, and we still weren't sure of the accuracy. Previously, information was integrated manually and, therefore, was not reliable or timely. That was at the heart of my needs."

- *Managing global operations.* Too many dispersed operations, not enough control: In order for a company to manage its local activities and to coordinate its worldwide operations, its technology systems must change. Three reasons dictate this need to change: stringent business conditions accentuated by channel and brand proliferation, the pressures of managing globally, and intense service demands by customers. Meanwhile, the span, scope, and intricacy of these global system implementations increases daily. For example, Dow-Corning's ERP installation includes about 1,400 concurrent users and 8,000 regular users in 84 sites across 17 countries.[5] Dow must be able to handle the currency, language, tax, and statutory requirements of many countries. The company's goal is to support these regional needs with a minimum amount of customization. Enterprise globalization has increased the performance pressure on a company as customers insist that manufacturers produce higher-quality goods with shorter delivery times and lower prices. To meet these demands, companies must have an accurate, timely information process.

• *Handling industry deregulation and regulatory change.* Too much change, no way to manage it: In many industries, new government policies, such as deregulation, often drive application requirements. For example, under the Telecom Act of 1996, U.S. telecommunications companies must resell local phone service to their competitors, forcing them to manage inventories, prices, and customer arrangements in formats not tracked today. Other government-driven regulatory changes were Y2K compliance and the conversion to the Euro.

• *Improving integration of decisions across the enterprise.* ERP links information application islands. Many companies have disparate, decentralized systems that prohibit various functional units from communicating easily. Financial applications don't communicate with the manufacturing system, which doesn't communicate with marketing. Until the advent of ERP, true system integration was difficult to achieve. As a result, most large enterprises find themselves contending with a hodgepodge of disparate, disjointed applications, creating an environment of confusion, misunderstanding, errors, and limited use of corporate information assets. The ERP model attempts to minimize information coordination problems by creating an integrated core of administrative and financial applications that serve as a focal point for all enterprise applications.

The first step in accomplishing these objectives is for firms to gain an integrated view of their business operations. The idea behind integration is quite simple: Use technology to develop process standardization across multiple business units in order to generate continued margin expansion and greater return on capital.

A significant factor in the second wave of ERP development was Y2K preparation, which was often cited as a major reason for ERP adoption. Hundreds of companies worldwide "went live" during 1999 as they switched off their legacy computer systems and turned on their newly installed ERP software. However, as these companies quickly realized, their ERP implementations represented only the end of the beginning. The next step in their technological growth would require adopting software solutions to support their e-business strategies.

Wave 3: Customer-Centric Integration (CRP)

Let's face facts. First came bricks, then came clicks. Now the challenge is integrating the two. Many of the companies that sell ERP software—including SAP, PeopleSoft, and troubled Baan, acquired by London-based Invensys—struggled once their markets became saturated and the demand for Web-based platforms surged. These companies are reinventing themselves as CRP (customer-centric resource planning) providers. Companies everywhere are racing to find the right combination of bricks and clicks.

e-Commerce is compelling companies to replace homegrown, industry-specific point applications with CRP applications. Why? Because traditional e-commerce configurations use cumbersome middleware to attempt to connect Web applications to back-end systems. This strategy involves the following drawbacks.

- It's expensive and time consuming. It is not unusual for ERP projects to cost hundreds of millions of dollars and to take more than 5 years to complete.

- A company's business rules and data are often scattered over multiple applications. In a multivendor world, data redundancies create inaccuracies and costly integration efforts.

- Upgrades are costly. Because multiple Web, middleware, and back-office vendors are involved with the implementation, accountability issues invariably arise when business rules conflict or technical problems occur.

Another key CRP driver occurs when a company changes its business model from a make-to-stock, demand forecast model to an e-commerce build-to-order, customer-driven model (see Figure 8.3). e-Commerce build-to-order and fulfill-to-order business models give customers more choices at a time when they have never been more confident that they can get what they want, when they want it, at the price they want. Traditional ERP solutions are ill-equipped to meet the business requirements of the build-to-order/fulfill-to-order business paradigm,

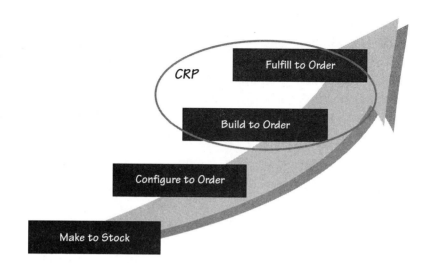

Figure 8.3: Evolution of Business Models

having been developed to meet the business requirements of make-to-stock/configure-to-order strategies.

ERP's business requirements have evolved from their focus on cost cutting, efficiency, and productivity to a new focus on customer value, effectiveness, and enhanced service delivery. Effective manufacturing and service delivery in the build-to-order/fulfill-to-order business world requires customer-centric planning and a unified, real-time transaction environment. CRP strategies assume that companies must plan continuously instead of the classic ERP assumption of long planning cycles.

Ericsson, the wireless giant, provides an excellent example of a company that recently implemented a CRP system to transform its service-delivery model. To support the company's migration from a purely functional to a truly integrated operation, Ericsson's manufacturing and distribution division made CRP a critical element of its business reengineering effort. Following the implementation of a CRP system from Glovia, Ericsson reportedly enjoyed the following significant operational improvements.[6]

- Sales order processing lead time was reduced from 1 hour to 10 minutes.

- Purchase order lead time was reduced from 1–4 hours to less than 5 minutes.

- Production scheduling run time was reduced from 18 hours to 30 minutes.

- Ninety-eight percent of orders are now delivered on time.

These benefits are quite impressive. Ericsson's CRP applications track cost accounting information related to sales orders, materials, money, labor, and asset utilization. The company's goal is to acquire a single, integrated view of all its information resource applications, including the general ledger, accounts payable/receivable, order entry, billing, sales, marketing, materials, purchasing, product data management, shop floor control, and manufacturing operations, to name only the most common.

Wave 4: Interenterprise Integration (XRP)

Your company has squeezed as many inefficiencies as possible out of operations but you're still getting trounced by competition. What's going on? The answer lies in supply chain integration. ERP apps are adapting to the e-business requirement that a company's partners benefit from the same seamless integration as the company itself. This fourth wave of ERP development, known as extended resource planning (XRP), extends the organizational foundation of an ERP backbone beyond the four walls of the enterprise to its customers, suppliers, and trading partners. Examples of XRP are B2B marketplaces. A main goal of an XRP implementation is to provide better synchronization with trading partners in order to reduce inventories, foster strategic pricing, improve cycle times, and increase customer satisfaction throughout the supply chain.

Current ERP systems offer little in terms of interenterprise planning. ERP has traditionally excelled at transaction management, the ability to manage the administrative activities associated with human resource, financial, inventory, and order processes. For example, although it has order processing functionality, an ERP system provides little or no information about the order's profitability or the best way to deliver the order to the customer. ERP differs from supply chain planning (SCP). Whereas the ERP approach asks, *Should* I take your order? the SCP approach asks, *Can* I take your order? Today's ERP systems are rudimentary. Data from ERP systems provides a snapshot in time of a business process, but doesn't support the continuous-planning requirements central to a successful SCP system. SCP's continuous-planning capability refines and enhances the plan in real time, adjusting the plan to accommodate any last-minute changes before the plan is executed. Attempting to devise an optimal plan using ERP-based systems has been compared to driving down a busy freeway while looking in the rear-view mirror.

XRP systems complement traditional ERP systems by providing intelligent decision support capabilities. An XRP system is designed to overlay existing systems, pulling data from every step in the supply chain and providing a clear, global picture of where the enterprise is heading. XRP-generated plans allow companies to quickly assess the impact of their actions across the entire supply chain, including the company's impact on customer demand.

The most daunting task when moving from an ERP-centric to an XRP-centric model is overcoming a company's information boundaries in order to understand and to connect with supplier's information and processes in meaningful ways. Like a good e-business strategy, a good plan is useful but not if you can't execute it. XRP initiatives must be supported by supply chain execution and selling-chain management practices, as these functions represent the external image of the enterprise. As business moves toward real-time supply chains, the integration of external and internal business activities will become critical (see Figure 8.4). An effective XRP strategy depends on tightly coupled decision making and execution. The message is loud and clear: collaborate or perish.

Benefits of ERP Suites

Companies are rushing to buy packaged ERP suites in order to address their critical business need for enterprise-wide shared services. Undertaking a shared-services initiative replaces old, autonomous departmental, or divisional services with a single, streamlined, corporate-level process. Shared-services projects take routine,

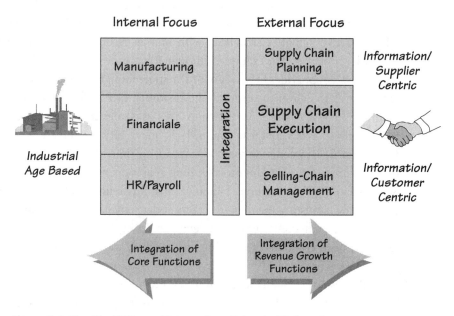

Figure 8.4: The Next Wave of Integration: Extended Enterprise

noncore business functions, such as accounting, that every business unit performs and define a common accounting process for all business units to use. Once the process is defined, the company establishes one IT infrastructure to manage the process efficiently. The shared-services business needs, which result in companies' selecting an ERP solution, are

- The need to create an application framework to improve customer order processing. Most companies, having ignored their back-office systems for years, are looking for solutions that will save them from their neglect.

- The need to consolidate and to unify relevant business functions.

- The need to integrate a broad range of disparate technologies, along with the business processes they support, into common processes and a common technology platform.

- The need to create a new technological foundation to support next-generation e-commerce applications.

ERP frameworks that are designed for a multisite, multinational company, such as Coca-Cola, are quite sophisticated. In order to function effectively, Coca-Cola must integrate business information across the organization, accommodate diverse business practices and processes that are integrated into a synergistic whole, manage resources across the enterprise, and support multiple languages, currencies, and jurisdictions. Automating even a small portion of Coca-Cola's global operations is a complex undertaking.

The decision to implement an ERP solution, however, is also complex and can make or break a company. Implementing an ERP package has been compared to enterprise architecture planning.

ERP Decision = Enterprise Architecture Planning

According to Jim Prevo, CIO of Green Mountain Coffee, "An ERP implementation is like the corporate equivalent of a brain transplant. We pulled the plug on every company application and moved to PeopleSoft software. The risk was certainly disruption of business, because if you do not do ERP properly, you can kill your company, guaranteed."[7] Green Mountain had no choice. The company was unable to manage its inventories electronically, even though its revenues grew by 30 percent annually. Green Mountain maintained extra-high inventory levels to ensure that orders could be filled. Increasingly, the management at both large- and medium-size companies must resolve their firms' enterprise architecture issues before selecting an ERP suite of products. In order to see whether ERP apps are a proper fit for their organization's business requirements, managers must ask, *What kind of company do we want to be?* rather than *What are each application's features?*

Getting the fit wrong can destroy an organization's competitive capability. FoxMeyer Drugs, a $5 billion pharmaceutical wholesaler, filed for bankruptcy protection following a bad case of ERP "implementitis." FoxMeyer filed a lawsuit against SAP's U.S. subsidiary and its implementation partner, Andersen Consulting, for $500 million each for allegedly making false assurances about the software. FoxMeyer argued that the implementation, which began in 1993, did nothing but drive the company to the wall. After filing for bankruptcy protection in August 1996, FoxMeyer was bought by competitor McKesson Drugs.

ERP implementations are rarely this bad, but corporate frustration with the inability to find the right fit between the ERP apps and their business needs is rising.

With horror stories like FoxMeyer and others, why do companies continue to invest in ERP software? The answer is simple. When implemented properly, ERP works. It streamlines business processes, facilitates better coordination within an enterprise, improves customer service, and, in general, enhances a company's bottom line. Often, the problem lies not with the ERP concept but in the management's demands for quick fixes and rapid cures to underlying structural problems, which cannot be fixed quickly or cured rapidly. ERP suites can't fix such problems, and companies that don't recognize this will fail at their implementations. Companies that recognize ERP's limitations , however, have gained significant operational benefits from ERP.

Remember that ERP provides a business foundation. Selecting and installing a new ERP solution is one of the most important—and most expensive—endeavors an organization will ever undertake. It's also the business initiative most likely to go wrong. A lack of alignment between a company's ERP apps and its business processes and e-commerce objectives can derail even the best-run firms. How should managers respond? Managers must be able to assess the technological, architectural, and business process issues involved with specific software. Unfortunately, most managers are unwilling to understand anything but the application's core functionality. They abdicate responsibility for assessing the solution's potential impact, turning the situation over to the company's IT department, with a mandate to "find an ERP system that will solve all our problems." This approach often results in a less than optimal solution.

Don't underestimate the difficulties in transitioning from old systems to new or overestimate the speed at which change can take place. Successful organizational change is a gradual process. Enterprise application initiatives require moving decades of corporate knowledge and information to a new technology platform. The case of FoxMeyer illustrates a key lesson that every manager must keep in mind: *Technology itself isn't the only challenge in managing transformation.* In an effort to stay ahead of the technology curve, managers tend to lose sight of their customers. FoxMeyer did. As companies adopt new technology, they must ask themselves, *Is this something our customers will recognize as valuable? Will it shorten the time between when the order is taken and order delivery? Will this system improve our product and our performance?*

An ERP implementation impacts far more than the company's software. ERP adoption significantly affects the company's culture, its organizational structure, and its business processes, staff, and day-to-day procedures. Executive management must understand the technical basis for business change and e-commerce functionality, in addition to the relationship between the new technology and its return on investment. The broadening of the ERP app market has meant that managers have a variety of choices as to the type of technological foundation on which to build. In order to choose wisely, managers must ask, *What business are we in? What are the key issues facing us today? What issues will be important tomorrow?* The ability to answer these questions fully and accurately is critical when considering an ERP solution.

ERP Software Decision: Build versus Buy versus Rent

Today, ERP apps define the overall corporate architecture. ERP implementations are enterprise-wide initiatives. It is therefore important for a company to decide whether to build the applications itself, buy them from a vendor, or rent them from an application service provider (ASP).

Traditionally, organizations have had two alternatives when selecting an ERP architecture:

- A highly complex, custom-designed application to meet the organization's specific requirements typically developed in a legacy environment.

- An off-the-shelf application designed to be amenable to a changing environment and to be implemented more rapidly at a lower cost.

Although custom-designed applications provide the desired degree of functionality, their size and complexity require lengthy design, development, and implementation efforts.

Both alternatives require substantial resources to maintain and often also the assistance of outside consultants familiar with the technology. In addition, custom-designed applications have limited flexibility to support diverse and changing operations or to respond effectively to evolving business demands and technologies.

To address the limitations of custom applications, off-the-shelf applications have been developed. They provide broad functionality, better integration with existing legacy systems, greater flexibility to change and upgrade, and a lower total cost of ownership. Most businesses are adopting these tools en masse. SAP, PeopleSoft, J. D. Edwards, Oracle, Lawson, QAD, and SSA offer by far the most popular off-the-shelf ERP packages available today.

Many firms are deciding to buy—rather than build or rent—commercial off-the-shelf (COTS) software from third-party vendors, for several reasons.

- Only organizations with deep pockets can viably maintain the high total cost of ownership and complexity associated with developing and maintaining custom-designed applications.

- Many current applications are technically outdated, and the ongoing redesign of business processes makes existing software functionally obsolete and a potential business impediment.

- Off-the-shelf solutions integrate the best business practices from a variety of industries. The ability to incorporate these best business practices into your firm's operations translates into bottom-line improvements.

- Companies realize that software development may not be a core competency. It's estimated that more than 70 percent of internal software projects fail. To minimize this risk, companies increasingly outsource software development activities.

Together, these trends ensure that COTS application vendors will sustain strong growth for years to come.

COTS solutions, however, come at a price. Companies must reengineer their established business practices to fit with software application constraints; or, applications must be customized, using costly, labor-intensive reprogramming to meet the company's requirements. These limitations result in an initial higher total cost to the organization, with the largest cost components being the consulting and programming resources needed to make the software work. The costs associated with these custom requirements will seriously challenge resource-constrained organizations.

As with most technology, COTS solutions do not provide a competitive edge for long, as any technology your company can buy today, your competitors can buy tomorrow. Every company must view the COTS solution within the context of its overall business strategy. *What business processes bring us our identity and our competitive advantage? How can we ensure that we enhance these with COTS solutions? How can we support our e-commerce initiatives with COTS solutions?*

The Capabilities of COTS ERP Solutions

COTS ERP solutions are extremely sophisticated and support effective e-commerce functionality with the following features:

- *Consolidation of the back office.* Consolidating back-office functions allows companies to better leverage their capabilities and to present a single face to suppliers. The goal is to centralize operations, which can be risky. Many companies have tried—and failed—to consolidate their software systems. Why is today's business environment different? Because executive management is now focused and paying attention to the benefits of technology consolidation.

- *Creation of a single back office that supports multiple distribution channels.* Consolidated back-office functions become even more important when firms must communicate with multiple customer-interaction channels. Companies need a seamless back office capable of supporting all paths to the customer. Why? Because it would be difficult to support new channels when existing ones are not integrated.

- *Facilitation of changes in business practices.* Trying to change encrusted business practices is extremely difficult. By taking the best practices inherent in various ERP apps, companies can bring about business practice change simultaneously with technological change.

- *Facilitation of changes in technology.* The ERP architecture is designed to mask the complexities of the underlying platform technologies, thus enhancing flexibility and simplifying software modification. Using flexible software toolsets, customers modify the application suites to accommodate their business practices, without concern for the impact on the underlying hardware, software, and network technologies.

Lower total delivered costs, excellent service to trade partners, and increased revenue growth are the broad benefits companies will see as a result of these changes.

ERP Use in the Real World: Three Case Studies

The success of the ERP solutions has been phenomenal. However, ERP is widely misunderstood as essentially production scheduling, which is simply not the case. The basic ideas behind ERP apps have a broad range of applicability to everyday business functions. What do we mean by everyday functions? As consumers, most of us are oblivious to the processes that produce the products we buy and use every day. We are also oblivious to the raw materials used to make them. But the acquisition of a product's raw materials, the accounts payable and receivable processes that fund its development, and the manufacturing and distribution processes that make and deliver it provide the basic building blocks for virtually every commercial product in existence. By examining how three firms in three separate industries—Microsoft in software, Owens-Corning in building supplies, and Colgate-Palmolive in consumer products—have used ERP in their organizations, we can better understand its benefits and issues.

Microsoft

In general, ERP software is used for division-wide or enterprise-wide integration purposes. Its purchase involves significant capital commitments. Microsoft spent 10 months and $25 million installing SAP R/3 to replace a tangle of 33 financial-tracking systems in 26 subsidiaries. As a result of the implementation, Microsoft estimates annual savings at $18 million, leading Bill Gates to call SAP "an incredible success story."[8]

Microsoft operates more than 50 subsidiaries around the world and continues to grow every day. In the early 1990s, its tremendous growth rate was straining the systems supporting the company's business. More than 30 separate systems supported the company's financial, operations, and human resources groups alone. These systems had been implemented in a piecemeal fashion over time, with significant customization in many of Microsoft's subsidiaries. Based on diverse hardware platforms, the applications communicated through a complex series of costly custom interfaces.

Microsoft's application environment was by no means integrated. Batch processes moved information between the systems. As the company grew, the time required to run the company's batch processes grew to more than 12 hours. Microsoft estimated that more than 90 percent of the more than 20,000 batch jobs that ran each month retrieved and processed the same information. The complexity of the older systems inhibited processing efficiency and didn't provide managers with easy access to the information they needed.

Management realized that it needed a new technology solution to support its core business, a solution that was both global and integrated. According to Microsoft's CIO, "What we needed was to develop a unified general ledger solution that streamlined and standardized the business processes around the world—one that would enable us to gain control over capital assets, establish worldwide business performance standards, and get rid of the multiplicity of legacy systems."[9]

The requirements were divided into three areas: financials, procurement, and human resources. The primary goals for the financials area were to simplify and to consolidate financial information and to bring together multiple systems into a single, standardized, worldwide chart of accounts. In the area of procurement, the goals were to increase transaction velocity, the number of procurement transactions handled at any given time, and transaction processing speed. The human resources requirements were to provide more accurate, timely, and consistent head-count information.

The SAP R/3 solution enabled Microsoft to keep pace with and support its growth. The company was able to capitalize on new business opportunities and also make the links with its customers and vendors more efficient and effective. However, moving from the company's legacy systems to a single global architecture required close coordination and extensive preparation. The requirements for the new system had to be thoroughly defined, and the solution had to be championed at the corporate executive level. Indeed, Microsoft's executives and IT group understood these challenges all too well because of the company's previous failed attempts at implementing ERP solutions in 1992 and 1993.

Going to ERP has proved to be a sound investment for Microsoft. Managers got better tools for making financial decisions, using the single chart of accounts. Consolidating the financial, human resources, and order management functions gave managers real-time access to accurate and timely financial information, which made it possible for Microsoft to close its books more quickly each quarter.

Owens-Corning

Building supplies manufacturer Owens-Corning is one of the world's top makers of glass fiber and composite materials, manufacturing fiberglass insulation, piping and roofing materials, asphalt, specialty foams, windows, patio doors, vinyl siding, and yarns. The company operates manufacturing facilities in the United States and about a dozen other countries.

In 1992, CEO Glen Hiner said that his goal was to grow the company from $2.9 billion a year to a $5 billion a year through a combination of acquisitions, overseas expansion, and more aggressive marketing of the company's traditional building products. The business goal: Owens-Corning should offer one-call shopping for all the exterior siding, insulation, pipes, and roofing material that builders need. As a work in progress, the process is fragmented. Customers call an Owens-Corning shingle plant to get a load of shingles but then must place a separate call to order siding and yet another call to order the company's well-known pink insulation.

One-stop shopping will give Owens-Corning the ability to integrate sales by allowing salespeople to see the inventories at any plant or warehouse and to quickly assemble orders for customers. Typical goals of sales order management include

- Accepting customer orders from any location worldwide into one system

- Assigning ship dates to available products

- Scheduling future ship dates for products not in stock

- Checking order status 24 hours a day, 7 days a week

Sounds simple, but like other large companies, Owens-Corning had operated as a collection of autonomous fiefdoms with an estimated 211 legacy systems.[10] Each plant had its own product lines and pricing schedules, built up over years of cutting deals with various customers. Trucking had been parceled out to about 325 carriers, selected by individual factories. Clearly, Owen-Corning's business needs had outgrown its practices, and the company required a platform that could handle present demands while serving as a long-term foundation for future growth.

The case of Owens-Corning illustrates how companies operate across a series of information islands. The tendency is for various departments to function as if they were independent empires. ERP can be used as a battering ram to break down such unhealthy rivalries and to pave the way to effectively integrating islands of information, ensuring total transparency.

For Owens-Corning to grow, it was critical to integrate order management, financial reporting, and distribution. The company chose to implement SAP R/3, requiring that Owens-Corning staff come up with a single product list and a single price list. The use of R/3 also allowed the finished-goods inventory to be tracked easily both in company warehouses and in the distribution channel. The estimated savings were more than $65 million by the end of 1998.

Colgate-Palmolive

An ERP implementation has rapidly become the spinal cord of Colgate-Palmolive, the world leader in oral-care products—mouthwashes, toothpaste, and toothbrushes—and a major supplier of personal-care products—baby care, deodorants, shampoos, and soaps. Palmolive is a leading dishwashing soap brand worldwide, and Colgate is a top producer of bleach and liquid surface cleaners (Ajax) outside the United States. The company's Hill's Health Science Diet is a leading premium pet food brand worldwide. Foreign sales account for about 70 percent of Colgate's total revenues.

To stay competitive, Colgate continuously seeks to streamline its business. At the same time, Colgate faces the challenges of new-product acceleration, which has been a factor in driving faster sales growth and improved market share. Also, Colgate is devising ways to offer consumers a greater choice of better products at a lower cost to the company, which creates complexities in the manufacturing and logistics process. To better coordinate its business, Colgate embarked on an ERP implementation to allow the company to access more timely and accurate data, get the most out of working capital, and reduce costs (see Figure 8.5).

An important factor for Colgate was whether it could use the software across the entire spectrum of the business. Colgate needed the ability to coordinate globally and act locally. Colgate's U.S. division installed SAP R/3 at end of 1996, a year or so ahead of most of its competitors. According to Colgate's annual report,

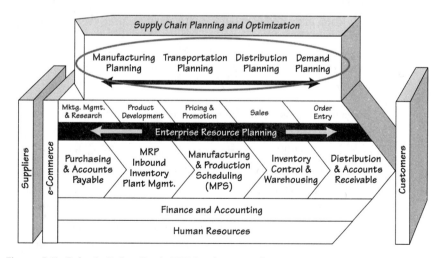

Figure 8.5: Colgate-Palmolive's ERP Implementation

"The implementation of SAP across the Colgate supply chain contributed to increased profitability. Now installed in operations that produce over 35 percent of Colgate's worldwide sales, SAP will be expanded to all Colgate divisions by 2001. Global efficiencies in purchasing—combined with product and packaging standardization—also produced large savings."[11]

The Colgate example proves that for organizations willing to navigate the difficult terrain of implementation, the benefits are quite measurable. The benefits from Colgate's ERP implementation are as follows.

- Prior to installing SAP R/3, Colgate had 75 data centers for its global business; now, the company has 2 data centers, employing only 40 people.

- Colgate used to take anywhere from 1 to 5 days to acquire an order and another 1 to 2 days to process it. Now, with SAP R/3, order acquisition and processing combined take 4 hours, not 7 days. Distribution planning used to take 4 days; today, it takes 14 hours. In total, the order-to-delivery time has been cut in half.

- Before SAP R/3, on-time deliveries used to occur only 91.5 percent of the time, and cases ordered were delivered correctly 97.5 percent of the time. Now, the figures are 97.5 percent and 99.0 percent, respectively.

- Using SAP R/3 has resulted in a one-third drop in domestic inventories, and receivables outstanding have dropped to 22.4 days from 31.4. Working capital as a percentage of sales has plummeted to 6.3 percent from 11.3 percent. Total delivered cost per case has been reduced by nearly 10 percent.

- After SAP R/3, accounts payable was consolidated into one location from eight, and three human resources administrative offices were consolidated into one.

Colgate's process streamlining has realized significant cost savings. But the biggest savings are expected to come as Colgate changes processes and organizational structure while implementing best practices in each region. Colgate and other companies in the consumer-products marketplace are in the early stages of making important changes to the way management runs companies and views its businesses. These changes will lead to improvement in profit margins, increased reinvestment in growing sales, further consolidation of the industry, and enhanced growth of economic profit. Clearly, Colgate-Palmolive is leveraging its ERP investment and aiming at the next generation of ERP—supply chain management, which is discussed in detail in Chapter 9.

ERP Implementation: Catching the Bull by the Horns

A combination of better products, time-to-market urgency, and thin in-house technical skills ensures that mainstream firms will embrace packaged ERP software. It's important to note that each ERP application suite has its own architecture, customization features, installation procedures, and level of complexity. Therefore, you can never approach the installation of all ERP packages in the same manner.

Take, for instance, SAP. Companies implementing SAP use a variety of implementation strategies:

- A *step-by-step approach,* in which one SAP module at a time is installed, tested, and integrated with other systems.

- A *"big bang" technique,* sweeping away all old systems at once and replacing them all at once.

- A *"modified big bang" approach,* in which various modules are implemented at one time, piloting them in one area of the company and then extending the program throughout the firm. Most companies use this method.

Even if the implementation strategy is right, setting up the ERP solution is not easy. Numerous obstacles—many of which are not technology related—hinder the organization's ability to move quickly. Consider the case of Brother Industries.

Brother Industries illustrates the complexity involved in translating strategy into execution. In early 1996, Brother Industries (USA), the U.S. typewriter and word processor manufacturing arm of Brother Industries Ltd. of Japan, figured that installing SAP's enterprise software in 8 months would be a snap. Brother would simply transfer data from its existing legacy applications into the new database. And while they were at it, why not migrate from a big mainframe computer to a client/server, desktop-centric model that nobody in the company had yet been trained to use? Oh, yes, and the information technology people could run most of the project.

Everything that could go wrong did. Members of the project team were technologists who didn't understand the business side of what the application was supposed to accomplish. For example, the team added up how many people worked on each assembly line and the volume of parts and materials ordered by each plant, figuring that simple arithmetic was enough to calculate costs. But the numbers proved far too vague for operations executives, who needed an accurate gauge of the cost of making each product. They needed to know labor and unit costs and waste rates at each plant.

As a result, implementation was far over budget and months behind schedule. After bringing in a new CIO to clean up the mess, Brother slowly fixed all the problems. Finally, the application began doing what it was meant to do: keep materials flowing, log orders in, send bills out, highlight the most efficient operations, and red flag the least. After taming manufacturing functions, Brother is expanding the footprint of the application to include a sales-and-distribution module that will convert sales orders to production orders. Next on the agenda is supply chain management. Brother is slowly and methodically building out the e-business blueprint.

Roadmap to Rapid Implementations: The Accelerated ERP Approach

As an old Chinese proverb warns, "Between here and the Promised Land can be a parched desert." Today's intense competitive pressures require fast response. Unfortunately, most ERP application suites can't keep up—systems take too long to install and, once installed, take too long to adapt to the ever-changing business processes vital to competitive success.

An analysis of many companies in a variety of industries reveals that success follows a simple implementation philosophy. Successful companies strive to understand their business processes, simplify them, and introduce automation. Unsuccessful companies start their ERP implementation effort with automation, bypassing the critical step of simplifying their processes. These companies believe that automation alone will improve performance and lead to productivity gains. Automating complex or non-value-added processes, however, will not increase productivity or provide measurable improvements in performance. Automation without simplification only immortalizes ineffective processes. In other words, a badly implemented ERP is like a broken rudder on a cruise ship: Everything is beautiful and expensive, but navigation is impossible.

Let's look at the ERP implementation methodology phases.

- In the *project preparation* phase, the project kickoff is organized, and all the arrangements for the project team are made. This phase also includes the estimation of project resources, costs, and duration of each activity.

- During the *blueprint* phase, the consultants document the requirements of the enterprise and its business process design, including interviewing potential users.

- In the *pilot* phase, the software is configured to match the structure of the company with the desired business processes. The technical team plans the interfaces and data integration infrastructure of the new system.

- In the *final* phase, all the work from the previous phases is consolidated, with the goal of preparing the system for final acceptance. This phase covers the final system test, user training, and final migration of the data to the new system. Moreover, all the conversion and interface programs are verified, as is the scalability of the system. Finally, the user acceptance tests are run.

- The *assessment* phase reviews the system to ensure that all business requirements were met. This includes checking the business processes and technical architecture, as well as checking with the end users, ensuring that their expectations were met. Finally, the business benefits of the new system are measured, allowing the company to determine the ultimate return on investment.

Using canned methodologies reduces risk and brings consistency to the overall project. Implementing ERP is just the beginning. By far the most important challenges facing any company are developing a new set of leadership and change management skills. At the same time some companies are facing problems by implementing ERP too quickly. Table 8.1 lists some potential problems.

Roadmap to New Leadership Skills

As companies find new ways to implement change, the management style that comes with issuing orders is giving way to one of coordination, or lateral leadership. Effective coordination management encompasses a combination of the following four capabilities:

- *Strategic thinking. How well does your ERP selection, implementation, and evolution strategy align with your business strategy?* To answer this question, you must first answer the following: *What are we trying to accomplish?* Companies selecting an ERP solution face a conundrum: *Should the priority be cost, functionality, or speed of implementation?* There is no easy or generic answer. The biggest mistake users make is getting caught up in the bandwagon effect surrounding some new technology without looking at what they really are trying to improve in their business. In fact, most failed implementations are doomed from the start by managers choosing the wrong system for their business.

- *Process reengineering.* Never underestimate the reluctance to change processes. One lesson that many managers have learned again and again is that you

Table 8.1: Pros and Cons of Rapid ERP Deployments

Advantages	Disadvantages
Up and running on ERP quickly	Inability to suitably customize software to match business operations
Less staff time spent on project	Small core group making key decisions without involving everyone
Less business disruption	Must understand business context and processes to implement effectively
Can be lower cost over time	Short time frame may limit IT staff's ability to support new software effectively; may require more up-front preparation costs

cannot implement large-scale systems without first changing processes. Process reengineering is essential to obtain the most benefit out of the software. This requires taking rules and procedures and mapping them in a logical manner into the software. An ERP system is really a collection of business rules and procedures (called *best practices*). Therefore, when implementing an ERP system, one set of rules and procedures is replaced by another. For this transition to work properly, a thorough alignment of both sets is a prerequisite. The decisions about which rules and procedures should be kept and which ones should be modified can quickly become a political nightmare.

• *Managing implementation complexity.* The complexity of implementing large-scale ERP systems is giving rise to a love/hate, "can't live with 'em, can't live without 'em" partnership scenario. Instances of ERP projects behind schedule and over budget occur with alarming frequency, as do cases of companies spending millions of dollars on a system and using only a small percentage of its capabilities. Most of these problems arise from lack of partnership governing. Most firms outsource their implementation, so effective overseeing of the outsourcing relationship is crucial. Increasingly, firms put in place a "gain-share" contract, which ties compensation to on-time completion. If Andersen Consulting—selected by Nortel Networks to do the implementation—delivers what it promises, achieving 80 percent accuracy, it gets paid an agreed-on amount. If Anderson does more, it is paid more; if less, the company is paid much less. Compensation is tied to deliverables.

• *Transition management.* Coordinating a smooth transition and overcoming employee resistance can be critical factors for the successful completion of a project. Even after effectively completing process reengineering, an implementation can fail. Who's at fault? Most of the blame for ERP installations has been leveled at the consultants retained to assist in the implementations, with software vendors running a close second. The vendors are often criticized for overselling the benefits of the new features packed into their systems and for underselling the amount of work involved in getting all the fancy tools to work. The consultants are accused of dragging out the installation process to rack up billable hours. Often, however, it isn't the consultant or the vendor at fault but rather the user. There is a logical explanation for this: the underestimated resistance to change. Top management often underestimates the amount of pain involved with large-scale ERP implementations. Like shooting the messenger bringing bad news, the consultant is unjustly made the scapegoat for the mess that implementation uncovers.

There are a few ways of making the pain of change disappear: Find ways of helping users understand the vision behind the change. Get them to participate in the implementation, and get pieces of the new system in front of them as soon as possible so they can overcome their fear.

ERP Architecture and Toolkit Evolution

Compared with those of even a decade ago, the ERP solutions that have become routine in corporate life today are pretty amazing. But have no doubt; they're nothing compared with tomorrow's. As a wise person once said, "The road to excellence is always under construction." So too is the ERP solution.

ERP architecture and toolkits are undergoing a fundamental shift. Architecturally, ERP products have become more loosely coupled and engineered for the Web. The old client/server paradigm is no longer viable. SAP and PeopleSoft enjoyed phenomenal growth during much of the 1990s because they foresaw the demand for the client/server model. These companies were behind the Internet curve, unlike Oracle, and that lethargy hurt them, along with a general slowdown in sales as businesses delayed purchasing new software while engineers dealt with potential problems caused by the year 2000 rollover.

Many ERP companies are recovering from the equivalent of a business hangover and are transitioning from the old architecture to new Web-based models. Consider PeopleSoft, which after 2 years of work released its browser-based PeopleSoft 8 suite. The company invested $500 million to reengineer the 7.5 release, including rewrites of more than 14,000 Windows-based user interface screens. The outcome for users: Instead of having to install a client version of PeopleSoft 8 on desktop PCs, customers will be able to give their end users access to the applications through a Web browser, a change that should make the software more portable and less costly to maintain and support.[12]

The long-term goal is achieving more flexibility in deployment and operations. The following crucial elements are required to achieve flexibility:

- *Components, not modules.* Historically, ERP systems have been built from interdependent modules. In the future, freestanding components will be capable of integrating seamlessly with one another, with legacy systems, and with third-party solutions. Why? Companies are outsourcing business functions, such as logistics, human resources, and accounting, in order to concentrate on areas that improve competitive advantage. Companies need applications that can be pulled apart, recombined, and distributed to match new outsourcing-based business models.

- *Incremental migration rather than massive reengineering.* ERP systems have traditionally taken too long to implement. This must give way to a ready-to-go product that allows companies to migrate in easy steps, moving steadily from one deliverable to another, rather than waiting long periods for completion of a total project.

- *Dynamic rather than static configuration of ERP systems.* Big ERP systems that are configured once and for all are no longer acceptable. ERP components must be dynamically reconfigured to suit changing business needs. No one vendor can presume to predict accurately and precisely how its customers will work and how their processes will flow. Technically, users will be able to influence the system's functionality and configuration simply by changing an underlying business logic template. Critical to such reconfigurability is the ability to create dynamic suites of applications out of best-of-breed components.

- *Management of multiple strategic sourcing and partnership relationships.* Rather than merely viewing the flow of processes, future ERP systems will model and monitor processes affecting the activity of the business, wherever those processes are occurring, up and down the supply chain. This is especially important in a business-to-business e-commerce environment.

The vision is turning into reality. Let's consider the ways in which ERP is evolving.

Hosted ASP Models: Hype versus Reality

The road to the most sophisticated, complex business capabilities, such as SAP or PeopleSoft (tier 1), used to be a long, capital-intensive journey. Only the largest, best-capitalized companies in the world could afford such world-class business capabilities. Implementing such tier 1 business applications involved high up-front costs and significant personnel investments and put the lion's share of project risk in the customer's lap. That is why many companies start with cheaper, tier 2 solutions, such as Mapics, American Software, or SSA applications. With their reduced functionality and limited scalability come fewer challenges and less cost. Unfortunately, companies adopting these solutions quickly outgrow them and must implement tier 1 applications thereafter.

At the same time, managing the complexity of ERP apps is itself a complex task. Implementations can last for months and stretch company resources. A staff of professionals, including systems administrators, DBAs (database administrators), and help-desk personnel need to be hired. Applications need to be implemented and then monitored and supported. A flock of vendors needs to be managed. Integration with other applications can be a nightmare. Software upgrades imply another round of intensive effort and major projects.

Into this world of ERP solutions comes the ASP pitch to large customers: Why spend lots of money and time and take enormous risks trying to put these programs together? Whether you are firmly positioned in the Fortune 500, a start-up, or somewhere in between, ASPs provide a rapid, fixed-fee implementations for tier 1 e-business capabilities for your company—today. ASPs, such as Corio, USInternetworking, and Oracle Business Online, tailor, implement, and maintain applications. For a monthly fee, ASPs deliver an entire integrated suite of e-business capabilities that will put your company on a level playing field with the best and biggest in your industry.

One such ASP is PeopleSoft eCenter, which gives customers a so-called tightly integrated, end-to-end ASP solution. The service offers single-vendor accountability for all of PeopleSoft's hosted applications, including customer relationship management (CRM), human resource management systems (HRMS), and financial management. The eCenter also hosts professional services automation (PSA), e-procurement, and the MarketPlace trading exchange.

So, what's the downside of the ASP model? Lack of flexibility and integration, especially in a large company with varying requirements. Hosted solutions work really well in a standard or start-up environment but tend to break down quickly when each division wants something different: a little variation or customization of the core solution. Each variant creates tremendous headaches as the solution gets deployed and enters maintenance. Soon, the users become hostages, not customers.

ERP Application Management and Maintenance: A Big Business

ERP implementation is crucial, but it is only half the secret of success on the Web. The other half is reliability. Yet a surprising number of e-businesses are failing to provide 24×7 availability, instantaneous scalability, personalized and easy-to-use self-services, and the fast and unerring reliability in transaction processing that the e-generation demands. ERP reliability solutions include software (tools) and methodologies that aid the implementation and configuration of applications to meet performance specifications required. As the complexity of ERP implementations increases, administrators want end-to-end management tools, realizing that the management of the applications is even more critical than rapid ERP deployment. In most cases, tools specific to ERP management simply have been neglected, weren't available, or were rudimentary.

Increasingly, companies realize that the best formula for managing complex ERP apps is to use a variety of management tools. Here's a look at the primary categories.[13]

- *Service-management tools* monitor the performance and availability of ERP apps, performing such functions as service reporting, availability, and performance management. For instance, how are you going to manage response time? This will require the ability to analyze the thousands of transactions that can occur simultaneously in an ERP system. Products in this category include Luminate and Envive.

- *Use-management* tools manage such functions as event monitoring, job scheduling, output, backup and recovery, and user access. Among the products in this class is IBM's Maestro.

- *System administration* tools manage network and systems for ERP and other network applications. Tools in this class perform inventory and asset management, software configuration, change management, and software distribution. IBM's Tivoli Enterprise, Computer Associates' Unicenter, and Hewlett-Packard's OpenView are among the offerings in this category.

As ERP software and implementations mature, managers are finding that application management—and the tools to make it happen—are essential to improving the return on what is typically a costly investment. Effective application management means making sure that response time, up time, and transaction volume are as fine-tuned as possible. There's little doubt that management tools are becoming a key requirement and will be an interesting area to watch in the future.

Memo to the CEO

ERP is ubiquitous and becomes bigger and more complex every year, and its development and management are essential components of competitive performance. The dramatic rise of integrated ERP apps form the technology backbone of e-business today.

The ERP phenomenon first surfaced in the late 1980s. Almost overnight, most Fortune 500 companies raced to implement ERP systems in order to reengineer their archaic software systems, which threatened to strangle their businesses. Companies feared that these older systems would make them noncompetitive against low-cost producers, such as the Japanese and other Asian competitors. ERP systems were viewed as the magic wand that with one wave would make process reengineering a breeze.

During the mid 1990s, enterprises were challenged to reduce product development time, improve product quality, and reduce production costs and lead times. Enterprises must meet these challenges in order to remain competitive in the e-commerce world. These challenges can no longer be met by making isolated business process and technology changes to specific functional units. The complexity of the challenges facing e-business today requires strengthening the relationships and interdependencies among various business processes, from finance to distribution.

With the choices e-commerce presents, companies can no longer afford to look at their operations in a vacuum. To achieve sustained growth, companies must be able to plan, execute, and control their business processes at every point. The advantages gained by companies implementing ERP solutions include lower costs and reduced inventory. ERP systems are enablers, but they aren't the answer in and of themselves. They essentially allow companies to streamline business operations. The next step is what companies do after their processes are streamlined.

Continually improving the ERP foundation is a significant challenge. How a company manages ERP's evolution within the organization is a complicated task. With few exceptions, no one person or department in the corporation has total ownership or responsibility for all the various functions ERP solutions govern. CEOs must appoint an ERP czar to oversee the entire organization. By so doing, the czar can better understand the effect that changing ERP conditions have on his or her business. Such an approach would help organizations to make informed decisions in alignment with their business goals.

As business needs change, so must ERP. Smart managers understand the process of enhancing and leveraging their company's ERP investment. In visionary organizations, the most critical element in business success and competitive advantage during the twenty-first century will be the strength and integration of the business community's ERP investments and e-commerce initiatives.

e-Commerce is forcing ERP apps to once again evolve to meet the changing needs of today's business environment. The resulting new innovations, such as XRP and supplier and customer integration, illustrate the rapidity with which technology and business processes are changing. The Internet's own contribution, the three w's—Web, work flow, and warehouse—are becoming integrated with recent ERP solutions. The power of innovation the Web and ERP represent is truly immense.

CHAPTER NINE

Implementing Supply Chain Management and e-Fulfillment

What to Expect

Starting an e-business takes ideas, capital, and technical savvy. Operating one, however, takes supply chain management (SCM) skills. A successful SCM strategy is based on accurate order processing, just-in-time inventory management, and timely order fulfillment. SCM's increasing importance illustrates how a tool that was a theoretical process 10 years ago is now a hot competitive weapon.

Let's face the facts. In today's "high customer expectations, gotta have it, real-time world," it's no longer fulfillment as usual. Companies are racing to find the right combination of click-and-brick supply chains, which is why you need to understand that SCM isn't a technology issue but rather a business strategy for creating new, interesting opportunities. Before implementing an SCM component as part of your e-commerce strategy, make sure that you've invested adequately in technology and in strong fulfillment. Also make sure that your company's order processing and its pick, pack, and ship operations are tightly integrated. What matters in the long run is execution.

In this chapter, we'll define SCM and ask the following questions: What will the supply chain look like in the years ahead? Do you know how to diagnose your company's supply chain problems—and cure the root problem? Is your company ready to design and implement new supply webs? Don't panic. The answers are here in the form of a supply chain roadmap.

And to make your job even easier, we also present eight steps to setting up your company's e-supply chain architecture.

Leading companies have the most innovative supply chains and are pulling ahead of their competition at breakneck speed. The following companies illustrate the impact supply chain management is having on modern business.

Bergen Brunswig is a major pharmaceutical and medical/surgical supply distributor. According to CEO Donald Roden, SCM has become his company's business. "We do $13 billion a year and handle billions of packages," says Roden. "We're no longer in the distribution business, but actually in the business of managing the supply channel. This means not just moving products, but managing information, and the ultimate cost-effectiveness of that supply channel."[1]

Dell Computer is built on a vision of customer-responsive order fulfillment. This vision requires a flexible supply chain that gets it made and gets it there. "We already have a quick-ship plan for large customers, where we can deliver a machine within 48 hours of an order," Michael Dell explains.[2] The frictionless flow of information through the supply chain is a central part of Dell's vision.

Procter & Gamble (P&G) plays its supply chain like a maestro plays the violin. P&G estimates that it saved retail customers millions of dollars through gains in supply chain efficiency. According to P&G, the essence of its approach "lies in manufacturers and suppliers working closely together . . . jointly creating business plans to eliminate the source of wasteful practices across the entire supply chain."[3]

Boeing Aircraft was forced to announce write-offs of $2.6 billion in October 1997. The reason? "Raw-material shortages, internal and supplier parts shortages, and productivity inefficiencies."[4] In other words, poor SCM created havoc with production at Boeing, resulting in extremely unhappy customers.

Nabisco, the food king, disappointed Wall Street with slow innovation and sales growth. The company's main problem was that its supply chains were not integrated. The supply chains for Nabisco Biscuit, the baked-goods segment, were handled by one software system, whereas the Foods Group division (LifeSavers and Grey Poupon) ran on another, resulting in unhappy retailers left waiting for Nabisco products to fill their barren shelves.[5]

During the Christmas season of 1999, *Toys "R" Us* couldn't commit to fulfilling customer purchases made before Dec. 24, even if the customer had placed an order before the retailer's Dec. 10 deadline. The company grossly underestimated the number of online orders it would receive. Those customers whose purchases weren't delivered on time were offered the option of canceling their orders or receiving $100 credit to shop at Toys "R" Us stores. The order delays resulted in unhappy customers, a class-action lawsuit, and a settlement.[6]

Today, companies must speed up their responsiveness to satisfy market demands. The most pressing issue facing modern business is no longer about reducing manufacturing costs and making the highest-quality product. The issue is about delivering value to the customer—what they want, when and where they want it, and at the lowest possible cost. Companies need rapid, cost-effective, flawlessly executed demand fulfillment in order to support this new value proposition (see Figure 9.1).

With e-commerce, the process focus is shifting inexorably outside the organization's four walls. Process reengineering, quality improvement, and other trends have all addressed the inner workings of the corporation. The next opportunity lies in the fusing of each company's internal systems to those of its suppliers, partners, and customers. This fusion forces companies to better integrate the interenterprise processes to improve manufacturing efficiency and distribution effectiveness. The managerial challenge? Integration must be achieved while simultaneously achieving flexibility and responsiveness to changing market conditions and customer demands.

There is no doubt that supply chain issues are getting the attention of senior management and even boardrooms. How should an executive respond? By first initiating supply chain education and then planning, execution, and measurement—in that order. Supply chain education is needed to address the SCM market's lack of definition and structure. No clearly defined SCM business requirements or application standards exist; even its buzzwords are poorly defined and confusing.

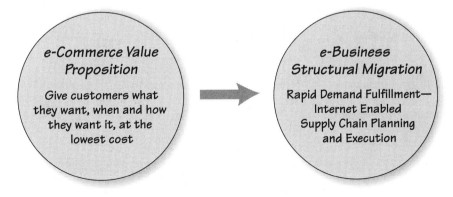

Figure 9.1: Cause of the Supply Chain Management Boom

The Basics of Supply Chain Management

Defining SCM

What will my supply chain look like next month? Next year? Ten years from now? Over the past two decades, SCM's evolution has been swift and sure. Before deregulation, every company had a traffic department responsible for deciphering the tariff and regulatory mysteries associated with moving freight. The emergence of the physical distribution management approach in the 1980s was an acknowledgment that transportation managers could not work in a vacuum, independent of their colleagues in purchasing, materials management, and warehousing. Logistics management evolved from physical distribution management to link sales order processes to manufacturing and distribution processes. In the 1990s, SCM represented a further expansion of logistics management.

In the simplest sense, the supply chain is a "process umbrella" under which products are created and delivered to customers. From a structural standpoint, a supply chain refers to the complex network of relationships that organizations maintain with trading partners to source, manufacture, and deliver products.

As you can see from Figure 9.2, a company's supply chain encompasses the facilities where raw materials, intermediate products, and finished goods are acquired, transformed, stored, and sold. These facilities are connected by

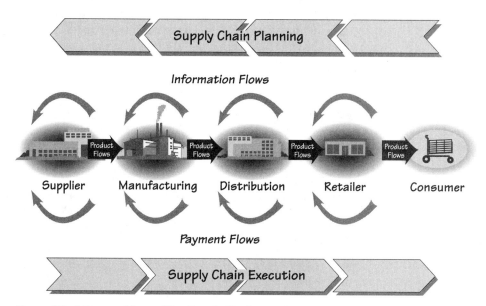

Figure 9.2: A Process View of the Supply Chain

transportation links, along which materials and products flow. Ideally, the supply chain consists of multiple companies that function as efficiently and effectively as a single company, with full information visibility and accountability.

At its most basic, SCM is the coordination of material, information, and financial flows between and among all the participating enterprises in a business transaction.

- *Material flows* involve physical product flowing from suppliers to customers through the chain, as well as reverse material flows, such as product returns, servicing, recycling, and disposal.

- *Information flows* involve demand forecasts, order transmissions, and delivery status reports.

- *Financial flows* involve credit card information, credit terms, payment schedules, and consignment and title ownership arrangements.

Interenterprise integration is a major focus of SCM. Since the late 1980s, businesses have focused on reengineering their internal processes to improve efficiency. Having succeeded, many organizations are now looking for other ways to gain competitive advantage, such as speeding up the time to market, reducing distribution costs, and getting the right products to the right place at the right time, cost, and price.

Surging demand, more frequent and shorter order-to-ship times, and increasing customer-compliance requirements are now the cornerstone of SCM. Today's enterprises are rethinking and reexamining their relationships with their suppliers, manufacturers, distributors, retailers, and customers. The market leaders realize that the more efficient their relationships with their partners, the greater the edge they will have over their competitors. As these partner relationships increase in efficiency, they become more dependent on the information flow. As with any relationship, the more communication there is, the greater the mutual dependence of the parties involved. This interdependency is creating sweeping changes in the competitive landscape. With the shift in focus from internal to external process improvement, competition of manufacturer versus manufacturer has become competition of supply chain versus supply chain. This change is forcing enterprises to solidify relationships with their own partners in order to remain competitive.

The SCM integration between Amazon.com and FedEx for distributing the book *Harry Potter and the Goblet of Fire,* one of the most popular books in publishing history, illustrates the challenges behind e-commerce distribution. Before the book was released, 350,020 copies were preordered at Amazon.com, making the title the retailer's largest advance order ever. The challenge became not only getting all those books to eager readers but also doing so in a single day. FedEx Home Delivery, in a deal with Amazon.com, delivered 250,000 copies of the Potter book the next day. To ensure a smooth distribution process, FedEx worked with Amazon for weeks prior to the ship date to integrate the firms' computer systems, to prepare labels, and to get the shipping data ready for "the largest single day distribution event in the history of business to consumer e-Commerce."[7]

Clearly, a supply chain perspective transforms a group of ad hoc and often fragmented processes into cohesive systems capable of delivering value to the customer. Such integration requires supply chain process optimization, which means minimizing the total cost of the order-to-delivery process by trading off the costs of inventory, transportation, and handling. Traditional business process optimization solutions succeed at minimizing a single cost, but they cannot handle the complex interdependencies that real-life business situations often create. Also, the business applications of the chain's players—manufacturers, distributors, transporters, and retailers—are designed to control the costs of the processes under the company's direct control, not the combined costs of end-to-end supply chain operations.

Until recently, no one player has had the information visibility needed to synchronize the entire channel. New versions of large-scale optimization applications make such process visibility possible. Consequently, supply chains everywhere hold more than double the product inventory needed to provide acceptable customer service. In addition, products are typically handled five or six times, and transportation carriers struggle to maintain the profitability of their equipment and to maximize driver utilization.

A variety of technological and process innovations have permitted simultaneous improvements to a number of steps in the supply chain process. Supply chain planning and optimization are enjoying a revival. The new generation of supply chain optimization tools, including I2 Rhythm and SAP's Advanced Planning and Optimization, provide an integrated approach through which demand prediction, inventory stocking, and transportation decisions are made cooperatively together. This new generation of software applications manages supply chain tasks more than they do costs and also optimize service, quality, and time factors that can strongly influence customer satisfaction.

An e-Supply Chain in Action

Cool Mint Listerine? All it takes to make and deliver it is syrup, a bottle, and a truck, right? Not quite. The supply chain dynamics, illustrated by the relationship between Warner-Lambert (WL) and CVS show how completely technology can be woven into the entire consumer product supply chain.[8] When you point and click on a bottle of Cool Mint Listerine at CVS.com or pick one off the shelf at the local CVS pharmacy, your act represents the culmination of a complex set of events and processes to ensure that the bottle is available for you. The mouthwash's journey begins in Australia, where a farmer sells his eucalyptus crop to a processing company. The company extracts the oil from the eucalyptus, then sells it to a plant oil distributor in New Jersey, which then transports the oil to WL's manufacturing facility in Pennsylvania.

Meanwhile, in a Saudi Arabian desert, natural gas is being drilled, producing the synthetic alcohol that gives Listerine its 43-proof punch. Union Carbide ships the synthetic alcohol to Texas, where it's refined into ethanol. The ethanol is shipped to the same WL plant in Pennsylvania as the eucalyptus oil. In the Midwest, farmers grow corn that is converted to Sorbitol, a sweetener that adds bulk to liquids. The Sorbitol is also shipped to WL's Pennsylvania plant. All these ingredients are then mixed, and the finished product, Listerine, flows through pipes to be packaged for distribution. The packages are shipped to CVS's warehouse and then distributed to its retail stores.

Imagine trying to manage and coordinate all these suppliers to ensure that every time a customer wants a bottle of Listerine, it's on the shelf or available to be distributed. The product order and its process, shipping, and final delivery constitute the basics of supply chain activity. It's a complicated process, one that consumers don't often think about but that successful companies understand is critical to their continued success. Many software systems are used throughout the supply chain cycle. CVS's merchandise transaction system calculates the exact quantities of Listerine needed at the company's pharmacy, generates a purchase order, and sends it via electronic data interchange (EDI) to WL. CVS's warehouse management system also receives the purchase order information so that it knows to expect the order.

At WL, the supply chain planning system analyzes manufacturing, distribution, and sales data against expected demand to determine how much product to make and consequently, how much of each raw ingredient the product requires. WL's capacity planning system schedules production and generates electronic purchase orders, which are sent to the company's suppliers. WL's SAP R/3 ERP package prices the order and also determines how much of the product to manufacture. The same day, the ERP system transfers the order to WL's transportation planner to also determine how best to consolidate order delivery and which shipping companies to use to minimize cost. Meanwhile, the delivery information plan is downloaded by the warehouse application for the warehouse staff to use for picking and packing purposes.

After the delivery arrives and the truck is unloaded, the CVS warehouse system generates an electronic receiving notice, notifying the CVS accounts payable department of the receipt from WL. The warehouse system also uploads the receiving notice to the company's data warehouse for purchasing, sales, and forecasting purposes and to the warehouse management system, which routes the pallets to the appropriate storage location. The pallets will remain in this location up to 3 weeks, until they're shipped to fill orders placed by CVS stores. The demand cycle starts again, with another purchase of a bottle of Listerine.

The ultimate objective of the CVS-WL supply chain is to "scan one, make one." A company's market share and revenue growth are increasingly dependent on getting the right product to the right place at the right time. The goal is to provide exemplary end-to-end service that will satisfy even the most finicky customer. Why? Because customer satisfaction creates more demand, requiring the production rate increase for in-demand goods. The phrase *in demand* is critical, as some businesses build products no one buys.

Some companies, such as WL, react quickly to customer demand by producing the goods customers want when they want them. Although a variety of businesses are already responsive, the supply chain can be streamlined further.

Supply Chain Investment Trends

Today, several forces are driving companies to expand Internet-enabled supply chain collaboration with trading partners:

- *The trend toward worldwide dispersion of manufacturing and distribution facilities.* The demand for customized products for local markets has increased.

- *Channel unpredictability.* New technologies are enabling firms to better manage local and regional demand, requiring sophisticated coordination of multiple distribution channels.

- *Responsiveness over efficiency.* The need for faster and more customized deliveries has disrupted traditional inventory management policies and transportation choices.

- *Companies' willingness to accept lower margins to maintain and increase market share.* Many companies are redesigning supply chains to drive out unproductive work and, consequently, eliminate delay, error, excessive cost, and inflexibility.

The advent of e-commerce has forced manufacturers and distributors to become more responsive to retailers and consumers. These same competitive pressures are forcing manufacturers to reduce costs, decrease order cycle times, and improve their operating efficiencies. As a result, manufacturers are under pressure to better manage the supply chain and to improve manufacturing efficiency and logistics operations while remaining responsive to changing market conditions and customer demands (see Figure 9.3). The increasingly complex global relationships among suppliers, manufacturers, distributors, retailers, and consumers compound these pressures.

The implementation of new technology helps to offset these pressures. SCM applications, built on new technology platforms, have enhanced the ability of organizations to integrate their processes through collaborative information sharing and planning. These innovations include the proliferation of Web sites, the introduction of point-of-sale devices to acquire data, the growth of data manipulation tools for large-scale data optimization, and the growth of data-dissemination capabilities.

Information is replacing inventory. Supply chain capabilities are rapidly growing to manage external inventory that companies can't see and don't own. Companies that are adept at managing information are less likely to carry costly inventory. Companies that don't understand how this trend lets them avoid inventory carrying costs will fail. The competition will move from a model of company versus company to one of supply chain versus supply chain. Learning to exploit the current chain-fusion trend will permit companies to achieve considerable advantage over their less adept competitors.

Figure 9.3: SCM Investment Areas

Internet-Enabled SCM

Strategies and structures vary from company to company, but the goal remains the same. *SCM will be a focal point of business strategy during the next decade.* With so many product options—from forecasting and purchasing to warehousing and shipping—and with countless variations in SCM terminology used relating to various supply chain functions, corporate managers often struggle to improve their SCM infrastructures. In order to relieve the confusion, it is important to understand that SCM's basics are the same whether companies make PCs or conduct financial transactions.

Interenterprise Integration

Interenterprise integration is the ultimate goal of SCM. As Figure 9.4 illustrates, SCM is evolving from the current enterprise-centric models, such as Nabisco in the food industry, to more collaborative, partnership-oriented models, such as

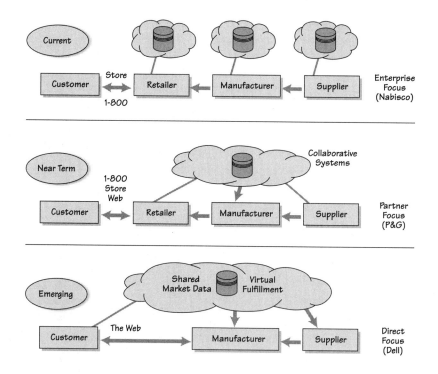

Figure 9.4: Three Supply Chain Strategies: (a) Enterprise Focus, (b) Partner Focus, (c) Direct Focus

Procter & Gamble's and Wal-Mart's continuous-replenishment model in the consumer packaged-goods industry. Leading-edge companies, such as Intel and Dell in the high-tech industry, have gone even further to create a streamlined supply chain model with mass-customization and customer-direct capabilities.

No company wants excess inventory. Much of the strategy behind inter-enterprise integration is focused on driving down inventory, production, and distribution costs. The basic economic reality, however, is that retail stores and distributors maximize their profits by the number of inventory turns. Inventory turns reflect the amount of goods sold. Inventory managers require frequent delivery of more product to replace sold stock—order cycles of less than 18 hours—whereas manufacturers maximize profits by longer production lead times—production cycles of many days or weeks. To manage the mismatch between the two, companies create stores of inventory in the supply chain, which is exactly the issue that manufacturers like Nabisco face.

Marketing promotions often drive supply chains. Historically, trading partners have engaged in various promotional pricing, purchasing, and diversion strategies in order to coerce one party or the other to maintain specific supply chain inventory levels. The supply chain retailers and distributors are closest to the point of product consumption by the consumer and, therefore, have access to the most accurate consumption data. When used in conjunction with the right replenishment optimization software, this data can provide the projected replenishment requirements of the supply chain *and* the production planning information so desperately needed by the manufacturers.

Today's customers are aware of their buying options, with the demands they place on suppliers often changing from order to order. In response to such an unpredictable customer order cycle, companies are looking to reduce excess or unnecessary inventory—deleting it entirely when using a zero-inventory model. Dell, for example, has had success using this strategy in its build-to-order scenario. The traditional method of forecasting future demand and developing a production plan based on forecasts no longer works in a service environment requiring shorter order-to-delivery cycles.

Collaborative and build-to-order direct supply chains seem to have magical effects because of the wonders of integration. It takes skilled managers to successfully engineer high-performance supply chains, ones that are built quickly, respond well, adapt well, and incorporate business intelligence. Thus, the three types of high-performance supply chains are responsive, adaptive, and intelligent.

Responsive supply chains quickly and accurately respond to customer needs. ATP (available to promise) is one important feature of their responsiveness.

Customer-oriented businesses need to know what product materials and production and distribution resources are available before they can promise a delivery date to the customer. ATP systems provide real-time integrated checks throughout the entire supply chain. ATP can help set realistic order-delivery expectations once the company has received the order and help companies perform against those expectations.

Adaptive supply chains can be rapidly reconfigured to adapt to changing consumer demand. They help companies to compete by accelerating the rate at which the companies identify and respond to changing business conditions and consumer requirements.

Intelligent supply chains are dynamic, not static, and are continuously fine-tuned to perform well. They are formed quickly as companies seek a slight edge over the performance of other chains. Adaptation implies that chains are formed and reformed in an attempt to strengthen the weak links in the chain.

Which supply chain type is your company trying to create in order to beat your competition? Improved service through SCM integration has become the Holy Grail for competitive advantage. Companies that are hard-pressed to outperform competitors on quality or price now attempt to gain an edge by delivering the right stuff, in the right amount, at the right time.

Evidence is mounting that inferior integration affects corporate performance. The lack of integration between supply chain planning and execution manifests itself in the following ways:

- Erratic customer service levels, from either too much or too little inventory

- No vision of future demand and its impact on production, owing to the production function's lacking confidence in marketing's forecast.

- Too many production changeovers, owing to the lack of agreement among customer service, distribution, and manufacturing on what products are required, when they're needed, and where

- Too many stockouts, from having inventory in the wrong place at the wrong time

A poorly integrated technology infrastructure presents the same problem to supply chain performance as it does to a company's internal performance. Poor systems integration mean reduced flexibility and cost control. A company's ultimate success depends on its ability to collect, organize, and analyze data and to disseminate this information throughout the supply chain in a timely, cost-effective way.

To facilitate integration among a company's supply chain participants, these partnering companies must deploy large-scale enterprise applications to address the chain's planning and execution needs. Collaborative planning applications use information to facilitate the delivery of the right products on time, to the correct location, and at the lowest cost.

SCM Planning and Execution

SCM is critically important to a successful e-business strategy. SCM is a business framework comprising multiple applications that can be divided into two application groups: supply chain planning (SCP) and supply chain execution (SCE).

- SCP applications integrate planning functions, such as demand forecasting, inventory simulation, distribution, transportation, and manufacturing planning and scheduling. Quality planning software improves forecast accuracy, optimizes production scheduling, reduces inventory and transportation costs, decreases order-cycle times, and improves customer service.

- SCE applications integrate execution functions, such as procurement, manufacturing, and distribution products throughout the value chain. Supply chain execution applications manage the flow of products through distribution centers and warehouses and help ensure that products are delivered to the right location, using the best transportation alternatives available.

Supply Chain Planning

SCP software modules can be grouped into the following general categories (see Figure 9.5). An *order-commitment,* or an *ATP system,* allows vendors to accurately quote delivery dates to customers by providing real-time, detailed visibility into the entire fulfillment cycle, from the availability of raw materials and inventory to production status and prioritization rules. Rather than relying on rule-of-thumb estimates, order commitment is connected to an iterative planning module to provide much higher order-promise accuracy.

Advanced scheduling and manufacturing planning modules provide detailed coordination of all manufacturing and supply efforts, based on individual customer orders. Scheduling is based on real-time analysis of changing constraints throughout the process, from equipment outages to supply interruptions. Scheduling is highly execution oriented and creates job schedules for managing both the manufacturing process and supplier logistics.

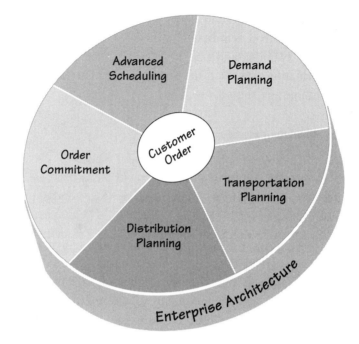

Figure 9.5: Elements of Supply Chain Planning

Demand-planning modules generate and consolidate demand forecasts from all business units within a large corporation. The demand-planning module supports a range of statistical tools and business forecasting techniques.

Distribution-planning functions create operating plans for a company's logistics managers. Distribution planning is integrated with the demand- and manufacturing-planning modules to provide a complete model of the supply chain and the operating plan for order fulfillment. This module also addresses customer-specified requirements.

Transportation planning facilitates resource allocation and execution to ensure that materials and finished goods are delivered at the right time, to the right place, at a minimal cost. This includes inbound and outbound, and intra- and intercompany movement of materials and products. This module analyzes such variables as loading dock space, trailer availability, load consolidation, and the best mix of available transportation modes and common carriers.

Supply chain planning modules help companies make better operating decisions. For example, SCP can help determine how much of a given product to manufacture in a certain time period, at what levels raw-material and finished-goods inventories should be maintained, at which locations to store finished goods, and what transportation mode to use for product delivery. Most of the data that SCP applications use to make the calculations is provided by the company's resource (ERP) backbone. However, many ERP and supply chain projects are not integrated, resulting in less than optimal performance and cost savings.

Today, as they cope with new customer demands, organizations require a certain flexibility across the supply chain that only a tightly integrated combination of planning modules can provide. Flexible SCP applications must be able to evaluate multiple planning strategies, such as

- *Profitable to promise:* Should I take the customer's order at this time?

- *Available to promise:* Is the inventory I need available to fulfill the order?

- *Capable to promise:* Does our manufacturing capacity allow for us to make an order commitment?

For example, when a priority customer places or changes an order on short notice, preference issues, such as color, size, style, and quantity, can have a widespread supply chain impact. Pricing may be affected by a change in product availability. Manufacturing may receive new production requirements and have to change job sequencing. Procurement may need to order new stocks of raw materials, which in turn affects suppliers. A transportation partner may need to have trucks available on a specified day.

SCP meets these needs by making the necessary adjustments to production and distribution plans. In addition, the applications allow information to be shared so that everyone is given the same information. This sharing is important, as many organizations lack one common information source. In such cases, manufacturing may have a production schedule that is not coordinated with marketing's promotions schedule or with the transportation department's shipping schedule. Without a common plan and information source, none of these departments is aware of the others' plans, making it impossible to efficiently coordinate activities.

Supply Chain Execution: e-Fulfillment

Focusing strictly on planning and managing inventory levels is not enough. Supply chain execution—the process of fulfilling customer-specific needs for goods and value-added services in a timely, efficient, cost-effective manner—is a key differentiator in increasingly competitive markets.

Several dot-coms in the furniture distribution business—Furniture.com, Living.com, HomePoint.com and GoodHome.com—underestimated the importance of fulfillment and are either struggling or have gone out of business. On its surface, the business appears to be an attractive one: Home furnishings are known for their high profit margins. But the truth is that home furnishing is a grueling business, one fraught with warehousing headaches, transportation complications, and increasing competition. For example, FedEx doesn't deliver large items, such as couches or cabinets, so furniture companies must pay expensive shipping fees to deliver large products by truck. The bulkier items also eat up valuable warehouse space. And running those operations on the Web adds multiple layers of complexity: dealing with servers, congestion, and customer service.

The economics of online furniture distribution are very complex. In its quest to drive customers to its site, for example, Furniture.com offered free delivery: Lamps, rugs, or other smaller items could be shipped through UPS, but larger pieces had to be moved by truck at exorbitant expense. According to a former employee, "There were many cases when we would get an order for a $200 end table and then spend $300 to ship it. When we started, we didn't anticipate how difficult the shipping was going to be. We never could figure it out."[9] Publicly, the company has said that delivery costs have equaled a third of sales, but the figure is estimated to be closer to 50 percent.

To keep customers happy, companies—both offline and online—must deliver as promised. Current trends show that companies need better access to detailed execution information in order to coordinate supply chain tasks. To manage sophisticated outsourcing arrangements, companies are turning to supply chain execution applications to provide fulfillment-pipeline visibility and to control orders, inventory, and assets. The market for supply chain execution applications is growing as a result of two major factors.

- Businesses that have maximized their internal efficiency are now working to achieve greater operational efficiencies in their relationships with supply chain partners.

- As companies look to achieve greater operational efficiency in their distribution relationships, they realize that planning applications aim for the ideal solution. To work in the real world, planning must have continuous access to transaction data.

Execution applications focus on the effective management of warehouse and transportation operations and their integration with planning systems and other enterprise software applications. Supply chain execution applications automate the order planning, production, replenishment, and distribution (see Figure 9.6) functions.

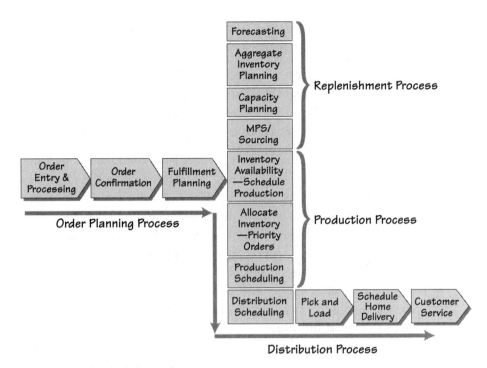

Figure 9.6: Supply Chain Execution

- *Order planning.* With rising customer expectations and short fulfillment deadlines, effective execution planning that breaks artificial boundaries and bridges the chasm between planning and execution is critical. The objective is to select the plan that best meets the desired customer service levels with respect to transportation and manufacturing constraints. Increasingly, firms have to plan backward from customer priorities and fulfillment deadlines. This implies that in order to generate a feasible plan, fulfillment planning must consider all supply chain constraints simultaneously, including transportation limitations, such as truck capacity and weight; alternative modes; and availability of downstream resources, such as loading docks.[10]

- *Production.* With the advent of modular designs, production functions are increasingly performed at dedicated warehouses, where workers perform light subassembly and sequencing, kitting, merging, packaging, and labeling work for specific products. The timing of final-product assembly drives the production plan for the product's subassemblies. Starting with the master production schedule for the finished product, a manufacturing resource planning system expands this schedule to derive when, where, and in what quantities various subassemblies are required to make each product.

- *Replenishment.* Production also includes component-replenishment strategies that minimize the amount of inventory in the pipeline and coordinate product handoffs among the various parties involved. Timely replenishment of warehouses is critical because customers no longer tolerate out-of-stock situations.

- *Distribution management.* Once a product is manufactured or picked, it is then distributed. Distribution management encompasses the entire process of transporting goods from manufacturers to distribution centers to the end customer. Recent innovations in distribution management have resulted in its integration with transportation planning and scheduling. Transportation planning coordinates product movement throughout the life cycle of the shipment and provides customers with the ability to track their shipments across a network of multimodal transportation. Distribution management applications give users easy access to shipping, tracking, and delivery data and also support the complex, ever-changing requirements of international trade, with its document generation and regulatory compliance features.

- *Reverse distribution or reverse logistics.* Rapid obsolescence and generous warranties have sparked a growing trend of customers' returning products. Damark International, a mail-order catalog firm offering products in computers, home office, consumer electronics, home decor, home improvements, and sports/fitness stated that in 1997, its merchandise returns from customers were approximately 14.1 percent of gross product sales.[11] This figure reflects the industry return rate. Reverse logistics means that because of customer dissatisfaction, items must be shipped, accounted for, and returned to the manufacturer or disposed of. Reverse logistics encompasses not only damaged or returned goods but also products designed for remanufacture, hazardous material, and reusable packaging.

e–Supply Chain Fusion

How do you create tightly woven supply chains? How do you migrate from existing, nonintegrated supply chain models to more effective, integrated models? Before we address the process of e–supply chain fusion, remember that many firms struggle when implementing an integrated supply chain strategy, because they must displace their existing supply chains, which are artifacts of the past.

Legacy supply chains are clogged with unnecessary steps and redundant stockpiles.[12] For instance, a typical box of breakfast cereal spends an incredible 104 days getting from the factory to the supermarket, weaving its way through an unbelievable maze of wholesalers, distributors, brokers, and consolidators, each of which has a warehouse.[13] Streamlining inefficient supply chains means changing the way the participating companies interact and could greatly affect leadership positions at some, or all, of the companies involved.

Diagnosing Root Causes of Supply Chain Problems

Before creating its e–supply chain architecture, a company must first diagnose the problems that prevent collaborative work. An example of an e–supply chain architecture is shown in Figure 9.7. The old axiom "If you don't understand the problem, it's hard to fix it" is true here. Fixing any business problem requires distinguishing an underlying structural issue from its symptoms. The following are typical supply chain issues:

- A lack of knowledge about the end-to-end demand planning function. This often results in an unstable demand quantity that changes frequently in the production schedule and can lead to expedited transfers and shipments.

- Inconsistent or out-of-date data, owing to a lack of integration with a company's ERP approach. This can result in reactive fire-fighting decisions based on inadequate information or poor decision-support tools.

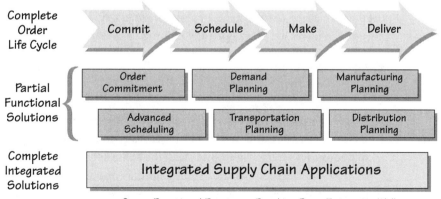

Figure 9.7: An Application View of the Supply Chain

• A lack of process integration across partners. Retailers are demanding more sophisticated purchasing, inventory management, and merchandising tools that enable them to distribute and to manage goods efficiently. Inventory management has become more complicated as retailers, distributors, and customers seek to reduce costs and to improve margins while replenishing inventory on a just-in-time basis. But until SCM is in place, it is difficult to execute an inventory management plan well.

Effective SCM deployment requires companies to make structural supply chain changes, as existing supply chain strategies are sadly outdated in an era when unnecessary inventories and costs must be eliminated. Historically, SCM applications have been mainly legacy applications. These legacy applications have been host-centric systems that operate on mainframe computers. These systems, developed and modified internally over many years or licensed from third-party vendors, represent considerable investments. However, they no longer have the flexibility to support diverse and changing operations within a company's business; nor can they respond effectively to changing technological innovation. Despite these limitations, many host-centric systems are still widely deployed, owing to their strengths in their targeted segments and to preserve significant hardware and software investments.

This situation is changing with the advent of better supply chain frameworks. Some companies, such as I2 Technologies and Manugistics, are creating solutions that provide integrated SCM functionality. These solutions are adept at handling large volumes of transactions, possess a high degree of reliability, can rapidly capture and analyze data, and can distribute information throughout geographically dispersed parts of the enterprise. Moreover, these solutions support the specialized requirements of global business, such as transportation planning and the increased prevalence of e-commerce.

Fixing the Root Cause

The evolution of supply chain fusion involves four stages.

1. *Enable information sharing.* This stage requires a solid communication process. For instance, more and more retailers are restructuring existing operations so that consumers interact effectively with the entire enterprise from a single store or Web site. Decision makers throughout the enterprise need to have a common base of readily available sales and inventory information, and in-store personnel need the ability to more rapidly respond to consumers' needs.

2. *Create joint performance measurement systems and collaborative planning processes.* Key challenges include creating performance measurements and developing a clear understanding of the costs and benefits involved in supply chain integration. We've seen partnerships and initiatives fail because they didn't address these issues. A procedure must be established for settling risk and achieving shared information.

3. *Realign work and collaborate fiercely.* In other words, what you used to do, I do now; and what you used to decide, I now decide for you.

4. *Redesign products and processes so that work becomes easier or more efficient.* A major challenge is including the entire supply chain in your interenterprise process reengineering efforts.

The majority of companies are in stage 1, the information-sharing stage, reflecting e-business's current state of the art. However, many forward-thinking companies are already using newer technologies to connect themselves. Once they understand the components of the supply chain, they'll use these technologies to create tightly coupled relationships and, at the same time, learn to create, use, and discard loosely coupled ones.

The coordination and integration of these information and work flows—within and across companies—form the catalyst for modern business. Managing these flows is a complex task because it involves coordination across multiple organizations within one company or many companies or with industries. In the past few years, the benefits from successfully coordinating and integrating information and work flows have attracted interest among managers, consultants, and researchers in academia and industry.

Management Issues in e–Supply Chain Fusion

The business world's understanding of SCM's management challenges is still quite primitive except in such companies as Dell, P&G, and Wal-Mart and in such industries as semiconductors, PCs, and peripherals. But the core concepts of using SCM to manage and to integrate the flow of products and services are only now beginning to invade corporate boardrooms. *Does your board and top management understand the SCM's benefits and issues?*

SCM decisions are really business design decisions. With customer satisfaction at stake, SCM is quickly becoming an executive and boardroom issue, not a technical, functional, or storeroom issue. Senior management is being asked to make complex strategic decisions in order to create integrated SCM solutions.

Increasingly, CEOs, CFOs, and line-of-business managers are being asked to make technical decisions that can help revolutionize their businesses. Where do they start? To make an effective supply chain design, you need to address the following four fundamental areas.

Determining the Right e-Supply Chain Structure

To meet customers' demands, keeping a large finished-goods inventory is an expensive approach to ensuring that your company can meet customer demand. What happens when the market demands something different from what you have stockpiled? The now obsolete product becomes a wasted investment. Companies must use supply chain planning to anticipate demand conditions and to act, not react, accordingly.

For example, in the computer supply chain, the consumer has a specific need for one of a thousand possible configurations of processors, hard drives, and peripherals. One manufacturer, Compaq, reacts by tying up millions of dollars to build an inventory of premade models, which the customer may not want, whereas another manufacturer, such as Dell, with its responsive supply chain, can quickly assemble every customer's order. Which manufacturer do you think pleases its customers *and* saves money?

In a classic article entitled "What Is the Right Supply Chain for Your Product," Marshall Fisher wrote: "Before devising a supply chain, consider the nature of the demand for your products," because "functional products require an efficient process; innovative products, a responsive process."[14]

Different strategic goals motivate companies to adopt different supply chain structures. Configuring the supply chain with a strategic view restrains the tendency to focus only on cost. A low-cost distribution network can be quite different from one designed for lead-time responsiveness. While analyzing strategies, make sure that the entire team understands and agrees on how to handle demand and capacity planning, strategic scheduling, and performance measurement.

The objective of any supply chain design is to please the customer and to make money. It's often easy to lose sight of the fact that the supply chain exists only to support a revenue stream. Businesses ought to focus their efforts on growing their revenue streams and not on reengineering the costs out of business processes.

Enabling Effective Differentiation Capabilities

Most profitable strategies are built on competitive differentiation, offering customers something unique that the competition doesn't have. But most companies, in an effort to differentiate themselves, focus their energy on only their products or services. *Supply chain strategies offer companies another opportunity to differentiate themselves.*

For example, build-to-order (BTO) business models are used to support delivery of the mass-customization value proposition. The basic goal of the build-to-order model is to trigger the entire buy-make-ship cycle only when a clear demand signal is sent by a specific customer. BTO provides vendors and suppliers with multiple avenues of differentiation by adjusting certain specific process variables, such as

- The velocity of moving goods throughout the supply chain

- Exposure to inventory carrying and depreciation costs

- Higher volatility in demand

- Transitions through product cycles

Supply chain differentiation makes even more sense when you consider the fact that most companies don't have just one supply chain but rather multiple supply chains running concurrently. Large companies, such as 3M, have more than 30 supply chain configurations. In such settings, differentiated policies that match performance standards to the cost and cycle-time realities of various products offer one of the most effective means for improving performance.

Facilitating Effective Order-Fulfillment Capabilities

Accurate order fulfillment is challenging and offers a great opportunity for reducing costs and improving customer service simultaneously. For example, marketing and production forecasting reduces errors that are often caused by multiple groups' developing forecasts independently. The various functional groups involved in forecasting have different business priorities and may have conflicting objectives. The classic example is the sales department that pads its forecast to ensure availability of a product, to the detriment of those trying to control inventory. Unless these conflicts are resolved, the supply chain can be pulled between two extremes, resulting in increased cost and poor customer service.

A precursor to effective fulfillment is order promising, which gives companies the ability to quote delivery dates to customers. The goal is to provide detailed visibility into the entire fulfillment cycle, from the availability of raw materials and inventory to production status and prioritization rules. Rather than relying on rule-of-thumb estimates, companies need to link into planning modules that provide higher order-promise accuracy. By reducing opportunities for errors, companies can save valuable time and money.

A tightly integrated chain is critical to successful order fulfillment. Well-run supply chains are built on the premise that order forecasts are merely plans—plans that will inevitably be wrong. Effectively run supply chains configure the chain to respond to orders. Planning establishes the level of resources—production capacity, labor, raw materials—required for a given time period. The effective deployment of these resources occurs when the chain responds to the pull of real orders, not the push of the plan.

Determining the Right Infrastructure Capabilities

Creating a real-time SCM infrastructure is a daunting and ongoing issue and quite often, a point of failure, for several reasons. The chief reason is that the planning, selection, and implementation of SCM solutions is becoming more complex as the pace of technological change accelerates and the number of a company's partners increases. SCM investments must be made tactically, while also bearing in mind the existing ERP and legacy infrastructure. Large companies invest in ERP systems to integrate such functions as purchasing, inventory management, production scheduling, and finance within the enterprise. The next step is to leverage these ERP investments to integrate the functions and information of multiple enterprises in real time.

SCM applications are in a continual state of flux. New technologies are fundamentally redefining the realm of what is technologically possible. Today, the Web and retail bar code readers, allow a wide variety of companies to track consumer demand. With point-of-sale scanners, information is captured accurately and cheaply and can be provided throughout the supply chain on a real-time basis at a reasonable cost. Similarly, on the distribution side, logistics providers have leveraged information technology to enhance their management capability. Predicting what new capabilities technology will provide is key to making solid investment decisions.

The SCM solutions market is in its infancy. In the early 1990s, software dedicated to SCM barely existed. Today, with SCM recognized as an important key to competitive advantage, the industry has boomed, and hundreds of software and technology suppliers are now competing. As more and more companies initiate internal and external supply chain improvement efforts, the industry is expected to explode in the coming decade. However, in this boom period, separating hype from true capability can be difficult. *Managers must be discerning.*

The Continuing Evolution of e–Supply Chains

As we enter the new millennium, a key issue for most managers is the nature of the supply chain in the coming decade. Several examples offer insight into the various ways modern supply chains are evolving.

Traditional supply chains, also called make-to-stock models, are particularly useful in mass-production environments. Production quantities and dates are provided by a sales forecast, with no concern for individual customer requirements. Instead, customers receive shipments from the finished-goods inventory. This means that the irregular demand flow resulting from various customer orders can be smoothed, produced, and warehoused downstream.

Some examples of make-to-stock users are Coca-Cola, Procter & Gamble, and General Mills. Typically, the resource utilization with make-to-stock models is modest, owing to a number of factors: inefficient parts purchasing, product overdesign, poor plant utilization, lengthy inventory pipelines, and lack of streamlined logistics.

Companies are now attempting to mitigate the problems associated with make-to-stock by using readily available process information to better coordinate the end-to-end supply chain. A more recent make-to-stock innovation is postponement, which configures the finished product to the distribution channel. For example, Hewlett-Packard configures its printers for each customer's order by adding the specific type of power supply, power cord, appropriate language instruction manual, and other materials to the box before shipment. However, some products have destination-driven features—particularly those for international customers—that are best handled in the distribution channel, not in production.

New methods, such as efficient consumer response (ECR), quick response (QR), or continuous replenishment have been introduced in the consumer-packaged goods industry, creating a customer-demand pull system that stretches across several companies. These just-in-time, or continuous-replenishment, methods vary in their levels of system integration, but all perform interorganizational boundary spanning aimed at coordinating activities in an integrated manner.

As the world moves from mass production to mass customization, supply chain requirements change. Build-to-order supply chains that are more suitable for the mass-customization world are emerging. Substituting inventory with information is another factor driving BTO supply chain innovation. This is especially true in the high-tech industry, in which components change continually, making product warehousing foolish. Firms want to be as flexible as possible so they can move components in and out of their warehouses quickly.

Integrated Make-to-Stock: Starbucks

A high-performance supply chain best achieves corporate objectives by balancing supply against demand. Seattle-based Starbucks Coffee[15] is one company that has succeeded at integrating the demand and supply sides to provide true end-to-end integration.

Starbucks's strategy is to be the most recognized and respected coffee brand in the world. Growth is part of that strategy, and technology is key to supporting growth. For instance, to determine the best locations for new stores, Starbucks uses customized real estate software. And to calculate how many green-aproned staffers are needed to serve coffee addicts, the company uses point-of-sale data for efficient labor scheduling. But the best use of technology occurs in Starbucks's supply chain.

Starbucks's supply chain supports three channels: specialty, direct response, and retail or joint ventures. The specialty channel supports airlines, such as United Airlines, and retail stores, including Nordstrom's. These specialty accounts don't fall under retail business unit operations. The direct-response channel serves customers through direct mail. Joint ventures provide opportunities to leverage the company's brand into innovative products. Recent joint ventures include Dreyer's Grand Ice Cream and Pepsi-Cola. These joint ventures create different supply chain opportunities. Starbucks created a centralized supply chain operations organization that supports each of these channels instead of running three separate business units.[16] The company recognized significant leverage in operating the supply chain operation in this way.

Starbucks is vertically integrated via the control of coffee sourcing, roasting, packaging, and distribution through company-owned retail stores (see Figure 9.8). The company uses automated manufacturing systems (Oracle GEMMS) to accomplish distribution planning and MRP. This helps determine its long-term buying requirements for coffee beans for roasting and packaging. Starbucks manufactures an estimated 85 million pounds of coffee a year at its facilities.

Dealing with multiple channels of distribution for similar products requires timely and accurate reporting of inventory, allocation capabilities, and maintenance

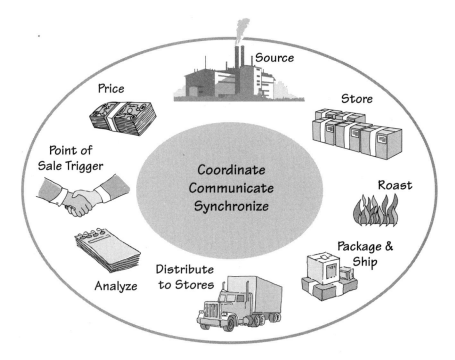

Figure 9.8: Starbucks's Vertically Integrated Supply Chain

of dynamic safety stock. To manage resource allocation, the company uploads nightly sales and inventory information from the stores to the Seattle headquarters. Instead of independent demand for finished goods—whole-bean coffee and coffee beverages—Starbucks is faced with an exploding sales forecast through a dependent component demand for its proprietary coffee extract and other coffee products. The sourcing network for these products can include as many as nine levels from grower to consumer.

The benefits of SCM to Starbucks include better allocation of critical resources, reduced overhead and material costs, improved quality, faster throughput, control of the complete material flow in the production process, and high-performance planning and integrated procurement, enabling faster time to market. Clearly, the objective of SCM at Starbucks is asset profitability, or putting the least money in to get the most profit out. Achieving this objective requires a commitment to invest in systems, people, and talent ahead of the growth curve. Starbucks's supply chain partners are challenged at every step. Starbucks envisions its role as providing the best tools to support the success of its partners while continuing to enhance the Starbucks experience.

Continuous Replenishment: The CVS Pharmacy–McKesson Demand Chain

CVS is a leading drug retail chain growing so rapidly that it may soon surpass Walgreens for the number-one slot. In recent years, CVS has made some significant drug chain acquisitions, such as Revco, to provide itself with excellent locations in new markets. The company converted these acquisitions to its own name and stocked them with CVS products. Figure 9.9 shows the entire CVS supply chain.

McKesson occupies the critical position in the CVS supply chain. Founded in 1833, McKesson is the largest U.S. distributor of pharmaceuticals, healthcare

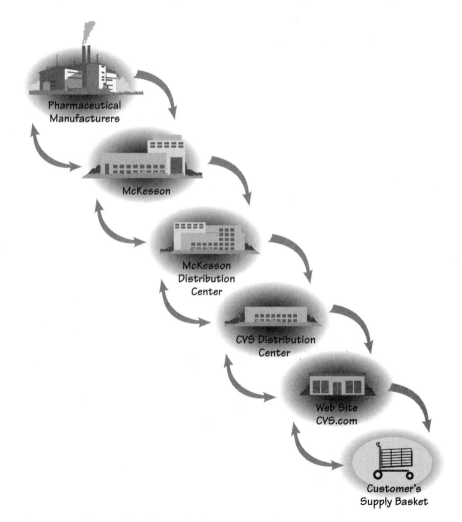

Figure 9.9: The Tightly Integrated Pharmaceutical Supply Chain

products, and medical/surgical supplies, with annual sales in excess of $20 billion. McKesson supplies pharmaceuticals and healthcare products to its roughly 35,000 customers and processes about 60,000 orders containing 1.6 million order lines daily. Customers include hospitals, independent pharmacies, chain drug stores, food stores, clinics, nursing homes, government facilities, physician groups, HMOs, and surgical centers. McKesson depends on e-commerce. Roughly 80 percent of all goods purchased by McKesson are ordered through EDI. Customers send virtually all orders in electronic form, using everything from handheld scanners to mainframe computers. In addition, all major movements of funds, including customer remittances and payroll, are handled through electronic fund transfers. Payments to larger suppliers are also handled in this manner.

In order to understand healthcare supply chains, you need to first understand the industry structure. Over the years, the drug distribution channel has experienced dramatic consolidation, with larger players purchasing smaller ones to complement their geographic and product positioning. In 10 years, the number of drug wholesalers has declined from 180 to less than 50.[17] As a result, the top five competitors account for 57 percent of the market. The chain drug stores are the largest customer segment of wholesalers. This sector has witnessed a number of consolidations, including the combination of CVS with Revco, and Thrift with Eckert Drugs. These chain stores continue to gain market share from independents.

Being in the midst of it all puts McKesson in a great position. Moreover, customers, including CVS, benefit from this paradigm shift by having the convenience of a single source of supply for a full line of pharmaceutical products, lower inventory costs, more timely and efficient delivery, and improved purchasing and inventory information. Better integration with McKesson is a key strategic move for CVS, as management sees significant potential for improving sales and margins through its enhanced pricing and promotional forecasting systems. Supply chain integration helps the retailer move from pull to push promotions by allowing category managers to plan promotions more effectively, using item history taken from historical point-of-sale data on a store-by-store basis. The integration with McKesson will substantially reduce the amount of time needed to plan and to stock inventory for individual promotions.

A major business objective in the CVS-McKesson chain is to improve performance through better supply chain integration. This requires much closer cooperation between McKesson and CVS, with McKesson even taking responsibility for stock levels. McKesson monitors CVS's store-level consumption and replenishes the inventory to meet the agreed-on service levels—true supply chain integration. This cooperative process between supplier and customer can be achieved only through seamless interenterprise process integration and sophisticated applications that link the customer directly to the supplier's production department.

What we learn from the McKesson-CVS relationship is that retail SCM is about interenterprise process integration. The objectives of interenterprise integration are improved customer responsiveness, strengthened supply chain partnerships, enhanced organizational flexibility, and improved decision-making capabilities. The CVS example also illustrates that to succeed in today's customer-dominated environment, companies must apply the same approach to intercorporate processes that they do to processes that reside within the company's own boundaries.

Build-to-Order: Intel, Solectron, and Ingram Micro

Ingram's core strength in logistics and order management and Solectron's efficient high-volume manufacturing process lets the two companies provide build-to-order (BTO) assembly services for PCs, servers, and peripherals. Why is business so excited about the BTO approach? In a traditional make-to-stock model, the demand plan is usually established and its implications embodied in a demand forecast. Supply plans are implemented to match the profile of the demand forecast while meeting the customer service targets, such as the order-fill rate. Revenue is a given, so only costs are minimized. Because demand is known, the focus is more on cost reduction than on profitability or market share growth. Changes in demand stemming from unforeseen circumstances often cause severe disruptions to the demand plan, resulting in lost sales, reduced market share, and unprofitable operations.

The concept behind BTO is matching supply with demand in real time. As customer demand becomes unpredictable, make-to-stock demand forecasting scenarios become unrealistic. In order to be effective, companies must integrate their supply plans with demand plans to best achieve corporate goals and maximized profitability. Enter BTO.

In the Ingram-Solectron supply chain (see Figure 9.10), Ingram receives a PC order from one of its reseller customers. The order is transferred electronically to one of nine worldwide manufacturing locations owned by either Solectron or Ingram. The PC is produced to specification at the manufacturing facility—probably married at some point with the associated peripherals—and drop-shipped to either the reseller or the end user customer. The entire process takes less than 7 days.

Intel, an Ingram-Solectron supplier, is at the heart of the PC value chain. Hundreds of raw-material suppliers, component manufacturers, assemblers, and

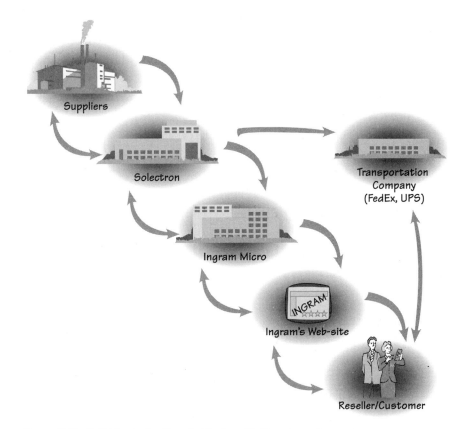

Figure 9.10: Build-to-Order Supply Chain with Zero Inventory

resellers depend on its continued success. In the past, Intel's success was clearly attributable to its relentless product innovation. Lately, however, Intel's supply chain practices with both suppliers and customers have taken a much more conspicuous role in the PC value chain.

Customers have begun to demand just-in-time delivery. This trend is forcing PC makers to aggressively eliminate slack and excess inventory from the supply chain. Making PCs to order eliminates unwanted stockpiles of components and finished product. But it also requires all participants in the PC supply chain—including Intel—to coordinate and to integrate supply levels, manufacturing capacity, inventory, and logistics data.

The enemy of an efficient supply chain is excess inventory, and in the fast-changing PC market, almost any inventory seems like too much. A PC maker's worst nightmare is an overstock of yesterday's PC languishing on warehouse shelves. Such situations force PC makers to sell their dated models at discount prices and to forfeit profits. Aiming to accelerate delivery speed while reducing inventory and costs in the PC supply chain, Intel established an extranet to communicate real-time inventory levels and demand to suppliers and customers. Intel has also implemented an ERP system to improve inventory control, product delivery, and business integration.

The Ingram-Solectron-reseller supply chain should benefit all parties involved, as it allows for time and cost savings by eliminating the associated handling costs, reducing shipping costs. It improves inventory management through the use of a more efficient pull-driven production strategy. Perhaps more important, it should help further drive industry consolidation, particularly within the distribution segment.

A Roadmap for Managers

SCM is a complex subject involving the flow of goods from upstream suppliers to manufacturers, distributors, and end customers. SCM involves many disciplines, from procurement and supplier management to multisite manufacturing, customer management, order processing, distribution planning, forecasting, demand management, warehousing, transportation, and managing final points of sale. Integrating all this is not easy; nor can it be executed quickly.

It's highly likely that, at this very moment, your company is either considering or attempting to design and implement a multicompany supply chain. Your company recognizes SCM's importance in providing the firm with greater control over order fulfillment processes, which is the primary path to generating customer loyalty and increasing market share. Following are key SCM questions that any major company should consider:

- *How do we define our interenterprise supply chain problem and scope of the issues involved? What is our supply chain, where is it broken, and how do we fix it?*

- *How do we make a business case for the reengineering of an interenterprise process that no one owns or fully understands?*

- *Do we start with a clean-slate approach or with an incremental-improvement approach?*

- *Should we build or buy? Which vendors and technologies should we consider? Should we consider best-of-breed applications or a single-vendor, integrated solution?*

- *What will the impact of each choice be on our legacy systems? How can we avoid the redundancy and a high degree of variability resulting from the lack of integration of various legacy systems along the supply chain?*

What is the SCM focus in your company? Are you forging an effective one-of-a-kind e–supply chain with your customers, distributors, suppliers, and outsourcing partners? Each company must cope with a confusing array of demands and choices when it develops a vision for the optimal supply chain. What can companies do today to prepare for the SCM world of the future? The following eight steps are crucial to turning tomorrow's promise into today's reality.

1. *Clarify your supply chain goals.* Companies must examine their SCM strategies as essential elements of their overall business designs. Companies must understand the extent to which their integrated sourcing, production, and distribution capabilities can be adjusted to drive superior value and customer satisfaction. If the value a company can provide is in production, the firm may choose to develop an operations-focused supply chain. If the value it can provide is in another area, the brand management/outsourced supply chain model may be more appropriate.

2. *Conduct a supply chain readiness audit.* Conducting a readiness diagnostic is the logical first step in implementing an SCM solution. The purpose of this assessment is to provide a company-specific roadmap for supply chain development. In it, your company must answer the following questions: Are you ready for the consumer demands, globalization, and mergers and acquisitions? What are you doing to promote supply chain coordination within the firm and with external partners? Are your performance metrics up to date? How do you compare with others inside and outside your industry?

3. *Develop a business case.* CEOs and boards of most companies remain unconvinced that an integrated supply chain approach will pay hard-dollar dividends. Making the business case for supply chain integration thus becomes a high priority for managers. The case must be made on both the strategic and practical levels, combining a clear sense of direction with detailed examples of the gains in service and cost to be derived from tighter integration.

4. *Establish a supply chain coordination unit.* Establish a hard-hitting but thinly staffed SCM team in your company. The objectives will be to provide corporate leadership in the analysis, design, and implementation of service and cost-effective solutions and to take them to new levels across the organization

and with the company's external partners. This team functions as a group of internal consultants, with top-management sponsors, to lower costs and to raise customer satisfaction. The team's participants must be trained in all aspects of the supply chain management: from procurement through manufacturing to customer service; the latest decision support tools; the best ways to establish win-win relationships with partners; and the facilitation techniques essential to collaborative teamwork.

5. *Begin supplier integration.* A supply chain isn't any good if you're the only one in it. It's imperative that you convince, cajole, even threaten your upstream suppliers and downstream distributors/customers into working with you. Persuade your external partners to plan now for Internet-driven supply chains. You may think that your industry isn't ready yet. If so, either you're missing key initiatives of which your competitors are already taking advantage, or you're sitting on a great opportunity to be first in your field. Have your marketing group talk to your supply chain participants to see how Internet orders can help drive distribution efficiencies.

6. *Develop a performance scorecard.* Don't rush into implementation without understanding supply chain performance measures. Work with your chosen suppliers to come to a common understanding of what the supply chain performance measures should be and what performance-related incentives and penalties should be implemented. Master the delicate balance between metrics, tactics, and strategy in a supply chain.

7. *Educate, educate, educate.* Invest in education and reorientation for your employees, vendors, and other members of the supply chain on the practices needed to optimize business processes. No person, team, process, or company ever knows enough. Make a company-wide commitment to creating and managing a more complex organization capable of tackling global business issues. Organizations must invest in ongoing training, mentoring, education, and feedback systems to keep their people current with the latest and best practices available.

8. *Learn to manage failure.* According to the law of averages, many supply chain projects are destined to fail in the coming decade. Many project failures are blamed on not involving users and on vendors' promising more than they can deliver. Whatever the reason, managers must become adept at identifying problems early on before they put the project at risk. The first step to turning any problem around is to admit that the project could be in trouble. This is

always simple in theory but difficult to practice, as egos, pride, and careers are often at stake. But the facts must be faced. Failure management can be extremely complex in an interenterprise setting.

Memo to the CEO

SCM is more than the latest craze; it's the new way to do business. Supply chain excellence requires an effective strategy, sustained management commitment, and changes in a company's attitude, culture, and organizational structure. Often, these actions must be undertaken simultaneously, making the supply chain implementation even more difficult. The participants must remember throughout the implementation process that the ability to integrate and to deploy SCM solutions is critical to remaining competitive.

However, the bewildering rate of technological change perplexes most managers, hindering supply chain initiatives. As a result, manufacturers, distributors, retailers, and consumers everywhere are reflecting on their roles within the supply chain and what changes to it would mean for them. Technology is not the only process variable that is changing. Competitive pressures, regulatory issues, pricing, and promotions, as well as causal factors ranging from demand origination to channel constraints, all contribute to a dynamic supply chain environment.

Today, we're seeing only the tip of the iceberg of how technology and other variables are affecting the structure of the supply chain process. Traditional supply chains have undergone a metamorphosis in the past decade in an effort to improve their competitive positioning through lower costs and accelerated time to market. Many companies have reexamined and restructured the way in which their products are designed, manufactured, warehoused, transported, and sold. As these changes occur, the old paradigm of company-versus-company competition is becoming less relevant, and success is measured in terms of supply chain versus supply chain.

Company efforts to streamline their supply chains are driven by several trends: ongoing e-commerce advancements, the globalization of the economy, the acceleration of corporate outsourcing, and the standardization of enterprise applications. The convergence of these trends is causing several changes to occur in the underlying structure of the traditional supply chain.

- Sales are becoming customer driven, as opposed to vendor driven, as demand generation shifts from push to pull models, such as build-to-order. These strategies require significantly less inventory to be carried within the supply chain. Although reductions in inventory levels are causing reactions at a number of component and manufacturing companies, reduced inventory levels should, in the long run, lead to lower pricing, a more stable product supply, and an eventual reduction in the severity of the traditional "boom-bust" cycles of many industries.

• Consolidation is accelerating within each segment of the technology supply chain to reduce the number of suppliers with which they interact and to establish a few key strategic supplier-partner relationships.

• As companies work to improve their competitive positioning, they're broadening the range of services they offer. Similar services are now offered at various points in the supply chain. Although this overlap of service offerings creates the potential for tension between supply chain segments, it also creates the opportunity for a number of interesting channel partnerships and mergers over the next few years.

• The dynamics of transferring information between trading partners have been irrevocably changed. As a result, companies must pay close attention to the world of interenterprise computing for new technological offerings, such as XML, as the next foundation for growth.

Supply chain efficiency will be one of the competitive battlegrounds for a wide range of companies over the next several years. Major changes in the business environment are already under way, and progressive managers must act now to ensure that they are preparing winning supply chain strategies as their firms enter the twenty-first century.

CHAPTER TEN

Demystifying e-Procurement: Buy-Side, Sell-Side, Net Markets, and Trading Exchanges

What to Expect

Inefficient and maverick buying habits, redundant business processes, and the absence of strategic sourcing are symptoms of poor procurement practices. For today's industrial-age companies to become tomorrow's e-business leaders, their current procurement practices must change. As with any successful e-business effort, efficient procurement strategies integrate a company's business work flow with a robust application infrastructure. Effective procurement strategies reduce the amount of paperwork a firm's employees must complete and lets them focus on their job instead.

The spread of e-commerce is changing the procurement landscape. The rise of Internet trading exchanges (ITE) represents one of the most exciting market developments of recent years. These exchanges alter the process by which raw materials and supplies are procured and supply chains are integrated. Businesses are using exchanges to automate and streamline their requisition, approval, fulfillment, and payment work flows.

This chapter discusses the new wave of e-procurement applications being deployed by companies seeking to radically improve their procurement processes. It explains the evolution of e-procurement practices from simple buy-side solutions to complex supplier/buyer marketplaces. The chapter discusses key e-procurement concepts, such as the ITEs and their relationship to a company's business processes and technology. The chapter also provides an easy-to-follow e-procurement roadmap to assist managers on their journey to the procurement model of the future.

The top 2,000 U.S. corporations purchase more than $500 billion of nonproduction goods annually. A typical company spends more than 5 percent to 10 percent of its revenue on office equipment, supplies, software, computers, and other so-called nonproduction goods. Many company purchase orders are for less than $500 worth of merchandise, a large percentage of which is now bought off contract or outside of the company's preferred buying channels. As a result, the level of purchase detail available for negotiating better supplier contracts is not available.

Among the Big Three automakers—Ford, GM, and DaimlerChrysler—transactions related to the buying and selling of car components is valued at roughly $500 billion per year. Such direct B2B exchanges comprise a significant market, exceeding several trillion dollars a year. This type of spending is nondiscretionary and is required for the company to do its job. Both buyers and sellers recognize that by creating a more efficient marketplace, they can streamline processes and lower costs.

Procurement is evolving from a support function to a valuable weapon in a corporation's competitive arsenal. Today's companies seek solutions that combat high procurement costs and lengthy order-cycle times while simultaneously ensuring that the delivery of materials or services goes smoothly. These businesses want to automate day-to-day purchasing tasks, such as performing catalog searches, processing purchase orders, and obtaining PO authorizations. By so doing, companies can free their employees to perform more important tasks, such as managing supplier relations, reducing inventory, and improving the quality of the parts coming in the door.

In the past few years, B2B procurement strategies have become a major top-management focus. Many executives realize that B2B is not so much a technological revolution as it is a business revolution enabled by technology. Business-to-business procurement initiatives are most often driven by a company's CEO or CFO, not just its IT executives. This level of executive involvement in procurement projects reflects management's awareness of the five key challenges facing corporate procurement functions today:

1. Reducing order-processing costs and cycle times

2. Providing enterprise-wide access to corporate procurement capabilities

3. Empowering desktop requisitioning through employee self-service

4. Achieving procurement software integration with a company's back-office systems

5. Elevating the procurement function to a position of strategic importance within the organization

A central objective of a company's e-procurement strategy is to better manage the firm's operational costs. As they seek to improve their margins, companies face unprecedented pressure to manage operating expenses as efficiently as possible. The dollar-for-dollar, bottom-line impact of the margin enhancement afforded by e-procurement is startling—especially when compared with only fractional increases in profits realized through revenue-focused initiatives. For example, according to *CFO Magazine*'s annual survey on sales general and administrative costs (SG&A), "slicing SG&A by $1 has the same bottom-line effect as boosting sales by $13," and "cutting 1 percent from SG&A will tweak earnings by 2.3 percent."[1] Clearly, there are few actions a CFO can take to deliver such disproportionate dividends.

Is your company pursuing a strategy to reduce its operating costs? Does your firm's management view the company's procurement process as a potential cost-saving opportunity? If so, has your firm implemented an e-procurement application framework that supports the development of the integrated procurement applications it needs? Is your company's management focused on developing and implementing a suite of software applications that support best-in-class procurement and financial practices?

Evolution of e-Procurement Models

The e-procurement marketplace is still young; however, the new business models required to serve this market are evolving rapidly. Table 10.1 lists the seven basic types of e-procurement trading models in use and shows their key differences. Note that each of the trading exchanges described in Table 10.1 can also be categorized as either a public or a private exchange. Private exchanges can vary widely in size, ranging from a single company automating its procurement function with its suppliers to a large, complex exchange, such as the online auto parts exchange, Covisint, created by GM, Ford, and DaimlerChrysler.

Public exchanges are most often referred to as portals. In these portals, a company or a group of companies list products or services for public consumption. Public exchanges vary in the degree of value they provide, ranging from product catalogs, order processing and approvals, to fulfillment management and customer care.

Table 10.1: Comparison of Various e-Procurement Models

Trading Model	Characteristics
EDI networks	• Handful of trading partners and customers • Simple transactional capabilities • Batch processing • Reactive and costly value-added network (VAN) charges
Business-to-employee (B2E) requisitioning applications	• Make buying fast and hassle-free for a company's employees • Automated approval routing and standardization of requisition procedures • Provide supplier management tools for the professional buyer
Corporate procurement portals	• Provide better control over the procurement process and let a company's business rules be implemented with more consistency • Custom, negotiated prices posted in a multisupplier catalog • Spending analysis and multisupplier catalog management
First-generation trading exchanges: community, catalog, and storefronts	• Industry content, job postings, and news • Storefronts: new sales channel for distributors and manufacturers • Product content and catalog aggregation services
Second-generation trading exchanges: transaction-oriented trading exchanges	• Automated requisition process and purchase order transactions • Supplier, price, and product/service availability discovery • Catalog and credit management
Third-generation trading exchanges: collaborative supply chains	• Enable partners to closely synchronize operations and enable real-time fulfillment • Process transparency resulting in restructuring of demand and the supply chain • Substitute information for inventory
Industry consortiums: Buyer and supplier led	• The next step in the evolution of corporate procurement portals

Pre-Internet Era: EDI Networks

Historically, large businesses have realized time and cost savings by linking with their major suppliers through private networks commonly referred to as electronic data interchanges, or EDIs. These systems automate the procurement process, support automatic inventory replenishment, and tighten the relationship between buyers and their primary suppliers. Some of the major EDI vendors are Sterling Commerce, Harbinger, and General Electric Information Services.

Because EDI was originally based on a company's private network, it required large capital outlays to implement, and adding each new supplier was costly. Smaller firms, unable to afford these costs, are prevented from establishing EDI connections as either buyers or suppliers. Thus, the savings accrued from implementing EDIs has been limited to large firms. EDI and extranets tend to operate best in strategic partnerships, specialized relationships, and rigid performance contracts. They don't do well in the open sourcing and flexible supply chain world.

B2E: Purchasing and Requisitioning Applications

Corporate purchasing worldwide is undergoing major structural change. The concept of implementing employee self-service procurement can seem futuristic when the majority of businesses are just now becoming comfortable using an office e-mail system. However, these next-generation procurement applications are taking hold in corporations, as the following scenarios illustrate.

- A key machine in a manufacturing company breaks, and a $100 part to repair it is needed immediately. The company loses $100,000 for every hour the machine is not operational. Bill, the factory foreman, uses the e-procurement system to expedite the replacement-part order. The system routes the PO to the supplier that has the part. The part is delivered to the shop floor within 4 hours.

- Ann used to fill out and submit requests for office supplies and then wait weeks for delivery. She now uses her firm's new e-procurement system to browse the catalog from the approved vendor list, make the product selections she wants, and drop them in her e-shopping basket. The system approves the purchase order, as it meets the company's predefined limits. The product ships overnight and arrives at Ann's desk the next day.

- At another firm, Lynn has just returned from a 3-month consulting engagement in Italy. To complete her expense report, she logs into her consulting firm's travel expense system. Instead of having to key in her credit card expenses, the totals are already tallied in the online expense report. Lynn simply keys in her out-of-pocket expenses and submits the report electronically. The report clears because it conforms to company rules.

For decades, companies have talked about improving everyday business transactions, such as ordering office supplies and processing expense reports. Why? Because the purchase of goods and services represents the single largest cost item for any given enterprise. It's estimated that for each dollar a company earns on the sale of a product, it spends about $0.50 to $0.60 on goods and services. More capital is spent on the purchase of materials and services to support the business's operations than on all other expense items combined. Billions of dollars are wasted every year in inefficient procurement practices.

Desktop requisitioning enables employees to purchase the products and services they need online. By hooking up the corporate intranet to a company's suppliers' Web-based commerce sites, a company can eliminate the paper-intense and costly purchasing process of traditional business. A company's buy-side software routes an employee's online purchase requests internally before they are turned into purchase orders and sent to the firm's supplier.

Consolidating the purchasing process with a few key suppliers capable of providing volume discounts can generate tremendous cost savings. For example, Ford reengineered employee requisitioning processes in an attempt to save billions of dollars spent purchasing office supplies and filing expense reports. Ford spends an estimated $15.5 billion each year on nonproduction goods and services, making it one of the largest purchasers of such goods worldwide. In order to implement its desktop requisition strategy, Ford revamped its purchasing process. In its old process, Ford received and distributed supplier catalogs from which employees selected the products they needed. The employees then manually completed a PO and submitted it for approval, a process that took days or weeks. Today, these same employees use the Web.

Ford's requisitioning software works like this: Sharon launches her Web browser and logs into the procurement site on Ford's intranet. She then clicks on Create to create a requisition form. She then browses through a customized catalog. When she finds an item she wants to know more about, she clicks on her product choice and views a screen containing a more detailed description and photograph. Sharon decides that she likes what she sees, so she completes the requisition form, specifying that she wants the product delivered to her desk and her reason for buying it. The form is routed to her boss for approval, then to the preferred supplier with which Ford has a negotiated contract. The purchase order is also automatically routed to Ford's accounting system. The supplier responds with a confirmation and a delivery date. Sharon comes to work the next day, and the item she ordered is on her desk. Talk about convenience. By using e-commerce to order goods from online catalogs, Ford expects to cut its spending and nonproduction transaction costs by as much as 30 percent.[2]

Ford also uses its desktop procurement applications to process the more than 1 million employee travel and expense reports submitted each year. Major firms, such as Ford, spend an estimated $36 processing each expense report an employee submits. With the Internet's ability to support the electronic downloading of credit card receipts, the cost per expense report drops to about $8, resulting in an approximate savings of $28 million annually.

As the example of Ford illustrates, the focus of today's requisition software packages is to reduce the costs associated with purchasing nonproduction goods. Table 10.2 lists the categories of operating resources and their characteristics.

Corporate Procurement Portals

After realizing the benefits of automating their requisitioning processes, many companies, particularly those with significant purchasing power like IBM, are choosing to implement procurement portals for buying both production-related

Table 10.2: Types of Operating Resources

Operating Resources	Characteristics
General and administrative: office supplies and books, furniture, and professional services and education/training	• Low dollar value/high transaction volume • Commodity products • Minimal tracking required • Large pool of requisitioners
Computer-related capital equipment: computer hardware and software, computer supplies, networking supplies, and copiers, fax machines, and telephones	• Close tracking of inventoried assets • Medium to high dollar value • Technical product specifications • Budget constraints • Hidden inventories difficult to track
MRO (maintenance, repair, and operations): machine parts, electrical controls, tooling, and shop supplies	• Critical to plant maintenance • Critical to factory and production operations • Off-site, distributed regions • Significant dollar volume • Careful tracking needed
Travel services and entertainment: airline, hotel, and car expense management; and entertainment analysis and catering	• High Dollar Value • Budget constraints and expense tracking • Multilevel approval process and spend

Table 10.3: Production- versus Nonproduction-Related Items

Characteristics of Production, or Direct, Materials	Characteristics of Nonproduction, or MRO, Materials
Production items: raw materials, components	Operating resources: office and computer supplies, MRO supplies, travel
• Scheduled by production runs	• Ad hoc, not scheduled
• Locus of operation: professional buyer's desktop	• Locus of operation: employee desktop
• No approvals required	• Approval required
• High degree of automation	• Almost no automation
• Driven by design specification	• Driven by catalog

and nonproduction-related goods (see Table 10.3). Production goods include all the raw materials, components, assemblies, and other items needed to produce a finished item. Nonproduction goods are items that businesses need to run day-to-day business operations, as identified in Table 10.2.

Procurement portals do a lot more than basic purchasing (see Figure 10.1). Until now, the terms purchasing and procurement have been used almost interchangeably. However, they differ significantly in their scope. *Purchasing* refers to the buying of materials and all activities associated with the buying process. Electronic purchasing addresses only one relatively minor aspect of the procurement problems companies face.

Procurement, on the other hand, is broadly defined to include a company's requisitioning, purchasing, transportation, warehousing, and in-bound receiving processes. Procurement is a closed-loop process that begins with the product requisition and ends once the invoice for the product is paid. Integrated procurement remains one of the truly significant business strategies, but its full potential could not be realized, given the technological limitations.

Early integrated procurement strategies sought to reengineer, even dismantle, traditional, hierarchically structured purchasing organizations. Many of these organizations had layer upon layer of approval procedures that slowed down the purchasing process. More recent procurement strategies focus on restructuring the entire order-to-delivery process rather than on specific tasks within the process.

The paper-based purchasing models of the industrial era are being replaced by the more effective online procurement practices. The new procurement models leverage a nearly ideal combination of volume advantages, flexible contracts,

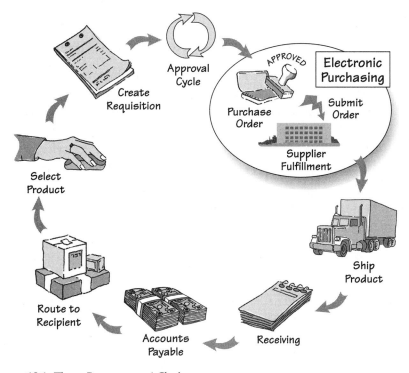

Figure 10.1: The e-Procurement Chain

and valuable supplier alliances, along with decentralized, user-initiated, and user-responsive purchases.

e-Procurement's benefits fall into two major categories: efficiency and effectiveness. e-Procurement's efficiency benefits include lower procurement costs, faster cycle times, reduced maverick or unauthorized buying, well-organized reporting information, and tighter integration of the procurement function with key back-office systems. e-Procurement's effectiveness benefits include the increased control over the supply chain, proactive management of key data, and higher-quality purchasing decisions within organizations.

Many companies are implementing e-procurement strategies concurrently with their integrated supply chain efforts. The Web provides the technological basis for achieving the supply and procurement chain management most firms seek. However, for many companies, development of a truly effective integrated procurement strategy is still far in the future. Relatively few firms have a clear vision of what a company must achieve when reengineering and integrating their procurement processes. Furthermore, no good roadmap exists for how such integration is to be achieved or what the ultimate destination is.

Trading Exchanges

First Generation: Communities, Storefronts, and RFP/RFQ Facilitators

Why build when you can outsource? The clunky procurement applications are giving way to sophisticated B2B portals called trading exchanges.

First-generation trading exchanges are *information and content hubs:* content communities that seek to attract any business professional responsible for researching and purchasing industry-related goods and services. These exchanges function like online trade magazines, offering daily insights into an industry and providing industry news and trends, product information, directories of industry participants, classifieds, and white papers. Other community-building mechanisms used by trading exchanges include chat rooms, discussion forums, bulletin boards, and career centers.

How do these trading exchanges make money? Advertising is a trading exchange's primary revenue source, given the highly focused nature of the community's participants. Advertising revenues include annual storefront fees, banner advertising, and event sponsorship. Some communities charge a subscription fee for membership. These e-markets can also receive lead-generation fees for product sales resulting from storefront traffic.

VerticalNet represents the largest grouping of trade exchanges to date, with 56 communities across 12 industry categories from solid-waste management to pulp production. VerticalNet's communities often have both a horizontal and a vertical focus (see Figure 10.2). The communities can be used for conducting commerce in direct goods—components or raw material—or indirect goods, such as computers, electrical equipment, and office supplies. The specific products and services offered through the various exchange communities tend to differ greatly.

VerticalNet offers its customers a comprehensive content package and facilitates the development of online storefronts for its supplier participants. VerticalNet's revenue model is dominated by advertising revenue related to the sale of online storefronts, sponsorships, and banner advertising. The liquidity, or participation, in VerticalNet's community and content e-markets is expected to grow over the next few years, owing to its recent alliance with Microsoft, which has committed to purchasing 80,000 storefronts. VerticalNet has also begun to capitalize on its targeted audience of small to midsize business communities by moving into e-commerce activities. VerticalNet is migrating from the advertising model to a transaction model.

Another form of the first-generation trading exchange is the Request for Proposal (RFP) and Request for Quote (RFQ) *facilitator exchange,* which operates a

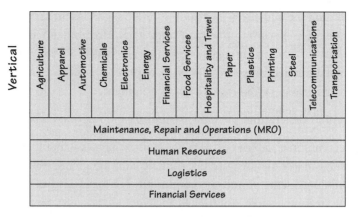

Horizontal

Figure 10.2: Horizontal versus Vertical Communities

centralized online marketplace. In this marketplace a preapproved group of suppliers submit fixed-priced, sealed bids in response to real-time RFQs issued by a buyer. The RFQs include both high-level and detailed requirements the supplier must satisfy. The exchange buyers do not necessarily select the lowest-priced bidder but opt for the supplier that best meets their specifications at a competitive price. The revenues generated by market makers using the RFQ/seal-bid mechanism can include subscription fees, fees for bids to be read, and transaction fees for bids submitted and/or successfully chosen.

In the energy sector, for example, WellBid has developed an online system to facilitate the procurement of oilfield services for the upstream oil and gas industry. WellBid's solution enables oil and gas production companies—the buyers—to electronically submit RFQs containing high-level specifications to preselected oilfield service companies—the suppliers. This online RFQ mechanism enables the suppliers and buyers to streamline their manual, paper-intensive commerce processes and to reduce the number of work-hours committed to this process.

Figure 10.2 illustrates the various vertical and horizontal marketplaces. Vertical marketplaces serve a specific industry, such as energy, hospitality, paper, and so on. These marketplaces focus on understanding industry practices and resolving industry "pain points," that is, inefficiencies that lower margins. Vertical marketplaces automate supply chains by digitizing and normalizing product catalogs, creating market liquidity by developing facilitator exchanges.

Horizontal markets, by contrast, span multiple industries. Horizontal marketplaces seek to make the procurement of common services more efficient because the audiences they address and the goods and services bought and sold over them are common to many industries. Horizontal market makers provide a venue for transacting such goods and services as MRO supplies, logistics services, media buying, outsourced human resources services, temporary workers, and excess inventory and excess capital equipment.

Second Generation: Virtual Distributors and Auction Hubs

A common criticism of first generation exchanges—that they were "an inch deep and a mile wide." As a result, content hubs are giving way to transaction hubs. Building a sense of industry community is a necessary but insufficient condition for creating a successful trading exchange. To succeed, an exchange must enable its participants to buy and sell products. Second-generation trading exchanges focus on obtaining their revenue from each buying and selling transaction that occurs within the exchange. Examples of these trading exchanges are virtual distributors and auction hubs.

Virtual distributors (VDs) offer one-stop shopping for a fragmented buyer and seller community by pulling together disparate product information from multiple catalogs and from multiple suppliers and/or manufacturers into one megacatalog. VDs generally do not carry any inventory or distribute products. Instead, they assist buyers in arranging for third-party carriers to transport the ordered goods. VDs help streamline the sourcing of direct goods, and thus lower transaction costs, by issuing a single purchase order and then parsing the order to each relevant supplier that ships the product direct. Many VDs are enriching the mix of services they offer, such as designing their software so that it integrates with a company's back-office operations, from order taking to inventory tracking.

One example is SciQuest, which serves the highly fragmented $12 billion U.S. life-sciences industry, with 100,000 labs purchasing product from more than 5,000 specialty suppliers and 1,500 distributors. Within that market, the customer, a research scientist, will suffer from a manual, time-consuming procurement process. Suppliers incur high sales and marketing expenditures from a dispersed buyer community. In order to address these market inefficiencies, SciQuest uses an online catalog to facilitate the search process for researchers and to streamline and to automate the procurement process for buying and selling organizations. By bringing the buyers and suppliers into one centralized marketplace, SciQuest reduces a supplier's customer acquisition costs by expanding its market reach.

Auction hubs are becoming a popular sales channel for "spot buying" unique items, such as used equipment, surplus inventory, and perishable goods. These hubs function similarly to a stock market. Buyers and sellers meet, usually anonymously, to agree on prices on commodities, such as raw materials, energy, or telecommunications capacity. These hubs can be driven either by sellers, such as AdAuction.com, which runs forward auctions of advertising space on the Web and other media, or by buyers, such as FreeMarkets, which does reverse auctions of industrial materials and equipment. Other auction hub examples are Altra Energy in the natural gas industry and eLance for matching freelancers with projects.

Auctions are of two types: forward and reverse. Forward auctions allow a multitude of buyers to bid for products/services from an individual seller on a competitive basis at below market prices. Forward auctions tend to be seller-centric. In this model, prices move only up. The seller lists the product or service offered, and bidders bid until a set time has elapsed. Before the auction begins, the seller sets a reserve price—a price that must be met for the seller to sell—and indicates whether he or she is willing to accept a partial-lot bid. If the bids fail to reach the seller's asking, or reserve, price, the seller is not obligated to sell the product or service. Auctions are commonly used as a mechanism for liquidating surplus inventory at the best possible prices.

In reverse auctions, or open-bid systems, buyers list the products or services they desire, and prequalified sellers bid on fulfilling the need. Reverse auctions last until a preset time has elapsed. The buyer is then obligated to purchase from the lowest bidder. Reverse auctions are the opposite of forward auctions, as prices move only downward. Reverse auctions are well suited for industries with fairly high fragmentation on the supply side and are also effective for industries that trade one-of-kind, nonstandard, customized products. Auction hubs can be independent dot-coms or backed by major industry players, but remaining neutral is key to their success.

Third Generation Trading: Collaboration Hubs

Transaction hubs are giving way to integration and collaboration hubs. These types of trading exchanges do far more than provide transaction functionality to participating companies, helping companies with end-to-end management of their supply chains. Collaboration hubs seek to create one common platform to enable all participants in an industry supply chain to share information, conduct business transactions, and collaborate on strategic and operational planning. The problem they are trying to solve is supply chain bloat: Most supply chains are overloaded with excess inventory because predicting the right product mix and inventory levels is difficult to manage correctly. As a result, the channel participants—raw-material providers, manufacturers, importers/exporters, distributors, and dealers—could better match production with demand, reducing excess inventories in the channel and speeding up cycle times. Collaborative hubs, in effect, attempt to substitute real-time, accurate information for inventory.

Collaborative hubs provide value-added services to continuously increase site "stickiness," generate multiple revenue streams, and increase competitive barriers to entry. For example, Bidcom provides a single online workplace for large contractors to collaborate with architects, store their blueprints, expedite the permit process, and purchase building materials. Bidcom's goal is to get projects done, from design through manufacturing to distribution. A collaborative hub must provide such services in order to sustain its market advantage and leadership. Additional value-added service hubs often include

- *Integrated commerce technology* that automates transaction processing and that can incorporate static pricing and/or dynamic pricing mechanisms

- *Brokering* services that offer logistic and financial services, including shipping, warehousing, credit, and insurance

- *Service and support,* including customer service support, returns processing, and warranty coverage

Collaboration hubs promise to enable supply chains to attain new levels of cooperation and information sharing whereby partners collaborate on strategic and operational planning. Collaboration efforts may include product planning and design, demand forecasting, replenishment planning, and pricing and promotional strategies. Of key importance is the role hubs play in recording historical trading data that can be analyzed in order to improve planning and forecasting, thus enabling further compression of the design and development cycle.

Industry Consortiums: Joint-Venture Procurement Hubs

Industry titans are striking back. They are tired of being typecast as dinosaurs, who are going to be extinct. They are asking: Why should some dot-com be allowed to recreate the supply chain? Larger firms have responded to the competitive threat posed by new start-ups by forming either buyers or suppliers. In a buyer consortium, a group of large companies combine their buying power to drive down prices. An industry's traditional leaders have two significant advantages over Net-born start-ups when creating trading exchanges for high-volume commodity goods: instant commercial activity and liquidity. For example, the oil and gas industry consortium, PetroCosm, has Chevron and Texaco as its anchor tenants.

The most famous consortium is the automotive hub, Covisint.[3] On February 25, 2000, GM, Ford, and DaimlerChrysler announced their intent to form a worldwide B2B marketplace. In April 2000, Renault and Nissan announced their intention to join the exchange. As a result, Covisint was established as an independent company, offering products and services designed to help automakers and suppliers alike achieve efficiencies throughout the supply chain.

Supplier-sponsored consortiums have begun to emerge in response to start-up exchanges and buyer consortiums. Similar to their buyer-centric relatives, supplier consortiums are forming in industries in which a few firms represent the highest concentration of market power. The big difference, however, is that supplier consortiums must give their sponsors the opportunity to promote and to differentiate the suppliers' products. The consortium must also provide an environment that compels buyers to purchase these products by aggregating the industry's key suppliers and providing significant levels of product depth, breadth, selection, and service.

Supplier consortiums are not new. The airline industry's Sabre is a successful example. The Sabre consortium forged links with travel agents, but over time, the airlines lowered the commissions paid to agents. More recently, the airlines started competing with the new "infomediaries," such as Expedia, and several airlines have created Orbitz.com, a Web site that will offer discounted fares exclusively.

How successful industry consortiums will be remains to be seen. Major issues related to consortium governance, technology, and antitrust concerns must be addressed. In order to resolve the governance issue, the traditional competitors must form an independent company that promotes the interests of all the consortium's participants. The technology issue relates to that of governance. With powerful traditional competitors, each with its own technology standards and systems, finding a common technological ground will be difficult. The new company will be twisting in the wind, trying to satisfy the requirements of all the members. Finally, the antitrust issue is a concern whenever cooperation among industry-specific giants is discussed. Many fear that collusion between dominant players will be at the expense of the industry's smaller firms. Other business issues these exchanges must confront are

- Under what conditions other industry players will be allowed to join an exchange once it is established

- Who is going to own, manage, and leverage the aggregated market data collected during the course of market operations

- What range of services and prices exchanges will offer

- How the exchange will maintain neutrality to avoid charges of collusion

In short, technology is no replacement for management or governance. These core business, legal, and ethical issues must be addressed before these exchanges can truly succeed.

Evolution of Procurement Processes

Before an e-procurement solution can be deployed, a company must undergo significant procurement process reengineering. Automating an existing procurement mess will only make matters worse.

The various e-procurement models all attempt to solve similar business process problems. These include the fragmentation of channels, managing by exception rather than by transaction, controlling maverick buying by automating the requisitioning process, and the integration of end-to-end processes.

A company must first clearly define the business problems its e-procurement solution is intended to address. e-Procurement initiatives can suffer from the same hype as e-commerce in general. Although many companies say that they want to implement an e-procurement strategy, they often do not know why. e-Procurement initiatives address a number of core business problems.

Reducing Channel Fragmentation

Maverick buying, inefficient processes, and nonstrategic sourcing are all symptoms of channel fragmentation. For example, one manufacturer has calculated that it spends $100 to process each purchase order. The company spends one third of its entire budget on nonproduction goods, with nearly 95 percent of these goods being purchased using people, fax, and paper-based, high-overhead processes. However, the company knows exactly how much it spends on the direct material used in its production processes. But don't ask the company how it spends approximately $1 billion a year on computers, office products, and furniture. *Does this remind you of your company?*

Most procurement processes are paper-intensive. For example, a large semiconductor manufacturer requires employees to fill out a paper form that has three copies. Employees keep a copy and give one to the purchasing department, which faxes a copy to the supplier. The supplier fills the order and ships it. The supplier collects these order forms, totals the charges, and bills the manufacturer. This process is neither efficient nor cheap for either party. Chances are, your company spends far more on PO administration than it does on the goods it purchases.

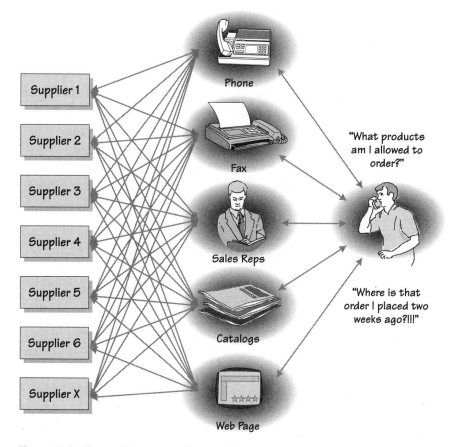

Figure 10.3: Channel Fragmentation Leading to Procurement Chaos

How much does it cost your company to buy something? Every purchase—from paper clips to spare parts for shop equipment—costs companies anywhere from $70 to $300 in administrative overhead in a paper-based procurement cycle.

Is maverick buying a problem in your company? Maverick buying occurs when employees buy products on their own, often charging the items they purchase to their corporate credit cards. As a result, the employees miss out on the volume discounts their companies arrange with preferred providers of products and services. Apart from the missed discounts, the additional administrative effort required to process these nonstandard purchases costs organizations an incredible sum.

Fragmentation can also occur during order fulfillment. Seldom is every product delivered on time, and incorrect, partial, and back orders are fairly common.

The customer must attempt to track the status of the order with the supplier through multiple offline channels.

As Figure 10.3 illustrates, the procurement inefficiencies resulting from channel fragmentation are astounding. Purchasing managers have a growing awareness of how to reduce maverick buying and to improve company profits. These managers know that they must reduce the need to service small-dollar orders by focusing on new and better contracts, obtain better purchasing information for contract negotiations, and negotiate with the knowledge of what has been purchased in the past. An e-procurement solution not only reduces off-contract buying but also frees purchasing to concentrate on strategic tasks, such as better contracting.

Hands-Free Procurement: Managed by Exception

Today's companies seek to transition the managed-by-transaction business model to the manage-by-exception model. Figure 10.4 illustrates hands-free procurement as the central business objective of e-procurement initiatives. The primary benefits are automating the mundane, eliminating the paperwork, and eliminating hidden procedures and other obstacles that keep employees from doing their real, productive jobs. Instead of dealing with the transaction process, employees can focus on completing their work.

For example, in summer 1996, Microsoft implemented MS Market, an online procurement engine. *Internet Week* quoted Bob Herbold, COO of Microsoft, as saying that MS Market is aimed at eliminating all paperwork company wide. In its first year, MS Market was used to purchase more than $1 billion in supplies. Some 6,000 Microsoft employees worldwide have used the system, in which the company invested $1.1 million.[4] MS Market reduces the personnel required to manage low-cost requisitions and gives the remaining employees a quick, easy way to order materials without being burdened with paperwork and bureaucratic processes.

In a case study published on Microsoft's Web site, Clay Fleming, a senior manager, elaborates on the procurement scenario: "We have a lot of dollars flowing into marketing and R&D. Unlike manufacturing companies, ours is a very distributed procurement environment. We get thousands of requests every week from all over the company for small purchases, from office supplies to business cards to catering services. The bottom line is that the majority of purchase requests from Microsoft employees involve relatively small amounts of money."[5]

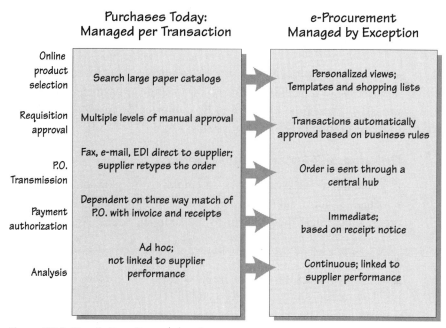

Figure 10.4: Hands-Free Procurement

Fleming points out that these "high-volume, low-dollar transactions" represent about 70 percent of total transaction volume but only 3 percent of accounts payable. Many employees were wasting time turning requisitions into POs and trying to follow company's business rules and processes—one of the biggest drawbacks to using traditional procurement procedures. Microsoft's managers sought to streamline the requisition process by using a requisitioning tool that automates all the controls and validations traditionally performed by the company's requisition personnel. Microsoft's employees requested an easy-to-use online form for ordering supplies that included interfaces to the company's procurement partners. The result is MS Market, a software application based on the managed-by-exception model.

It's estimated that more than 1,000 orders a day worth over $3 billion annually flow through MS Market. MS Market's business benefits are phenomenal. The purchase cycle was reduced from 8 days to 3 days. The employee overhead related to the requisition process was reduced from 14 to 1.5 full-time employees. Employees in charge of processing POs were redeployed so that they could concentrate on higher-level procurement functions, such as analyzing procurement data and cutting deals with vendors.

e-Procurement Infrastructure: Integrating Ordering, Fulfillment, and Payment

The end-to-end procurement process comprises three separate work flows: the order work flow, the fulfillment work flow, and the payment work flow (see Figure 10.5). These processes need to be supported by customer service and backward integration to accounting systems.

Ordering: Self-Service Requisitioning

In a traditional purchase process, an employee ordering something must fill out a requisition form, submit it, wait for it to be approved, and receive a purchase order, which must then be sent to the supplier. Sound familiar? Most organizations have *many procurement guidelines and rules that employees must follow but that are increasingly archaic given the technological options available today.* At many companies, little help is available from the purchasing department, and purchase orders can take weeks to fulfill. The new generation of procurement software automates everyday business purchases by using efficient Web-based applications.

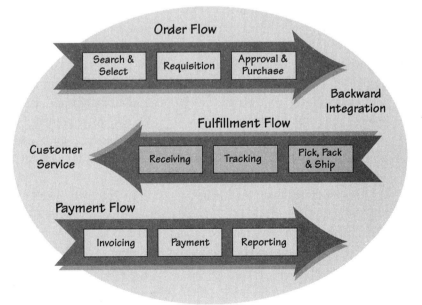

Figure 10.5: Three Critical Process Flows

Self-service order work flow functions enable transactions to take place and to clear once customers click the Buy button. Order work flows include the steps in the purchase order process through approval routing. Once a requisition is submitted, it's routed for approval based on the company's business rules. The approvers are notified of any pending approval requests via e-mail and can choose to approve, reject, or forward the request to another approver. Approver spending limits are also monitored and enforced, minimizing fraud during the approval routing process.

Figure 10.6 depicts the buyer side of the requisition process in greater detail. Using the software's easy point-and-click interface, employees can create, submit, and track several types of requisitions—including catalog, off-catalog, blanket, and preauthorized purchases—right from their desktops. Preapproved shopping lists speed ordering supplies for new employees or for repeat purchases. The interface must be powerful enough to meet the needs of a broad range of users, including casual users, purchasing professionals, and system administrators.

1. *Secure personal login.* Each requisitioner is given a secure personal login code containing user profile information, such as job title, default department, accounting codes, and default ship-to and bill-to information. These profiles are also used to customize the software's screen display so that requisitioners can access and order only those catalog items they are authorized to purchase.

2. *Browse authorized supplier catalogs.* Requisitioners can use powerful search and browse capabilities to peruse multiple supplier catalogs. Catalog information can be viewed for a specific supplier or by functional product category across all suppliers. Only contracted products and prices are shown. Purchasing administrators can add product detail to help steer requisitioners to preferred products or to indicate which products require approval prior to purchasing. Requisitioners can also order services and place requests for nonstandard product sourcing.

3. *Create requisition/order.* When using self-service requisition software, requisitions are created in real time and can include products from one or more suppliers. Requisitioners can then add products to a requisition by searching the product catalog or by adding products from their personal favorite-product list. In addition, requisitioners can copy existing orders and modify them for requisitions that approximate past purchases, further speeding the process.

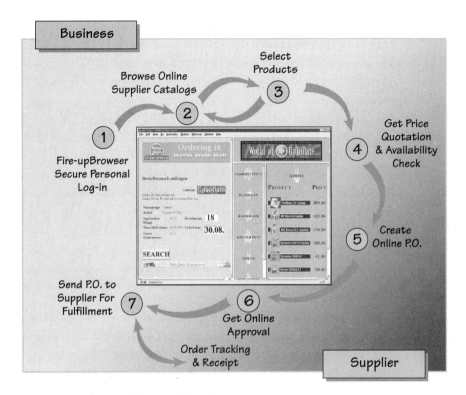

Figure 10.6: The Buy-Side Requisitioning Process

4. *Submit requisition/order.* Payment options that procurement software supports include a blanket purchase order, a new purchase order number, or procurement/credit card, limited by what each supplier accepts. Requisitions that fall within the company's purchase controls are broken out into one purchase order per supplier and sent to the appropriate supplier for fulfillment.

5. *Enforce purchase controls and approvals.* A company's purchasing managers should control which products are available for purchase by employees, where these products can be purchased, and who has responsibility for approving an order. With these controls in place, purchasing managers can then choose which level of empowerment makes sense. Embedded purchase controls ensure that requisitioners cannot purchase restricted items or place orders beyond specific limits, such as a stated dollar amount per order or dollar amount per period. Requisitions that violate purchase controls are required to be routed for approval to the appropriate individual or group.

Usability is critical in self-service applications. Every e-procurement solution must be designed for casual use by untrained employees. If users don't like the system, the whole application will fail. Even if users love the system for various reasons, such as ease of use, it must also meet the needs of the company's purchasing managers. Its behind-the-scenes operations must provide extensive support for the company's professional buyers, including management controls, reporting, and integration with existing systems.

Fulfillment: Order Management and Supplier Integration

Electronic linkages between trading partners' back-office systems expedite order entry, order fulfillment, and status inquiries. In addition to the ability to place orders with suppliers via electronic data input, fax, or e-mail, a procurement system should provide a seamless transition from requisition to purchase order, with no rekeying of orders. Fulfillment work flow includes the following steps:

1. *Order dispatch.* Cross-supplier requisitions are broken down into one purchase order per supplier and sent to each supplier via a range of order formats to match the supplier's preferred method of receipt. Copies of the purchase orders are sent to the purchasing system for reporting and tracking. As the orders are fulfilled, suppliers send back an order acknowledgment, the order's status, and shipment notifications.

2. *Accounting back-office systems connectivity.* Procurement touches virtually every aspect of an organization and the software systems used to run it. Unless a procurement system can elegantly integrate with existing corporate financial, production, distribution, and human resource applications, duplicate efforts will be required to maintain the same data in multiple systems. Instead of tedious, time-consuming, and error-prone data entry, the accounting information is converted and exported in real time to an ERP system.

3. *Supplier connectivity.* These applications streamline and automate all interactions between a company and its suppliers—from creating and updating catalog pages to issuing purchase orders directly to the suppliers' systems. In order to better manage the movement of resources—materials, services, knowledge, or labor—through the procurement chain, successful firms have created direct linkages with their suppliers. These direct links remove the rigid barriers that have historically dominated outmoded procurement practices.

4. *Order tracking.* Requisitioners are notified via e-mail of an order's status, including whether the order has been approved, an order acknowledgment from the supplier, and the order's shipment status. With most Web-based procurement applications, requisitioners can also access online order status information to review detailed order and line-item status histories.

5. *Receiving.* The receiving functionality is used to track delivered goods and services from suppliers. Receiving is responsible for storing/staging inbound items and initial quality and quantity checks. For each delivery from a vendor, a record of receipt is entered into the corresponding purchase order. As products are received, the quantity received is entered into the corresponding PO line item in one of three ways: enter the quantity received for a single line item; mark the line item as completely received; mark the entire PO as fully received. The quantity received for all line items will automatically be entered as the quantity ordered.

Receiving, in turn, kicks off the payment work flow. The accounts payable department is responsible for processing the invoices received from suppliers and then releasing payment to those suppliers under agreed-on terms.

Payment: Invoice Management

No company can afford to survive without monitoring payments and open invoices. Although such services and features can be brokered to third-party providers, it is the responsibility of the market sponsor to create the payment work flow. The software should also support billing, shipping status, and term-contracts functionality so that the procurement process—from order placement to order fulfillment—is one integrated, end-to-end service. The specific functionality in the payment work flow includes

- *Invoicing and billing.* This module is designed to look after all aspects of entering and processing invoices from multiple suppliers. The long-term recording of all incoming and outgoing invoices allows you to check all invoices. In addition, payment conditions for customers and suppliers are stored so that they can be accessed by other programs. The billing system provides the mechanisms for billing account management, including functionality that enables such tasks as account setup, product subscriptions, statement processing, and account review.

- *Payment.* Payment processing is a key component of any successful procurement software package. The software's payment module must support extended capabilities, such as credit card processing, providing line of credit, placing payments in escrow, withholding taxes, and any cross-border trade requirements that apply in order for the full potential of e-procurement best practices to be realized.

- *Reporting.* Solid, accurate reporting of information is the key to process optimization and cost reduction. A good procurement system should track what was purchased, by whom, from whom, at what price, and how long it took to complete each step of the cycle. This information is invaluable when negotiating with suppliers and for month-end reconciliation.

e-Procurement Analysis and Administration Applications

Buy-side functionality alone is not enough. Procurement professionals also need more sophisticated technology to increase their effectiveness and to extend their responsibilities beyond their traditional role in purchasing direct production materials and shop-floor MRO spending.

Figure 10.7 illustrates the detailed requirements for succeeding as a procurement professional. The core competency of a successful and effective procurement strategy is the application of spending analysis and planning across the entire spectrum of procurement activities.

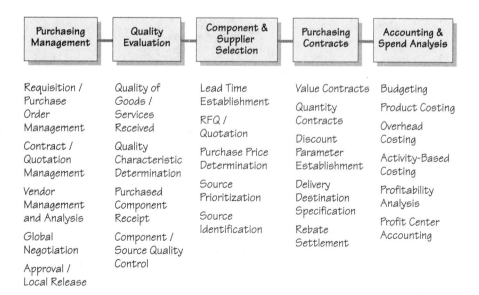

Figure 10.7: Detailed Breakdown of Functionality for the Procurement Professional

Spending analysis and procurement planning provide the procurement professional with the information needed to purchase wisely and to measure the cost savings. Spending analysis and procurement planning include the following functions:

- *Data collection.* Professional buyers need to collect and to generate comprehensive data on all purchasing activities, such as spending to date against budget, spending pending approval, activity by geography, supplier on-time delivery compliance, items received, and weekly, monthly, quarterly, and annual historical spending data.

- *Market analysis.* A thorough market analysis helps buyers to better understand their spending, their business requirements, and their market. Procurement professionals use predefined, procurement-centric online analytic processing (OLAP) reports to view the vast amount of data collected for forecasting, trend, and what-if analyses. This reporting and analytic capability provides organizations with the ability to interpret their transaction data in ways that are most productive for them. Figure 10.8 illustrates the key objectives of any multidimensional market analysis.

- *Supplier management decisions.* Management can use a variety of criteria to analyze transaction data in useful ways and for making informed decisions.

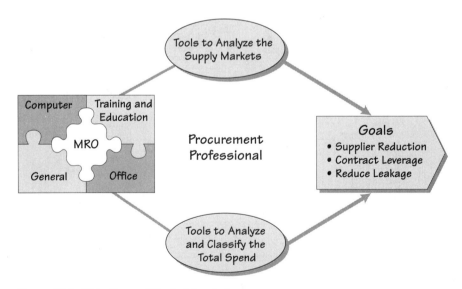

Figure 10.8: Objectives of Market Analysis

Typical supplier management decisions include determining which products to include in a given catalog, whether to restrict the procurement of certain goods to meet fiscal and business imperatives, or renegotiating volume contracts for more favorable discounts. Without such procurement intelligence and visibility, purchasing professionals have a more difficult task when interpreting business data and making decisions that benefit the company.

- *Configuration of spending controls.* No data, analytical tool, and decision support capability is useful if the procurement professionals within a firm cannot reconfigure their company's spending controls in real time. Today, the horizon for completing purchasing transactions is relatively short—1 to 2 weeks—making the ability to enact process controls quickly. Professional buyers must be able to change catalogs and the procurement work flow in real time so that spending patterns can be altered to meet a firm's purchasing and business imperatives. In other words, a company's buyers—not its IT department—must control the procurement process.

- *Continuous feedback.* In order to close the spending-analysis loop, procurement professionals must be able to view, in real time, the results of their process controls through subsequent data collection and analysis. This feedback allows them to further refine the controls they've implemented, if necessary.

Clearly, procurement administration is central. If you don't know where your firm's money is spent, it is impossible to get control over your procurement process. Automating procurement processes alone does not provide the depth of data collection, reporting, analysis, and control that companies must have in order to implement best practices across a global enterprise. Without the ability to measure, control, and provide continuous feedback to the procurement process, it's extremely difficult to measure the process's performance.

Marketplace Enablers

Marketplace enablers exist to help other companies create marketplaces on the Internet. Most market enablers supply software and consulting expertise. Others also seek equity stakes in the companies or exchanges to which they provide technology. Table 10.4 shows the market segmentation from a market enabler's perspective. Two preeminent infrastructure providers—Ariba and FreeMarkets—provide excellent examples of marketplace enablers.

Table 10.4: Enabler Market Segmentation

Market Segment	Infrastructure Provider
B2B exchange software	Ariba, I2, Commerce One, Rightworks, Claris Oracle
B2B order management	Spaceworks, I2, Yantra
B2B catalog management	Requisite, Saqqara, Cardonet
B2B third-party services	eCredit, Order Trust, Ligistics.com
B2B auctions	FreeMarkets, OpenSite, Moai
B2B integration to suppliers	WebMethods, Vitria, Neon
B2B content management	OnDisplay, ec-Content, WIZNET

Ariba: Tools for Enabling Marketplaces

Ariba was the first company to market its nonproduction procurement solution, which it named the Operating Resource Management System (ORMS). Ariba came into existence because its founders asked, How can firms automate their day-to-day purchasing of nonproduction-related items?[7] Ariba's executives knew that although many firms have well-established procedures for production-related purchasing, little procedural or technological innovation had taken place during the past 50 years to reduce the costs of nonproduction procurement.

Ariba quickly realized the tremendous market opportunity that auto-mating nonproduction procurement processes provided. At least 30 percent of a typical company's spending goes to nonproduction purchases and is managed via a maze of paper-based processes. Therein lie opportunities for automation, control, and leverage. For example, automation in travel and entertainment not only reduces the cost of processing expense reports—from more than $36 to less than $8, as we have seen—but also shortens the cycle time, from 22 days to 3 days.[8]

Ariba did a very smart thing. Realizing that customer requirements are a fast-moving target, Ariba did not write a single line of code until it understood what the customer value proposition was. Ariba focused on customer need, conducting interviews with more than 55 prospective customers and gathering feedback from several Fortune 1,000 companies. Ariba did not fall into the trap many businesses do when executing an application design strategy. Too often, companies fail to see that innovation is not in the eye of the manager or inventor; it's in the eye of the user. Let's look at the market pain—the people, paper, and process-intensive nature of procurement—that Ariba focused on.

Ariba's revenue model is quite interesting. Ariba has four revenue streams:

1. *Transaction-based server capacity license.* Ariba charges a fee for its software, based on the transaction volume a customer expects to conduct using the software each year. Typically, a customer pays roughly $1 million for a license to pass 100,000 million line-item transactions each year. If the transaction volume exceeds this limit, the customer will be required to buy additional server capacity. Transaction volume is based on the number of line items— one line on a PO—created. For example, a PO that has a request for three pens and one computer has two line items.

2. *Software license fees.* The software module license fees are charged for licensing the ORMS adapters. Usually, the server-capacity license fees and the software module license fees are bundled together and negotiated as a package. The server-capacity license fees are usually less than 75 percent of the total license fees.

3. *Network fees.* The network fees include the subscription fees to the Ariba network, the maintenance and support fees, and transaction fees. The network fee is approximately 15 percent of the capacity-based license fee.

4. *Other fees.* These include implementation fees and education fees and are based on time and materials.

In the past few years, Ariba has transformed itself from a pure buy-side solution provider into a technology platform for building and powering Internet trading exchanges. Ariba accomplished this transformation by acquiring Tradex—an exchange solution—and TradingDynamics—an auction solution. Ariba is expanding its product offerings from automation of the transactional buying activities of indirect materials/services into automation of strategic and direct materials buying by acquiring SupplierMarket.

To fully capitalize on its new profile, Ariba has also partnered with sell-side solution companies, such as InterWorld and CardoNet, and supply chain management companies, such as IBM and I2 Technologies. With these relationships, Ariba platforms now cover buy-side, sell-side, exchange and auction, and supply chain optimization solutions.

FreeMarkets: Auction Enabler

FreeMarkets operates a buyer-centric auction exchange focused on the $4–$5 trillion procurement market for industrial parts, raw materials, and commodities.

Industrial parts, raw materials, and surplus assets represent attractive B2B opportunities for the following reasons.

- *Direct materials are often custom-made with no standard price.* These inputs are mission-critical, as they are used in the production and manufacturing of finished goods. Buyers must screen suppliers carefully, as low-quality inputs result in low-quality finished goods, and unreliable deliveries can halt production lines and result in lost revenues. Screening suppliers based on price, quality, delivery, and other parameters is a time-consuming and expensive process. Therefore, buyers screen only a subset of the complete universe of potential suppliers and select from the few that qualify.

- *The current procurement process is inefficient.* Buyers have traditionally been limited to a list of approved suppliers to ensure product quality and timely delivery—limiting market liquidity, competitive pricing, and potential quality and service improvements from new or unknown suppliers. Therefore, buyers often purchase inputs at a premium—restricting potential for margin expansion and greater profitability. Furthermore, the phone- and fax-based methods of purchasing are time consuming and costly to process. Location-based auctions for various supplies are often chaotic, and it costs suppliers money to fly in and participate.

- *Traditional asset-disposal methods are plagued by imperfect product and pricing information.* With asset disposal, companies would advertise the surplus or used assets in a directory, solicit inquiries, send equipment and machinery specs by phone or fax, and then solicit and negotiate bids from buyers—a process that may last several months. Companies often choose to write off inventory, owing to the difficulty, time, and costs associated with finding buyers.

FreeMarkets service, which it calls market making, creates a custom market for the direct materials or other goods that its client purchases in a particular auction. FreeMarkets combines its BidWare technology with knowledge of supply markets to help its clients obtain lower prices and make better purchasing decisions. FreeMarkets offers two sets of solutions—Industrial Auctions and Surplus Asset Exchange—to automate and liquidate the procurement process and disposal of surplus assets. FreeMarkets supports 26 auction formats in 36 languages in 100 vertical markets, ranging from printed circuit boards to tax consulting services. [9]

Industrial auctions are buyer-driven, downward-price auctions in which suppliers continue to lower their prices until the auction is closed. Given the fragmentation and information-intensive nature of direct materials, FreeMarkets integrates an interactive auction process with technology and domain expertise to generate cost savings for the buyers. Before each auction, FreeMarkets works with its client to identify and to screen suppliers and to assemble a request for quotation that provides detailed and consistent information for suppliers to use as a basis for their competitive bids.

Surplus asset auctions are seller-driven, upward-pricing auctions targeting the $200–$300 billion new- and used-equipment and excess inventory market. As with its buyer-driven auctions, FreeMarkets provides surplus sellers with real-time bidding technology, active market-making support, and bidding results implementation. In March 2000, FreeMarkets acquired iMark.com, Surplus Records, and SR Auctions to expand into the surplus-asset market.

FreeMarkets has two methods of earning revenue. The first method earns revenue by charging a subscription rate based on estimated auction volume potential per customer. The fixed rate is generally a percentage of the estimated revenue. A 1- to 5-year contract is then negotiated. The second method is an incentive provision, written into the contract, that allows for additional revenue if the annual savings or volume is higher than the negotiated threshold. Between 1995 and 2000 alone, the company has conducted $10 billion in auction volume—generating more than $2 billion in estimated cost savings.

A Roadmap for e-Procurement Managers

Managing a procurement chain is a little like playing chess. There are many components on your procurement chain chessboard, and you must move all of the pieces strategically to win. In this section, we look at the key pieces in the procurement chess game.

Chief procurement officers (CPOs) are looking to deliver the maximum business impact at the lowest possible cost. The business objectives of CPOs are fourfold: (1) leveraging enterprise-wide buying power, (2) quick results and low risk, (3) supplier rationalization, and (4) cost reduction by automating best practices in strategic procurement. To achieve these goals, CPOs are coming to the conclusion that e-procurement is where the action is. Simple in concept, e-procurement applications are powerful when applied to the large number of products and services that companies buy. Consolidating the buying of these items and rationalizing the procurement chain can add tens to hundreds of millions of dollars directly to the bottom line. Take this systematic roadmap with you on your journey to e-procurement success.

Step 1: Clarify Your Goals

Enterprises should make sure that the business problem or the goal is well understood. Every company wants to improve its procurement chain, but you can't get there if you don't know where you're going!

What is your company's specific e-procurement goal? The critical first step in designing, reengineering, or optimizing your procurement chain is to assemble your team to define precisely what goals you want to achieve. The typical goals of e-procurement include

- Automating the selection and purchase of goods

- Cutting costs significantly throughout the organization

- Quickly and accurately reporting company-wide purchasing patterns

- Eliminating purchasing by unauthorized employees

Is your goal a comprehensive and consolidated business solution? Successful e-procurement must encompass all of a company's major cost areas while also augmenting a company's existing investments in its accounting, financial planning, and human resources systems. It's easy to automate distinct procurement stages using stand-alone, or point, solutions. However, these address each segment of the procurement life cycle individually, missing the point entirely, and ensuring none of the significant cost benefits that accrue from a comprehensive e-procurement strategy. As Figure 10.9 illustrates, today's businesses need an integrated e-procurement management solution.

What are you trying to improve? At some point, it's important to set numerical targets for the processes you are implementing. It's not uncommon, for example, to take 10 percent to 15 percent of your procurement chain cost out of the system by process reengineering. This is tangible, hard capital that can be saved and deployed toward other strategic projects. The key is to examine the procurement chain elements essential to your company and to set achievable goals that are in harmony with the organization's overall objectives.

Step 2: Construct a Process Audit

With strategic goals in place, it's important to understand your current procurement process and the factors that affect, impede, and interact with it. Take time for a procurement chain audit to ensure that you have an accurate big-picture model. This is a critical step in the process of moving from where you are today to where

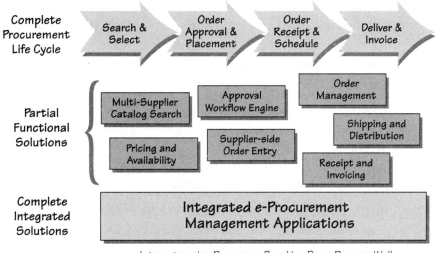

Figure 10.9: e-Procurement Management

you want to be tomorrow. The first phase of the procurement chain audit consists of modeling the work flows in procurement. Modeling the procurement work flows identifies key bottlenecks, creates shortcuts, and streamlines the purchasing process.

Finally, ask yourself, What kind of buying do you want to support? The type of buying influences the type of e-procurement solution. There are also three types of buying.[10]

- *Strategic buying* involves supplier selection, contract negotiations, and supplier management. Strategy buying is oriented toward establishing a long-term relationship between buyers and sellers.

- *Transactional buying* involves purchasing products according to existing contracts and processing the transactions. Transactional buying is essentially "paper pushing."

- *Spot buying* usually involves one-time deals. Spot buys occur when existing contracted suppliers cannot fill the order, when there is a rush order, or when the order is one-time only and the order size is too small to justify the contract negotiation process.

Which type of buying are you trying to automate? To get a good picture of the current spend, collect data. Remember, the collected data isn't only numbers but also information about people, procedures, and processes. Once the data is collected and analyzed for consistency and accuracy, it can be compiled into a model representing the current procurement chain. This model represents a baseline that is used to drill down to the next level of analysis, during which key areas can be studied to ensure that

- Current processes are consistent with the organization's strategic goals and objectives

- The procurement chain processes meet customers' needs

- Current procurement chain processes promote efficiency

Through these analyses, you will identify critical success factors and key performance indicators. You will also assess problem areas and areas of vulnerability. The results of these assessments can then be inserted into the mix—let's call it the "global procurement chain optimizer"—to help determine the proper direction for the design phase.

Step 3: Create a Business Case for e-Procurement

Putting a return on assets (ROA) business case together for e-procurement can be useful because it forces you to systematically analyze your business. Companies should understand the requirements without overanalyzing them. Some organizations still have a tendency to overanalyze technology solution decisions.

Business case analysis forces you to understand your context. If you don't understand your environment, you can do very little to fix it. The process of putting a business case together forces you to articulate hidden assumptions. One widely used technique in creating an e-procurement business case is ROA, which uses the following formula:

$$ROA = (Revenues - Expenses)/Assets$$

To increase ROA, you need to increase revenues, decrease expenses, or keep the asset base as small as possible.

Whereas increasing profitability by generating revenue requires substantial investment in capital equipment, marketing, and sales, increasing profitability through e-procurement requires only a relatively limited additional investment. Implementing an e-procurement solution commonly saves at least 5 percent of operating resource costs.

Decreasing expenses can be accomplished by identifying inefficiencies in the procurement chain, which enables companies to reduce expenditures, such as inventory carrying costs. By reducing the amount of captive capital in the procurement chain, a company becomes profitable more quickly. Cost improvements are not just cutbacks. Enhancements are often made through better coordination and communication. For instance, many companies have to expedite operating resources by shipping "premium freight" in order to get an order to an employee on time. With proper planning, this cost can be avoided.

Improving asset utilization can be accomplished by reducing working capital. The amount of assets companies have captive in the procurement chain affects the profitability of the company directly. Working capital can be reduced in two ways: (1) eliminating warehouses to maximize stock availability and to minimize inventory holdings and (2) eliminating excess inventory to reduce leakage or hidden inventory.

Companies are beginning to move from optimizing within the four walls of the enterprise to optimizing the entire procurement chain. The goal is not just to support an integrated business process that connects the customer's customer to the supplier's supplier but rather to increase the velocity at which the virtual enterprise operates.

Step 4: Develop a Supplier Integration Matrix

Without supplier commitment and involvement, the road to e-procurement is a long one. In today's world, with its ever-increasing velocity of change, few organizations want to commit to long-term relationships. Conventional wisdom says that if a company encumbers itself with long-term agreements, it will lose the flexibility to react to new opportunities. What if something better comes along tomorrow? But the reality is that this approach may be costing your organization money.

What's needed is a supplier integration matrix (SIM). A SIM helps determine the best type of relationship to have with individual vendors. In the complex procurement environment, a company must define favorable relationships to have with vendors in order to optimize the procurement chain. Any organization that applies only one relationship structure to all vendors, either consciously or unconsciously, is shortchanging itself. A SIM helps evaluate suppliers according to how each contributes to the current or future success of the company, classifying suppliers into the following categories:

- *Strategic-collaborative.* A supplier offering a unique or scarce product or service is a candidate for a collaborative relationship. This relationship might entail long-term commitments by both parties to procure future production or investment. These suppliers become strategic partners, and the technological systems set up to share information with them are often critical components. Examples are MRO suppliers.

- *Strategic-cooperative.* A supplier that offers a strategic product—but not a unique or scarce product—is a candidate for a cooperative relationship. This might entail incentives for the supplier to invest in improving the procurement chain, such as reducing the number of suppliers to increase the volume of business you give to each. Cooperative relationships may be short-, medium-, or long-term relationships. Examples are computer suppliers.

- *Nonstrategic-limited.* A supplier that provides products or services that are not strategic to your organization's success and are limited in supply is a candidate for a short-term, nonstrategic, limited relationship. In this situation, you look at the quality and the value provided by the supplier versus the availability of similar products and services from other suppliers. Examples are administrative and professional services, such as temp agency services.

- *Nonstrategic-commodity.* A supplier offering a nonstrategic product that is in plentiful supply will have a nonstrategic, commodity relationship with your company. With these kinds of products or services, you can tolerate price variations without feeling a critical impact on your strategic products or services. These relationships are usually short term, with minimal commitment. Examples are office and book suppliers.

When using a SIM, review your supplier set on a periodic basis to determine whether external or internal factors have changed enough to require moving suppliers to a different classification. A good SIM model can prevent roadblocks in the procurement process.

Step 5: Select an e-Procurement Application

Enterprises should wade through the vendor hype. Obviously, there is much to consider in selecting an e-procurement application. However, many of these issues can be addressed by asking the following questions:

- *Will it support my procurement process?* Optimization of the business process is the goal. The application choice must support that goal. For instance, a proprietary catalog system might create more problems than it solves. Careful evaluation of the application support for the buy-side process must be done.

- *Does it leverage my other application investments?* You've probably already made multimillion-dollar investments in enterprise resource management systems. Therefore, it is imperative that the procurement solution build on these investments rather than recreating the same functionality.

- *Will it work seamlessly with other applications?* Procurement is a complex chain of events. The solution must interface with the various integration points along the procurement chain. For example, it must exchange accounting information with the general ledger system. Likewise, the receiving function must feed accounts payable and asset management systems.

- *Is it extendable?* Can it accommodate technology from other vendors? With technology innovation being unpredictable, it is important that the solution be scalable and extendable in new directions. For instance, can the solution leverage new best practices as they emerge? The solution must keep the door open to take advantage of new twists and turns in technology.

Table 10.5 presents a quick checklist to help evaluate various solutions. Taking the time to do the spadework will save a lot of heartache downstream.

Step 6: Remember: Integration Is Everything

You must absolutely avoid gathering requirements, disappearing for 6 months, and then launching the "completed" portal. This strategy is doomed to failure. The ideal goal for managers should be to continuously iterate toward the target—the integration sweet spot (see Figure 10.10). By focusing on each of the areas of operating resource management (ORM), none will be left out of the integration effort. This will ensure that the requirements of employees, suppliers, and buyers are considered when you are building your integrated ORM application.

Enterprises should iterate development and deployment. We can't stress strongly enough how critical it is to the success of your e-procurement chain that you not take an exclusive buy-side or sell-side viewpoint. Companies implementing

Table 10.5: Evaluation Checklist

Function	Questions for Evaluating Vendor Solutions
Requisition management	• Are the selection and purchase of goods automated right from the desktop? • Can requisitions be created without data entry? • Can users pick from noncataloged items?
Catalog management	• Does the solution provide multisupplier search capability? • Can it access supplier-maintained, Web-based catalogs? • Can it control the number of preferred suppliers, eliminating unauthorized purchasing by employees?
Transaction management orders?	• Are requisitions seamlessly converted into purchase • Is there a log of every activity associated with the order? • Is the approval process easy to navigate?
Supplier management	• Is there seamless flow from the employee to the supplier and back? • Is there real-time connectivity to check for product availability? • Does it electronically send and receive the full range of requisition documents from buyers—purchase orders and requisitions, invoices, advance shipping notices, and acknowledgments?
Back-office integration	• Does the system easily interface with other applications? • Does the system provide easy administrative tools for management?
Overall sophistication	• Does it integrate the sourcing, ordering, and payment processes into one end-to-end solution that takes advantage of current buyer/supplier relationships? • Does it reports quickly and accurately about organization-wide purchasing patterns?

ORM solutions often choose one or the other. In our experience, we've found that this does not lead to good integrated solutions. You must collaborate with the supplier. Collaboration means both the buy-side and sell-side applications must dance cheek to cheek for effective procurement.

A significant issue in development will be integration with other back-office systems. Even amid a flurry of partnerships with ERP vendors, the integration of procurement applications with older legacy applications could be a big challenge. ERP and middleware companies are working to improve this situation.

Figure 10.10: The Three Faces of ORM Applications

Step 7: Educate, Educate, Educate

How much of a change in behavior does using your marketplace require on the part of suppliers and buyers? The less, the better. Change often generates opposition. If opposition slows the e-procurement project down or alters its direction, major problems occur, among them schedule slippage, higher costs, and poor morale. Senior management must deal with this problem by listening, communicating, selling, and, when all else fails, firing. If senior management can't do this, the project will fail. The opposition will grind down the project team to an expensive crowd of people wandering around accomplishing nothing.

Failure to take care of the "soft" implementation roadblocks—people—may be the most common reason that projects don't succeed. Why do companies let this happen? Why don't they work on the soft stuff? Because it's difficult. It's so much easier to get all wrapped up in the software modules and the transaction and processing speeds of the new computers. We see this frequently when companies are implementing ERP systems. Enormous amounts of staff time, mental energy, and dollars are devoted to working on the software, and relatively little time is devoted to people. The result: resistance, subpar results, and a lot of money spent for not much payback.

Finally, enterprises should not underestimate the effort and costs of deployment. Remember that your procurement chain is a dynamic, living organism. It consists of people, information, technology, and systems. The key point here is that it never stops changing. At today's maddening pace, it is critical that we keep in mind that procurement is a continuous process and not merely discrete elements. To be successful, continuous improvement is absolutely key.

Memo to the CEO

The world of e-procurement is changing at a dizzying pace. Executives know that their companies have to operate, day-in, day-out, buying components, raw materials, services, and supplies; collaborating and negotiating; maintaining their distribution capabilities; and translating their customers' interests into advanced designs and dependable products. And B2B procurement is rapidly becoming the most efficient way to conduct all these modes of business.

Regardless of the industry, today's competitive pressures and unrelenting focus on profits mean that operational cost reduction is more than just a nicety. Three catalysts driving growth in the e-procurement space are

- *Cost savings.* Applications reduce purchasing costs by nearly 90 percent, which translates into dramatically better margins for buyers. Centralizing procurement activities concentrates the total spending and improves negotiating power.

- *Improved efficiency.* Focus purchasing on strategic, value-added upstream portions of the business rather than on transactional, downstream activities.

- *Control.* Increase purchasing's role in the company's total spending, including such nontraditional areas as operating resource procurement. Web-based procurement exchanges provide better inventory management, faster time to market, and use less working capital than traditional means of procurement.

The e-procurement suite of Web-based cost management solutions provides employees and purchasing professionals with an opportunity to deliver cost savings and to increase bottom-line results. By directly reducing your operating resource costs, e-procurement affects your bottom line. e-Procurement also decreases cycle time by focusing on enterprise processes untouched by automation, streamlining the costly, time-consuming, paper-based processes associated with acquiring most goods and services and replacing them with an automated, easy-to-use system.

By providing improved visibility into the process flow, e-procurement can strengthen management control. e-Procurement reduces maverick buying, ensures compliance with corporate policies, and institutionalizes a company's best business practices. While improving accountability and control, implementing e-procurement can improve productivity. End users know the status of requests and receive approval sooner, so they get the goods and services they need more quickly. e-Procurement can build strategic supplier relationships and use aggregate buying to gain volume discounts from suppliers.

The advances in e-procurement applications are promising, with the potential to turn the management of purchasing into a strategic weapon. Most important, the savings gained from procurement automation drop directly to the bottom line to deliver a substantial boost to profitability. However, for e-procurement, there will be several years of "tire kicking," during which most organizations test and pilot solutions but do not fully deploy them. We expect significant e-procurement deployments to take place in a couple of years. As other companies deploy their solutions, they can learn from the best and worst practices mentioned here and leverage their experiences in their own e-procurement efforts.

CHAPTER ELEVEN

Business Intelligence: The Next Generation of Knowledge Management

What to Expect

Conventional wisdom says that knowledge is power. An undifferentiated mass of information is not knowledge. Intelligence results from a company's using its intellectual resources and capabilities to bring focus, clarity, and meaning to the large volumes of information and data made available by today's technology. However, attempting to harvest knowledge without having the necessary analytical tools can render a company powerless. As companies adopt responsive, event-driven e-business models, they have to invest in new knowledge frameworks to help them respond to changing market conditions and customer needs.

The challenge is how to transform the incredible amount of valuable data locked away in a company's applications, storage platforms, and databases into new revenue opportunities. Converting data into knowledge is the job of applications known as business intelligence (BI). BI is an emerging group of applications designed to organize and to structure a business's transaction data so that it can be analyzed in ways beneficial to company decision support and operations.

In this chapter, we examine BI's capability to tailor information content, format, and interaction to the needs of individual users. The BI trend provides customized and personalized information to customers and other end users through a variety of channels: e-mail, pagers, faxes, and Web pages. We review the basic elements on which BI is built—personalization, analysis and segmentation, reporting, what-if analysis—that form the foundation of BI applications. We also examine several areas in which BI is being used, including employee benefits management, customer management, and information retrieval. The chapter concludes with an easy-to-follow manager's guide for establishing a BI framework in your firm.

> The main objective in war, as in life, is to deduce what you do not know from what you do know.
>
> — The Duke of Wellington

In business, knowledge is neither a product nor a capability. Rather, knowledge is a critical framework of a fully evolved information economy. Let's consider two examples.

A multibillion-dollar retailer of electronics with more than 5,000 stores nationwide delivers an online weekly sales report to managers, who use this report to identify "hot spots"—locations where products are selling at a faster rate than in the rest of the country. By identifying these hot spots, the retailer can inform its manufacturing partners what products are in demand in which regions, enabling them to manage inventory levels in response to real-time sales events.

An insurance claim software provider offers more than 200 auto insurance companies the ability to access and to analyze insurance claim data via the Web. Its consumer database alone includes profiles of more than 1 million consumers. Auto insurance companies access and analyze nationwide insurance claim data, including repair-cycle times and the amounts paid for vehicle parts, and compare their claim-resolution performance against industry averages and historical trends.

These companies and many more like them are running "about the business" applications. For example, Wal-Mart, which operates more than 2,400 stores, supercenters, and 450 SAM's Clubs in the United States and more than 725 stores internationally, has developed a 100-terabyte data warehouse that monitors and captures each transaction in each store. The company's goal is better inventory management and improved collaboration with suppliers, which in turn enables Wal-Mart to merchandise each store on an individual basis and to provide superior local shopper satisfaction.

Wal-Mart's software, Retail Link, gives suppliers access to sales, inventory, and pricing information at Wal-Mart stores and SAM's Clubs. More than 7,000 suppliers access the data warehouse via Wal-Mart's Retail Link, enabling suppliers to know exactly what is selling where, plan their production accordingly, and keep inventories under control. With sales and in-stock information transmitted between Wal-Mart and their suppliers over the Internet, buyers and suppliers have a single source of information, thereby saving a significant amount of time over more traditional systems.

The Wal-Mart data warehouse, powered by NCR's Teradata servers, runs more than 30 business applications, supports more than 18,000 users, and handles some 120,000 complex queries a week.[1] As Wal-Mart captures shoppers' transactions, the data warehouse receives 8.4 million updates every minute during peak times—detailed data on each item purchased. Wal-Mart's sophisticated knowledge management strategy is based on a simple premise: Success comes from anticipating customer needs—even before they do.

Whereas the first generation of e-business applications focused on buying and selling goods via the Web, second-generation e-business applications focus on organizations' gaining insight from the data collected with each transaction. These applications analyze data more effectively to develop customer loyalty and to enhance profitability, analyzing a business's customer interactions and helping optimize its customer relationships. Second-generation e-business applications aid in both interpreting what has happened in past transactions and using this knowledge to support decisions about which direction the company should be headed.

Evolution of Knowledge Management (KM) Applications

You've got operational data, transactional data, and a boatload of e-commerce data. Today's companies are looking for application solutions to help make sense of the information gathered. Companies want to know

- How to make effective use of raw data

- How to convert raw data into revenue

For example, FedEx reengineered its database marketing process from marketing and campaign planning to customer segmentation, evaluation, and refinement. A knowledge application has been instrumental in FedEx's efforts to automate its database marketing process. FedEx reports a time reduction in direct-marketing campaign cycles and a major improvement in "prospecting" campaigns.[2] Companies are demanding more than access to data. They want processed and refined information that will help reach effective tactical decisions.

At Best Buy, it used to take months to profile customers and to reasonably predict their purchasing behavior. Now, the company's new Web-based applications take less than half that time. The Web browser has become the de facto interface for the "information at your fingertips" paradigm. The browser's speed enables the retailer to direct services to its most valued customers much more aggressively in a highly competitive marketplace.

The foundation of any KM framework is information sorting, extraction, packaging, and dissemination. Retailers, manufacturers, and financial institutions have spent millions of dollars to build data warehouses containing masses of information about their customers and their transactions. At headquarters, managers use query engines and reporting tools to extract useful information from data warehouses. The reactive, data centric world of today is gradually changing into the proactive, query-driven knowledge world of tomorrow. Figure 11.1 shows how KM has evolved in the past decade. This evolution has occurred in five waves, the last two of which are ongoing.

Wave 1: Group Memory Systems

Most companies will tell you that their two greatest assets are employees and the knowledge they possess. In its broadest sense, group memory is the sharing of information throughout the company. Group memory systems included discussion boards or bulletin systems, such as Lotus Notes and corporate intranets. This technology provided a company's employees with instant access to data and reporting information that had previously taken days or weeks to obtain.

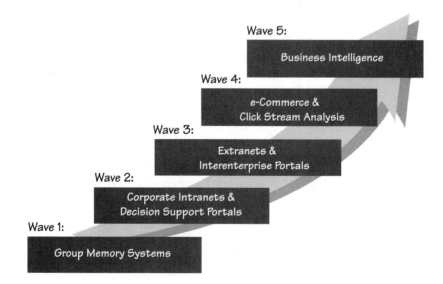

Figure 11.1: Evolution of Knowledge Management Applications

For example, Intraspect, a knowledge management start-up company, used its applications to integrate collaboration, organization, searches, and subscription in a single location called a group memory (GM). Contribution and subscription to the group memory is easy because of GM's tight integration with the company's e-mail and desktop applications. Search tools help locate and reuse information in the group memory, the company's Web servers, and legacy databases.

Lotus Notes and Intraspect applications form the core of group memory systems. The main goal of GM is to enable companies to use their own data to determine best practices, to retain the tacit knowledge and experience of individuals, and to classify employee expertise. GM also makes it easier for corporations to react more quickly and decisively to problems, as well as to competitors. The methods and combinations of products needed to implement a GM application, however, vary widely.

Although GM was the buzzword of the 1990s, it failed to live up to its promise, being long on cost and short on results. Consequently, companies have been reluctant to adopt the technology, for the following reasons.

- *Few can define it.* Vendors of document management systems, data warehousing applications, and push technology all claim to provide GM tools, but some consulting firms help clients indiscriminately develop GM strategies for virtually any process without consideration for the enterprise-wide scope that is needed. Firms are faced with a deluge of contradictory and confusing efforts.

- *Software vendors are distancing themselves from GM as a product.* Riding the corporate fascination with the GM wave is no more. GM was to the late 1990s what reengineering was to the early part of the decade, a fad spawned by consultants and vendors to generate demand for their products and services.

- *Costly group memory efforts aren't delivering expected returns on investment.* The efforts of one company have produced a number of knowledge databases using Lotus Notes. The most widely used is the "gossip and rumors" database. In fact, GM is referred to as the "knowledge scam," owing to the miniscule ROI that firms receive from their GM efforts. At most companies, GM-like efforts have evolved into corporate intranets.

Unfortunately, GM's hype and failure have resulted in businesses' throwing the baby out with the bath water. However, new ideas and approaches, once suppressed, have a way of reappearing in new forms. *Does your company have a group memory effort? What have results been so far?*

Wave 2: Corporate Intranets and Decision Support Portals

Using corporate intranets and decision support portals, companies seek to create more complete and uniform linkage of the data resources scattered throughout the organization. The technology enabling this development is the corporate intranet. Moving from departmental solutions, in which data and reports are developed for small, specialized communities of users, to a corporate intranet opens up a company's data resources to a broader base of users by using the browser as a standard interface.

However, dumping reams of information on employees' desktops isn't effective. Key information should be disbursed just in time when the user needs it. For example, a large software company improved its sales-close ratio when it tracked the sales force's progress in the sales cycle and then distributed competitor intelligence or industry-specific information only at relevant points in the sales cycle.

Clearly, corporate intranets alone do not create knowledge, much less manage it. For knowledge to be created, data aggregation must be complemented by data analysis. One trend is to perform data analysis by using decision support portals. With databases growing larger every day and the time available for in-depth business analysis shrinking, automating the predictable components of a decision maker's routine, where possible, makes a lot of sense. Managers also use decision support portals to conduct data mining, the process of analyzing large quantities of data to discover relationships and patterns to support better decision making.

Decision support portals built on corporate intranets are a prerequisite for creating a responsive business model. For example, Home Depot, the do-it-yourself building supplies retailing giant, is pushing knowledge to the staff level. Home Depot carries a diverse inventory in its more than 500 stores. Most of its stores have installed Home Depot's Mobile Ordering platform, a radio-frequency-transmitted data warehouse link. The system uses cart devices to let floor clerks and department managers access data analyses of the store's past and present inventory in order to make merchandise ordering decisions while standing in front of the merchandise itself.[3]

As this example illustrates, decision support applications streamline the process of turning decision into action. The objective is to help users address any critical issues facing their businesses by answering highly focused, industry-specific management questions.

- *Retail:* What products or groups of products should our company sell? Where? At what price? How much shelf space should be allocated for specific products? How much promotion should each product receive? Which products sell well together? How much inventory should be carried? What was the in-stock position and stock-to-sales ratio of the ten most profitable and ten least profitable items?

- *Banking and finance:* What are the 100 most profitable customers by branch, and how are they contributing to income? What portion of the contribution comes from fees? Interest income? Overdraft charges? Whom should I target for direct-marketing efforts? What is the proper pricing strategy for a given set of financial products? Which customer groups are credit risks? How much fraudulent activity is occurring?

- *Telecommunications:* Of the customers who have switched carriers in the past month, what are their average call volumes and dollars spent since they signed up with my company? What are the same metrics for the 3 months before they quit?

- *Healthcare:* What is the range of outcomes for a given treatment? How frequently is this treatment prescribed? Which drugs, hospitals, doctors, and health plans are most effective? Which patient groups are most at risk? How efficient and effective is a given technique for treating a specific illness?

The promise of intranet-based decision support applications is to offer decision makers the opportunity to ask and to answer mission-critical questions about their businesses, using transactional data assets that have been captured, but not exploited, to their fullest extent.

Wave 3: Extranets and Interenterprise Portals

As companies begin to implement supply chain strategies, they will move select parts of the internal corporate information infrastructure outside the firewall so that suppliers and trading partners can access them. These extranets are driven by fast information access, customized data, and responsiveness.

Extranet-based interenterprise linkages create new requirements: the ability to manage huge data volumes, data breadth coverage, cross-platform support, response-time speed, and a broad range of interface choices. For example, every day, DaimlerChrysler's massive Mopar parts operation ships about 220,000 items from 3,000 suppliers to its 15,000 dealers. A logistical nightmare, the operation is a monitoring and forecasting balancing act to ensure that the parts pipeline stays just full enough but not too full. Dozens of planners and forecasters manage atop this network, making decisions about how many engines to ship to Phoenix or correcting an undersupply of brakeshoes in Boston. If the pipeline is constricted, customers go without the parts they need, meaning that costs rise as parts are rushed to them. If the pipeline is full, DaimlerChrysler ends up paying for needless inventory. Viewing these transactions in real time using a Web browser provides invaluable data to DaimlerChrysler's management team to make pipeline adjustments as the parts are distributed from the group's 15 distribution centers.[4]

Extranet-based applications encourage trading partners to improve profits by managing inventories in the supply chain. In order to obtain information visibility and reliability, a company's partners may be willing to offer more favorable terms, invest more in comarketing, make available increased levels of supplies, provide more shelf space, or pay higher prices. The extranet-based KM strategy goal is to give preferential treatment to one another in exchange for detailed ordering and inventory information that provides greater process reliability and visibility up and down the supply chains.

For example, Lexmark, which manufactures and distributes laser and inkjet printers for the office and home markets, is using extranet-based solutions from Microstrategy to help customers manage their inventories. Through Lexmark's data warehouse and an inventory management application called the Retail Management System (RMS), Lexmark aims to help dozens of large retailers manage their inventories of printers. The company is using an approach called vendor-managed inventory (VMI), which is used by the retail packaged-goods industry to track inventory. VMI helps replenish inventory before it's depleted. In contrast, stores without VMI often don't order inventory until after it runs out, because they're too busy to act in advance.[5]

Potential users of Lexmark's RMS application include a firm's vendors, distributors, partners, outsourcers, resellers, and financing sources. Initially, the RMS project was used to provide customer inventory information to about 35 field salespeople but later was expanded to provide management reports to about 75 top executives and line managers at headquarters. The number of potential supply chain DSS users can range from hundreds to tens of thousands.

In addition to boosting sales, RMS gives Lexmark a better idea of where its customers are and the best locations for its products. The data warehouse replaces a system in which inventory figures were compiled by paper. Using the data warehouse, sales and inventory information that once took 4 or 5 days to turn around is now compiled in half a day.

Lexmark's RMS application is an example of an interenterprise knowledge portal. As such, it provides access to valuable retail sales information that can be used to design new products, refine marketing campaigns, develop optimal pricing schemes, rationally allocate inventory, and proactively schedule factory production.

Wave 4: e-Commerce and Click-Stream Analysis

Successful online interactions with customers don't happen by chance. The rise of e-commerce has helped new forms of KM management to emerge, such as user click-stream analysis, e-mail management, and multichannel knowledge portals.

User Click-Stream Analysis

Click-stream analysis provides the electronic footprints that show where people go on the Web, what they do or buy, and when they return. What marketers need is the ability to always be aware of every customer activity and purchase, as well as to be able to analyze and to understand their buying preferences and to anticipate their changing expectations.

Collecting and analyzing all the mouse clicks of a company's prospects and customers is a nightmare for companies ill-prepared to handle this amount of information. How can businesses prepare? User click-stream data is accumulating so quickly at some Web sites that it's testing the limits of conventional approaches to database management. As a result, a new generation of much larger, faster-growing databases in the 5-, 10-, or even 15-terabyte range is being developed, forcing managers to invent new roadmaps on database design, storage, backup, and archiving.

e-Mail Management

Another rapidly growing KM area is intelligent e-mail management. Companies providing these applications include eGain, Kana Communications, and Siebel. Until recently, a company's relationships with its customers and partners were based on in-person, telephone, or written interactions. In order to communicate effectively, companies invested substantial resources in call centers. Typical call centers were customer service oriented, often using costly technology, and were not scalable. Also, outbound direct-marketing calls are expensive and only minimally effective in their conversion and response rates. With the advent of new channels and the proliferation of e-mail, business communications with customers and partners has fundamentally changed.

KM infrastructure enables companies and their partners to interact at any time through a variety of communication channels, including the Web, e-mail, telephone, and the storefront. The KM infrastructure should provide e-businesses with the ability to track and to manage millions of daily interactions and permit the companies to analyze, report, and launch customized initiatives in response. A KM infrastructure combines automation, business rules, artificial intelligence, work flow, analytics, and advanced messaging-analysis technologies to allow e-businesses to deliver information and to respond to customer requests rapidly and accurately.

Knowledge Portals (KP)

Multichannel knowledge portal software lets users search, process, and present data in corporate intranets, using a standard Web browser. Among the growing number of portal vendors are Brio, Business Objects, Cognos, DataChannel, Plumtree, Portera, and Viador.

How do knowledge portals work? A call center manager uses a KP to monitor customer service agent productivity in approximately 30 call centers using more than 500 queues. Call center managers can use KP to gain a detailed understanding of how various agent activities relate to call center performance and to measure the effectiveness of the center's various training initiatives. The insights gained from the KP analysis enable managers to understand historical service trends and customer service patterns, quickly identify problem areas, and ultimately increase customer-retention rates.

Another example is a sales manager who is using a KP application to quickly analyze and report on sales productivity, providing each division on-demand access to any relevant reports via the Web. The portal permits the manager to drill down into sales data by individual agent, product, and service, as well as to monitor sales performance trends and product churn at the division level.

Wave 5: Business Intelligence

Data analytics, coupled with broadcast engine technology, is the foundation for proactive business intelligence: any time, anywhere, and any place. As companies gather information from their own activities, they also seek to syndicate and to resell that information. For instance, credit card firms do not restrict themselves to processing individual sales transactions but also actively package the transaction information for sale to other customers. The commercialization of individual transactional data raises significant issues of privacy, intellectual property, and pricing. These issues will dominate discussions of BI as new business models are designed to capture, consolidate, and resell consumer information, business transaction records, and financial data.

BI, based on personalized information, is proactive and data driven. Personalization is the use of technology for the proactive capture, organization, and delivery of information to individuals. For instance, at the National Weather Service, reports on pollen count, in conjunction with patient profiles, alert specific asthma patients to renew their allergy medication prescriptions. BI automates the delivery of information to customers by using exception conditions and recurring schedules as triggers for communication.

Traditional decision support applications do not personalize information. As a result, decision support applications must change to include new personalization and distribution capabilities. An example of this trend can already be seen in MicroStrategy's DSS Broadcaster, a database add-on that uses push technology to send subscribers information based on predefined parameters. Preset queries are run against the company's data warehouse. Users can either receive all reports or receive an alert through e-mail, fax, or pager when an exception occurs. For example, a customer deposits $50,000 into a direct deposit account. A message is automatically sent to a marketing representative so that he or she can act on this potential cross-sell opportunity.

Figure 11.2 shows the new end-to-end model for converting data into transaction revenue. BI's five components—information, analysis, personalization, multichannel delivery, and transactions—when properly configured, form a robust, scalable, and flexible BI platform. These new applications turn the traditional query-and-response paradigm of decision support on its head. With this new generation of applications, the logic is reversed: What if the system didn't wait for the end user to ask a question? What if the system just asked the question for them and sent them the answer? For example, a customer's desire to receive news on Federal Reserve rate changes can be leveraged by a bank to package it with an offer for a low-interest home loan.

True personalization demands that each customer experience be tailored to the type of communications device. Using a powerful personalization engine, a company can provide a unique experience to the same customer on a variety of

| Customer-Centric Information | Analysis and Segmentation | Personalized for Each Customer | Multi-Channel Delivery | Facilitate Interaction or Transaction |

Figure 11.2: The End-to-End Model

communications devices. BI applications assume that customers dislike information clutter and that given a chance, they will indicate their preference for the type of information they receive, the frequency of subsequent communication, and the medium for communication.

The next generation of BI applications will use e-commerce technology to open up the world of the data warehouse to hand-held devices. Prior models relied only on static information about customer transactions. BI assumes that corporations will shift their capital priorities in order to invest in a "sense and respond" infrastructure to serve customers better. These applications allow firms to not only collect but also analyze data for use in building more profitable supplier and customer relationships and to increase profitability through revenue growth.

However, for information-based business intelligence models to function well, an integration framework must tie together the various classes of knowledge applications. Without this integration framework, companies may not reap the benefits they expect from their knowledge investments.

Elements of Business Intelligence Applications

Business knowledge doesn't just happen. Several key KM elements must come together before a data jungle can be transformed into a revenue-generating asset. Figure 11.3 illustrates the elements of KM:

- Data/content organization and collection

- Analysis and segmentation

- Real-time personalization

- Broadcast, retrieval, and interaction

- Performance monitoring and measurement

Data Organization and Collection

Imagine the following scenario: A customer visits a brick-and-mortar store and at checkout, gives the clerk her e-mail address. Later, at home, the customer receives a "thank you for visiting" e-mail, along with a special offer. Intrigued, the customer clicks on the embedded URL to access the online store and views other products or complementary products to those previously purchased. A few days later, the customer is alerted by e-mail about an evening special available only to

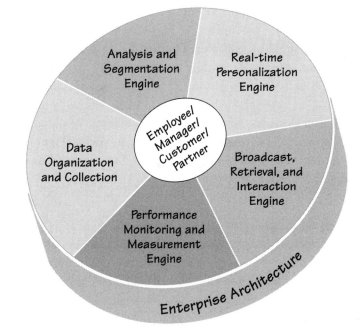

Figure 11.3: Elements of Knowledge Management Applications

online customers. The customer makes a purchase online and picks up the package at the store next day.

In order to provide this level of customer access and "push" technology requires preparation. A data warehouse initiative is often the first requirement for a successful BI strategy. Following are a few examples of companies undertaking such initiatives.

- 3M has a data warehouse with 5 terabytes of capacity for storing and analyzing financial, customer, sales, and inventory data. This data helps achieve consistency of facts and definitions across various corporate functions.

- Office Depot has a multiterabyte data warehouse loaded with sales transaction information used for market analysis and demand forecasting.

- Travelocity has invested in a multiterabyte data warehouse to solve the following problems: growth exceeded data warehouse capacity, long queries, high overhead, poor data quality, and validation. The company's goal is to better manage the customer life cycle and buying cycles and to target customer promotions and offers.

BI initiatives require visibility into an organization's activities with both its external and internal constituencies. Today, however, data about customers, partners, and suppliers is captured and stored in many locations throughout the enterprise. Integrated views are needed to enable companies to recognize and to respond accurately to customers, whether they purchase products through a physical store, telephone call, or Web site. BI also helps coordinate information between brick-and-mortar and online initiatives. BI initiatives depend on integrated data from a variety of information sources (see Figure 11.4): Web sites, call centers, customer profile and transaction history, transactional systems, operational databases, ERP systems, and third-party data.

The following factors are critical to the success of large-scale data integration efforts:

- *Scalability.* Companies tend to underestimate the effort and volume of the data required to develop a complete view of their transactions, customers, and visitors. Companies must assume that they'll need terabyte-sized customer-centric information storage. Click-stream data alone can consume several

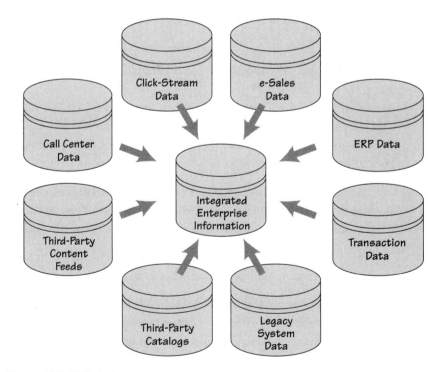

Figure 11.4: BI Data Sources

gigabytes a day, with transactional data and third-party data adding exponentially to the volume.

- *Flexibility.* The BI initiative must accommodate multiple data models and database architectures and allow for integration with other back-end information systems. This helps create a rich picture of every customer as more transaction data is gathered. Without this flexibility, the usefulness of BI efforts will diminish over time.

- *Performance.* Information queries need to be completed in minutes rather than hours or days. Fast and accurate access to customer and transaction information ensures a dialogue with customers at every touchpoint, presenting a single face to the customer. In addition, the ability to aggregate information at differing levels of abstraction, such as transaction, customer, and zip code, makes it possible to discern patterns of customer behavior—for example, the sizes sold by zip code.

Although data organization can be difficult, the payoff is worth the effort. Companies that have an incomplete view of the customer will suffer harsh consequences. In presenting customers with inappropriate offers, they dilute customer loyalty and trust and increase customer dissatisfaction.

Analysis and Segmentation

Analysis and segmentation applications offer tools for data mining. The goal of data mining is to improve pricing, retain customers longer, and find new revenue streams. For example, Travelocity, an online travel site, taps a database of information on its 19 million customers to develop travel offers that are e-mailed to segments of the company's customer base. Travelocity applications perform analysis, segmentation, and prediction to ensure that these communications take place in a personalized manner.

Many Internet businesses don't have a clue when it comes to understanding customer behavior on their Web sites. They collect gigabytes of customer clickstream data each day but don't have the applications to answer even basic questions, such as Which referring sites are most effective in getting customers to my Web site? At which times do we get the most users? Table 11.1 shows how analytical applications take advantage of the unified data set to ask questions about frequently repeated customer behavior and preferences in a retail setting. Consequently, these findings can boost the effectiveness of any marketing campaign's formulation, execution, or testing. For any e-business marketing campaign, the emphasis has got to

Table 11.1: Analytical Applications in a Retail Setting

Question	Analysis and Segmentation Activity	Technical Application
Who are our most frequent shoppers online and offline?	Frequent shoppers (precise targeting of customer segments)	Query the database, applying statistical function to determine top 20% of frequent shoppers
What do frequent customers have in common?	Attributes of frequent shoppers	Using data mining tools, identify trends in the frequent-customer segment
How do we identify products that provide a healthy return and those that have low margins?	Link frequent-shopper bills to products	Establish relationship between shopper attributes, bills, and margin of products being purchased
How can a campaign be constructed to reach these segments to cross-sell new products?	Identification of segment details	Query the database for detailed customer information on the new segments

be order size and margin. You must get customers to spend more, and to spend it on the most profitable stuff. Money spent attracting the customer and shipping goods is wasted if he buys a $10.00 item and never returns.

Several industries are eager to exploit the opportunities made possible by analysis engines. The telecom industry is using analysis and segmentation applications to increase profitability. For example, BC Telecom, Canada's second-largest telco, faced many challenges in marketing its services and managing customer relationships across their life cycles. One challenge was the need to shift its focus from product marketing to customer-centric marketing. Although it had made a major investment in a multiterabyte data warehouse, BC Telecom believed that its processes and marketing systems were not well integrated with the transaction information available, and the company's large investment was not generating optimal returns. To solve these integration problems, BC Telecom implemented a customer optimization service. Within 3 months, the company had achieved significant results from targeted marketing campaigns aimed at its 1.7 million customers. This example illustrates how relationship mining begins with developing a clear picture of customer behavior.

Without analytical tools, massive volumes of customer-centric information become useless. For example, in the banking industry, the history of a customer's transactions offers insight into his or her lifestyle. Analyzing customer information is not simple. The information is scattered throughout the various functional areas of the bank, where it is stored according to the rules governing each functional area. Even when customer data collection is centralized, it's still a challenge to transform that information into knowledge capital for use in building profitable, long-term relationships with customers. Data warehousing has been promising this KM benefit for some time but has focused primarily on the technology rather than on the value of the knowledge that can be extracted from the warehoused information.

Real-Time Personalization

The personalization of customer information is possible because of the convergence of e-commerce and real-time relationship management. Personalization capabilities help companies better understand and respond to each customer's needs, behaviors, and intentions, ensuring that customers get exactly what they need—when they need it.

Customers want to interact with companies whose products and services fit their needs. Customers don't want to be treated as part of a crowd, a mass. Recent research indicates that 39 percent of online shoppers failed in doing what they set out to do. A staggering 66 percent of loaded online shopping carts were abandoned before the checkout process. Less than 5 percent of visitors became customers.[6] Therefore, a new breed of personalization applications is emerging to meet the following needs: a business that is responsive to customers, shows interest—knows who they are, keeps them informed—knows their needs, appreciates their business, and makes them feel valued (see Figure 11.5).

A personalization application makes it possible to customize products and services in a cost-effective manner by lowering the marginal cost of personalization. Until now, personalized attention and service were labor intensive and not scalable to serve a large customer base without high costs. Most companies provide personalized attention to a small group of their best clients. Today, every Amazon.com customer gets recommendations for books, owing to Amazon's personalization technology. The addition of thousands of customers to Amazon's customer base has had a minimal effect on its cost to sustain this excellent level of service.

Personalization involves using user-defined information filters and specifying events as triggers for information delivery. Time-sensitive information, such as a stock quote, can be personalized in a number of ways. Both BI and KM applications support multiple output devices—e-mail, Web page, fax, pager, cell phone—with the appropriate device-specific formatting, so data can be sent to specific end users, based on their needs. Personalization also involves delivering information using natural-language sentences rather than traditional report formats.

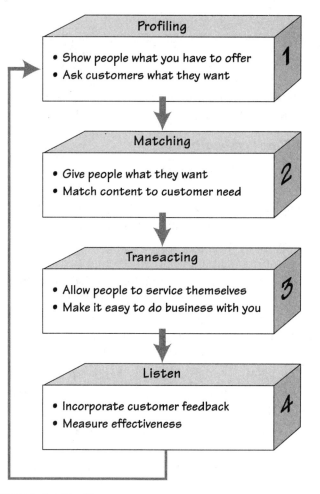

Figure 11.5: Personalization Step

Personalization applications allow you to

• Provide each customer with a personalized Web page—a portal—that allows the customer to interact, transact, and collaborate with the company. For example, provide customers with one-click access to all related activity—from support requests and credit checking to sales questions and order-status information.

• Display only the information you want individual customers to see. For example, all customer cases—inquiries, trouble tickets, purchases, and so on—can be stored in the same database, but each customer sees only his or her own.

- Proactively notify customers of product improvements and upgrades, promotions, and service enhancements relevant to them. Your most loyal customers are automatically provided the highest level of service and managed in a distinct business process.

- Tailor information and recommendations according to each customer's individual preferences. For example, prefill service or sales requests with customer data, saving them and you time from having to repeatedly ask for the same information.

- Deliver personally relevant information related to the products that customers own. Avoid overwhelming customers with unrelated information.

A key component of the next wave of e-commerce is personalization. Personalization increases efficiency and customer enthusiasm when interacting with your company. *Is your company considering implementing the technological foundation for personalizing its offerings?*

Infrastructure for Broadcast, Retrieval, and Interaction

This infrastructure proactively delivers information to every customer via the medium of his or her choice. For example, Microstrategy's DSS Broadcaster, which was implemented at Sabre, books $66 billion in travel reservations a year. Sabre has built a 2-terabyte warehouse of airline bookings, which will grow to 4 terabytes when hotel and rental car bookings are added. About 1,000 Sabre employees access at least some of the data, as will the airlines that presently buy tapes of Sabre's raw booking data. Using Broadcaster, Sabre plans to sell e-mailed reports to travel agents and companies that want control of their travel costs. The recipients can use the data to analyze who books an inordinate number of expensive, last-minute fares.[7]

Although use of the Web is becoming more and more widespread and 24/7 the corporate standard for customer access, few customers are online all day. However, they can be reached through other communication devices, the number of which is expected to quadruple per customer in the next 5 years. Corporate use of wireless technology will also quadruple in the next 3 years. A successful KM strategy requires an engine that will reach millions of customers wherever they are—via phone or WAP phone pager, television, or e-mail. A scalable broadcast infrastructure built on an open architecture and supportive of all communication devices enables this level of customer interaction.

Both prefabricated and custom-made software can be integrated into the platform to provide services to millions of customers. Equipped with such a communications infrastructure, companies can continually create significant customer value at Internet speed, automating the who, what, when, where, and how of sales and marketing.

Performance Monitoring and Measurement

Performance monitoring and measurement applications provide the information that managers need to improve operations and strategy. By using key performance indicators (KPIs) linked to a balanced scorecard, companies can continuously monitor process performance against its strategic targets. An effective monitoring system is the best way to translate strategy into action.

For example, its Interactive and Reporting Information System (IRIS), permits British Telecom (BT) to track more than 10,000 ongoing development projects. IRIS provides up-to-the-minute project information, helping managers make accurate spending and management decisions. IRIS enables BT to perform program management strategy, which groups together projects with a common business theme. However, IRIS requires a new business framework that includes more sophisticated analysis and reporting capabilities, including precanned reporting, data analysis, modeling, and forecasting and other knowledge-oriented functionality.[8]

BT has chosen SAP's Strategic Enterprise Management (SEM) suite, a set of applications enabling executives to make informed decisions in a corporate war-room environment. SEM's Management Cockpit, the system's core, displays key performance monitors graphically on large color-coded screens, similar to military war rooms in which a tremendous amount of battlefield information is processed for decision making.

SEM generates information to help executives make quick decisions. SAP's Business Warehouse application feeds the Management Cockpit with all relevant data, including information from transaction systems and external sources, and also provides executive teams with up-to-the-minute corporate data in continuous view. The goal is to let executives see external market trends and interrelationships in cross-functional business data and to receive early warning signs of missed targets.[9]

What Web-enabled performance monitoring and measurement solutions is your company considering?

Business Intelligence Applications in the Real World

Every company sits on a wealth of data. The question is how to transform this wealth into knowledge capital and profit. Knowledge applications help organizations understand customer buying patterns, identify growth opportunities for sales and profit, and improve overall decision making. Successful KM enhances profits in

- *Customer service.* A company's service function often encompasses the key customer touchpoints necessary to run a successful business. Examples are customer inquiries, order fulfillment, and problem resolution. We use an example from the telecommunications industry to illustrate how BI can benefit customer service.

- *Business planning.* A company's business-planning function examines the company's operations, including customer service, in order to determine how company operations could be streamlined in order to achieve higher levels of customer satisfaction. We use a retail example to illustrate BI's business-planning benefits.

- *Business operations.* A company's operations attempt to deliver efficiency and quality to both its internal and external customers. Business operation strategies differ across industries. For example, determining the efficiency and quality of operations in the banking industry might focus on ATM and online transactions. In the telecom industry, the focus might be on phone calls; and for the retail industry, the focus might be on a strategy to include supply chain management. We use a healthcare industry example to illustrate BI's potential benefits to business operations analysis.

BI in Telecommunications: Combating Customer Churn

Today, telecommunications companies offer services that to consumers seem nearly identical. Not surprisingly, consumers have tended to accept the next best offer to come along, switching carriers on the basis of a better price or for more convenience. Known as the *churn factor,* this changing of service providers is an expensive form of customer turbulence that forces providers to process a steady stream of service starts and stops.

Churn management is the process of ensuring that profitable customers stay with a particular company. Advanced churn management techniques include the ability to predict a given individual's tendency to select another service provider and to define the correct course of action to retain the customer.

Customer churn is a challenge in any industry, but the problem is most acute in the ultracompetitive wireless industry. For example, 360 Communications provides wireless voice and data service to 2.4 million customers in more than 100 markets in 15 states. The company applies business intelligence techniques to cross-selling cellular and long-distance services, credit analysis, and churn-factor analysis and reduction. The company's credit analysis application determines the customer profile for customers who are likely to default, then uses this profile to predict future defaulters and default rates. Customer profile analysis is performed by the company's software proprietary tools that rate a customer's level of credit and churn risk.

Telecom carriers, such as 360 Communications, focus on customer retention, acquisition, and win-back and use data warehouses and information to support these efforts. Why? Because it's estimated that it costs $300 for a wireline carrier and at least $500 for wireless carriers to acquire a new customer and $50 per year to retain that customer. Churn costs European and U.S. telcos close to $4 billion each year, and the global cost of customer defection may well approach a staggering $10 billion per year. Annual churn rates of 25 percent to 30 percent are now the norm, and carriers at the upper end of this spectrum will get no return on investment for new subscribers, because it takes 3 years to recover the cost of replacing each lost customer with a new one.

All telecom carriers must establish a customer base that is not just price driven. BI data mining tools analyze call-detail records and other customer data to reveal the best prospects. With an average annual churn rate of 20 percent to 25 percent, a 1 percent reduction in churn can amount to millions of dollars in retained business, which quickly pays for the original data warehouse investment. Data warehousing also provides managers with easy access to customer profile information to understand customers better. Using these customer profiles, companies can design new promotions to help retain existing customers and to cost-effectively attract new customers. Companies can also build accurate predictive models to determine which customers are most likely to switch to a competitor and take appropriate action to fix any internal problems that contribute to customer churn.

With deregulation and competition, telecom providers must differentiate themselves in what is a commodity business. To become full-service providers, these companies must use business intelligence applications to help them deliver a better variety of distinctive services both now and in the future. BI applications can be used to analyze call volumes, bills, equipment sales, customer profitability, and costs and inventory; to gain purchasing leverage with suppliers; and to manage frequent-caller programs.

BI in Retail: Capturing and Reporting Sales Data

The world's largest department store chain and third-largest retailer, Sears, Roebuck and Co., has clung tenaciously to its industry lead despite the inroads made by discount mass merchandisers. Founded in 1886, Sears became synonymous with U.S. retailing, only to be caught by surprise in the 1980s as shoppers defected to specialty stores and discount merchandisers. Today, Sears is adopting new forms of technology to support its regeneration as a more flexible, market-responsive company.

In the early 1990s, Sears's technology infrastructure was based on 10- to 20-year-old sales information systems packed with redundant, conflicting, and sometimes obsolete data. For example, the system was configured to show Sears's locations in ten geographic regions but didn't reflect any closed locations or Sears's new operations, which are divided into seven regions. Sears's finance, marketing, and merchandising departments used their own systems, which were not integrated with the sales systems. As a result, a sales manager might come up with a different sales figure than the accounting department for the same region. Even within departments, information was scattered among numerous databases, forcing users to query multiple systems for even simple questions.

In order to survive as a company, Sears was forced to embrace BI on a dramatic scale. Sears's executives decided that a single data source for its key performance indicators—sales, inventory, and margin—was a strategic imperative. The goal of the initiative was to implement a technology that could capture sales data and generate accurate, reliable sales reports. Sears's Strategic Performance Reporting System (SPRS) includes comprehensive sales data; information on inventory in stores, in transit, and in the distribution centers; and cost per item, which provides users with the profit margin on a daily basis by item and location. The SPRS application can also be used for analysis of scanner check-out data; tracking, analysis, and tuning of sales promotions and coupons; inventory analysis and redeployment; price-reduction modeling to "move" product; negotiating leverage with suppliers; managing frequent-buyer programs; profitability analysis; and product selections for granular market segmentation.

One of Sears's most significant initiatives was constructing a sales knowledge application that uses a massive, 1.7-terabyte data warehouse and replaces 18 major databases, each of which previously ran on separate systems. This new application tracks sales by individual item and location on a daily basis to fine-tune buying, merchandising, and marketing strategies with precision. The benefits are measurable. Sears managers use the knowledge application every morning to check on the previous day's sales and can check at the national, regional, district, store, line, and stock-keeping unit—Sears's equivalent of an individual item—levels.

Sears also has freshened the merchandise mix in its mall-based stores to reflect its awareness of modern-day demographics. Long viewed as male oriented, Sears changed its image when market research revealed that a large portion of buyers for its merchandise were women shopping for their families. The retailer began reconfiguring its stores to emphasize women's apparel, rolling out "the Softer Side of Sears" as its marketing strategy. The technological transformation of Sears is not over, for it has yet to address the rapid rise of e-commerce and how its knowledge applications can be used to provide competitive advantage in this new environment.

BI in Healthcare: Employee Benefits Management

Every company seeks new ways to streamline its business functions and to use them to gain a competitive advantage. Many companies have selected employee benefits management as a focal point for differentiation. These companies have done an extensive job attempting to meet their employees' needs with more flexible benefits, new disability products, efficient HMOs, and 401K programs. There has been a transition from paper-based to automated systems, as labor costs for this processing-intensive industry are the biggest benefits a company incurs.

Unfortunately, many of the new benefits have made program administration difficult and time consuming for the employees. Whether the benefits transaction is a promotion, an update, a life-event change, or a termination, it often involves many other department or even organization entities outside of the company's human resources department. To make benefits management more accessible, HR departments are moving toward self-service knowledge applications. One company exemplifying this trend is Employease, in the HR transactions arena, which is attempting to replace costly, labor-intensive, paper-based processes with self-service solutions.

In the healthcare benefits management area, employees in the United States are confronted by multiple provider choices, poorly kept information, and limited access to information and support resources. Consequently, employees are unable to make well-informed decisions about their healthcare or to obtain the information they need. Today, although healthcare processes are automated, primarily through the insurers' and hospitals' mainframe systems, information access is still difficult, with limited connectivity between participants, and coordination of care across the continuum of services is poor. The result is inefficient benefits management, duplicate processes, high costs, poor services, and poor-quality care.

No longer willing to put up with status quo, employees are demanding greater value, better service, demonstrated quality, and lower cost for their benefits programs. Before improved service and greater value can be provided, the numerous parties involved in benefits management must be able to communicate with one another. An estimated $200+ billion is spent annually on administrative expenses, moving data through organizations using paper-based management systems, and on an undifferentiated mass of proprietary technology that is making it impossible for insurers, doctors, and patients to communicate easily.[10]

All the stakeholders in the employee benefits process must have access to software that weaves them together in a seamless network. The Web makes such integration possible. The solution to the employee benefits' problem lies in a knowledge-centric business model that allows both service providers and employees to meet halfway. Self-service architecture allows consumers to drive their own transactions, such as plan analysis and claims processing. Using self-service, employees can perform

- Managed-care functions, such as membership management, network management, care management, premium billing, and claim/encounter processing

- Historical tracking of employee and benefits information via access to a centralized HR system on which employee data is maintained

- Eligibility checks, referral scheduling, and authorizations

- Claims submission, information access, and reporting

The next generation of human resource systems will be self-service applications. These applications connect all the players in the employee benefits arena—consumers, providers, payers, and employers—in a common end-to-end solution, independent of location and platform. By providing access to information, supporting common transactions across business boundaries, and moving mission-critical functions out of the legacy environment and onto the Internet, information flows between organizations and individual entities can be simplified and their efficiency enhanced.

Technical Elements of the Business Intelligence Framework

The pieces are finally falling into place to create BI frameworks that address challenging business requirements. To meet the challenge of creating a unified BI framework, organizations must integrate a number of applications. The BI architecture is built on a three-layer platform (see Figure 11.6):

- *BI solutions,* which include the ability to deliver informational views, queries, reports, and modeling capabilities that go way beyond current offerings

- *Enabling technologies,* such as data mining, query processing, and result distribution infrastructure, which include the ability to store data in a multidimensional cube format for online analytical processing, or OLAP, to enable rapid data aggregation and drill-down analysis

- *Core technologies,* such as data warehouses and data marts, which include the ability to extract, cleanse, and aggregate data from multiple operational systems into a separate data mart, or warehouse

Putting all the above pieces together isn't as difficult as it once was. Having discussed earlier the solutions BI can provide, it is important to understand how BI enabling and core technologies work.

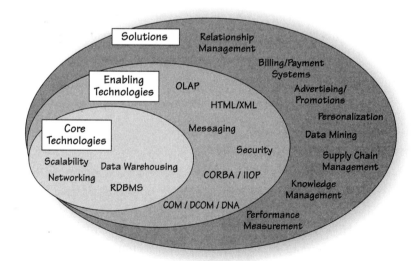

Figure 11.6: Three-Layer BI Solutions Architecture

Enabling Technologies: Online Analytical Processing (OLAP)

OLAP, a key component of BI, is increasingly used to improve business analysis. Historically, OLAP has been characterized by expensive tools, difficult implementation, and inflexible deployment. However, with new innovations, OLAP is seeing more widespread use in a wide array of applications, ranging from corporate reporting to advanced decision support.

OLAP solutions provide a means to analyze complex data by using a more intuitive set of business rules and dimensions, such as profitability analysis by product, channel, geography, customer, or fiscal period. In addition, by insulating the user from the technical aspects of data storage and data structures, OLAP solutions enable less technically sophisticated users within an organization to perform their own analyses.

Typically, OLAP solutions provide complex computational capabilities, including time-series analysis and ad hoc, drill-down, and interactive analysis. For example, a marketing manager identifying a market-share reduction can drill down to isolate the problem to a specific product at a specific store.

OLAP is an umbrella term for a range of approaches (see Table 11.2). OLAP

Table 11.2: OLAP Types and Terminology

Table 11.2: OLAP Types and Terminology

Definition	Sample Products	Uses	Best Fit
Desktop OLAP, or client-side OLAP: Products that pass data from a server to a desktop client to perform most of the processing locally. Often linked to query and reporting tools that create specialized views from within larger data sets for particular end user needs.	Business Objects, Brio, Cognos	End user report viewing and drill-down analysis	Small, customized data sets; offline usage on laptops or portable devices
Relational OLAP (ROLAP): Places the emphasis of data query processing and delivery within the relational database. The ROLAP engine submits automated, highly specialized, iterated queries to the database and handles the delivery of the information to the users.	MicroStrategy DSS Products Server, Information Advantage, Platinum Technology	Retail market analysis, health-care information processing, customer relationship analysis, Web-based information stores	Data warehouse analysis, analysis of transaction records, rapidly changing data or very large data sets

(continued)

Table 11.2 (Continued)

Definition	Sample Products	Uses	Best Fit
Multidimensional OLAP (MOLAP): A specialized server-based database that takes relational data from a transactional system and physically stores it in a unique format to enhance query access. Typically, data is summary level and contains defined dimensions or data characteristics.	Arbor Essbase, Oracle Express, Seagate (Holos), and SAS	Financial budgeting and forecasting	Fast response times on consolidated data records; data analysis needs combined with data updates
Hybrid OLAP: Products that combine the characteristics of MOLAP and ROLAP approaches. For example, supporting both server- and client-based processing or processing both within the standard relational format and in special data storage structures.	IBM DB2 OLAP Server, Microsoft Plato	Emerging range of selected MOLAP and ROLAP uses	Data center or LAN processing of operational data stores

consists of desktop OLAP, relational OLAP, multidimensional OLAP, and hybrid OLAP. The core process for each of these applications is essentially the same. Data that is entered into a database system is offloaded, reformatted, or accessed in specialized ways to enhance the processing of complex queries that are beyond the capabilities of the standard database.

Core Technologies: Data Warehousing

Today, a majority of Fortune 2,000 enterprises have constructed or are constructing data warehouses to serve as networked data hubs for optimizing their business operations. Data warehouses are repositories of summarized historical data, often extracted from disparate departmental or enterprise databases. The idea behind data warehousing is to gather all company data together in one place to give greater business process visibility, learn more, and improve organizational performance.

Warehouse data supports management's decision-making process. This process is *subject-oriented, integrated, time-variant,* and *nonvolatile.*[11] Simply put, this means that the data warehouse is focused on a business concept, such as sales, rather than on a business process, such as issuing invoices, and contains all the relevant sales information gathered from multiple processing systems. This information is collected and represented at consistent periods of time and is not changing rapidly.

Companies of every size are finding that data warehouses are essential for running their businesses. For example, over the past 30 years at General Motors (GM), the company installed centralized databases that were "best in class" in their day but are now considered legacy. The unforeseen high transaction volumes of today's computer environment and the complexities of day-to-day operations have rendered these systems nearly useless. Moreover, the data access tools accompanying these older databases were either too unsophisticated for detailed data analysis or too difficult for the average end user to use. These legacy systems also segregated the company's operational data and data query activities from its production databases.

Data warehousing helps users identify business trends, find answers to business questions, and derive meaning from historical and operational data, all of which enhance decision support in the enterprise. In the early 1990s, GM began gathering all vehicle and vehicle order data and putting it into the data warehouses. This effort resulted in a common, comprehensive historical view of GM's operations. Users can search, aggregate, and manipulate the data as they see fit.[12]

How Data Warehousing Works

Data warehouses take production data, such as a customer transaction, edits and organize the data, and put it in a place appropriate for user browsing, analysis, and decision making. The process usually involves centralizing a variety of data sources or extending the value of a central repository so that more can be done with the existing stored data, enabling the data to be mined, transformed, or analyzed and depicted visually. The result is practical access to critical data and decision support.

Data warehouses store data in a format optimized for analysis and are used in conjunction with query and reporting tools designed to perform predefined queries and simple calculations. This level of analysis, however, is limited. For example, query and reporting tools generally are not designed to perform time-series analyses, such as calculations of the weekly changes in market share by region. Tools that do these tasks often require users to understand the technical aspects of data storage and data structures. As a result, the use of data query and reporting tools is often limited to highly trained technical users.

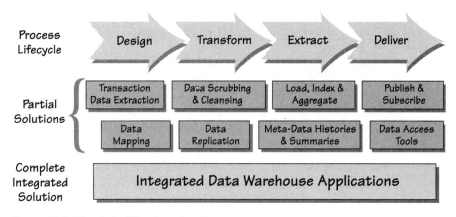

Figure 11.7: The Data Warehousing Process

Data Warehouse Components

Figure 11.7 provides a complete picture of the data warehousing process. The components of the data warehousing process include

- Transactional applications to ensure that source data can be stored in any format, from modern relational databases to traditional legacy sources

- Extraction and transformation tools that read data from transactional systems, make the data consistent, and write it to an intermediate file

- Scrubbing tools to further cleanse raw data

- Movement tools that move data from the intermediate files to the data warehouse, while automatically managing data volume and cross-platform issues

- Repository tools that maintain the metadata—information about the data—in the warehouse and monitor transactional applications so that if a data record changes, the data extraction and transformation tools are updated

- Access tools—on the user's desktop—that retrieve, view, manipulate, analyze, and present data: spreadsheets, query engines, report writers, and even Web browsers

- Data delivery for continuous customer access, including instant messaging among all manner of devices—browsers, e-mail, pagers, fax, Palm Pilot, Windows CE, and wireless—regardless of the communications medium

A Roadmap for Managers

Development of a Web-based BI framework requires serious management attention. Figure 11.8 depicts the four elements of the knowledge framework: users, applications, analytical tools, and data sources. Use the following steps to guide your company in setting up its knowledge framework.

1. *Identify the goals of the BI project.* Once you've established the objective, make sure that goals are actionable and that the business can put the knowledge to use. For example, Works.com's B2B marketplace uses Brio's Enterprise, a knowledge portal tool, to monitor and to report on customer activity. The tool can monitor activity throughout the "sales funnel" process—from the point customers enter the portal, set up an account, and begin placing orders all the way through the registering of additional requestors and the establishment of procurement and approval procedures. *Can you define your BI implementation goals clearly?*

2. *Determine where knowledge resides in the company.* Part of what makes BI such a difficult concept to grasp and to put into practice is that knowledge is ubiquitous. It can live inside a myriad of databases, a fact that illustrates why data warehousing is such a crucial component of business today. Some company knowledge is difficult to locate because it is often hidden and undervalued in

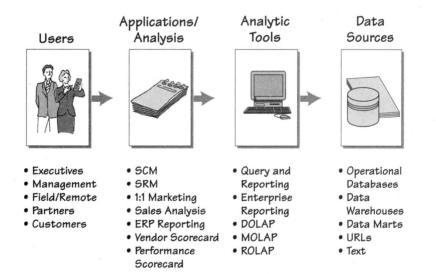

Figure 11.8: Blueprint for Knowledge Management

the minds of employees, or it might dwell in the relationships your colleagues have with people at other companies.

3. *Determine what information the company needs to capture.* Despite what you might have read, knowledge isn't just about "knowing what you know." It's more important to learn what you need to know. Help employees capture information by employing "journalists"—analysts with knowledge of or experience in business operations—to help determine what information needs to be captured and how to apply knowledge already captured to improve specific business processes.

4. *Collect, clean, and prepare data.* Obtain the necessary data from the company's internal and external sources. Check and resolve data conflicts, unusual or exception values, missing data, and any ambiguity. Use conversions and combinations to generate new data fields, such as ratios or rolled-up summaries. These actions require considerable effort, often as much as 70 percent or more of the BI implementation effort. If you already have a data warehouse, especially one that contains detailed transaction data, you have a head start on data collection, integration, and the cleansing process.

5. *Balance external and internal data.* Historically, business enterprises have focused primarily on information about their internal operations. As today's markets become more dynamic, this perspective becomes less viable. Peter Drucker often admonishes executives for not looking outside their company's four walls. He points out that the single greatest challenge is for companies to "organize outside data because change occurs from the outside." His prediction is that the companies obsessed with information about their own internal operations will result in their being blindsided by start-ups.[13]

6. *Develop new approaches to categorizing information.* New firms are developing capabilities to categorize information across their core business applications, including ERP systems. A key success factor when categorizing company information is to develop a categorization scheme with business relevance.

7. *Build the data model.* The model-building step involves selecting the appropriate data-mining tools, transforming data, generating samples for training, testing, and validating the model. The key activity for validating the data model is to test the model for accuracy. The model is first tested by using an independent data set, one different from the set used to create the model. Then assess the model's sensitivity and pilot test the model to ensure usability.

8. *Deploy the model.* For a predictive model, use the model to predict results for new cases; then use the prediction to change your company's market behavior. Deployment may require building computerized systems to capture the necessary data and to generate a prediction in real time so that a decision maker can act on the prediction. For example, a model could determine whether a credit card transaction is likely to be fraudulent.

9. *Monitor the model.* As the environment changes, so must the model's data with which it is analyzed. The BI models a company uses for its knowledge management work must account for changes in the economic, product, and competitive environments in which it operates. Any of these socioeconomic forces can alter customer behavior, making a model accurate today and useless tomorrow.

10. *Measure the ROI.* Quantifying a return on BI is difficult. Although several new companies offer software to help with quantifying BI, it will always be difficult to put an exact value on a company's knowledge resources. Companies that fail to put their knowledge capital to use often come up with ideas and decisions haphazardly rather than systematically through a carefully organized approach.

Memo to the CEO

In its most basic form, Business Intelligence (BI) is a strategy, not a piece of software. Companies have accumulated vast stores of transaction data over the decades. In the wake of this information deluge, ERP, CRM, and other applications generate even more information about a company and its relationship with its customers. Most of this information remains dormant, residing in unused databases. BI applications let companies put this dormant asset to use as a valuable resource. BI's competitive advantage lies in its ability to analyze large amounts of data, determine the personalized preferences of customers, and then contact these customers with the information relevant to them, wherever they may be.

Next-generation BI applications are now freeing up the underused data assets and making them accessible to large corporate audiences, down to the line-level employee. The extensive deployment of PCs and connected servers has fueled the demand for easy-to-use BI applications and for access over the network to key corporate data previously locked away in the company's mainframe. BI can deliver efficiency gains by making information assets open and visible to any constituency a company selects.

Why do we need "about the business" BI applications? First, to compete in today's real-time economy, businesses must be able to quickly identify and respond to changing market conditions and customer needs. Today's business runs 24×7, creating a new business need for BI applications that work nonstop to collect a real-time flow of information and data that never stops. To take advantage of the opportunities this information provides, technology must be able to collect, organize, access, and analyze large volumes of data—quickly.

One-to-one marketing is another reason about-the-business applications are key. In order for one-to-one marketing to succeed, companies must determine a customer's value and this customer's specific needs. A one-to–one marketing strategy requires significantly more information about customer behavior and preferences than do other market strategies. Until recently, companies didn't capture detailed customer behavioral information. Even if they did, it was not easily accessible from a single source. New BI applications address these needs.

The *"information at fingertips"* revolution is yet another way BI applications are so important. With the advent of the Internet, the universe of connected customers, suppliers, and employees has expanded exponentially. At the same time, many companies have flattened their organizational structures, delayering their hierarchies and empowering employees at all levels to make decisions. This change has resulted in two critical expectations.

1. Companies want their employees to spend less time compiling data and more time analyzing it to identify key customer trends and preferences.

2. Employees and partners expect high-quality information, around-the-clock access, and lightning-fast application performance.

A final reason for considering a BI solution is *return on information investment.* Today's business management expects a significant return on its data warehouse and other technology investments. Businesses' data warehouse investments have resulted in vast amounts of internal financial and operational data and historical data on customers, projects, and suppliers. However, much of this information is sitting in a database gathering silicon dust. Most of it is not being used to effectively manage companies.

In conclusion, innovation in information delivery is creating new functionality that has not existed until now. For example, the real-time delivery of information has been made easier by Web-based and wireless technologies. Traditional knowledge management models focused on data analysis. More recent innovations couple data analysis with data delivery, resulting in a structural migration from data access applications to a new generation of proactive business intelligence tools capable of responding quickly and accurately to changing business conditions.

What does all this mean? Knowing how to manage a company's knowledge assets can make or break a business. For this reason, business intelligence—the harnessing, organizing, and delivery of information assets—has become critical to the future of business. The convergence of the Web, BI decision support systems, databases, and newly integrated back-office infrastructures is leading to a business intelligence renaissance.

CHAPTER TWELVE

Developing the e-Business Design: Strategy Formulation

What to Expect

We are just a few minutes past the e-business "big bang." e-Business technology is creating a seismic shift in the way companies do business. e-Business innovation is a "top of mind" issue for most business leaders, driven in part by the rapid rates of innovation in customer, internal, and supplier-facing processes. Also, the next wave of Internet development—the integration of offline and online assets—requires novel strategies.

An urgency to innovate is sweeping across all industries as managers search for the next big idea that will transform their businesses or rewrite the rules of competition. Just knowing the importance and structure of e-business is not enough. You need to create and to implement a plan that allows you to make the transition from an old business design to a new, e-business design.

The e-business planning process may sound like common sense, but doing it right requires an ongoing, unrelenting commitment of time and energy. Many, if not most, companies are unwilling to make the commitment. Yet in a dynamic marketplace, that's a perilous strategy because the distance from hero to zero is rather short.

This chapter is designed to help new entrepreneurs and managers in traditional companies unlock the mysteries of e-business strategy formulation. The chapter is meant to help organize and gather the information managers need to initiate a highly focused e-strategy aligned with corporate goals. By answering the questions posed here, managers can gain a better understanding of issues, tradeoffs, bottlenecks, and traps in setting an appropriate direction.

> The monster was upon him. One of the snake-like heads darted out at him. Swinging his sword, Hercules cut it off. Immediately two new heads grew from the Hydra's bloody neck. Hercules cut them off also—but four new heads grew in their places. Hercules gasped, "I fear that before I am finished it will have nine hundred heads!"
>
> —*The Twelve Labors of Hercules*

Creating an e-business strategy is like fighting the multiheaded Hydra. For each challenge you resolve, many more rise to take its place. Creating e-solutions requires simultaneously melding multiple disciplines—business strategy, enterprise applications, and technology implementation. Pursued alone, none of these three by itself is sufficient. A synergy of all three is needed to create sophisticated digital solutions to intricate business problems.

When preparing their e-business designs, the key strategic issue confounding today's managers is *how to transform an old business design, based on the physical realities of business-as-they've-known-it, into a new design rooted in the digital requirements of tomorrow.* The requirements of the old business design tend to focus on implementing cost-cutting, back-office improvements. The requirements of the new, digital-based business design focus on implementing revenue-enhancing, customer-facing improvements, such as new ways of selling to help spur profit growth by making it easier for businesses to market products, to fully utilize customer data, and to manage relationships with suppliers and consumers.

Few traditional companies still deny that technology will change the way they do business. So, why is it that many say they want to change but most stay mired in the old way of doing things? These companies are paying lip service to the idea that reinvention is a core doctrine of e-business. History has taught the lesson again and again: Successful companies can go from winning to losing rather quickly. Clearly, managers of profitable companies must anticipate the need for self-transformation and change when they can, not when their backs are against the wall. A company's refusal to change can mean stagnation and losing its ability to generate new value through innovation. We call this "the legacy effect."

At the same time, we caution managers not to treat e-business as a silver bullet or as a corporate cure-all. e-Business is simply another technique for reinventing business—appropriate in some circumstances but not in others.

Consider the transition under way at Intel. Founded in 1968 by a trio of engineers, Robert Noyce, Gordon Moore, and Andy Grove, Intel revolutionized the electronics world with its innovative chip designs. Quietly toward the end of 1990s, Intel began transforming itself from a chip-maker into the leading "building block supplier" to the Internet and wireless Web. Fearful of sluggish growth in its traditional PC microprocessor business, Intel is storming into the new markets of networking, wireless appliances, communications equipment, and Web hosting. It's spending billions of dollars to buy Internet-related companies and invest in start-up ventures. In short time, Intel snapped up 22 companies for over $9 billion. The largest deals: Level One for $2.2 billion, DSP Communications for $1.6 billion, and Giga, an optical-networking firm, for $1.3 billion. Financial metrics are dictating the strategic move from a dominant chip company to a communications and server company. As the traditional PC market slowed and Internet related networking grew, Intel's healthy 30+ percent revenue growth rate over the 1990s slipped to a lukewarm 15 percent in 1999. The aggressive transformation of Intel from a PC-centric giant into an Internet-centric company bears careful watching. Bottom-line: Few companies in history have successfully undergone such sweeping changes. At stake is the long-term health of one of the pillars of the new economy.

Moving Physical to Digital: The Case of OfficeMax

An excellent example of a company's successful transition from a legacy infrastructure and culture to an e-business infrastructure and culture is OfficeMax, one of the largest high-volume, deep-discount office products superstores. The company operates more than 780 full-size stores featuring more than 10,000 office products, computers, and related items in more than 330 markets. Office-Max also operates CopyMax and FurnitureMax, store-within-a-store modules devoted exclusively to print-for-pay services and office furniture, respectively.

With the launch of OfficeMax Online in 1995, OfficeMax became the first office products retailer selling products over the Internet. In addition to a vast assortment of products, OfficeMax.com offers search and browse features, customer order and usage reports, and customized express-order templates. The e-channel is supported by call centers 7 days a week, 24 hours a day, and 17 delivery centers around the country guarantee next-day delivery. Clearly, success requires integration of online and offline components.

OfficeMax has invested more than $50 million to upgrade its online systems and process controls, and the company intends to continue investing aggressively in infrastructure to support growth. A replatforming project, FutureMax, will provide the firm with integrated applications and technology. The project will implement three major application suites: merchandising, inventory management, and financial systems. Their integration will provide seamless connectivity to a number of special-purpose applications delivering comprehensive, decision support information in a timely manner.[1]

If you're like OfficeMax, you're probably in the early stages of transitioning your company to a digital future. You and your firm find yourselves at the beginning of the twenty-first century, unsure of the next steps to take and of your ultimate destination. You struggle with the question: *What is the right strategy for our company in a highly uncertain business environment?* For some executives, shaping their companies' future means high-risk, high-return investments. Other, more conservative executives hedge their bets by making a number of smaller investments. Still others favor investments in flexibility to allow their companies to adapt quickly as markets evolve. *Which e-strategy is right for you?*

Roadmap to Moving Your Company into e-Business

The answers to five questions—who, what, when, where, and why—form the foundation of your e-business strategy. Even in a technology-crazed world, a good business strategy comes first. Many organizations fail to create an effective e-business strategy detailing their end goal and target before choosing the map they'll use to get there. As a result, they risk pouring valuable resources into an initiative that will eventually fail. You must first decide on your destination before attempting to map your e-business journey.

But don't underestimate the implementation task that lies ahead. Talking about e-business is easy; making it happen is the difficult part. The methods for achieving e-business success are simple to grasp. After all, isn't it obvious that you should serve your customers better? Implementation is difficult because it *forces you to not only question your past business behavior but also to change it.* You have to look at what you do in a different way, throwing out traditional methods and acquiring new skills.

Making e-business a reality involves three key elements: the e-business strategy, the e-blueprint formulation, and tactical execution. e-Business strategy helps figure out the why and what of customer value creation. e-Blueprint formulation is the how and when of customer value creation. Tactical execution is where the rubber hits the road and things happen.

In Chapters 12–14, we discuss each component's role in the roadmap to e-business success. In this chapter, we delve into strategy formulation. In Chapter 13, we detail how to turn your e-business strategy into a blueprint for action. In Chapter 14, we reveal how to turn your blueprint into executable projects.

e-Business Strategy Formulation

In this phase a company builds awareness and makes a plan to create a new customer value. To do so, you need to develop a clear vision of what the customer needs are and what the customer is looking for. Develop a clear understanding of what capabilities you need in order to address the customer needs. At the same time, take a critical look at yourself. Formulating an e-business strategy requires a company to be conscious of its own abilities and limitations. The last thing you want to do is fight a high-tech war with sledgehammers.

e-Business strategy formulation—what to do—includes the following phases.

- *Knowledge building* helps the company understand what the customer is looking for and where the industry is going. This phase opens a window on the future and provides an opportunity to really understand what customers value.

- *Capability evaluation* defines the existing business and identifies what capabilities it has today and what capabilities it needs to have tomorrow. This phase allows companies to question whether they have what it takes to serve customers' changing priorities.

- *e-Business design* asks what value proposition a business must provide to take advantage of digital capabilities. How is this value going to be packaged into products, services, or experiences? This phase involves developing a coherent design that lays the foundation to address the new customer needs. The design is also a roadmap that helps the company get where it needs to go.

Formulating an e-business strategy can seem like a mystical exercise in which the truth is difficult to pin down. However, following a few guidelines can help managers to reduce the mystique. We present these guidelines in the form of strategic questions. Spend a few quiet hours contemplating and answering them. The answers will form the foundation of your e-business initiatives. Once you have worked through the questions, meet with other senior executives and compare answers. This meeting will reveal gaps—the closing of which is your starting point on your e-business journey.

The Process of e-Business Strategy Formulation

According to Niccolo Machiavelli, the sixteenth-century Florentine philosopher, "There is nothing more difficult to take in hand, more perilous to conduct, or more uncertain in its success, than to take the lead in the introduction of a new order of things. For the reformer has enemies in all those who profit from the old order."[2]

e-Business has a lot of similarities to the quality revolution in the 1970s. The quality wave dramatically changed the way many organizations conducted business. For example, Xerox watched its share of the U.S. copier market drop from a dominant 85 percent in the early 1970s to 13 percent in the early 1980s.[3] Other companies experienced similar crises. Quality, as many businesses quickly learned, was a matter of life and death. Some of the biggest casualties of the quality war were U.S. consumer-electronics manufacturers, many of which went out of business before they could react.

Today, established companies face a similar transition as they urgently attempt to revitalize their businesses as to adapt to the new economy. e-Business strategy is about addressing the requirements of an uncertain, as yet defined, future. e-Business strategies are based on our assumptions and beliefs about what this future will mean to our businesses. It helps us reflect on the changes our companies must make as customer priorities shift, technology advances, competition increases, and new core competencies must be developed.

Three popular approaches to formulating an e-business strategic plan are top-down analytical planning, bottom-up tactical planning, and continuous planning with feedback. Top-down analytical planning takes a broad view of the business environment, identifies the company's options, and then defines the firm's mission and strategic direction. Bottom-up tactical planning takes a narrower view of the business environment, identifying and performing the activities required to produce short-term results in specific areas. Continuous planning with feedback is a mix of both approaches. However, before selecting an approach for creating an e-business strategy, a company must first define where it wants the strategy to take it and the concrete business results it seeks to achieve.

The most important question: What result do I want to get? Creating an e-business strategy confuses even the most seasoned managers. We are continually amazed at how experienced managers who achieve incredible results on a daily basis and who are extremely customer and market focused in their thinking are at a loss when required to create an e-strategy. These managers suddenly shift their orientation from meeting customer needs to meeting the needs of Wall Street and the company's stockholders. These managers become concerned with what to tell the market analysts about the decision to develop an e-business strategy and the financial message this decision sends. They want to demonstrate the revenue opportunities the strategy makes possible and also to gloss over the fact that these revenues may not be realized for months or even years.

e-Business strategic success requires focusing on the business results you want, not on what others—the markets, the stockholders—think. Managers must function as change agents helping their firms transition to an e-business future. The primary purpose of an e-strategy is to guide the corporate change effort in the direction the company knows it must go.

The first priority when defining an e-strategy is the change effort's destination. Think of the e-strategy creation as a journey on which you take your company. Your company starts at point X and ends up at point Y. Whenever you take a trip, the first thing you want to know is where you're going, because that directs all your planning—the type of transportation you take, your accommodations, expenses, and clothing. In our planning process, we call the destination point Y. It's where you want your company to be when your e-business implementation is complete.

What's your point Y? Try to answer in this form:

- When we are done, my *customers will* _____ or

- When we are done, my *employees will* _____ or

- When we are done, my *company will* _____.

Fill in the blank with one or two words to denote a single, specific destination. However difficult it may be to narrow your focus, it's an essential discipline. A single destination can be observed and measured. However, the process of setting this destination can differ dramatically, depending on the planning approach chosen. Let's look at the three different approaches to planning in more detail.

Top-Down Analytical Planning

The top-down method attempts to systematically define a vision of the business's future. This objective is to define a vision as precisely as possible in order to assess cost and to prepare a capital budget. This approach values creating a data-rich environment and is numbers driven and analytically based. Managers review alternative future scenarios, testing how sensitive their predictions are to changes in key variables. The goal of their analysis is to identify the most likely outcome and to create their strategy based on it.

The top-down approach serves companies well in stable business conditions that lend themselves to predictive analysis and modeling. As with wood that's been eaten by termites, the troubles facing companies in the e-world aren't obvious in a top-down planning model. Revenue is growing, spending is under control, and systems function well. The e-world is anything but stable and predictable. It is characterized by its customer-centrism and the rapid execution required to fulfill changing customer needs. When such stresses are applied to an apparently stable company, problems quickly become evident. When there is greater uncertainty about the future, top-down planning is only marginally helpful and often extremely risky.

The separation of strategy formulation (analysis) and implementation (execution) is the single greatest problem with top-down planning. It can lead to the following flawed plans:

- *The never-seen-again strategic plan.* Once-a-year top-down strategic planning is often a joke, a "paralysis by analysis" bureaucratic nightmare. Too many businesses invest countless hours of their top managers' valuable time in endless meetings. They spend thousands of dollars creating a plan only to file it away and never use it.

- *The no-goals strategic plan.* A strategic plan with no targets and goals is worthless! Successful plans need to include specific performance goals that the company must meet and use as a baseline measure the following year. Also, a strategic plan is simply a wish list unless you identify the software applications needed to meet its goals and the resources—human, technological, and financial—needed to develop these applications. Many companies are great at top-down planning but falter when it comes to crossing the chasm and implementing the plan.

- *The no-feedback strategic plan.* The absence of accurate feedback from customers, suppliers, and employees leads to disaster in environments in which sensitivity to changing needs or requirements is key to success. Traveling on the wrong road never leads to the right destination. Because e-business deals with future opportunities, much of the information required to make strategic decisions is at best uncertain and at worst unreliable. Customer requirements are continually changing, and new opportunities are always being discovered. What looked like an excellent project 6 months ago can suddenly be not so promising. Continuous feedback is essential for identifying course corrections that need to be made.

No matter how intelligently drawn the big picture is, it is a static creation. Today's volatile environment does not lend itself to systematic analysis. Organizations and industries face tremendous structural change, uncertainty, and decisions with huge opportunities and risks. Making smart choices in this environment demands creativity, insight, and intuition more than systematic thought.

Bottom-Up, "Just Do It" Planning

Today's unstable, often chaotic business environment has eroded faith in traditional strategic planning. The idea of planning as an orderly process assumes the future to be a continuation of the present. At a minimum, strategic planning assumes that the future will arrive slowly, at a predictable pace, allowing plenty of time to adapt. In many industries, these assumptions are rarely true.

In an environment in which change is the norm, the insights of employees on the front line take on new importance. Salespeople and others who deal directly with outside clients are the first to be aware of changes in customer needs. Organizations with hierarchical decision-making structures have few mechanisms in place for ensuring that the insights of front-line staff reach the strategy makers. This limitation makes it nearly impossible to respond quickly to the demands of the marketplace.[4]

As a result, bottom-up strategic planning is flourishing. Managers are abandoning the analytical rigor of traditional planning processes and are basing their strategic decisions on solving immediate needs. Often, many individual projects are heroically executed. Frequently, however, no integrated plans link these individual projects into a cohesive program designed to achieve corporate-wide objectives.

A bottom-up strategy can result in a fractured pattern of authority, with individual managers basing their strategic decisions on their business units' needs, not the needs of the enterprise as a whole. This approach impedes comprehensive planning and the systems integration required for successful e-business initiatives. For example, when brick-and-mortar banks invested in Web banking in the mid 1990s, they failed to integrate their existing channels into their strategy.

Many Fortune 1,000 corporations have grown dissatisfied with the first generation of applications developed to support the "just do it" approach to e-commerce. These applications were implemented without considering how they would work with the rest of the service/delivery infrastructure. Companies are now pausing to ask how e-commerce fits with the rest of their corporate strategy.

Continuous Planning with Feedback

We believe that the most successful e-business strategy is one in which planning is an ongoing company activity using feedback from the company's customers, suppliers, and staff. In a fluid business environment, the best approach may be to allow strategy to evolve through the discovery of what works and what doesn't.

Why integrate planning and execution through a feedback loop? The landscape in which companies operate has changed. Everything moves much more quickly today, which means that there is a lot less room for error. As a result, the hard distinction between formulating and implementing a strategic plan will blur. Planning cycles will shorten and become more organic as plans are adapted to business environment changes. The perceived distinction between strategy and tactics also blurs, especially because conditions often require such quick responses that tactics will dictate or at least shape strategy.

Under the continuous-planning approach, e-business councils are responsible for the tactical execution of the strategy. These cross-functional teams set clear priorities, establishing target areas for execution, and then allocate resources for the most important projects. The feedback allows the teams to respond quickly to change, unlike implementations following highly structured, hierarchical models. However, this approach is easier to describe than to follow.

Continuous-planning success depends on feedback. Successful e-business strategies evolve as new customer needs are identified and the company's technological infrastructure adapts to serve them. Most companies are uncomfortable with feedback-driven, fluid project planning revision. They want guarantees about their return on investment (ROI), which are difficult to provide in the unpredictable world of e-business. This demand for quick success and maximum ROI often derails e-business projects undertaken by established firms. Concern over short-term ROI becomes more important than the long-term benefits.

Another form of continuous planning is "trigger-point planning." This approach supports decision making in rapidly changing environments. In the absence of clear long-range plans, companies establish contingency plans based on multiple visions of the future and then determine the "trigger points"—a competitor's decision to extend its product line, for example—that will signal which contingency plan should be put into action. Finland's Nokia Corporation used the trigger-point model in the timing of its successful decision to become the first major wireless company to adopt code division multiple access (CDMA) as a standard for digital wireless communication technology.[5]

Trigger-point planning is becoming more widely used as the technology becomes available to keep up with triggering events. Lucent, Xerox, and Ericsson routinely use the Web to monitor real-time data from their customers, suppliers, and channel partners to help them know when to pull the trigger. The trigger-point process also requires the continuous sharing of information throughout the corporation. Compaq's cross-functional strategy team meets weekly to pore over updated information and, if necessary, realign strategy.

Trigger-point planning is a tool—a means to an end—not a goal in itself. Its successful use involves people throughout the organization. Trigger-point planning allows companies to focus on those business activities that are a direct response to events in the business environment. This tool is intended to help senior managers face difficult strategic decisions, set company priorities, and eliminate extraneous business activities and directions rather than initiate new ones.

Knowledge Building

"Nothing endures but change." Heraclitus said this almost 2,000 years ago, but he could have been talking about business today. The business environment is changing quickly as new technologies and competitors push firms and industries to reinvent themselves or pass into history. In order to survive in a world of change, the first step in any transformative journey is knowledge building.

Knowledge building enables managers to understand their priorities by gathering information on how customer needs change over time. By understanding their customers' present and future priorities, business leaders align their businesses with those priorities and grow market share.

Knowledge building is difficult. The first mistake many companies make is underestimating the amount of knowledge and data needed to make a strategy effective. Strategy must be based on fact, not on opinion, but often isn't. The typical corporate strategy session is conducted in intense 2- or 3-day off-site planning meetings dominated by opinions rather than facts.

How does my company develop its strategy? A major challenge facing firms seeking to develop their e-business strategies is how to implement a fact-based rather than an opinion-based strategic development process. A fact-based approach involves the following core activities: idea generation, collection, and evaluation and screening.

Does your company use ideas, data, and facts to support strategic decisions? Without understanding the surrounding environment and developing an internal frame of reference to serve as a roadmap, managers often develop the right strategy for the wrong problem.[6] The best-laid strategies go awry when the roadmap fails to correctly chart the realities of a business situation, when one or more of management's beliefs are incorrect, or when internal inconsistencies make the overall business design invalid.

The *knowledge-building exercise generates ideas.* Once gathered, the ideas are then screened for potential core strategic ideas, using several criteria (see Figure 12.1).

What data or facts do you use? Every company has its own set of data for planning, but in general, data should address the following key areas, as outlined in Table 12.1. Data from these areas is segmented and analyzed to determine the key

Figure 12.1: Idea Screening

opportunities in each. The focus on objective business data helps remove personalities and subjective opinion from the decision-making process and improves buy-in.

Once selected, the core idea is developed further. The next step in the idea management process involves answering a sequence of questions (see Table 12.1).

Table 12.1: Questions to Ask When Starting an e-Business

Understanding the customer	1. *Who are my customers?*
	2. *How are my customer priorities shifting?*
	3. *Who should be my target customer? How will the e-business help reach my target customer segments?*
Customer value and relationship trends	4. *How can I add value to the customer?*
	5. *How can I become the customer's first choice?*
	6. *How does my product reach customers?*
Technology trends	7. *Do we understand the environment and industry trends?*
	8. *Do we understand technology trends?*
Supply chain trends	9. *What are the current priorities in the supply chain?*
Competition	10. *Who are my real competitors? What is my toughest competitor's business model? What are they doing really well?*
Core competencies	11. *What capabilities do we have today?*
	12. *What capabilities and resources do we need to speed up our execution?*

As you can tell from the sequence of questions, we believe that it's a good idea to begin by analyzing the customer and business environment first, performing an outside-in rather than inside-out analysis. This approach forces managers to take a broader perspective by answering questions such as these: *How are my customers changing, and how will that affect me? What are the new trends that will make me obsolete in 5 years? What are the decisions that have to be made to sustain the growth of the company?*

Who Are My Customers?

Managers often think that they know their customers because they sell products or services to them. But more often than not, what executives think they know about the customer is more likely to be wrong than right. Understanding your customers is a full-time job. To do this job right, you need to care deeply about them.

Understanding the customers requires careful, thorough analysis. However, you must first categorize your customers into distinct groups, or segments, whose behavior can be analyzed systematically. The following customer segmentation model devised by Charles Schwab, the discount brokerage powerhouse, illustrates behavioral grouping:

- *Life-goal planner.* This investor is interested in trading mutual funds for long-term growth and wants tools for financial planning and portfolio optimization. A stable financial service provider is more important to this customer than the latest in technical analysis.

- *Serious investor.* This data-hungry investor is an active trader who values high-quality information, investment tools, and research. She or he wants one, integrated, easily accessible place to get help in deciding what to buy.

- *Hyperactive trader.* Low-cost trading, a simple interface, and fast execution are keys to this market junkie. This frequent trader doesn't even want to have to reenter a password on every order.

- *One-stop shopper.* This convenience-minded consumer wants a comprehensive package of financial products—stock trading, mutual funds, credit cards, bill payment, and checking. Breadth of offerings and ease of use are important to him or her.

Charles Schwab built his business the way Henry Ford built his; by taking what had been a luxury product and making it available at reasonable prices to the masses. By understanding its customer segments, Charles Schwab is able to focus its e-business strategy and to tailor it to the needs of the distinct segments. Now take the time to identify and write down a description of each of your customer segments. Once you've done so, answer the following questions: *What is important to each customer segment?*

One approach for conducting a segment analysis is to examine customer behavior in complementary markets. Customers who buy from you also buy many other products and services. By extrapolating from their behavior in complementary markets, you can apply this information to your industry. Answering the following questions will help better understand customer behavior: *What are five new products or services in your industry that have become popular in the last 5 years? What customer segments are buying these products or services? Why do these customer segments like these products or services?*

Answering these questions will also help you assess your customers' needs, which is where any outside-in analysis and new value proposition must begin. Need is the opposite of flash: substantive, not superficial. Need remains when everything else is stripped away. For Amazon.com, customer needs include convenience, consistency, reliability, and innovation. Customers have two types of needs: spoken, or explicit, and unspoken, or implicit. The most difficult challenge in customer analyses is understanding the unspoken needs of the customer. Again, take the time to write down the spoken and unspoken needs of your customers.

In the airline industry, distinctive customer needs comes down to a few basic services: efficient ticketing, polite in-flight service, convenient schedules, competitive fares, on-time arrivals, baggage that arrives when you do, and quick recoveries that get you on your way after bad weather, or heavy air traffic, causes unforeseen delays or cancellations. With the arrival of e-business, the focus is still on distinctive customer service, with faster online booking, new computer systems that speed up the boarding process, roaming agents with hand-held computers to provide in-transit passenger support, easier self-service administration of loyalty programs, and easier ways to record customer feedback, or the "voice of the customer." *Can you identify the basics of customer service in your company?*

Finally, answering the question "*Who are my customers?*" influences how your company's performance should be measured. For example, if you believe that your distributors are your customers, you might measure performance based on only what distributors care about. Are the products they distribute in stock? What are the discounts and payment terms? In short, you must understand who your real customers are, what they expect, and what they value. Take the time to write down the performance indicators relevant to each of your customer segments.

How Are My Customers' Priorities Changing?

Customer priorities have a natural tendency to change, often catching firms off guard. Peter Drucker, in his classic book *Managing for Results,* describes this moving target conundrum eloquently: "The customer rarely buys what the business thinks it sells him. One reason for this is, of course, that nobody pays for a product. What is paid for is satisfaction. But nobody can make or supply satisfaction as such—at best, only a means to attaining them can be sold or achieved."

Many companies find that the absolute best place to start is by improving those things that your customers would like you to improve. Collecting these ideas and acting on them has been an unexpected gold mine for many companies. Take the time to *write down the five things your customers ask for most often.* Is your company doing anything about them?

A company that doesn't understand customer priorities is running blind. The scene in Lewis Carroll's *Alice's Adventures in Wonderland* in which Alice asks the Cheshire Cat for directions speaks volumes about business today:

> *"Would you tell me, please, which way I ought to go from here?"*
> *"That depends a good deal on where you want to get to,"* said the Cat.
> *"I don't much care where—"* said Alice.
> *"Then, it doesn't matter which way you go,"* said the Cat.

Until you know your customers' priorities, which define where your company wants to go, you can't create a way to address them and reach your destination. *Is your company in a similar situation of knowing it wants to go somewhere, but "where" has never been clearly defined or communicated?*

Are your customers seeking an experience, not just a product or a service? How will you add value for them? Once customer priorities are defined, you can work to put the means for addressing them in place. Remember, your company must intuit how technology can and will change customers' needs and alter markets. For example, Jeff Bezos, CEO of Amazon.com, believed that once bibliophiles and time-starved businesspeople were comfortable using the Internet, they would be interested in buying books online (see Figure 12.2). Everyone, even die-hard e-commerce visionaries, was surprised at how great this unspoken need was and how quickly people bought books online.

Take time to answer the following question: *How has your customer changed in the past 5 years, and how do you think the customer will change in the next 3?*

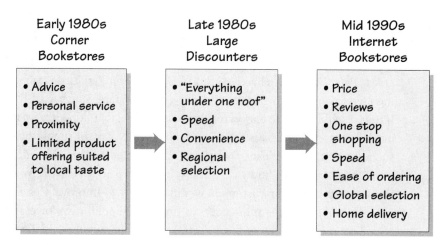

Early 1980s Corner Bookstores	Late 1980s Large Discounters	Mid 1990s Internet Bookstores
• Advice • Personal service • Proximity • Limited product offering suited to local taste	• "Everything under one roof" • Speed • Convenience • Regional selection	• Price • Reviews • One stop shopping • Speed • Ease of ordering • Global selection • Home delivery

Figure 12.2: Value Migration in Book Retailing

Who Is My Target Customer?

Once you understand your current customers, their priorities, and how these are changing, reflect on how to grow your customer base. Are there new groups in the market that value what you do? Can you jump a step along the value chain and serve your customers' customers?

Creative customer selection is a central element of value reinvention. Amazon. com's affiliate program, Digital Associates, is an interesting variant of creative customer selection. This reseller network, estimated to include more than 100,000 commercial and amateur Web sites, attempts to lure first-time cybershoppers, consumers who might stumble on member companies' Web sites. For member sites, there seems to be nothing to lose by being part of the network, as there are no joining fees and the only cost is maintaining banner ads and product information on their own sites. And there's a bonus: Each affiliate earns a commission of up to 15 percent just for enticing online shoppers to click over to Amazon.com's online superstore and buy something.[7]

In 1998, Dell was encroaching on Compaq Computer's market share in the desktop computer marketplace by using a direct-delivery model to reach its customers. In contrast, Compaq's customer was the reseller. However, vendors such as Compaq can no longer afford to support multiple sets of hands between their operations and their end users. Compaq was forced to make a strategic choice and chose as its target customer the end user, not the reseller. However, going direct proved to be disastrous for Compaq. In the meantime, Dell has perfected

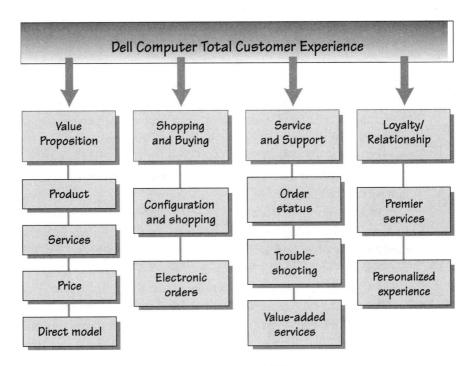

Figure 12.3: Dell Computer's Total Customer Experience

the direct model of delivering a comprehensive customer experience (see Figure 12.3). Take the time to answer the following questions: *Am I targeting the end user, distributor, or value-added reseller? In order to grow my company, whom should I be targeting? What are the needs of this new target customer base?*

How Can I Add Value for My Target Customer?

Customers want innovation, value, and savings. Which do you offer? Take the time to write down the answer to the following question: *How do I add value to my target customer base? Do I save money? Offer convenience? Offer new forms of value?*

Understanding how they add value concerns many early pioneers in B2C and B2B e-commerce. These business pioneers have gotten the public's attention and created demand. But do these companies have real businesses? Are these firms making sure that they add value and make a difference? Are they making sure that they're not one of many companies offering the exact same product, at lower and lower prices? Are they making sure that they really do offer a smarter, more convenient way to buy goods and services? Are they making sure that they don't ignore the details, such as ensuring that the product gets delivered to the person who bought it? Are they making money?

Understanding how your company adds value is especially important in times of transition, when a company seeks to move from its bread-and-butter business to a different technology or service channel. When Thomas Edison perfected the electric lamp, there was a panic among gas companies all over the world. Pundits proclaimed that the gas industry was dead. It was not. The gloomy gurus simply underestimated the heating potential of gas. How can a company provide increasing value for its customers while simultaneously reinventing certain parts of its business?

Another way to keep industry assumptions from stifling your firm's creativity is to avoid focusing too much on the competition. Rule breakers tend to be creative. They often lead in the creation of value as Starbucks, America Online, and Yahoo! They are often ridiculed, as was Wal-Mart during the 1970s and 1980s, when most business analysts thought that the company would fail.

Rule breakers also refuse to allow industry assumptions to become a barrier to innovative thinking. For example, the palm computing industry was initially written off as unprofitable by venture capitalists and most consumer-electronics firms. But in 1998 alone, Palm Computing sold 5 million Palm Pilots. The Palm Pilot had become the fastest-selling computer product in technology history. The trend has since accelerated. Not bad for a product written off by many as a dead category.

How Do I Become My Customer's First Choice?

Every customer contact creates for the customer a moment of mediocrity, a moment of misery, or a moment of ecstasy. *How do your customers experience contact with your firm?* You can be your customers' first choice if you dazzle them with unexpected service. The Ritz-Carlton hotels are a good example. At the Ritz-Carlton, quality service is a way of life. But it's no longer enough to just offer mints on the pillow. These hotels have created ways to continually surprise guests with quality, to build customer loyalty, and to ensure repeat business.

It all starts at registration. Guests' preferences, noted in a central computer, can be recalled when they visit any Ritz-Carlton hotel. The system tracks room preferences, favorite newspapers, even what radio stations they like. Ritz-Carlton has embarked on an aggressive effort to improve service further. It hopes to reduce the number of defects per thousand overnight stays from 48 to 3. A fizzled battery in a TV remote counts as a defect. The hotels are now staffed with technology butlers on call to help when a guest's hard drive crashes or when there is a problem getting online. Companies that continually surprise and dazzle customers with superior quality build customer loyalty that is difficult, if not impossible, for competitors to challenge.[8]

In order to become your customers' first choice, you must offer incentives. Airline loyalty programs started in the early 1980s as a simple way for airlines to build loyalty by rewarding repeat customers with free flights, upgrades, and other incentives. These programs have become a major battleground for business over the years. All the large carriers now offer various gimmicks, sign-up bonuses, and reciprocal-partnership perks in an effort to win clients' bookings. *What incentives does your firm offer its best customers?*

At your company: *How do customers make decisions about buying your firm's product or service? What has your company done to retain customers and deepen the customer relationship?* Understanding the customer choice process means knowing who will buy the service or product, when, in what form, and how.

How Does My Product Reach the Customer?

Understanding how products and services are distributed and marketed is crucial to business success. If a good product doesn't reach its intended customer, the company will flounder or fail as surely as a business delivering a bad product.

The process for sending flowers from one city to another seems reasonably straightforward. But when you look behind the scenes, you see how involved the process is. You call your local florist, who places a call to another participating florist, who selects and delivers the flowers. The participating florist ordered these flowers from a distributor, which got its flowers from a wholesaler, which bought the flowers from a farmer. By the time the flowers are delivered, they're 8, 9, or even 10 days old. Ruth Owades, CEO of the upscale floral company Calyx & Corolla, changed the flower-delivery industry by asking a simple question: Is it possible to bring the experience of the catalog business to the flower industry, even though the product is perishable?

Before Owades, everyone simply accepted this traditional, time-consuming process as a given (see Figure 12.4). The secret of her success was looking at an existing process from an entirely different perspective and knowing when and how to break the rules. She reengineered the process to remove nonessential steps. Calyx & Corolla customers call a toll-free number and order flowers. The order is transmitted by computer directly to the farmer, who has a talented flower arranger right on the farm. The order is packed in special containers and delivered the next day by FedEx. In creating the direct-from-the-grower model, Ruth eliminated three unnecessary steps and the associated costs, and the recipient has flowers that are up to 9 days fresher.[9]

Traditional Cut-Flower Industry Chain

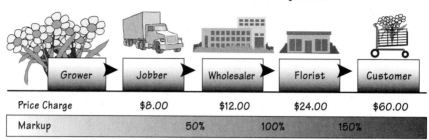

Price Charge		$8.00	$12.00	$24.00	$60.00
Markup			50%	100%	150%

Calyx & Corolla's New Cut-Flower Industry Chain

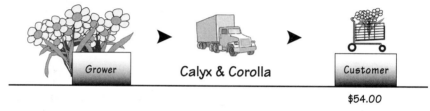

$54.00

Figure 12.4: The Reengineered Flower Industry Supply Chain

At your company: *How are your company's products delivered? How many steps do they go through before they reach the customer? How many of these can be eliminated? How can this distribution and delivery process be streamlined by using the Internet?*

Do We Understand the Environment and Industry Trends?

Technology alone isn't driving most companies toward investments in e-business. Rather, creating a corporate structure that allows the company to deal with rapid business change is. To build an effective structural foundation, managers must first carefully evaluate their business environment. Managers often lose sight of the big picture, given all the demands on their time. However, quality strategic planning and long-term decision efforts begin with developing a broader business perspective. Conducting an environmental analysis helps business executives see the forest from the trees and enables the business to

- Take a fresh look at its business environment and see how it's changing

- Define critical industry and customer issues so that decisions can be made against the backdrop of a broader context

- Correctly position the firm within the industry and identify the most critical industry issues

A well-done environmental scan provides invaluable insights, as it forces the company to step outside its own limited perspective and to examine general trends in business and society and assess their impact. It's a good idea for an enterprise to conduct an analysis frequently in order to spot major discontinuities.

How do you conduct an environmental analysis? Typically, you would arrange a series of sessions with a qualified industry expert who is familiar with the latest trends in technology, competition, customers, demographics, legal and regulatory developments, and local, regional, and national economic conditions and their potential industrial impact. Participants in these sessions benefit immensely, gaining a deeper understanding of industry issues and a shared vision of the future, based on their shared, in-session experiences with colleagues. Participants must come out of these sessions understanding the ramifications of the industry issues discussed.

By identifying key economic, political, social, and technological trends, companies and their business units can develop better-informed strategies for the future. However, if not well facilitated, an environmental analysis can be a tremendous waste of time. Managers often view discussions about potential business scenarios in which the company may compete as a strategic planning activity. Although the sessions are used to develop a context within which strategic decision making can occur, they are not, in themselves, strategic planning meetings.

Do We Understand Technology Trends?

Predicting which technology will next capture the market is difficult. Some companies hedge their technology bets, entering into many new e-business ventures simultaneously, some embracing e-commerce 100 percent.

The 1890s present a good example of the perils of trend prediction. Mark Twain knew a thing or two about the book business. He observed that authors wrote books faster than they could be printed. Twain sank his entire life savings into a new technology for typesetting. He was right about the printing revolution that was to come. However, he put his money into the wrong printing technology. A year later, an inventor came up with a process, Linotype, which became the book printer's technology of choice, and Twain went broke. Soon thereafter, he was back to being a writer. Twain's story has its parallels today. We're all betting on which technologies are going to transform our future. But as Twain discovered, the risk is great when you put all your eggs into one technological basket.

Consider CompuServe, one of the original Internet online pioneers, which was founded in 1969 as a computer timesharing service and introduced its first online service in 1979. In 1994, CompuServe was the largest online service, with double the number of customers of America Online. Yet the management of CompuServe failed to react to the emergence of the Web as a competitive threat. According to Scott Kurnit, formerly second in command at Prodigy, the rise of the Internet "turned the model of the online services industry upside down."[10] CompuServe floundered and watched helplessly as the number of its subscribers fell and as competition escalated. The ultimate indignity was its acquisition by America Online. What went wrong? Why didn't management react to the threat from technology change?

Take time to write a description of the core technology on which you are betting your future. *Is it going through a transition? If so, do you have a transition plan? Are you putting all your eggs in one basket, or are you diversified?*

What Are the Priorities in the Supply Chain?

Coordinating all the players throughout the supply chain requires a detailed understanding of a company's partners. At your company: *Do you understand what your upstream suppliers need from your company? Do you know what your suppliers' current capabilities are? How can we better partner with them to deliver value more effectively? For example, can we deliver products in 2 days if it takes the competition 3 weeks?*

When reviewing your suppliers' priorities, be practical and balance supply chain expectations with reality. The Internet was supposed to link buyers and sellers directly—ushering in an era of frictionless commerce. In this scenario, the role of traditional wholesalers, distributors, and other middlemen would be minimized, eliminated, or replaced with more efficient technology. Consumer prices would go down, even as the sellers' profits rose. Instead of falling prey to disintermediation efforts, middlemen have maintained their role in the supply chain. Some manufacturers realized the difficulties they would have selling directly to consumers over the Web. Most manufacturers, from clothing to toys, get 99 percent of their business from middlemen. Selling directly to consumers would alienate their most important customers. As a result, major companies, such as Levi Strauss and Rubbermaid, have dismantled their Web-direct operations, owing to lack of profitability and the channel conflict issue. *At your company, is there a channel conflict problem?*

Take time to write a description of your supply chain. Your company may have several supply chains. Focus on describing the three most important ones, assessing their importance in terms of how they affect customer value. For each of these, answer the following questions.

- What's our cycle time? How can we compress it? How can we streamline our supplier and transportation relationships to respond to customer demand more quickly than anyone else in our industry?

- What's our lead time? How does it compare with that of our closest competitor? How can we reduce lead time yet increase the time spent adding value to products?

- What's our average inventory level for finished goods? Work in progress? Raw materials? What would it take to increase inventory turns?

- How effectively do we use our warehouses? What would it take to increase throughput if orders are being generated online?

- What channels are ideal for selling and marketing our products, and to whom should we sell them? How should we support these products to keep our customers happy?

You must carefully think through each of these questions in order to shape an e-fulfillment model.

Who Are My Competitors?

Take the time to write a description of who your competitors are. This isn't an easy exercise. Competitors aren't just the other companies in the same business as you. If the only companies on your list are firms in your industry, you risk making the same mistake the telephone industry made when it ignored an emerging technology called Internet telephony.

In the business world lurks a competitor that will attempt to render your business model obsolete. For example, the history of modern retailing reflects drastic business model changes in less than 50 years: Main Street in the 1950s, malls in the 1970s, superstores in the early 1990s, and e-commerce in the late 1990s. Each time the business model changed, a new group of market leaders emerged. Woolworth's never really escaped Main Street. Sears, for the most part, remains stuck in the mall. These incumbents and many others missed the early warning signs. Who paid attention when Sam Walton opened the first Wal-Mart Discount City in 1962? Who really understood the impact that Wal-Mart would have on the distribution chain? Similarly, business analysts everywhere initially dismissed Home Depot as an insignificant player, and now it's a category killer.[11]

When conducting a competitor analysis, companies frequently miscalculate the boundaries of their industries, do a poor job of spotting competition, and make erroneous assumptions about competitors. By focusing on the most visible aspects of a competitor's operations, strategists often end up with an incomplete assessment of the competitors' capabilities and boundaries. They anticipate a competitor's moves, based on past behavior. In so doing, they simplify the situation, assuming that the competitor's actions will follow historical patterns of behavior or that the competitor shares the same worldview as the company does and will behave accordingly. When simplified assumptions and partial information are substituted for clear understanding, a variety of strategic errors occur.[12]

At your company: *Which are your firm's top competitors today? Which are the five upstart companies that will become fierce competitors within the next 5 years? How sure are you that your firm really understands its competition?*

Capability Evaluation

Before selecting its future direction, a business must first assess its business objectives, organizational structure, and current capabilities. The old adage "Know thyself" is vitally important in plotting a course for the future. When assessing your company's objectives, structure, and core competencies, ask the following questions: *What do we want to accomplish? How should we structure ourselves to be most effective? What capabilities do we have today? What capabilities and resources do we need to acquire in the future?*

What Is My Objective?

What do you want your e-business efforts to accomplish? Every business wants results from e-business, but the type of result or change can vary a lot. For example, e-business can be effective as a way to solve nagging problems in customer service. Then again, you may want to create a new business opportunity that defines the rules in your business. Each of these scenarios could lead to different e-business efforts.

Based on the scale of impact on the organization, we've defined three broad levels of strategic objectives: process improvement, strategic improvement, and business transformation (see Table 12.2).

- Process-improvement objectives are appropriate if companies face relatively low levels of uncertainty and are content with incremental, gradual change. With the process-improvement approach, a company maintains a committed focus on conventional process measures, such as capacity utilization or throughput, and on basic customer service.

- Strategic-improvement objectives are appropriate for companies bringing about enterprise-wide, end-to-end change. With the strategic approach, a company maintains a committed focus on such measures as the reduction of process variation, customer-centricity, and leveraging cross-business opportunities.

- Transformational objectives are appropriate when the company faces significant uncertainty, is seeking to change the competitive game in the industry, and must address substantial customer, channel, or competitive challenges. Transformational strategies require companies to reinvent themselves, based on limited, inadequate information about the likelihood of the transformation's success. The company must redefine its product or market position, how it invests in technology, the configuration of its business systems, and industry partnerships.

Of course, many companies are tempted to try accomplishing all three strategic objectives. However, the skill requirements for successfully executing any of these three strategies differ radically. By identifying which strategy is the appropriate driver for your e-business efforts, you will arrive at the best strategic choice for your firm.

Table 12.2: Clarifying Your Strategic Objectives

Objective	Characteristics
Process improvement	• Reducing costs • Decreasing rework • Shortening processing time • Fixing specific errors
Strategic improvement	• Enhancing supply chain efficiencies • Web-enabling strategic operations • Decreasing time to market • Improving customer satisfaction
Business transformation	• Changing the rules of the game • Creating a customer focus • Abandoning old ways of doing business • Major culture change

What is the Best Way to Structure Our e-Effort?

What segments or functions within my firm should be involved in our initial e-business efforts? Restructuring their companies to accommodate e-business is by far the most difficult problem facing chief executives today. The most common e-business structures are

- *Internal.* The e-business activity is given to an internal group that has to mobilize and execute simultaneously. Examples are BellSouth and GE.

- *Autonomous.* The e-business activity is given to a subsidiary or an autonomous online division. Examples are Office Depot and Charles Schwab.

- *External.* The e-business activity is a pure e-play. These companies have no offline baggage and are usually venture-backed, Web-savvy, and super-aggressive. Examples are Webvan and Amazon.com.

Which e-business structure is right for you? Which is feasible in the current organizational environment? When determining feasibility, there are almost always tradeoffs. The main factors influencing a particular structure's feasibility are

- *Resources:* Time, budget, people

- *Centrality:* Is this core to the business or just another strategic initiative?

- *Scope:* Does this require a massive change or an incremental change?

- *Time frame:* How quickly do you want results?

What Internal Capabilities Do We Have Today?

Depending on the structure you select, it is important to assess your firm's internal capabilities. *In fast-moving business environments, it is essential for companies to select a strategy based on what they know is possible for them.* A capably executed strategy delivers better results than a seemingly more elegant one that does not reflect an organization's strengths. It makes sense for a company to choose a sound strategy that meets its financial goals and that provides the best fit with the abilities of its top managers.

In determining a company's strategy, it's critical to conduct a corporate self-examination of the firm's strengths and weaknesses (see Table 12.3). This readiness assessment can be an extraordinarily useful exercise when taken seriously, for it challenges long-held beliefs.

Table 12.3: Areas of Assessment

Customer Interactions	Production and Fulfillment	People	Technology	Core Infrastructure
• Sales channels • Marketing • Customer service • Call centers • Distribution channels	• Manufacturing • Distribution • Supply chain management • Production scheduling • Inventory management	• Culture • Skill sets • Training • Knowledge management • Executive commitment	• ERP systems • Legacy apps • Networks • Web site and intranets • Security • IT skill sets • Help desk	• Financial systems • Research and development • Human resources

Because strengths and weakness are both relative concepts—relative to the competition and to customers' expectations—yesterday's strengths may have become today's weaknesses without anyone in management having noticed. A thorough corporate self-examination clarifies your readiness in each business area, your existing e-business environment, and your vulnerabilities and risks.

When assessing your company's infrastructure, remember that technology implementation can either accelerate or impede an organization's ability to adapt to changing business conditions. Today's technology solutions must fully meet business requirements. Their underlying design must be flexible enough to integrate new and emerging technologies without compromising the existing enterprise architecture. Easier said than done.

At your company: *Does business philosophy differ from the philosophy of the IT department? Is the infrastructure organized around application "stovepipes," owing to political reasons?* Companies in which the application infrastructure isn't aligned with the business objectives usually struggle and fail.

What Capabilities and Resources Do We Need to Speed Up Execution?

Capability assessments identify what you need to acquire, improve, or build to make your vision a reality. As mentioned earlier, alignment between a firm's vision and its capabilities is a precondition for sustainable success. With the strategic direction defined, each function must specify the capabilities it will need in order to successfully deliver the targeted benefits.

The company must develop transition plans describing how each function must change or expand in order to meet the strategic objectives. The transition plan should also integrate each functional area's individual strategies with the company's overall strategy. A thorough transition plan details how the business operation will continue to function while change occurs, providing a sense of stability to the markets as the firm moves from its current state to its future state.

Companies must develop solid enterprise architecture. They must develop or acquire the skills needed to develop an enterprise architecture. A solid enterprise architecture provides a logical, consistent plan of activities and coordinated projects. The enterprise architecture guides the progression and development of an organization's application systems and infrastructure from their current state to the desired future state.

Most organizations claim to have an enterprise architecture in place, but most often what they have is a bunch of stand-alone solutions that don't talk to one another. The introduction of unproven, often untested, and sometimes unapproved technology into the corporate IT environment exacerbates the situation and destabilizes the existing architecture. The presence of unauthorized technology in turn delays introducing other applications that are capable of significantly improving business operations, as the environment is too chaotic to introduce them effectively. To minimize chaos, companies must detail the overall strategy or blueprint while also providing guidelines on how individual project teams should integrate in order to achieve e-business goals.

e-Business Design

Once a company has completed its capability assessment, it must then define its e-business design. The company must define the specific acts it will take to ensure that it maximizes customer value and, in the process, make a profit.

Selecting an e-Business Design

Following is a listing of common e-business designs.[13] Larger companies attempt to accomplish several of these simultaneously. Which of these comes closest to what you're trying to accomplish?

- *Category killer:* This design uses the Internet to define a new market by identifying a unique customer need. A company must be among the first to market and to remain ahead of competition by continuously innovating. Examples are Amazon.com and Yahoo!

- *Channel reconfiguration:* This design uses the Internet as a new channel to directly access customers, make sales, and fulfill orders. It supplements, rather than replaces, physical distribution and marketing channels. Examples are Cisco and Dell.

- *Transaction intermediary:* This design uses the Internet to process purchases. It is a transactional model, including the end-to-end process of searching, comparing, selecting, and paying online. Examples are Expedia and eBay.

- *Infomediary:* This design uses the Internet to reduce search costs. It offers the customer a unified process for collecting the information necessary for making a large purchase. Examples are HomeAdvisor and Auto-By-Tel.

- *Self-service innovator:* This design uses the Internet to provide a comprehensive suite of services to the customer's employees to use directly. It gives employees a direct, personalized relationship with the company. Examples are Employease and webMD.

- *Supply chain innovator:* This design uses the Internet to streamline the interactions among all parties in the supply chain to improve operating efficiency. Examples are McKesson and Ingram Micro.

- *Channel mastery:* This design uses the Internet as a sales and service channel. It supplements, rather than replaces, the existing physical call centers. An example is Charles Schwab.

e-Business Design Refinement

After a company selects its e-business design, it should review the questions raised in the sections Knowledge Building and Capability Assessment. Knowledge building and capability assessment results and requirements may vary, based on the design selected. Several areas of critical questions to consider are

- *Customer selection.* Which customer segment do I serve? For what features are these customers looking? What capabilities do I need in order to provide these features?

- *Customer experience.* Are there unique experiences that I can offer my customers that competitors would be hard pressed to match?

- *Customer capture.* How will I retain my customers so that they don't migrate to more powerful competitors? What features do I need to attract and to retain customers?

- *Scope of design.* What are my company's critical activities and product/service offerings? Which activities will I perform in-house, and which ones will I outsource?

- *Ease of doing business.* What process design should I embed within our business applications to make it easy to do business with my company? Ease of doing business is a key catalyst in changing industry rules.

- *Organizational systems.* What organizational capabilities are critical to my translating the answers to these questions into marketplace success?

Clarify the Differentiation Levers

How is my firm positioned in the market? What is my company's differentiation strategy? Market positioning identifies how you want to compete for customers. Identifying a company's positioning in the market determines the capabilities needed to achieve differentiation. Market positioning requires a firm to excel in at least one of the following major dimensions of differentiation:

- Aesthetically appealing or functionally superior product features

- Marketing channels that provide the desired levels of responsiveness, convenience, variety, and information

- Service and support tailored to end user and channel member sophistication and urgency of need

- Brand or image positioning that imbues the company's offerings with greater appeal on critical selection criteria

- Price, including both net purchase price and cost savings available to the customer through the use of the product or service

Some companies have become successful by focusing heavily on one or two of these dimensions. Which ones does your company focus on? It's a good idea to reexamine every dimension of differentiation in the preceding list frequently, to see if they still make sense for your firm.

In summary, it is important to revisit your company's business design often. Even if the design seems solid, ask yourself regularly: *What in our business environment can render it ineffective?* The *Titanic* was supposedly unsinkable. It wasn't the collision with the tip of the iceberg that sank it but unseen shards of ice beneath the water that sheared rivets off the ship's hull. Today's corporations face similar unseen dangers beneath the economy's surface. No company is unsinkable, and many icebergs lurk in the form of changing customer priorities, new technology, and competition. By remaining flexible and through consistent business design reexamination, companies can avoid the *Titanic*'s fate.

Case Study of e-Business Design in Action: E*TRADE

E*TRADE illustrates the value of identifying and focusing on specific dimensions of competitive differentiation. E*TRADE is a leading provider of cost-effective online financial services. As a self-service innovator, E*TRADE has become synonymous with the term "online trading" by being one of the first to establish a leading, branded destination Web site that offers self-directed investors compelling prices and direct access to high-quality, real-time information.

As a start-up, E*TRADE illustrates an interesting aspect of e-business design: the tension between incumbent firms and start-ups. Incumbents and new entrants have different sets of advantages. Incumbent trading firms, such as Merrill Lynch, have cash, financing, customers, production assets, and brand. New entrants, such as E*TRADE, have a clean-slate business design, an entrepreneurial culture, and nimble decision-making processes.

Table 12.4 captures the key differences in strategic planning between successful large firms and innovative start-ups. At E*TRADE, the role of management is to create change through creative destruction. It's the classic "ready, fire, aim" so typical of the entrepreneurial spirit. Too often, in large companies, it's "ready, aim, appoint a committee." Another difference between the start-ups and established companies is the payback period. In most traditional planning models, payback is often 5 to 10 years, with a conservative ROI of 10 percent to 15 percent.

Table 12.4: Planning at Traditional versus Start-Up Companies

Traditional Planning Framework	Entrepreneurial Framework
• Analyze industry trends. • Analyze enterprise business processes to identify gaps between firm and best-practice leaders.	• Develop and build a working implementation that solves a critical customer problem. • Analyze customer pain to find market opportunity.
• Design incremental organizational change, taking into account the existing customer base and channels, industry contacts, and capital resources.	• Develop an e-business infrastructure, services, and applications to make the business model more efficient. Acquire or merge with firms that provide complementary solutions to transition from point solutions to integrated solutions.
• Implement and execute plans to bring about organizational change.	• Use e-business architecture to attack new market segments. Continuously improve e-business architecture. Be nimble.

Start-up companies often aim for a payback of 2 to 3 years, with an exponential ROI in excess of 100 percent.

Up-and-coming companies, capable of a faster time to market are taking the lead, albeit for a short time. To understand the success of such underdogs as E*TRADE, we must examine why start-up companies are successful in creating an e-business strategy. For start-ups, the logic of e-business differs from that of established firms when addressing the five basic dimensions of strategy: assumptions about customers, customer segments, customer value, resources and capabilities, and product and service offerings.

Customer Assumptions

Customer assumptions determine which questions managers ask, what opportunities they pursue, and how they understand risk. As an online brokerage pioneer, E*TRADE did not take industry conditions as a given. E*TRADE added value to the traditional brokerage business by offering 24-hour service, a significant price discount because of cost advantages inherent to the Web, and direct access to such information as stock quotes, news, and charts.

E*TRADE's initial goal was to optimize the quality of the information it offered and to break down barriers to information across product lines better than anyone else in the brokerage community. Today, E*TRADE is evolving from an online trading firm that pushes trading to one that places a premium on asset accumulation. The firm's growing mutual fund center and acquisition of Telebank and an ATM network are primary examples of this strategy. Also, E*TRADE is opening brick-and-mortar offices in SuperTarget discount stores. The 500-square-foot E*TRADE Zone is designed to draw in shoppers, especially female customers, to talk to customer service reps to trade or to make deposits into E*TRADE Bank accounts.[14] These days, it often takes bricks to really click with customers.

The lesson: Many companies take their industry's conditions as a given and set strategy accordingly. e-Business innovators have no industry conditions to assume, as the ventures they undertake usually have no precedent.

Customer Segments

E*TRADE's customer base is highly active. More than 25 percent of E*TRADE's customers go online every day and trade an average of 25 times per year! Online trading has gone from a novelty to a fixation in the span of a few years—in homes and offices.

Many companies seek growth by retaining and expanding their customer bases. This approach often leads to finer segmentation and greater customization of product and service offerings to meet specialized needs. e-Business innovators follow a different logic. Instead of focusing on customer differences, e-business innovators build on the new qualities that a market niche values.

E*TRADE understands how important customer service and product depth will become as price premium deltas decline. Competition for customers among online brokers is running at a fever pitch. More than 160 Web brokers are now vying for customer investment dollars, ranging from no-frills Datek to the sites of full-service houses, such as Morgan Stanley Dean Witter and Merrill Lynch. With so many online brokers around, E*TRADE is under tremendous pressure to keep customers from leaving.

Thus, building customer loyalty is critical, as is creating a situation in which the customer perceives the switching costs to be high. Strong front-end systems, automated data accumulation, and management are critical to E*TRADE's success in this arena.

While e-business investment funds and brokerage services have developed business models focused exclusively on creating online service, traditional brokerage houses face the challenge of launching online services while continuing to support their existing business models. This situation replicates the tension between start-up and established firms within the confines of one company and presents an internal, competitive conflict for channels, people, and resources.

Customer Value

E*TRADE didn't let competitors set the parameters of its strategic thinking but instead compared its strengths and weaknesses with those of the competition and focused on building advantages. E*TRADE realized early that although investing appeals to a broad audience, each investor has his or her investment objectives and risk tolerance. This gave E*TRADE the opportunity to create unique one-to-one relationships at a lower cost than traditional full-service brokerages.

Whereas full-service brokerages pride themselves on service, the cost model is dramatically higher, owing to both labor and brick-and-mortar expenditures. Many discount brokerage houses provide relatively low-cost trades but less service. E*TRADE provides low cost and high service, enabling the company to attract customers from both brokerage segments.

However, as the market matures, E*TRADE is pushing to penetrate the financial advice space through a joint venture with Ernst & Young (E&Y). This could close a gaping hole in E*TRADE's product lineup and provide a lure for attracting clients with higher net worth. E*TRADE had an interesting strategic choice. Building its own financial advisory capability would be prohibitively expensive after factoring in the heavy technology, personnel, and real estate investment required to make any market headway. Beyond the cash, E*TRADE is set up to embrace the brick-and-mortar model favored by Schwab, Fidelity, and Merrill Lynch. But by partnering with E&Y, whose financial and tax-planning network counts some 20,000 clients, E*TRADE has the opportunity to quickly gain a major product line. The lesson: e-Business innovators redefine core competencies needed to compete.

Resources and Capabilities

Many companies view business opportunities through the lens of existing assets and capabilities. They ask, Given what we have, what is the best we can do? In contrast, e-business innovators ask, What if we start anew?

E*TRADE has taken a clean-slate approach to the brokerage business. This is not to say that e-business innovators never leverage their existing assets and capabilities. They often do. But more important, innovators assess business opportunities without bias or constraint. This approach gives them insight into where to create value for customers—and adroitness at figuring out how value changes—and how to create value quickly.

E*TRADE's first priority is to maintain its momentum through innovation. Customer acquisition and retention get more expensive as competition intensifies. Therefore, E*TRADE is reinvesting a large portion of its revenue into sales and marketing, launching aggressive advertising campaigns aimed at full-service and discount brokerages.

E*TRADE's plan is to build a presence in the top 20 markets worldwide via partnerships. It believes that collaboration with online content companies with technology know-how will provide a significant first-mover advantage and reduce its risk. The company has already established franchise relationships in Canada and Australia. A typical international franchise deal with E*TRADE includes up-front fees of $2 million, plus participation in future revenue streams.

The lesson: To keep up with new entrants, traditional brokerage houses and banks are adjusting their business models to take advantage of online opportunities and to invest heavily in technology development. In the meantime, E*TRADE is investing heavily in building brand-name recognition and adding products and services that go beyond basic trading capabilities to maintain customers.

Product and Service Offerings

Conventional competition takes place within clearly established boundaries defined by the products and services the industry offers. e-Business innovators often cross those boundaries and think in terms of the total solution customers want. From there, the innovators brainstorm ways to overcome the compromises that the customers are forced to make.

E*TRADE is expanding by forging relationships with other financial service providers in order to increase the depth of its products. For example, the company hopes to provide electronic bill payment as an option for its customers. New products and services serve the dual purpose of providing added value to customers while diversifying revenue streams and reducing the potential for volatility. E*TRADE has aggressively extended its services to include the ability to purchase mutual funds online and to make initial public offerings. It has also launched subscription services that provide consumers with valuable information, such as research by Wall Street analysts, sophisticated charting and modeling capabilities, and personalized investment advice.

The lesson: Although competition is certainly on the horizon, E*TRADE is working diligently to maintain its advantage. Hence, while competing brokerage firms struggle to adjust their cost structures in order to support $8 to $20 trades, E*TRADE is developing complementary financial services and marketing partnerships designed to create customer loyalty and to increase perceived switching costs.

Future Opportunities: Rethinking Organizational Structure

As E*TRADE evolves from a start-up to a more mature company, it is facing a host of new pressures that make differentiation key in a fight for long-term viability. E*TRADE is fighting back by creating an e-business strategy that integrates diverse parts of its operations—marketing, sales, trading, banking, product development, and finance—to facilitate decision making and quick market response. Tight integration ensures that when decisions are made, the parts come together quickly to form a cohesive whole that meets customer expectations in real time.

e-Business impact isn't limited to product development and distribution but extends to organizational structure as well. For example, E*TRADE is beginning to cross-sell new financial services to its highly proactive, self-directed customer base. The company is taking advantage of this opportunity because it's focused on gaining market share by scaling its back-end processing engine in order to dramatically lower its cost structure. In order to take advantage of cross-sell opportunities to mainstream customers, E*TRADE must make a shift from being a pure-play to a click-and-brick company.

The lesson: The forces of e-business are creating a structural upheaval in business processes, a shift that rearranges value propositions more than mere hardware or software ever can. This new world has its own distinct opportunities and its own rules. Businesses that play by the new rules will prosper and become market leaders; those that ignore them, won't.

Memo to the CEO

Peter Drucker noted, "A time of turbulence is a dangerous time, but its greatest danger is the temptation to deny reality."[15] Most executives recognize that they must leave past practices behind. They realize that a tollbooth is at the entrance to the new economy. Not all firms will be able to pay the toll, because it requires a new type of currency—e-business leadership. Admission will not be granted to firms that hold steadfast to yesterday's assumptions and practices.

With large-scale technological and environmental change, companies in all business sectors are faced with the same basic questions: *How should we compete in our industry? What are our important objectives? How do we achieve long-term focus in an increasingly competitive and sometimes downright hostile business and technology environment?*

The answers to these questions form the essence of strategic planning. However, aligning innovation with strategy, coupled with disciplined execution, is the most significant way to create value. It's not difficult to see why. By its very nature, innovation requires out-of-the-box thinking. The challenge lies in nurturing this sort of thinking while ensuring that it does not conflict with the strategic goals of the company.

Some people use e-business strategic planning to create a written document that will only gather dust on a shelf. At its core, strategic planning isn't a written scheme but a systematic way of understanding what your company is trying to accomplish, identifying the best ways to accomplish your company's goals, and effectively communicating the specifics of accomplishing these goals throughout the corporate hierarchy. Unfortunately, this straightforward process can be time consuming, difficult, even unpleasant. As a result, most companies either don't execute strategic planning well or do something that passes for strategic planning but really isn't. In addition to out-of-the-box thinking, we need the heart and discipline to make our strategies a business reality.

The difficulties of creating e-business strategy are often compounded by executives' being too short-term focused to pay attention to long-term issues. Because the stock market places great emphasis on the quarter-by-quarter results, executives often concentrate on peripheral elements—financial management and growth through acquisition and consolidation. Although important, these elements don't advance the company's core value. Strong companies are built on innovation and new products that customers care about.

How do we turn the tide? The challenge is to create a planning process that is customized, results in collective organizational learning, and increases knowledge about your business. The case for devising an e-business blueprint strategy and creating a strategic plan is compelling, yet justifications for not doing it abound.

- Management and staff are too busy putting out today's fires to worry about tomorrow's problems or business opportunities.

- Managers rationalize that their solid market niche protects them from the marketplace turbulence, saying, "Why waste time planning for a future when we are making so much money today?"

- Managers rationalize that because the future is inherently unpredictable, there's no way to prepare for it. In other words, what will be will be.

The logic behind these thoughts is flawed. Any manager who believes that his or her business will be unaffected by the Internet is asking to be blindsided. The unpredictability of the future is no excuse for failing to plan. A business can influence its own destiny in even the most changing environment. As the start-ups and new entrants demonstrate, rapid, unpredictable change and disarray usually present unparalleled opportunities.

Businesses with the will to win are a dime a dozen. The truly successful ones are those with the will-to-prepare. Preparing to win is what strategic planning is all about. Thoughtful planning is difficult to fit into today's busy schedule, but keep in mind that a characteristic of every successful business is disciplined preparation and execution.

CHAPTER THIRTEEN

Translating e-Business Strategy into Action: e-Blueprint Formulation

What to Expect

Interestingly enough, many managers plan ingenious strategies in response to competition and marketspace innovations. Yet few firms excel at translating strategy into action. If you ask these same managers how well their organizations have executed past projects and to assess their ability to reach strategic goals, you'll hear a litany of frustration and little hope for success. This problem is getting worse as companies race to integrate physical assets and online capabilities.

The problem has often been a lack of tools for managers to align both their long-term and short-term e-business strategy and the processes and application frameworks that will help them implement it. The e-business blueprint provides the tools to support management in implementing a solid long-term foundation. The e-blueprint creation process covers both infrastructure and application projects and provides a roadmap to help companies translate their e-strategies into actions.

An enterprise blueprint is a plan for the long term. A well-planned blueprint of interconnected applications is a prerequisite for e-business. This chapter explains how to span the gap between e-business strategic planning and execution using e-blueprints. The chapter also

- *Details the steps involved in building an e-business blueprint*
- *Presents the business case for making e-business investments*

- *Discusses the management issues and challenges you must confront when developing an e-blueprint business case*
- *Provides a business case checklist and the top ways companies fail at turning strategy into action*

Why is it that converting e-strategy into action, high on management's priority list, is not well understood? Could it be that most managers underestimate the real challenge: getting their ambitious Internet plans off the drawing board and onto the implementation road? Is top management slow to realize that whereas designing a high-level e-business design—identifying the journey—might take a few months, building a comprehensive e-business architecture—getting to the destination—is a long, bumpy road?

It has been our experience that e-strategy discussions ignore the link-application infrastructure between strategy formulation and execution because executives fail to see it as part of the big picture. Unfortunately, most people don't find application infrastructure to be a very exciting subject. As a result, many companies miss the opportunity to make an educated choice between a "real" strategy that they can execute well and an "ideal" strategy that may demand capabilities they simply do not possess. So it should come as no surprise that many "ideal" strategies have trouble getting executed in the real world. How do you fix this alignment problem? How does a firm arrive at a "real" strategy?

A good analogy to the "ideal" versus "real" dilemma can be found in everyday life—fitness. Fitness isn't an option in today's sedentary e-lifestyle. It's a necessary part of our daily routine. To become fit or to maintain fitness, many individuals set goals, often at the beginning of the year, to stick to a disciplined regimen. Yet few follow them. The strategy is great, but the execution is poor. To execute better, experts have been advocating a whole new way of thinking about exercise—one that goes beyond regarding fitness as a fad or the province of marathon runners and instead considers it as a necessary part of our daily routine. Again, good concept. But to get there requires not only major shifts in personal behavior but also an effort to systematically change structural and process impediments to leading more healthy lives.

Everybody knows they should exercise. So why do so few people actually do it? This fitness dilemma is very similar to e-business execution dilemma. Many firms fail to establish connection between their strategy-planning processes and the processes they use to identify, select, implement, and deploy individual projects (see Figure 13.1). Companies often fall prey to the "business fad of the day" syndrome and often throw away discipline and bet the company on the silver

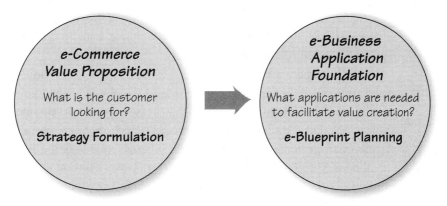

Figure 13.1: Linking Value to e-Blueprint Planning

bullet. *This lack of discipline at the enterprise level creates deep-rooted structural and coordination problems in a world in which the time between planning and tactical execution is increasingly compressed.*

Based on our experience of observing what works and what doesn't in large companies, we have come to the conclusion that lack of a disciplined approach to execution is often the cause of failure. To overcome this problem, we have created the concept of e-business blueprints as a missing link between strategy and tactics. An e-business blueprint is defined as the whole fabric of applications, processes, and services that shape and sustain customer value. The traditional model of different silos with different applications has restricted the development of holistic strategies for building more integrated and efficient e-businesses.

So what lies ahead? In the previous chapter, we detailed the questions that managers need to ask before they can create an e-business design. The purpose of this chapter is to add to the e-business roadmap detail that can help bridge the chasm between high-level e-business strategy and effective execution. Read on and learn what others are doing about the challenge and, most important, what your company can do!

Setting the Stage for e-Blueprint Planning

Clarifying the e-Blueprint Problem

In medieval times, cathedrals were usually built without any blueprints. The master builder had a vague idea of a plan and began to build. As he proceeded, the builder or his patron—a bishop, a king, or a rich nobleman—might alter the plan. Rather than start anew, the builder incorporated the changes and continued until something resembling a cathedral was complete. Usually, the finished product looked nothing like the initial design.

Today's corporate e-business efforts resemble the construction of a medieval cathedral. A "vague idea" substitutes for cohesive management and a well-developed plan. Intuition rather than reason directs development of new applications. The e-business strategy's success hinges on the creative ability of the artists—management—rather than on the inherent solidity of the design.

Today's typical corporate infrastructure comprises a diverse mixture of application packages, legacy systems, and custom apps. The problem is not so much the diversity but the absence of a cohesive approach to creating sustainable business designs. The CIO of Chase.com stated it well: "We're not trying to be a winner on the Internet. We're trying to be one of the best-positioned companies to take advantage of opportunities in the new economy. It is a much bigger battle we're trying to win, and a massive opportunity to change the way business is done."[1]

e-Blueprint planning links your e-business strategy with the technology, resources, and company capabilities required to make the strategy happen. As technology spending accelerates, e-blueprint planning becomes more important and difficult, for the following reasons.

- Without an e-business blueprint, technology investments are not often linked to a definable e-strategy. The business risk increases, as poor investment decisions can be costly and detrimental to an organization's competitive position.

- The strategic use of technology, the widening scope and complexity of decision making, and the speed of innovation make it difficult for organizations to make technology-related decisions effectively.

- The successful analysis and implementation of technology projects that meet stated objectives is rare. Failure, on the other hand, can be devastating.

- Greater technical complexity and the proliferation of vendors offering a variety of solutions have made understanding emerging technology, and anticipating its impact, more challenging.

Technological complexity and the associated fiscal risks mean that more companies are searching for better ways to manage the task of aligning their business models with their decisions about technology spending. Such alignment takes skill and depends largely on which type of strategy—process improvement, strategic improvement, or business transformation—is being pursued. The skills required to execute each of these strategies, although not mutually exclusive, are rarely present in a single company.

Strategic alignment is further complicated by the widespread corporate habit of managing a group of poorly integrated individual projects rather than a portfolio of projects carried out in support of a specific strategy. This project portfolio detailing a master plan for implementing multiple concurrent projects is the e-blueprint.

The e-blueprint lays out a plan for execution. This may require companies to overhaul project management. For instance, in an SAP R/3 financial application project, McKesson chopped an unwieldy 40-member business steering committee down to 4 executives: CIO, CFO, the controller, and the vice president of shared financial services. At the same time, McKesson transferred the week-to-week project management from a single business executive to a four-person "project office" that had business knowledge, SAP knowledge, and a deep understanding of the complex legacy systems. No one person had all this knowledge. There wasn't even a person who knew two aspects.[2]

Focusing on e-Blueprints, Not Single Projects

In most companies, e-business projects are treated the same as any other initiative. Each e-effort is undertaken *one project at a time in isolation from other projects,* with little forethought given to achieving economies of scale and scope or shared resources. Without a shared strategic vision in place, each initiative goes in its own self-defined direction. This problem is compounded by mergers and acquisitions. As a result, many companies have serious application infrastructure problems, and these problems have worsened in recent years.

The end results of the single project focus are

- Resource competition, resulting in political fights

- A failure to embrace commonality of purpose and technology across the organization

- Uncoordinated system designs, with lack of compatibility and standardization among initiatives

- Inconsistent customer experiences when one common experience would suffice

- Expensive in-house-developed technology serving a single project

- Business processes with essentially the same specifications but subtle differences so they are not reusable

An e-business blueprint can easily become chaotic and dysfunctional when it is developed and managed one project at a time (see Figure 13.2). In most companies, the political will simply is not there. Without such political courage, the institutional obstacles to well-thought out, comprehensive, and integrated e-blueprints will remain. Like good politicians, top managers rhetorically support common initiatives every chance they get—but then do next to nothing to make it happen for fear of the consequences.

Departmental resistance is often the reason individual projects take precedence over enterprise-wide need. Departmental incentive structures are often driven by parochialism, group loyalty, and a stubbornly rooted culture based on the concepts of profit center and individual P&Ls. As a result, the business lines are loath to implement common projects. This attitude is tremendously harmful when you are creating solutions for a common customer.

The experience of Microsoft provides an alternative to the single-project mentality. Most readers probably own a PC powered by Microsoft Windows running Microsoft Office. There is a good reason for this. Microsoft drove most of its competitors, such as WordPerfect and Lotus, out of the word processing and spreadsheet business by developing consistent and common product platforms for its major product families. Microsoft did the same to Novell in the

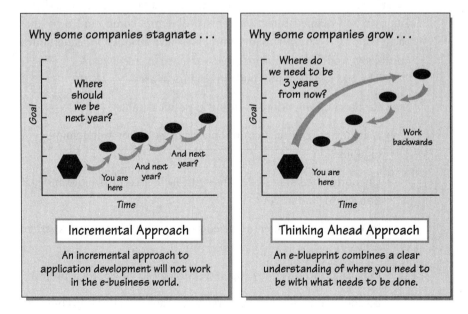

Figure 13.2: Approaches to e-Blueprint Planning

networking business by making local area networking part of its operating system. Microsoft overtook Borland in the development tools business by emphasizing consistency and broader integration. Microsoft overtook Netscape also by using its platform to provide integration, consistency, and ease of use. In area after area, Microsoft's relentless pursuit of improvement excellence, coupled with its focus on providing better integration for the customer, has proved to be unstoppable.

Beginning the e-Blueprint Journey

Imagine taking a caravan of thousands of people on a journey with no map, no plan, no one in charge, no logistical support, no way to keep everyone informed, no scouting reports to assess and update progress, and no navigational instruments. Sheer madness, yet that's how most companies handle the transition to e-business. The purpose of the e-blueprint is to map a course for creating an integrated design and to avoid the dead ends that are typical when you don't plan where you're headed.

The e-blueprint translates strategy into action (see Figure 13.3). Integration of the following drivers into a comprehensive application framework is the essence of blueprint planning:

- *Organizational,* such as consolidation, the need for operational efficiencies

- *Business,* such as mergers and acquisitions, new business initiatives

- *Customer,* such as changing customer priorities

- *Technology,* such as the availability of new technology, legacy applications

GE, Wal-Mart, Microsoft, and Intel seem to excel at this. For instance, during the 1980s and 1990s, Wal-Mart turned the discount-retailing business into a pure game of tactical execution by excelling in information technology, logistics infrastructure, and front-line execution. Market leaders know that however excellent a strategy may be, it will not succeed without disciplined execution.

Blueprints also must support the "value" goals: customer focus, highest quality, lowest cost, and shortest lead time. For instance, e-blueprints must support the necessary application integration required to deliver value to customers. How? By determining the strategic elements of its application infrastructure and translating these to an enterprise-wide, unified foundation that is both efficient and flexible, allowing the company to adapt, change, grow, and innovate.

In your company, who lies awake at night thinking of the integration of technology and applications across all the business units?

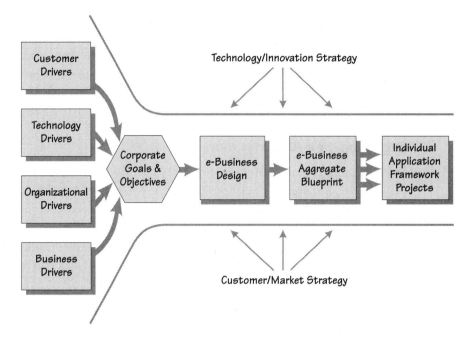

Figure 13.3: Translating Strategy into Action

The relationship between value creation, innovation, and integration forms the core of e-business blueprint planning. Are your blueprint planning efforts able to

- Balance the opportunities for improving application infrastructure by prioritizing technology appropriately in accordance with the corporate strategy

- Achieve the right project mix to support the company's strategic direction while allocating resources appropriately

In addition a company can take two possible approaches when justifying its blueprint. *Which of the following is your company doing?*

- A short-term approach whereby a company patches together an e-blueprint plan incorporating the company's existing applications

- A longer-term approach whereby a company starts over with an entirely new group of applications as the core piece of its e-blueprint plan

Companies with groups of complex information systems must adhere to a structured and disciplined approach when managing the risks associated with enterprise framework planning and investment. Corporate managers can learn from builders. Any builder will tell you that designing a house from the ground up is often a breeze compared with adding on to an existing structure. When starting from scratch, you can pick and choose the features you want. But adding on can be a headache because you have to mesh new and old structural elements, and often the old structure dictates the materials, design, and extent of the addition.

To Patch or Not to Patch?

What is the optimal blueprint for traditional brick-and-mortar organizations? Whether a company chooses to patch together its existing applications framework to support its e-business strategy or to start with an entirely new framework, neither choice reduces the workload or the difficulty. There are no shortcuts when creating seamless integration across enterprise applications. For this reason, many established firms are vulnerable to competition from start-ups.

For example, Citibank is a pioneer of online banking. When formulating its e-business blueprint, Citibank decided to abandon many expensive, proprietary computer systems it had built in the past decade and to create a new Internet banking and investment service. Citibank aims to replace the core back-office computer systems on which it keeps customer accounts—systems that it had built and maintained at a cost of hundreds of millions of dollars. The bank is taking such a radical action to catch up with a new generation of competitors, such as E*TRADE and more nimble, established companies, such as Charles Schwab, that have seized the initiative on Internet financial services.[3] Citibank had to address the question of *whether to create a fresh new infrastructure* or *to patch the existing infrastructure. Based on your experience, is discarding legacy systems the best way for larger companies to compete with newer firms?*

Large firms face three challenges when deciding to patch or not patch their existing infrastructure:

- Integration of their legacy infrastructure

- Building a seamless infrastructure on a fragmented application base

- Knowing when to walk away and start over

Many companies must deal with the first of these challenges. For large, established companies, updating and integrating their existing infrastructure is often their only choice. According to the CIO of Delta Airlines, "A Web site is like an iceberg. What you see looks small and simple, but below it you have infrastructure integration issues with maybe 40 or 50 databases. So building a Web infrastructure can be a pretty serious risk for older companies."[4] In the case of large firms, the e-blueprint provides a logically consistent plan for implementing coordinated projects to take a company's application infrastructure from its current state to the desired future state.

The second challenge requires large companies to make sure that the front-end experience for customers is a seamless, well-integrated service-delivery platform. Such platforms mark a fundamental change in the way a business runs. Integration is not simply an IT issue but means creating the right structural foundation to facilitate e-business.

The third challenge is knowing when to walk away and start over. If the company has chosen to patch its existing infrastructure, senior management has the responsibility to monitor whether such change is sufficient to meet the goals of the company's e-business strategy. When incremental change is insufficient, the company must be prepared to make the fundamental changes required to reshape the application foundation on which the company operates. The e-blueprint assists companies in overcoming the inertia and cultural resistance that often come with the decision to undertake radical technological change.

As companies become customer focused, an effective blueprint differentiates successful companies from other firms because it enhances their ability to deliver value. Blueprints help launch new integration efforts, not just implementing patches to existing initiatives. Information, process, and data integration across applications is where the battles will be fought and won in the next 5 years.

Evaluating Your Company's e-Business Blueprint Process

It is important to regularly assess how your firm is managing its e-business blueprint formulation. Following are several red flags indicating that the process is in trouble:

- Platform projects take too long. When asked why, managers point out how everyone is working as hard as possible, but people are stretched across too many projects. Too many "strategic" projects in the pipeline results in project gridlock.

- Many substandard projects have been in the pipeline for years, have lost their value, and are siphoning off resources from more worthwhile efforts.

- Nearly all the projects you are implementing are long-term, multimillion-dollar, big-bang efforts. Many of the projects are high reward but also high risk, implying that there's a high probability of technical or commercial failure.

- Almost all projects you are implementing appear to reinvent the wheel, resulting in wasted effort and overlap, and no one takes advantage of previous work or already established key elements.

- Too much procrastination when making decisions. The complexity of today's technology—proliferating layers of servers, operating systems, application languages, network protocols, databases, middleware, hardware, and software—makes it more and more difficult to ascertain the long-term impact of any technological choice.

- Project interdependence is difficult to manage. Increased integration among business units and functions means that changes in one system often affect dozens of others, some in other organizations.

- Lack of communication and business-side buy-in. IT often deploys technology without user management's buy-in, and users resist it. Adoption is slow or just nonexistent.

Having a disciplined e-blueprint process can help address some of these issues. For example, we estimate company sales-revenue losses of approximately 25 percent on average, stemming from order rework, incorrect orders, and errors from a lack of integration. *At your company, how much money could cross-business integration save?*

Basic Phases of e-Blueprint Planning

A company's e-blueprint is a dynamic portfolio whereby a business's list of active projects is created, continually updated, and revised. By filling in the gap among strategic planning, organizational capability, and application infrastructure, a blueprint strategy brings discipline to the chaos of e-business change, providing a common language that executives from marketing, information technology, and manufacturing can all understand and participate in. The e-blueprint joins the business design, supporting applications and performance objectives into a cohesive whole. An enterprise blueprint is a plan for the long term. Thinking ahead avoids short-term fixes that may need to be redone in the future.

An enterprise blueprint is composed of multiple projects. For instance, an ERP implementation in a company like Intel is a project. The value of having a blueprint lies in the fact that it brings order to chaos: how new projects are evaluated, selected, and prioritized; how existing projects may be accelerated, devalued, or killed; and how resources are allocated and reallocated to the active projects.

Once projects have been screened for inclusion into the enterprise blueprint, they are evaluated by balancing the optimal investment mix of risk and return, cost reduction versus growth, and short-term versus long-term goals. The ideal process for doing this is a detailed project business case that is evaluated by the committee that oversees the overall blueprint. This is the final stage prior to implementation, so it's important that the business case be clearly defined.

Once the committee has approved the project, it is time to move to the messy part: execution. Clearly, the battle is won not in the boardroom but in the trenches—in programming shops, on factory floors, and at service counters. Execution is the defense against competitor attacks. Companies that fail to execute are vulnerable to attack.

Figure 13.4 shows the three basic phases to blueprint planning:

- *e-Blueprint creation.* This step defines the e-blueprint strategy and related initiatives. The step also selects goal-focused—customer-centric—rather than means-focused—product-centric—projects.

- *e-Blueprint facilitation.* This step creates the business case for the project(s). This step also identifies which projects are worth pursuing and how these can be justified to management.

- *e-Blueprint execution.* This step creates a tactical execution plan for the e-blueprint. This step also determines how approved projects get executed and brought to market.

Many enterprises place greater emphasis on the e-blueprint creation—what needs to be done—than on either e-blueprint facilitation—who does what—or e-blueprint execution—when and how it is done. Here, we'll look at e-blueprint creation and facilitation in more detail. Chapter 14 will delve into e-blueprint execution.

e-Blueprint Creation: Defining the Blueprint in Your Company

e-Business design drives the blueprint. The goals of the e-business design—process improvement, strategic improvement, or business transformation—dictate the composition of the blueprint.

A great blueprint starts with clear ideas. If done well, e-blueprint creation helps ensure long-term success with your e-business design by helping institutionalize

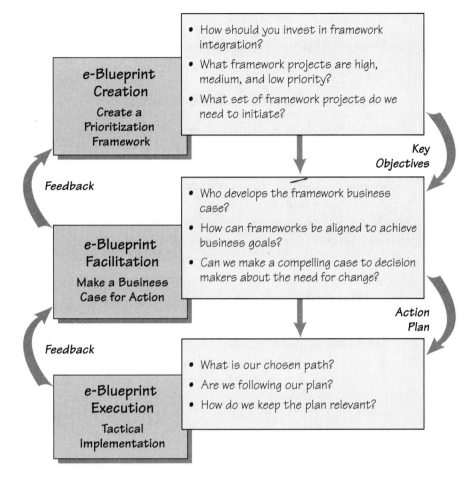

Figure 13.4: The Roadmap to e-Blueprint Planning

change with the organization, providing a framework for managing technology and innovation so they yield sustainable growth. Over time, e-business designs change by proactively adapting to streams of technological and process innovation. A well-developed blueprint must also change accordingly.

e-Blueprint creation has five steps.

1. Establish the aim of the overall e-business design.

2. Establish the scope of the effort.

3. Classify and analyze the application frameworks.

4. Prioritize what needs to get done.

5. For each application framework, design the execution plan.

Let us now consider each step.

Step 1: Establish the Aim of the Overall e-Business Design

The blueprint escalates in complexity, depending on the scope of what is being accomplished in the business design. For instance, "We want to go from brick and mortar to click and mortar" requires very different blueprint from "We have to connect our systems to systems of our business partners."

No e-business journey can be successful without knowing the destination. Figure 13.5 charts five general destinations in developing e-business blueprints, ranging from cross-functional process integration to multicompany integration. *Where does your organization want to be in terms of these?* Each destination has a different scope and degree of complexity come implementation time.

Let's examine the five destinations of e-business design.

- *The cross-functional business unit.* The business goal of the firm is to produce dependable, consistent, quality products and services at the lowest possible cost. In order to accomplish this goal, companies typically focus on automating existing functions and tasks. Most companies are striving to reach this level.

- *The strategic business unit.* The business goal is to serve the customer end to end, for example, in order acquisition and fulfillment. Here, companies are

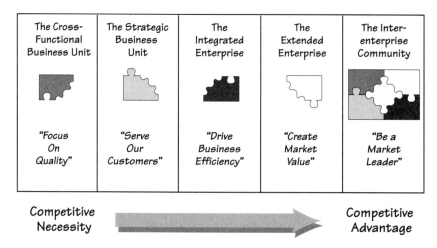

Figure 13.5: Roadmap to an e-Business Architecture

beginning to consolidate their supply chains in some areas, such as combining distribution and transportation into logistics, and manufacturing and purchasing into operations, with the ultimate goal of better meeting customer demand. In the past decade, strategic business units (SBUs) have increasingly taken the role of application strategy formulation away from corporate headquarters. The shift makes sense: SBUs are closer to customers, competitors, and costs. American Express is an example of this type of company. However, in a high-velocity environment rife with mergers and acquisitions, SBUs can fail to create organizational agility by losing their focus on the organization's priorities and capabilities.

- *The integrated enterprise.* The business goal is to focus mostly on cost reduction and internal efficiency. The driving goal is to be highly customer responsive, leveraging the ability to quickly deliver high-quality products and services at the lowest total delivered cost. Such companies become highly responsive by investing in operational flexibility as well as integrating their internal supply chains, from the acquisition of raw materials to the delivery of product to the customer. Companies implement a strategy of decreasing costs by achieving "preferred partner" status with key suppliers. Dell Computer is such an integrated enterprise.

- *The extended enterprise.* The business goal is to creating market value. *Extended enterprise* describes a multienterprise supply chain with a shared information infrastructure. The extended enterprise enables supply chain integration, more effective outsourcing, and self-service solutions for both internal and external users. The extended enterprise allows for sophisticated online business processes that interweave line-of-business apps with other internal and external information or sources. The goal is profitable growth, which some companies accomplish by providing customer-tailored products, services, and value-added information. This differentiates them from competitors. Cisco with its intricate relationships in the IP world, is an example.

- *The interenterprise community.* The business goal is to market leadership through complex collaborative arrangements. Companies consolidate into true interenterprise communities whose members share common goals and objectives across and among enterprises. These companies are able to streamline their business transactions with their partners to maximize growth and profit. Intel, in our opinion, is an example.[5]

At each destination of e-business design, it is very important to align the scope of design with the nature of the blueprint. If the scope of the e-business design is restricted to a single strategic business unit, it makes no sense to create a grandiose blueprint plan that goes across 20 other business units. Often, companies create visionary designs that don't get implemented because of the misalignment between the scope of the design and the magnitude of the application integration problem. In other words, application integration via a blueprint must be closely aligned with the e-business design.

Step 2: Establish the Scope of the Effort

A blueprint is a reflection of the e-business design. When assessing the scope of such an effort, it's important to map your company's e-business design into the three types of improvement: process improvement, strategic improvement, and business transformation. Each type of e-business system is defined by the degree of risk associated with it.

Process-improvement systems are low risk and often are derivatives, add-ons, and enhancements of existing designs. These process-improvement systems include incremental feature changes with little or no major structural changes. These systems often require fewer resources and entail less risk because they leverage existing systems and enhance their functionality. If you look around your company, you can find a lot of these projects.

Strategic-improvement systems are moderate to high risk. The systems create new structural foundations that can be leveraged across multiple areas of the business. These systems also create an infrastructure on which various strategic initiatives can be undertaken, such as e-commerce, supply chain management, and others. The move toward enterprise framework systems is driven by business—companies see the need for being able to move quickly through configurable building blocks.

Business-transformation systems are high risk and involve substantial changes in the foundation of the firm. These systems often spearhead the entry of the firm into a new area of business. These systems are often risky and have a high probability of failure. Breakthrough systems are usually undertaken by start-ups because such firms are more open to a clean slate and starting over with a new applications approach.

To get the most bang for the buck, e-business blueprint efforts should focus on either strategic improvements or business transformation. Table 13.1 captures the distinction between these types of systems.

Table 13.1: Types of Blueprint Efforts

	Strategic Improvement	Business Transformation
Focus of Change	Build exceptional internal capabilities	Gain unusual insight into the customer and market needs
Skill Development	Distinctive process thinking	Excellent strategic decision making
Implementation Approach	Highly linear	Entrepreneurial
Measuring Progress	Efficiency targets	Market share

Step 3: Classify and Analyze the Application Frameworks

In this step, a company must break down its blueprint into logical application frameworks. In Chapter 5, we described in great detail the emerging application frameworks that are shaping the business landscape. We have defined the architecture of the integrated landscape as comprising various application frameworks: CRM, SCM, and ERP (see Figure 13.6).

The blueprint, which includes the entire set of application frameworks, must be viewed as one system. In the words of W. Edward Deming: "A system is a network of interdependent components that work together to try to accomplish the aim of the system."[6]

However, during the process of application framework analysis, companies must think through how to deal with their existing infrastructures. As companies race to implement their e-business strategies, the old infrastructure creaks and groans under the strain. Fixing its problems requires careful and deliberate investment in integration. How should companies prioritize the projects in which they will invest while maintaining the existing application infrastructure?

In established companies, framework projects are the norm today. Figure 13.7 represents an example of a framework project: a B2B portal with an end-to-end transaction management infrastructure. Once built, this platform can be leveraged to service the customer in unique ways. This is a high-risk project, given the scope, complexity, and high-level integration required. In this figure, one of the things that should strike you right away is the number of applications involved in delivering value to customers. In the foreseeable future, we do not anticipate one integrated application to deliver the end-to-end engage/transact/fulfill/service requirements in satisfying customers' needs. Various applications will need to be integrated to work seamlessly.

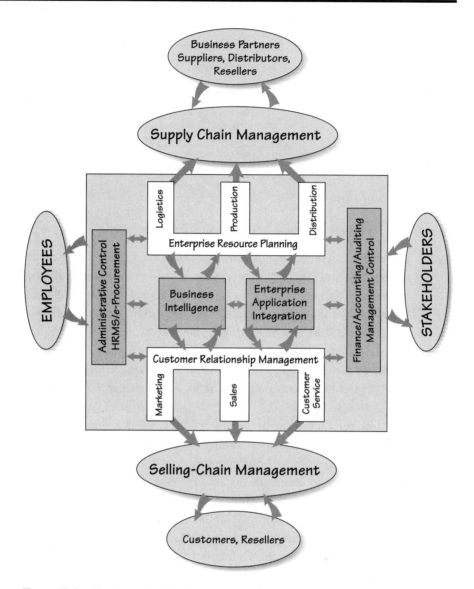

Figure 13.6: e-Business Application Frameworks

Step 4: Prioritize What Needs to Get Done

Whereas corporate architects look ahead several years, project prioritization still tends to be an annual ritual. Once a year, corporate headquarters asks its various operating units to submit application spending wish lists. Line-of-business managers, in turn, pose three questions to their subordinates.

- *Where do we need to spend money on application enhancements?*

- *How much will each of these enhancements cost us?*

- *What will we get for the money we spend?*

The result of this process is a separate wish list for all the various divisions—far too many for review. Each division checks for inconsistencies and redundancies among the wish lists prepared by its own sites and functions. Once problems are resolved, each division forwards its wish list to corporate headquarters, where a quick summation typically reveals that full funding of all of the requests simply is not in the cards.

What target should we set for next year's capital spending? Answering this question often involves hours of discussion and negotiation among a company's highest levels of management and finance. Once the capital-spending target is set, a portion of it is allocated to each operating division in the form of a capital budget.

The managers tend to make a game of the system. They know that rarely will every project on the wish list get funding. Instead, each sees the other lines of

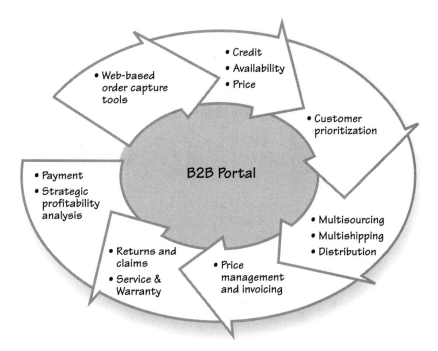

Figure 13.7: An e-Business Framework Project

business as competitors for a limited pool of dollars. Experienced managers tend to be even more sophisticated players of the capital-spending game. How they are measured, rewarded, and penalized largely determines how they spend capital. For example, leaving capital on the table at the end of the budget cycle is considered to be bad management in most companies, despite advances in performance-measurement techniques during the past decade.

Therein lies the paradox: Application integration is mandated from the top but gets lost in the jungle of capital budgeting. How do you fix the current way of allocating resources? The first step in developing a blueprint plan is to clearly define the types of projects a company needs.

Figure 13.8 depicts an e-business funnel, which is an excellent way to prioritize various infrastructure projects. The e-business blueprint evolves from a high-level design into execution through a series of review and decision points called screening criteria. An example of a screening question is, *To what degree does the project align with the company's strategy?*

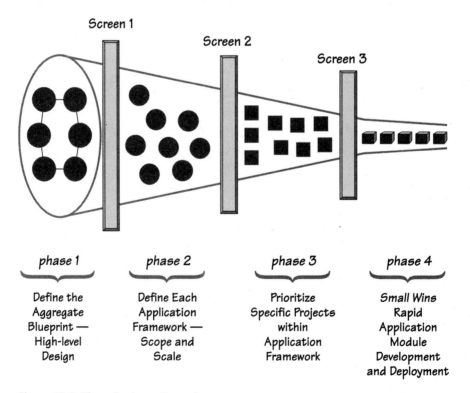

Figure 13.8: The e-Business Funnel

To successfully create an integration e-blueprint, companies need prioritization processes for capital budgeting, investing in new technologies, and allocating scarce resources among competing business groups. Senior managers should be responsible for deciding how to allocate resources among the various enterprise framework projects to achieve strategic objectives. Like money managers, they need to build a portfolio that optimizes their application investments.

Step 5: For Each Application Framework, Design the Execution Plan

Once you have a blueprint design that has been improved through several iterations of the "aim-scope-classify-prioritize" methodology, you should ask: What is the one best way to bring it to market? In the past, the development of application frameworks, such as SAP R/3, were implemented slowly. However, in today's competitive world, companies can't afford that luxury. Given their complexity and scope, application framework implementations can either accelerate or impede an organization's ability to adapt to changing business conditions.

Table 13.2 illustrates four execution imperatives: speed, efficiency, flexibility, and innovation. To succeed, implementations must be responsive to changing customer demands and competitor moves. This means that they must have short time-to-market cycles. The ability to identify opportunities, organize execution, and bring to market new capabilities quickly is critical to effective competition. At the same time, firms must bring new capabilities to market efficiently. Resource allocation among competing projects is critical.

Between the broad architecture of application framework and the details of specific work tasks lies a set of choices a firm must make about the overall

Table 13.2: The Execution Imperatives

Required Capabilities	Driving Forces	Implications
Fast and responsive	Changing customer expectations; accelerating value migration	Shorter time-to-market cycles
High execution productivity	Scarce resources; wrong moves can destroy company	Make better management decisions about resource allocation and project selection
Flexible configurations	Continuous innovation; changing customer needs	Make architectural decisions that allow flexibility
Innovation	Demanding customers; intense competition	Creativity combined with integrated solutions

execution process. Figure 13.9 illustrates these choices, which form the foundation for creating an execution plan, are

- *Creating a development blueprint.* Define the types of enterprise framework projects covered by the aggregate e-blueprint: how projects should be sequenced, how work should be organized, how efforts should be led and managed, what milestones should be established, how senior management will interact with the project, and how problems should be framed and solved.

- *Creating a customer blueprint.* Analyze and assess the current infrastructure and customer priorities to help clarify the e-blueprint definition. Identify the customer problems and issues the blueprint must address. Specify how the plan supports differentiation throughout. Decide which enterprise framework projects to undertake.

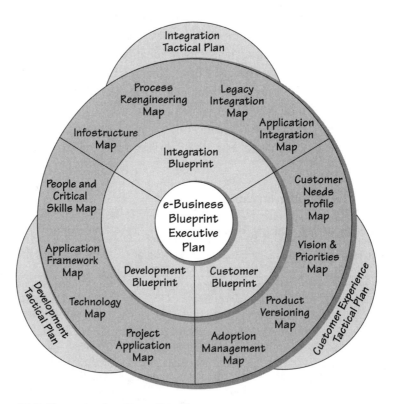

Figure 13.9: Elements of an Execution Plan

- *Creating an integration blueprint.* Review your own portfolio of active projects across the firm. Avoid reinventing the wheel. Establish the desired future mix of enterprise framework functionality by type: e-commerce, SCM, or CRM. Establish forward and backward integration to ensure a smooth customer experience.

These steps take time to do well, are not easy, and require senior management's focused effort and attention in understanding the scope and time frame required for execution. However, these steps provide an excellent foundation for creating an aggregate e-blueprint plan, as they force the level of detailed planning necessary for the blueprint's success. Remember, e-business success or failure is decided largely in the first few steps that precede execution.

e-Blueprint Facilitation: Making a Business Case for Action

Entrepreneurs use business plans to get funding from venture capitalists. Managers use business cases for garnering funding for projects. Business cases provide justification for investments.

With the blueprint ready, a company needs to create a detailed evergreen business case supporting the blueprint's various initiatives (see Figure 13.10). An evergreen business case serves as a bridge between a blueprint plan and the blueprint's

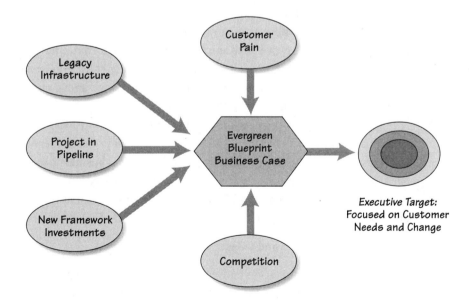

Figure 13.10: Need for an e-Business Case

execution. A good business case provides a foundation for tactical decision making and technology risk management.

Constructing a business case for a new e-business blueprint is difficult. However, the process of detailing a business case helps clarify the overall effort's purpose. This clarity of purpose permits the required resources—human, capital, and technological—to be targeted for maximum results. A properly developed e-business case ensures that the work will be done right the first time and also makes it possible to orchestrate simultaneous progress by diverse team members across all key functions in the enterprise.

A good business case challenges conventional viewpoints and provides concrete, actionable business advice. It eliminates two problems: the tendency to do nothing ("Let's wait and see") and the tendency to treat e-business as just another run-of-the-mill project. Most managers will not move until an opportunity is crystal clear. By then, it's often too late, because the competition didn't hesitate and is either enjoying the lion's share of the market or has so much momentum that it's difficult to attack them. e-Business is as much about creating and shaping customer needs as it is about serving well-identified customer requirements.

Often, when a new technology, such as the Internet emerges, invariably people ask, "Why develop a business case? Aren't the benefits obvious? Shouldn't we automatically stay up-to-date with technology?" Even when the benefits of new technology are significant and visible, a business case is a powerful tool for establishing corporate direction. Management will not commit any money unless absolutely convinced that it's the way to go. A strong business case channels and accelerates project approval and implementation by coordinating work across functional silos, creating buy-in by most users, yielding consensus and clarity of objectives, earning active top-management sponsorship, and communicating critical information among diverse participants.

Finally, e-business projects should not be treated as business as usual. Because managers already handle a number of traditonal projects, there is a strong tendency to adopt the same planning procedures for e-business projects. However, the planning sequence for traditional projects is based on well-understood execution and deployment capabilities—factors that may not apply to new Web applications.

Who Develops the e-Business Case?

In established companies, executives still think of technology as a tool. That is, design the strategy and then pick the tool. Unfortunately, it does not quite work that way anymore. Technology influences business design. The answers to such questions as "What business model makes sense?" and "What strategy makes sense?" are a function of the technology choices and assumptions about where technology is headed.

More than ever, the ability to integrate and to deploy e-business projects is critical to remaining competitive. In order to create e-business solutions built on a technology infrastructure, complex choices have to be made by senior management. Furthermore, as e-business becomes a more integral part of day-to-day operations, the absolute dollar expenditures spent on technology will increase. As this happens, more managers, including CEOs and CFOs, will become involved in the decision-making process.

The blueprint's sponsorship should include the following key roles:

- *Chief executive officer, president, chief operating officer, or general manager.* The senior executive of the organization plays the critical role because implementations of this type often impact most of the organization. The senior executive sets the overall tone for the organization and is critical to the decision-making process.

- *Chief information officer and the information technology organization.* Initially, the IT group leads the effort in researching the technical blueprint, thus playing a critical role in developing the business case. The IT organization provides the guidance needed to understand e-business application features, the enterprise's IT architecture, the technology infrastructure, and the resources required to implement e-business software.

- *Chief financial officer and the finance organization.* The CFO and the finance organization are usually involved in the decision to undertake a reengineering and/or enterprise application effort. The finance organization provides the analytical skills necessary for estimating costs and benefits. Often, the CFO and the CIO together provide the overall leadership for developing the business case.

- *Operating vice presidents and their respective organizations.* The involvement of senior-level management is critical in developing a credible business case. Each representative must be highly familiar with his or her organization's business processes and the potential for enhancing them.

- *The role of the board.* Achieving a return on investment (ROI) from an e-business application implementation requires the board to effectively guide and support the project. Significant change cannot occur or be sustained without the visible, active support and involvement of the board.

How the world has changed in a few short years! Historically, IT managers have purchased entire solutions from one large vendor, such as IBM or SAP. Today, however, they must evaluate a variety of rapidly evolving new products and technology platforms from multiple vendors. As a result, it has become increasingly difficult for organizations to efficiently formulate decisions, leaving them at the mercy of consulting firms.

Also, it would be dangerous for companies to let their consulting partners or IT functions make "bet-the-company" application infrastructure decisions in isolation. Decisions about how to deploy network applications, ERP software, and other e-business systems should be increasingly participatory, with line-of-business managers, marketing executives, and corporate leaders joining IT professionals in the technology review and decision-making process. However, we are not advocating decisions-by-committee but rather a core group of cross-functional yet fast-moving individuals.

The blueprint management challenge: finding the appropriate mix of executive and management participation to ensure project success while avoiding bureaucratic unresponsiveness just when you need decisions to be made quickly. By forcing senior management to take full ownership and not delegate too much authority to a large number of managers, decisive sponsorship is ensured.

Key Elements of an e-Business Case

An e-business case is crucial to obtaining top-management support. This is the chance to solidify the different concepts, budget, and design, in order to avoid costly mistakes. The content of a business case includes justification for the project, assessment of the preliminary scope of the project, and assessment of the project's feasibility.

The scope and complexity of reengineering business processes and implementing new technology often require a solid business justification before senior management will commit the time, resources, and funding for the initiative. Assuring management that its investment in enterprise applications will create value is of key importance. To achieve this, the business case should demonstrate how the investment is consistent with the overall strategy of the firm and how it will be efficiently managed.

The e-business case provides justification for the project along strategic, operational, technical, and financial lines (see Figure 13.11).

- *Strategic justification: "Where are we going?"* This section of the business case identifies the significant new capabilities required to achieve business

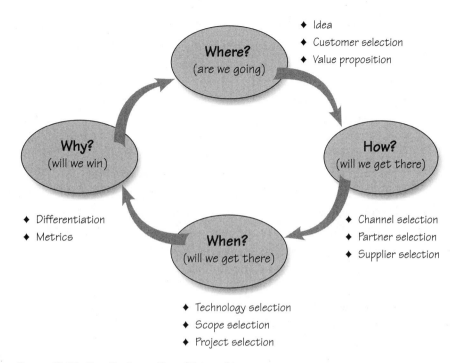

Figure 13.11: Key Business Case Dimensions

objectives. This section also summarizes the competitive landscape and the market gaps. Using this information, the reviewers of the business case can project the business future standing once the project is complete.

• *Operational justification: "How will we get there?"* This section of the plan identifies and quantifies the specific process improvements expected to result from process reengineering and integrating new enterprise applications with the reengineered processes.

• *Technical justification: "When will we get there?"* This section identifies how the implemented enterprise applications support the overall technology strategy of the company and demonstrates how the new technology will enable improvements in the cost and capability of the IT infrastructure.

• *Financial justification: "Why we will win?"* This section outlines the costs and benefits of the proposed application and process framework and quantifies these benefits in performance measures meaningful to the organization, such as net present value, internal rate of return, or return on investment.

A detailed, technical appraisal in the e-business case must focus on the plausibility of a project. In other words, customer needs and wish lists must be translated into technically and economically feasible solutions. This step might involve some preliminary design work, perhaps a prototype demo or walkthrough, but it should not be construed as a full-fledged execution project.

A strong technical appraisal diffuses objections along technical grounds, avoids analysis paralysis and conflicting agendas, reduces participants' unwillingness to share information, and dissolves technological mistrust. An operations appraisal also must be done, investigating issues of integration, including cost, and the amount of investment required. Finally, a detailed financial analysis is presented to assist senior management in making its decision.

Changing a firm's business strategy is tantamount to committing money and human resources in the face of business risk and uncertainty. A preliminary assessment of scope can mitigate these concerns. The preliminary assessment proposes piloting the project in a clearly defined, limited area of the business. This allows the project team to identify issues that may arise before rolling the system out on a larger scale.

By deciding on an initial set of project boundaries to present in the business case, you define the project's preliminary scope. Key elements to consider are

- *Organizational.* Which business units, locations, organizations, and processes will be included? Which business functions, activities, and modules will be used?

- *High-level application architecture.* A firm should develop a high-level application architecture to support the needs outlined in the business case. This enables management to assess an e-business application's degree of potential fit with the desired business process capabilities of the organization.

- *High-level project plan.* The plan should include estimates of the implementation process, timetable, key milestones, and benefits. Each of these components is essential for supporting the discussion and decision-making process.

- *Resource requirements.* The business case is a powerful tool for identifying the internal skills and resources needed for action. In addition, a business case can be used to determine whether outside resources are required for specialized tasks or to overcome limitations in internal skills.

After the preliminary scope of the project is set, you must then do detailed feasibility analysis along the following dimensions:

- *Financial.* Assess whether the project's benefits outweigh the cost or risk of the implementation. State the financial analysis in fiscal terms. Other considerations, such as mission criticality, should be a part of the analysis.

- *Organizational and cultural.* Assess the ability of the organization and the culture to accommodate a new way of doing business. Try to assess resistance. When it comes to creating an e-business blueprint, the resistance comes from the IT units and the line of business. Be sensitive to these conflicts and sell the project strongly to the IT and business units.

- *Technical.* Assess whether the data, component, and application infrastructure can support new applications. Cost, risk, and benefit of alternative technology investments should also be considered.

- *Suppliers, partners, and customers.* Assess the impact of the new apps on these different players in the supply chain.

Once project feasibility is established, the political process of aligning support for the project begins. A sound business case is invaluable for communicating, educating, and garnering widespread acceptance of a project.

e-Business Business Case Checklist

Setting the business direction shouldn't be an academic exercise and should be preceded by a realistic look at the marketplace and at the company's circumstances. Once that is accomplished, the managers responsible for developing the business case should follow the following guidelines.

- *Develop a goal statement.* A goal statement is fewer than 20 words, succinctly defines the project, details who benefits from the project's implementation, and states how the project fits with overall corporate strategy.

- *Set measurable goals.* Once the goal statement is complete, determine how each goal will be measured. Using a consensus process, prioritize each goal according to its importance to the business.

- *Set objectives.* An objective is an action statement of what is to be completed under each goal during a specified time frame. Again, use a consensus process to prioritize objectives.

- *Develop short- and long-term action plans.* Action plans consist of time lines, process changes, technology planning, roles and responsibilities assignments, and budget allocations. It's desirable and possible to achieve both short- and long-term results. When properly balanced, the two complement each other.

- *Gain approval.* Review action plans with management. Get buy-in from key players. Make necessary revisions or adjustments. This step requires constant, regular communication with top management. Be brief. We recommend that when presenting the business case to review boards, managers should be succinct. Experience shows that summaries of around ten pages, supported by as much additional detail and analysis as warranted, make up a workable package for senior managers.

Some managers think that building an e-business case is simply an exercise in getting funding, and it is. But as you've learned from this chapter, it should yield considerably more important results. Building an e-business case speeds implementation, reduces risk, and helps maximize, or optimize, the benefits to be gained today and tomorrow. Unfortunately, few firms provide managers with effective guidelines for preparing an e-business case. Keep this chapter as a resource in mapping future cases.

Communicate, Communicate, Communicate

Once senior management is convinced of the validity of the business case, the next step is to build organizational consensus—the buy-in needed to move a company toward an e-business architecture. Top-down management is not the best way to approach consensus building. Obtaining stakeholder buy-in is critical to any project's success.

Before beginning your e-business implementation, work out the details of the e-blueprint and develop a list of initiatives. Each of these projects may have to be sold to the affected stakeholders. Once buy-in is complete, execution can begin. However, if buy-in does not occur, the project can be still canceled before financial commitments have been made.

To sell your e-business case, follow these rules.

- *Create an elevator pitch.* In the average time it takes to complete a ride on an elevator, answer the questions: *What value are we creating with our e-blueprint? How does this blueprint contribute to our corporate goals? Is the blueprint flexible enough to keep up with changing customer needs?* Remember, the vision needs to be clearly and repeatedly communicated. This is the most commonly overlooked step in the scramble to keep pace with IT demands.

- *Create a cross-functional e-blueprint team.* By allowing members of the business units to participate in discussions about the e-blueprint and its effects on the company, you're more likely to get buy-in. Think of the team members as your ambassadors. They can help sell the benefits and foster support at the grass-roots level.

- *Take baby steps.* One way to sabotage the effort is to start talking about major changes. You have to ease into this type of change, or you'll face resistance. Start small by demonstrating the positive effects of the new e-blueprint. Get buy-in by selling the benefits of streamlining inefficient systems or improving turnaround on time-consuming tasks. Baby steps help win converts because they demonstrate your sensitivity to the change's impact.

- *Clearly communicate plans and the benefits of the new e-blueprint.* Regularly publish an e-blueprint strategy statement. This document will allow business units to have a handy reference of exactly what technologies your organization is pursuing. Many companies update these statements on a quarterly or as-needed basis to keep up with changing demands and trends.

- *Document success and publish the results.* Company intranets and newsletters are good forums for some positive PR. Highlight tangible results, such as increased access to legacy information, faster turnaround time to data queries, or improved customer satisfaction scores. This publicity is also an opportunity for managers to show how technology is benefiting their units as well as the company.

Stakeholders are often concerned about the project's definition, often subjecting the business case to a number of "must meet" and "should meet" criteria. Here again, consensus agreement must be reached on a number of key items before the project proceeds with implementation. The items to be addressed include definition of scope, specification of an integration strategy, delineation of product benefits to be delivered, and agreement on essential and desired features, attributes, and specifications.

The Serious Business of e-Business Blueprint Planning

Aligning strategy with e-business execution is a serious undertaking. Even the best ideas are rarely implementable as is. Enterprise innovation requires a master plan, or e-blueprint, to build a creative work environment in which a steady stream of high-potential ideas can emerge and be manifested through the enterprise's infrastructure and strategy. Top management should play a strong role in the blueprint-planning process, for three reasons: Blueprint decisions are among the most important a company makes, may cut across several product lines or divisional boundaries, and frequently require the resolution of cross-functional conflict.

One problem with creating an e-blueprint is that each participant in the process has a different perspective on the end result.

- The chief strategist sees an "ideal portfolio" to support the corporate vision.

- The chief financial officer sees optimally allocated financial resources.

- The chief information officer sees the right infrastructure in place to support the business.

- The chief marketing officer sees better customer retention and greater sales.

- The chief executive officer sees competitors kept at bay and positive financial results quickly delivered.

e-Blueprint creation can do all these things and more *if* top management is committed to it. At your company, *how committed is your management?*

The Problem of Leadership

For large, established companies, the single biggest impediment to e-business blueprint planning is lack of consistent sponsorship from top management. Without deep investments of time and energy from senior executives, companies simply cannot achieve the cultural, strategic, and technical changes required for e-business success. The top three most frequently cited reasons for project failure are poor planning or poor project management, change in business goals during the project, and lack of business-management support.[7]

The root cause of bad planning is overdelegation. We know, good managers delegate. But in the case of e-business, there is often a lack of understanding of which responsibilities can be delegated and which can't. The following senior management responsibilities can't be delegated:

- Sitting on the blueprint committee, a group many companies form to guide and to coordinate their e-business initiatives

- Approving the strategic direction and corporate vision it supports

- Setting the project's goals

- Participating in the deployment process

- Personally reviewing performance against strategic goals, just as they've always reviewed performance against sales and profit goals

Creating a blueprint is a pervasive, all-encompassing task. It's more than selecting the projects necessary for meeting strategic needs or allocating project resources. Top management's participation is needed because making good blueprint decisions requires making complex tradeoffs in a variety of areas. e-Business blueprint planning influences the products and services that a company will introduce to market over a 5- to 10-year period, the types and levels of capital investment to be made, and the integration agendas for the company's suppliers.

At your company, *does your management team have the vision to take the right roads on your e-business journey?* Media hype and stellar initial public offerings have made the road to e-business look smooth, inviting, and easy to navigate. Plenty of consultants are ready to take companies to the Promised Land with the "one-minute guide to e-business glory."

Don't believe it for a moment. Around the first curve, conditions start to change, the road gets bumpier, and after a while, you begin to see that the road you're on won't take you where you want to go because earthquakes, such as changing customer priorities, have altered the terrain. You plan your alternative routes while keeping in mind Robert Frost's observation, "Two roads diverged in a wood, and I took the one less traveled by and that has made all the difference."[8] Similarly, executives face many forks in the road to successful e-business implementation.

Ask yourself the following questions about your company's executive commitment:

- *Is senior-level management involved in e-business decision making? Is the CEO promoting the CIO to the role of a key adviser?*

- *Is top management attempting to sell the value of integration to decision makers?*

- *Has my company recognized that improving e-business investment management is a long-term process and should be planned accordingly?*

- *Has my company ensured that e-business investment decisions are strongly linked to strategic business objectives?*

- *Has my company built a shared e-business vision through various management levels? Has the e-business vision been presented in terms relevant to line-of-business managers?*

The real test of a blueprint is what happens when things don't go according to plan. At this point, when the going gets tough, the senior executive's commitment becomes clear.

Why e-Business Initiatives Fail

Companies without effective e-blueprint management plans in place will face several challenges. First, weak blueprint management can set the company adrift in a sea of too many projects. If there is no consistent mechanism for evaluating and, if necessary, killing weak projects, these projects take on lives of their own. Further, new projects are added to the initiative's scope without considering whether resources are available to support it or how other current projects will be affected. The result is a total lack of focus and a strain on available resources.

Will we never learn? With a lack of focus and too many active projects, resources and people are spread too thin. As a result, projects are starved for resources and end up in a queue—a serious bottleneck in the process—and the cycle time increases. Suddenly, there are complaints about projects being behind schedule and taking too long. Then everyone starts to scramble, with predictable results: Quality of execution starts to suffer. Not only are the projects late but also their success rates drop.

Lacking effective blueprint management also means an absence of rigorous and tough decision points, leading to poor project selection decisions. Excessive reliance on ROI to rank projects pushes cost saving and incremental-improvement projects to the top of the list, while breakthrough projects languish. This emphasis often results in too many mediocre projects that yield only marginal value to the company, while valuable projects are starved for resources. Soon, they fall behind schedule or never achieve their full potential, costing the company to miss out on numerous opportunities.

Without a rigorous blueprint, the wrong projects often get selected for the wrong reasons. Some companies' investment decisions have more to do with high-clout sponsorship than good business sense. In these instances, instead of decisions being made on fact, they are based on politics, internal disputes over territory, and emotion. This environment stifles innovation at the execution level, forcing lower-level executives to work outside normal channels.

If your business faces any of these problems—long cycle times, a high failure rate, lack of strategic alignment—perhaps the root cause can be traced back to ineffective blueprint management. Following are 12 classic reasons why e-business projects fail.[9] Does your organization have any of these symptoms?

1. Design the application blueprint on your own, in your own department—in a vacuum. After all, you know best, and cross-functional teams are a waste of time!

2. Don't do any homework or auditing. You already know what the problems are in the company, so jump immediately to a solution.

3. Don't bother looking at other companies' methods, such as their best practices, business models, execution snafus, and so on. You have nothing to learn from them.

4. If you do assemble a task force, meet several times in private. Then present your grand e-business design and expect other managers to applaud, even though they haven't been involved.

5. Don't seek outside help. Just read trade magazines and design your blueprint based on a generic model. If you do seek help, hire a brand-name guru who knows nothing about technology or blueprint management.

6. When other managers have questions, become defensive and rail at these "cynics" and "negative thinkers" who simply don't get it! Refuse to deal with objections—even valid ones—and never modify initial designs, because they belong to you.

7. Don't worry about communicating. Most of this e-business strategy stuff is obvious anyway. Anyone can get it if they think hard enough.

8. Speaking of communication, make sure that the blueprint document is three binders thick, full of checklists and spreadsheets. If in doubt, overwhelm the reader with volume.

9. Don't bother with the process or project management, because the e-business design is so good it will be automatically implemented.

10. Don't waste time taking baby steps to execute. You want the big-bang effect. Turn off the old set of applications, and completely switch the organization over to the new way of doing things.

11. Don't factor in periodic feedback as an opportunity for course correction. All too frequently, business priorities change over the course of developing a blueprint. Also, newer, more powerful technologies supersede the technologies proposed as solutions to problems identified early in the process.

12. Don't factor in existing projects. Many blueprint efforts lose sight of the fact that backward integration must be maintained and projects have to be delivered while the new stuff is under development. Any blueprint approach must allow the delivery of key functionality to meet short-term business needs.

Memo to the CEO

Let's take a deep breath and examine our current predicament. Managers everywhere have been given identical marching orders from top management: Create a blueprint for the integrated enterprise and, in the process, develop supporting information and application architectures.

Customer-centric process integration is becoming a business transformation initiative. The pillars on which this process integration stands is the new integrated application frameworks. Top management at many companies now recognizes that application frameworks are critical to carrying out business strategies across a dispersed organization. Many profound changes are forcing organizations to rethink and to broaden their views on integration.

- Heightened competition and increasingly sophisticated customers are forcing companies to present a single, near-real-time view of their customers and their relationship to the company, even though information about them is spread across multiple stovepipe applications.

- Current integration approaches are no longer timely enough for many applications. This is particularly apparent in supply chain management, where competitive advantages increase with the availability of near-real-time data and its propagation.

- A new style of event-based application is emerging. Activities in one area, such as a debit to inventory, cause a number of other applications in formerly unrelated areas—from replenishment applications to modeling spreadsheets—to perform a related action.

- Mobile and wireless computing are quickly becoming part of the landscape, but unfortunately, they are fundamentally incompatible with legacy application architectures.

Integrated applications, in which the e-commerce front end integrates tightly with the back office, represent the next step in the evolution of online systems. The ability to deliver integrated applications is a significant competitive differentiator in many industries and an operating requirement in others. Just to maintain parity in their industries, businesses will soon need to move beyond their current family of legacy applications.

Are companies going to build from scratch in order to achieve end-to-end integration? Not necessarily. Most organizations are finding more value in purchasing packaged applications and modifying them to suit their needs. As a result, the structural foundations of many companies are made from such frameworks as SAP, Siebel, and PeopleSoft. They're connected over the Internet in new, more sophisticated ways that enable them to exchange information more quickly than ever before. This connectivity accelerates business processes in which multiple departments or multiple companies work together. However, it accentuates the need for careful integration planning between these disparate application frameworks.

The process of blueprint creation, facilitation, and execution is an enigma and a source of frustration in many companies. Senior executives often invest in week-long retreats, extensive market research, and expensive outside consultants trying to develop the strategic plans that lead their companies to a prosperous future. Too often, though, these plans never come to fruition—the expected results never materialize. At times, the failures are outside the firm's control, such as when a competitor wins the race to the market or when changes in consumer tastes or trends occur. Frequently, though, the cause of failure is the lack of a comprehensive blueprint: the internal processes and events needed to bring the strategy to life. By nurturing and supporting the processes outlined in this chapter, senior management can develop organizational expertise that is truly difficult to match and a source of long-lasting competitive advantage.

CHAPTER FOURTEEN

Mobilizing the Organization: Tactical Execution

What to Expect

Every business has two needs: (1) to develop a strategy for achieving future competitive advantage and financial success, and (2) to execute this strategy quickly enough to beat competitors to the desired markets. However, in the e-business environment, meeting these needs is a complicated task, as planning and execution often occur simultaneously.

Tactical execution means making the e-business blueprint operational. As discussed in Chapter 13, the e-blueprint is the link between a company's e-strategy and the strategy's execution. The e-blueprint consists of the priorities, projects, and resources required to bring a proposed strategy to market. Tactical execution is how a company's e-blueprint becomes a business reality.

Successful tactical execution requires risk taking, attention to detail, and discipline. The demand for e-commerce, e-business, and m-commerce projects is growing rapidly. In attempting to respond to this increasing demand, today's IT organizations are frantically managing multiple projects, resources, and customer relationships in a fast-paced, and sometimes hectic, business environment.

To do so without an effective, disciplined project management approach in place can make e-business initiatives feel like a "juggling act" in which it's only a matter of time before something gets dropped. Disciplined project management means setting a clear project direction, committing the necessary resources to those projects, and defining and managing a quality product development process. This chapter highlights some of the most common e-business project implementation pitfalls and lays out the roadmap for successful tactical execution.

"There are few original strategies in banking. There is only execution."
—*John Bond, chairman of HSBC Holdings[1]*

Visionary companies, such as GE, Wal-Mart, and Enron, consistently outexecute their competition.

- GE has continually cut costs and raised quality with its now-famous Six Sigma quality blueprint. Building on this success, GE is racing to become an e-company. A variety of initiatives are under way to integrate e-business and quality and to further reduce costs. For instance, to cut costs, GE implemented an e-procurement system that eliminated paper requisitions, forms, and the manual preparation of daily requests for low-value items. GE uses the system to purchase more than $1 billion from more than 1,400 suppliers. As a result, the RFQ cycle dropped from 7 days to 1. In addition, GE has realized a 15 percent reduction in total purchasing cost and the lowering of purchasing headcount.[2]

- Wal-Mart, the world's largest brick-and-mortar retailer, opens new stores and conducts smaller-scale market tests more quickly than its competition. Based on these test results, the company then makes the necessary tactical adjustments to optimize profitability. Although Wal-Mart is exceptionally well managed, the company can do nothing to change the fact that it's in an incredibly tough industry, as evidenced by its miniscule net margins. Without a lot of room for error, Wal-Mart's excellent management helps keep errors to a minimum.

- Enron, the world's biggest natural gas and electricity trader, has developed a network platform to facilitate energy trading. Enron is on its way to create what may be the world's largest online business: Transactions could hit $400 billion, about half of Enron's total sales of gas and electricity. Much of that will be new business stimulated by the Web's speed and price transparency. Enron Online is expanding into new markets, such as wireless bandwidth and network capacity.

These visionary companies tend to combine a winning strategy, the talent and execution needed to support the strategy, and the integrated transition from old to new ways of doing things that are so critical. This coordinated combination of strategy and execution, occurring quickly, not only scores quick wins but also demoralizes the opposition. It leaves competitors wondering what hit them.

Execution—how, what, and when—is the focus of this chapter. Execution requires tactical leadership; that is, a company must have the ability to identify and to quickly execute on opportunities. Only a talented team with strong managers can craft a winning strategy and connect it with the executional excellence necessary to make it work.

In the e-business world, fast turnaround of projects separates winners from also-rans. The financial cost of delayed or mismanaged projects is huge. More significant, the lost-opportunity costs of being late to market, such as market exclusivity, leadership positioning, or thought leader and advocacy relationships, are even higher. Yet companies can get their product to market faster and with a competitive edge with a simple yet underused strategy: bringing a tactical mindset to the implementation of e-business programs.

Examples of bad e-business execution are plentiful but get buried in the corporation. Take for instance, Kmart, whose late arrival to the Internet was not so much a strategic move as it was bad execution. The company had tried its hand at e-commerce twice before, but the sites it launched were so poorly executed that they were abandoned before they made much of an impact. Kmart is trying yet again with Bluelight.com, a reference to its old spur-of-the-moment "blue-light specials," when customers in the store were alerted to head to a certain aisle to get extra-low prices on selected items. The BlueLight.com site carries typical Kmart merchandise, such as home furnishings, toys, and electronics. But the company plans to enhance the site, adding more products than it could ever fit in its stores. Bluelight.com is also adding new services, such as free Internet service and travel and financial services. The jury is out on this one.

Roadmap to Tactical Execution

Kmart has not been short of vision but has fallen short in tactical execution and its ability to get customer adoption. What most brick-and-mortar companies don't seem to understand is the changing nature of tactical execution. Building an e-business requires well-integrated processes—order entry, order management, fulfillment, and service. However, these process are not built on a traditional foundation of people but on software.

Software applications are the soul of Web-related ventures. The e-business design and software projects must be closely intertwined. The questions to focus on are: *Do the tactical efforts support the business model? Do the tactical efforts reflect changes in thinking about the business model?* The answers to these seemingly common-sense questions are often the root causes of failed strategies.

Figure 14.1 illustrates the e-business roadmap. A company's vision and e-business strategy define *why* a company chooses a specific e-business direction and *what* that direction will be. The company's e-blueprint defines *how* and *when* a firm's e-strategy will become a business reality and *who* is responsible for successfully completing the e-business initiative and *where* within the company the initiative will be carried out. However, it is how well a company executes its e-business blueprint—tactical execution—that defines whether the firm will be an industry leader or a follower.

Tactical execution and adoption management are key components of an effective e-business strategy. As an organization begins execution of its plans, it must confront required increases in the rigor in its technology delivery processes, increased use of new and rapidly changing technologies, and adoption management issues associated with new and redesigned business processes.

However, realization of an e-business vision is an iterative process. As an organization's e-business vision crystallizes, architectural models and associated

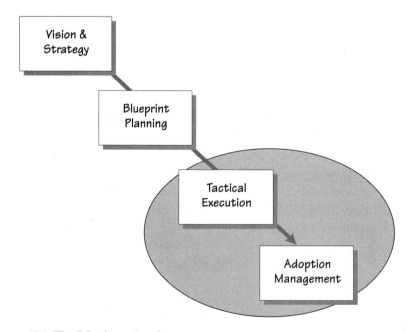

Figure 14.1: The E-Business Roadmap

strategies must be refined to hone the vision. Introspection and assessment of the organization lead to strategic and business model adjustments.

e-Business Tactical Execution

Southwest Airlines turns airplanes around on the ground much more rapidly than its competitors do. Its short ground time and fast execution of between-flight tasks makes its equipment more productive and the airline more profitable—even with much lower fares, especially on the short routes. The recipe—time on ground equals lost revenue—is no different for e-business.

Building enterprise-scale e-business applications is incredibly difficult. But it has to be done. The risk is disruption of business, because if you do not plan and execute properly, you can kill your company, guaranteed. To succeed, e-business tactical execution must carefully manage the five components illustrated in Figure 14.2.

- *e-Project management.* This component includes project oversight, product management, and software version and release management. e-Project management ensures that the goals of the project(s) are clear, valid, widely understood, and shared.

- *e-Development.* This component addresses the rapid software development methodologies available to speed up software implementation.

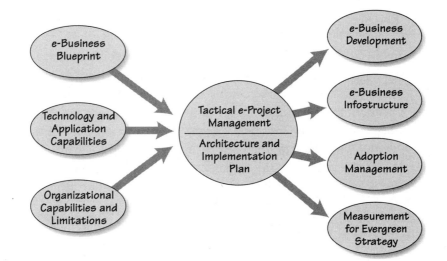

Figure 14.2: Elements of Tactical Execution

- *e-Infostructure management.* This component focuses on the production capabilities required by the project(s), such as software and process scalability and reliability, outsourcing via application service providers (ASPs), hosting, storage, and security.

- *Adoption management.* This component addresses change or transition management.

- *Performance measurement.* This component discusses the tools and metrics used to quantify e-business project success. Performance measures help monitor real progress, set benchmarks for continuous improvement, and establish key performance indicators to ensure accountability.

Tactical e-Project Management

Corporate e-business applications are quickly moving from drawing board to reality; however, that's only half the battle. A transition to e-business needs a tightly coordinated approach. Coordination flies in the face of traditional application execution, which is characterized by a number of groups working on various aspects of an issue but not talking. This approach is like building an airplane by having one group go off on its own to design the wings, another to build the landing gear, and still another to develop the fuselage, with no group ever communicating with the others. *Would you fly in a plane built in such an ad hoc way?*

e-Project management attempts to bring order to chaos. It is a formal methodology in which projects are planned and executed, using a systematic, repeatable, and scalable process. It is a series of techniques to help people efficiently manage projects, with a focus on specific results and deliverables, time, and resources.

A major reason a company may need project management is that knowledge is being lost at a time when the need for expertise is growing. Knowledge drain results from technological change, turnover, downsizing, outsourcing, and retirement. Project knowledge replacement is becoming more difficult, owing to labor shortages in critical jobs and new technologies, lengthening orientation time for new employees, decreasing response times for market changes, and many other factors. Recruiting and integrating new people and getting them up to speed are very difficult to do in a hard-deadline setting.

What's different about e-business project management? Project management is project management; there is no difference for e-business projects. *Not true.* Managers who are involved in tactical execution know that times are changing and that nothing is as it seems. Although the steps of project management may seem fundamentally the same, new challenges make e-project management a much bigger headache. e-Business projects must confront five project management challenges:

- *Speed.* Working in Internet time is like living in dog years. Traditional application development projects took 1 and 2 years to complete. Internet projects are estimated in months, sometimes even weeks.

- *Resources.* When working against aggressive deadlines, recruiting, hiring, training, and retaining team members is extremely difficult. Project team competency and morale are greatly affected when team members leave.

- *Requirements.* Gathering customer requirements has been a traditional challenge for IT project teams. This is even more difficult in the e-world. Customers are seldom clear on what they want and present the project team with a continually moving target when attempting to define their requirements.

- *Release cycles.* Traditional software release dates were scheduled every quarter. In the new economy, they are scheduled monthly. Version control, change management, and coordination with rollout teams become even more important.

- *Technology.* The only thing more challenging than keeping up with the latest in technology is attempting to implement an e-project while the technology is changing.

Finally, because the business model and e-business are intertwined, managers must continually ask themselves: "Do the projects reflect changes in thinking about the business model of the company?"

Process Overview

Watching over e-business projects requires keen conceptual ability, a mind for details, a sense of urgency, and plenty of energy. Figure 14.3 illustrates the key phases of e-project management: define and organize the project, plan the project, and implement and track the project.

Define and Organize the Project

The success of a project is often determined by clearly stated, fully achievable objectives. It is critical to define the desired outcome, the desired results, and the project's scope. Many times, projects fail because the desired outcomes were poorly defined, and the organizational structure and supporting processes required to accomplish it were neither well understood nor communicated throughout the company.

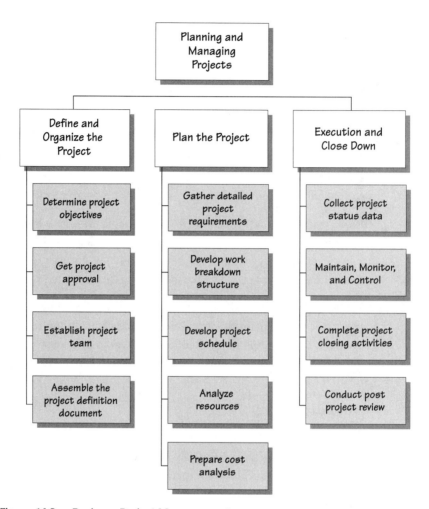

Figure 14.3: e-Business Project Management

Further adding to the possibility of failure are unclear assignments, confusing roles and responsibilities, unproductive meetings, poor communication, interpersonal conflict among team members, and the lack of follow-up.

Plan the Project

One source of tension for each project is producing a credible project plan. Customers often need the project completed "yesterday," and aggressive time lines are set to meet the demands of the customer as closely as possible. The project schedule targets the customer's desired completion date. How the major deliverables will be developed and the availability of resources to do so are key considerations when preparing the project schedule.

When creating a credible project plan, the project manager must know what is "in scope" for the project and what is "out of scope." A project's scope defines what the project seeks to accomplish and what it will not accomplish. Both the project scope and those tasks that are outside its purview must be documented and reviewed by the customer before a project plan can be completed.

Without a clear, written definition of the project's scope, the risk of "scope creep" increases, which can lead to missed project deadlines and dissatisfied customers. A credible project plan must be based on a reliable, systematic process that produces schedules managers trust, a risk statement they understand, and assurances that the project can be delivered on time and under budget.

In addition to clearly defining the project's scope and potential risks, a comprehensive communications plan should also be developed. In it, all project stakeholders should be identified, communication responsibilities and checkpoints outlined, and an internal marketing plan developed.

Execution and Closedown

During the execution phase, the project team implements the project plan. All the tasks associated with the application's development and rollout are completed. The communications, quality assurance, risk management, work break-down structure, and resource components of the project plan are carried out and tracked. The project manager directs and monitors these activities and modifies the project plan as needed.

Keeping a project on track is an even greater challenge than developing the initial project plan. Successful project management requires proper follow-up and adherence to the project schedule. Otherwise, projects can quickly fall behind schedule and lose momentum. Well-executed project management means

- Monitoring project scope: planned performance versus actual performance, planned versus actual budget, quality, and project communications

- Controlling changes in project scope

- Reviewing project risk, project team skills, project status, milestones, and accomplishments

- Discussing and resolving challenges, problems, and issues

- Conducting status and performance review meetings

One part of project management that is often overlooked is postproject review. Project managers and team members are often too busy working on the next project to formally close out a project. Closing out the project offers an opportunity to learn from data collected during the project. Typical project close-out activities are

- Ensuring that the customer has approved and accepted the final deliverable

- Reviewing project practices that were effective and not effective

- Identifying possible process improvements for future projects

- Completing project documentation, including developing and validating an unresolved-issues list

- Acknowledging the team's contributions

In addition, distributing a customer satisfaction survey to key customers that the project team interacted with on a regular basis can help assess project success from the customer's viewpoint.

The Intangibles: Continuous Project Communication

Powering up for e-business is no small undertaking. A solid communications plan keeps management, the project's customers, and team members informed of the project's status and of any milestones at risk of being missed. A project communications plan

- Identifies all persons concerned with the project and develops follow-up activities to keep them involved

- Assigns communication responsibilities and a process for keeping everyone informed

Project communication is often inadequate, of poor quality, or unidirectional. Project work entails two essential ingredients: people and the effective exchange of ideas. Project communication is like engine oil. For a project to function like a well-oiled machine, frequent, consistent communication must be a priority. If a machine is not oiled, it will not start or, if it does, it will quickly falter and grind to a halt. Its oil, like a project's communication, must be continuously recycled and regularly replaced with new oil, as the old oil becomes no longer usable. Ask yourself: *How much managerial attention in your company has been focused on project communication?*

e-Development Process

No new e-business development process is exactly the same as another. Two processes may have similar steps, but the underlying semantics of the process are determined by the specific company culture. e-Business project development can be broken down into the general categories illustrated in Figure 14.4.

Opportunity Generation: What Customer Pain Are We Solving?

Every project must be built around opportunities for addressing a customer problem. Developing and using all sources for potential opportunities are vital. The ability to reduce the vast number of opportunities into a more realistic figure is a key issue at most organizations.

One way to classify opportunities is to think about what kind of problem you are trying to solve. Are you attempting to create a multivitamin supplement, headache relief, migraine relief, or cancer-fighting drug? Most early e-commerce efforts tended to fall into the multivitamin-supplement opportunities. Although multivitamins are good to take, no one notices if customers stop taking them. As e-commerce matures, it is more willing to tackle significant problems—the headaches—customers face. *Where do your projects fall in this customer-pain continuum?*

The most significant opportunities are also the most simple: transactions in everyday life that you would like to see be made easier. That's often a good target

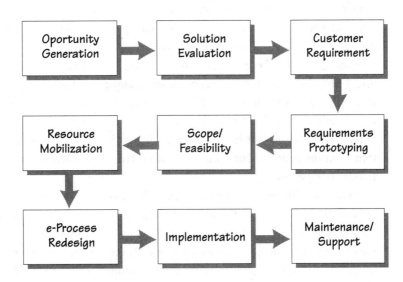

Figure 14.4: Generic e-Business Development Process

for opportunities. Opportunities about how to relieve customer pain may be collected passively, but we also recommend that the firm explicitly attempt to generate opportunities. As a way of tracking, sorting, and refining these opportunities, we recommend that each promising idea be described in a short, coherent statement. Some of these opportunities may be expanded, refined, and explored. Often, this exploration is done informally by someone who emerges as the "champion" of a particular idea.

There are many ways to identify opportunities. One company uses an annual management brainstorming/planning retreat for this purpose and to prioritize which opportunities will have the greatest impact on the customer. Another organization encourages its employees to develop opportunities, going as far as to grant stock options. A third company starts with a strategic document outlining the opportunities the company will pursue. The strategy provides "slots" based on competitor analysis. Each slot is filled with a new idea. After review and approval, the ideas that fit with the company's overall strategy are selected for development. Yet another organization hires a consulting firm to survey its customers about their wants and needs and uses this feedback to develop opportunities. The consulting firm documents the market opportunity, the estimated return on investment and capital requirements, and any competitive issues.

We have learned through numerous strategy engagements that looking at opportunities from the customer's perspective is not done by executives. Companies develop opportunities by thinking about how to solve their own pain. One large bank had us review its e-strategy to prioritize opportunities to pursue. We asked who the target customer was and what "pain" it was suffering. It was amazing to see the blank stares and silence. Most of the opportunities were pain reduction for themselves. For instance, they wanted to put all reports online. When asked why, they said that the customer kept calling and bothering them and that this would alleviate the continual calls. Once the reports were online, the customers called and asked whether the bank did not want to talk to them anymore. Sure, the online reports had made their life easier but had alienated their customers in the process. The bank was not looking at opportunities from the customer's perspective!

When brainstorming about opportunities, always ask: *What is the customer pain we are trying to solve.* For small and large projects, hundreds of opportunities will be collected. Some of these opportunities probably do not make sense in the context of the project, and in most cases, there are simply too many opportunities for the firm to pursue at once. The second step in the tactical planning process is therefore to select the most promising opportunities to pursue.

Solution Evaluation: How Can We Allievate the Customer Pain?

Solutions are built from opportunities. Once the viable opportunities are selected, they must be further developed, examined, and prioritized before the select few solutions proceed to full design. Solution evaluation includes development of a formal business plan with forecasts, initial requirements, project schedule, and resource requirements. This plan must include the elements listed in Table 14.1.

Different companies use different solution evaluation criteria. One company has two hurdles that must be passed before the design phase is entered: the business plan approval and the solution review. The business plan approval includes action items, such as strategy alignment, competitive positioning, sourcing plan, resource identification, design-to-cost analysis, return on investment analysis, risk assessment, and a preliminary process plan. Once the business plan is approved, the solution is given a formal review.

Another organization's solution evaluation phase centers on a formal executive approval. Once the top opportunities are selected, they are developed further, as well as costed. The costing activity requires that the team forecast cost within a certain percentage. At the same time, the developers assesses the feasibility to make sure it will be able and ready to design and implement. Major questions that must be answered before formal approval include: *How are we going to build this? What technologies are we going to use? Where are the impacts going to be?* This information is placed into a detailed project plan and presented to the executive team.

Table 14.1: Elements of Solution Evaluation

Element	Questions
What	• Which customer processes are involved? • What is wrong? • What is the opportunity in terms of customer problems, competitive pressures, internal inefficiencies, lack of new features in products, or unmanageable complexity in processes?
Where/When	• Where do we observe the problem? • Are there any service or infrastructure implications? • Under what conditions do we observe the problem?
How Big	• How big is the problem/opportunity? • What is the cost of these problems in terms of lost revenue, expenses, speed, or morale? • How will we measure it? • Will the solution require the customer to change process or culture?

Getting Detailed Requirements Right

e-Business project success is linked to an understanding of customers' needs and wants. The identification of new improvement opportunities is related to the activity of identifying customer needs (see Figure 14.5). Some proactive approaches are to

- Document the process frustrations and complaints that customers experience

- Interview top users, devoting attention to innovations introduced by these users, including modifications these users may have made to existing products

- Systematically gather suggestions from customers, perhaps through the sales force or customer service system

- Perform competitive benchmarking by carefully studying competitors' products on an ongoing basis

- Track the status of emerging technologies to facilitate the transfer of appropriate technologies from research into product development

Successful e-business strategies are fueled by a deep understanding of the customer processes and pain points. Most people tend to ignore the importance of fully understanding customer requirements before moving into development. As Lynn Lorenc, VP of Marketing at Footlocker.com puts it: "Lack of attention at this step will cause problems downstream that result in project derailment."[3]

Most failed strategies are fueled by the lack of ability to see below the surface. It is also important to realize that technology changes quickly but that underlying customer needs do not. Gather the customer requirements and organize them into four categories:

- *Strategic,* "forward-thinking" requirements that the market has not asked for yet

- Customer-driven, "requested" requirements

- Technology-driven requirements

- "Feature-complete" requirements for adding more bells and whistles to existing requirements or providing fixes

Once general requirements are identified, they must be prototyped to derive detailed requirements. Front-end prototyping work is to avoid requirement surprises so you need not cope with them later. It is a pay-now-or-pay-far-more-later

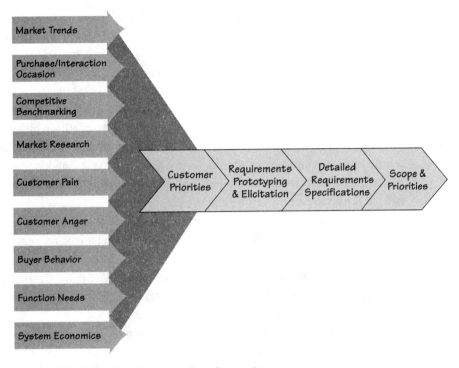

Figure 14.5: Gathering Customer Requirements

situation. Requirements prototyping is essential for generating detailed requirements. Here, the development team solicits a response from potential customers in the target market. This type of testing is used to select which of two or more opportunities should be pursued and to gather information from potential customers on how to improve.

Setting Scope

Determining the scope of a project and narrowing the focus are the first and most important step. *Understanding the total project scope is essential to managing its development.* This usually requires communication with the customer and/or users to ensure both correct interpretation of each defined need and unambiguous wording of the responsive requirement. You must know what the customer *really* needs or wants, not just what you think was stated! *If the requirements don't reflect the needs, the customer will never be satisfied.*

The scope of many e-business projects is fuzzy. For example, a statement of project scope might begin with the following: "The creation of a new customer experience through the integration of customer fulfillment needs and the optimization of product production and delivery." Such an all-encompassing scope indicates that the company has failed to assess its own capabilities for achieving its stated strategy. Very few who have ventured down this path have succeeded, although many have declared victory.

When the scope is just too grandiose, the breadth of change and resistance frequently overcomes any project team. The solution is to partition big problems or projects into manageable chunks. Think big, but prioritize and implement in small steps. This also helps keep the team focused and interested. Achieve early victories to sustain momentum. It allows achievements to be realized and internalized at a faster rate.

Project scope can be rigid or flexible. At a number of organizations, the scope is frozen when requirements are developed and set. Minor changes, refinements, and tuning can occur but only to a certain extent. Other organizations never completely freeze the design and are open to change even after they have gone to production. If a change is determined to be necessary and vital to fulfilling customer needs and expectations, the organization will make the change.

To change the original requirements, some form of approval is required. This can range from upper-management review to individual functional area review to team consensus. Changes usually are monitored to determine whether the quality has been increased or if the design meets customer requirements to a greater extent.

Garnering Resources: Mobilize, Mobilize, and Mobilize

Building on the requirements, the *resource mobilization* phase defines the project management team, resources, and time line necessary to realize the requirements.

The first step in mobilization is organizing project teams. Today's enterprises depend on quality project management to complete projects on schedule and within budget. It is likely that the firm cannot afford to invest in every development opportunity. As timing and resource allocation are determined for the most promising projects, too many projects will invariably compete for too few resources. As a result, the attempt to assign resources and plan timing usually results in a return to the prior evaluation and prioritization step to prune the set of projects to be pursued.

The second step in mobilization is careful resource planning and allocation. Many organizations take on too many projects without regard for the limited availability of development resources. As a result, skilled developers and managers are assigned to more and more projects, productivity drops off dramatically, projects take longer to complete, projects become late to the market, and profits are lower. *Careful resource planning* helps an organization make efficient use of its resources by pursuing only those projects that can reasonably be completed within the budgeted resources.

Figure 14.6[4] illustrates a common problem in e-business project resource allocation. Most firms allocate resources well for the up-front activities, such as strategy formulation. However, firms tend to either underestimate or underbudget for the downstream activities, such as production system: rollout, maintenance, and enhancement. In our experience, a project rarely comes in on time and on budget. A significant part of the problem is changes in requirements, scope, and technology. Estimating the resources required for project phases—strategy, blueprint planning, prototype development, and production rollout—forces the organization to face the realities of finite resources.

Although the resource planning process is often linear, the activities associated with selecting the most promising projects and allocating available resources

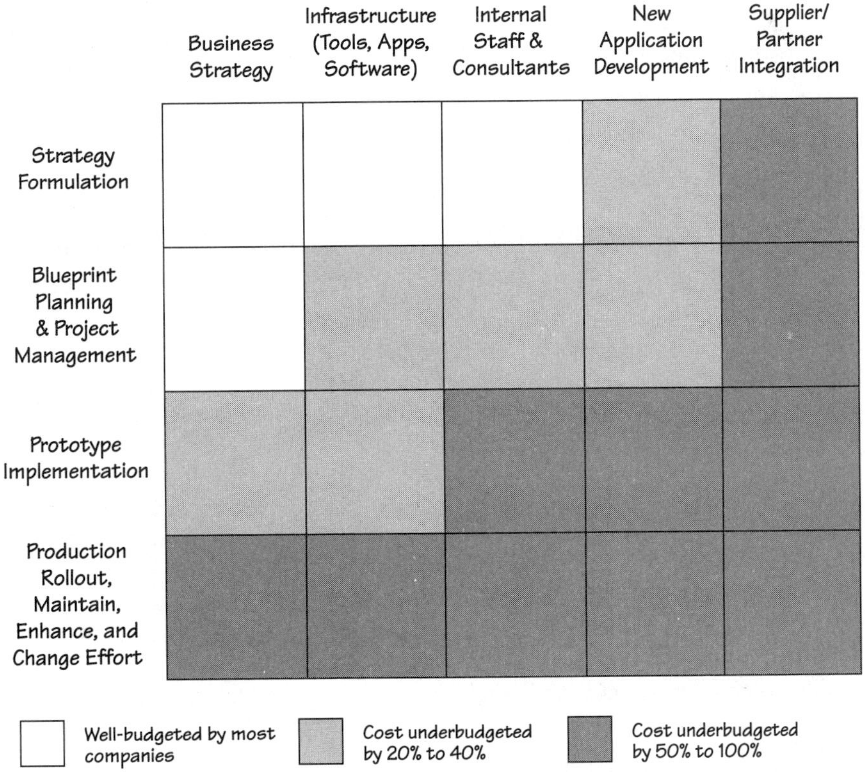

Figure 14.6: e-Business Resource Allocation Problems

to them are inherently iterative. The e-blueprint plan must be reevaluated frequently to further refine or cull the projects it recommends, based on the budgeting and scheduling realities and the latest information from the development teams, marketing, and the company's service organizations. The ability to adjust the project plan over time is vital to the long-term success of the enterprise.

e-Process Redesign

Imagine that you have been given the job of creating a B2B portal for the healthcare industry supplying hospitals, surgery centers, and physician offices with products ranging from medical equipment to soaps. Your mission is to improve the end-to-end process of procurement. How will you start? First, you will have to develop a good understanding of the current operation, the activities that take place in the purchasing process, and the tasks involved in each activity. You will also need to understand the various products that need to be offered and the reasons why customers would buy them from you and not from your competitors. Do you have lower prices, faster delivery, higher quality, or a better catalog that allows your customers to buy everything they need from one source? Only after understanding the physical process itself, how it links to the performance of the customer, and the level of performance required by customers can you begin to look for e-business opportunities to build the B2B portal.

Most e-business projects require some form of business process reengineering. The effective implementation of new technology is contingent on optimized business processes being in place. Business process reengineering involves the following main activities: identify your business's core processes, define the customers these processes serve and their expectations, and create detailed and high-level maps of how these processes function. Figure 14.7 lists the detailed components of each of these tasks.

Most managers have trouble when analyzing and redefining the existing business processes because it requires them to take an honest look at how the company performs its work, what their customers' expectations are, and how all the company's processes work together. Unfortunately, in a busy world, which manager has the time for this?

But self-examination is a necessary step. Only by examining its current state of operations can a company begin to envision how its operation could improve. When looking at how a company works, it is important to ask such questions as: *Why are we doing this process this way? Can we streamline this business process with the aid of technology? What does the customer experience look like? Why are we not*

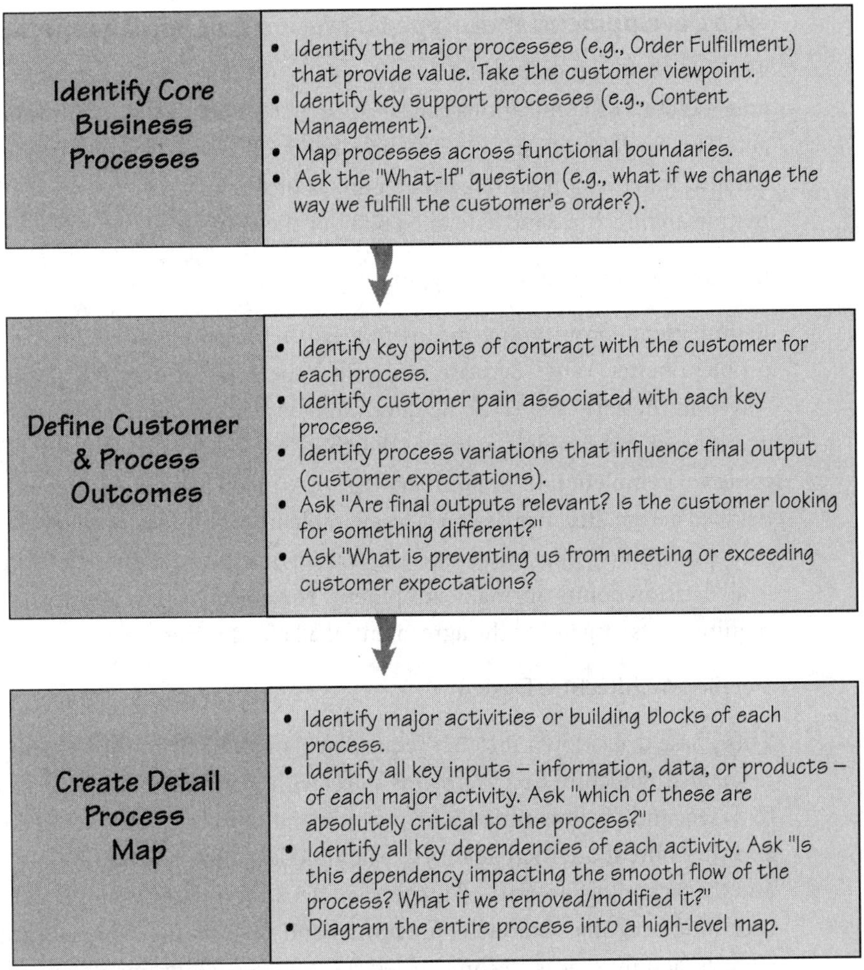

Identify Core Business Processes	• Identify the major processes (e.g., Order Fulfillment) that provide value. Take the customer viewpoint. • Identify key support processes (e.g., Content Management). • Map processes across functional boundaries. • Ask the "What-If" question (e.g., what if we change the way we fulfill the customer's order?).
Define Customer & Process Outcomes	• Identify key points of contract with the customer for each process. • Identify customer pain associated with each key process. • Identify process variations that influence final output (customer expectations). • Ask "Are final outputs relevant? Is the customer looking for something different?" • Ask "What is preventing us from meeting or exceeding customer expectations?
Create Detail Process Map	• Identify major activities or building blocks of each process. • Identify all key inputs – information, data, or products – of each major activity. Ask "which of these are absolutely critical to the process?" • Identify all key dependencies of each activity. Ask "Is this dependency impacting the smooth flow of the process? What if we removed/modified it?" • Diagram the entire process into a high-level map.

Figure 14.7: Creating the Process Map

sharing data across functional lines about common customer experiences? Are these activities necessary?

Process change often takes much longer than expected. For example, e-tailing technology was quickly adopted by many retail companies, but the business processes that it supported took more than 5 years to evolve and to stabilize. New business processes take years to develop, adopt, and integrate with the firm's culture. This is the primary reason why many dot-coms are failing. They expected the world to change at their speed.

Web Development: Prototype Validation and Implementation

The goal of this phase is to create a plan with specificity and completeness of coverage so that the applications can be constructed and tested on time and on budget. This includes designing the user experience and specifying the content, detailed functional requirements, technical blueprints, data requirements, information architecture, and a detailed plan for the application.

Detailed Requirements Prototyping

Requirements prototyping means that effort must be made to understand the problem better. Why? Because more time spent in refining the problem being solved in the early stages of the development process reduces the probability of project cost and schedule overruns. Further, two thirds of system cost is predetermined at completion of preliminary design, with 80 percent predictable from the detailed design. Because design is inseparable from the development and support processes, prototyping ensures consideration of its impact on their ultimate costs at all decision points during development. The objective is to quickly define stable requirements by gaining the agreement of all affected parties.

Detailed Architecture Design

This phase drills down into the requirements identified in the scope phase. The detailed architecture design process starts with planning, what is to be achieved, by when, and for how much. The purpose and objective, the intended audience, and the content are then analyzed. The function and presentation are designed, and the technology to be used is specified. This allows the developers to detail the user interface, object model—functional and data requirements—data conversion, legacy interfaces, technical design, security requirements, standards and processes, and the engineering phase work plan for each of the applications. Web architecture answers the following questions: *What is the purpose of the project? Who is the intended audience? What process flows need to be supported? What information content will be presented? What are the presentation devices, styles, and form that will used? What about security and client and server specifications?*

Application Development

In this phase, developers develop, enhance, integrate, and refine the applications until they are completed and ready for testing. Most Web projects use iterative development. This means that the entire development process is repeated several times before the software is released. This reduces the risk associated with tight deadlines because the higher-risk features are implemented first, and the less complicated features are saved for last. The other methodology often used for more traditional software development projects is the waterfall method, which involves finishing each phase of the project completely before moving on to the next phase. The reality is that application development in large organizations is a complex process, especially when dealing with Web, middleware, and legacy and database apps. These applications cannot be knocked out in days or weeks. One year is considered a short development cycle for a complex Web transaction system. Unfortunately, a year-long development cycle may be too slow from a business perspective. Therein lies the dilemma of Web development: rising expectations from the business side, inability to deliver complex applications quickly from the development side. In-depth discussion of the nuances of Web-ware application development is a critical one and is beyond the scope of this book.

Quality Assurance and Testing

QA ensures that the applications meet all functional requirements and perform as expected. Once the applications have successfully met these requirements, they're ready to be deployed. QA in the Web development world, unlike other development, requires a quicker turnaround while testing a seemingly endless combination of test cases. Among other differences from other development, a Web application is subject to continuous evolution, often introducing requirements creep. An adapted Web testing approach is necessary. This exploding market for Web sites and iterative application development requires effective techniques and means to conduct testing. This testing is vital in order to help the organization or company avoid huge amounts of lost revenue in the event that the Web site or application is nonoperational (nonavailability issues), nonusable (usability issues), or nonfunctional (functionality issues).

Field Testing

Before the application is rolled out into a production setting, it must be field tested. There are two types of field testing: (1) A small amount of a new application is built to ensure that it works and meets customers' needs, enabling the team to resolve a majority of problems early in the process; (2) A larger amount of the application is produced so that formal internal and field testing can occur. These prototypes usually are close to how it will appear during production. Another form of field testing is to select test sites to roll out the new concept. Once the site has been selected, proper training is given to employees so that they understand their roles and responsibilities. The application is then implemented and tested with collected measures to assist in fine-tuning the process and to make clear its impact on the customer and employees. Any changes to the process are implemented during the test run. After all the tests are completed and the process has been verified, the product is rolled out to other selected sites.

Release Management

Once the final release is verified and approved, the application is launched into production. A scale-up period normally is required before full production can begin. Individuals from numerous functional areas are needed to ensure a smooth transition.

Several items normally are required before production can begin:

- A production rollout and deployment plan

- A formal hosting plan

- A support and help-desk plan

- A detailed maintenance/upgrade plan

- An end-to-end quality plan to ensure that all processes conform to specifications/customer needs

Typically, once the application is ready to launch, the project manager coordinates with all technical people related to the deployment of the product in a production environment. In the next section, we discuss the challenges of outsourced Web development projects and what can go wrong.

Managing Outsourced Web Development Projects

A large retail company journeys into e-commerce with a large e-business consulting/computer company. The outcome: Scope is too large, project takes too long, and project costs too much. Let's look at one example. (The business names have been changed to protect the not so innocent.)

For its third generation of six e-retail sites, Sports.com chooses WebVendorX, for two reasons: the first, its product—WebAce—an out-of-the-box bundle of retail software, and the second, its prior e-commerce experience. WebVendorX stated that it had built more than 30 e-commerce sites. Of the consulting firm proposals Sports.com reviewed, WebVendorX's was the highest priced.

It took WebVendorX 12 months to assign a dedicated development team to the Sports.com project. The team consisted of 18 people. Few had relevant e-commerce experience, including the project lead, who had never built an e-commerce site. The senior technology staff consisted entirely of consultants to WebVendorX, not the company's full-time employees. After gathering the Web sites' requirements over a 3-week period, Sports.com received a document that included less than half of the sites' requirements and was so poorly written that it was incomprehensible. After 3 more weeks of requirement meetings, Sports.com received another incomplete requirements statement. By this point, the cost of building the sites had increased 100 percent since the project's beginning. WebVendorX argued that most of the requested functionality, including a product adviser, gift certificate, and gift center, would have to be customer developed, as it was not part of the out-of-the-box solution WebAce provides. Because it took 6 weeks instead of 3 to define Sports.com's specifications, the project was now delayed by 3 months.

Sports.com was under contractual obligation to build the next-generation family of sites by August 1, 2000. Sports.com asked WebVendorX to prepare a time and cost estimate, using the current site-requirements document to build one site instead of the original six. WebVendorX returned with an estimated cost of $6.5 million and a proposed launch date of August 17, 2000. However, the launch date was not guaranteed. When asked why the cost was so high, WebVendorX's representative answered, "This is the cost of doing business in the e-commerce space today."

Sports.com fired WebVendorX and purchased a competing product, a comprehensive, out-of-the-box suite of enterprise-class applications. In addition, Sports.com hired an implementation firm. The total cost for this software and its implementation was $1.6 million. The last of the six sites was built in 90 days, launched on August 1, 2000, and included more functionality than had originally been specified in the WebVendorX requirements document. When choosing your development partner, do so wisely and carefully.

Application Service Providers

A company's development resources are continually stretched thin in a variety of directions. IT managers are seeking development solutions to relieve the stress of too few qualified personnel to meet too many development needs. Application leasing through application service providers (ASP) provides a company with the power of large application frameworks such as ERP, CRM, and e-procurement. In addition to providing these frameworks, ASPs maintain these applications themselves.

Over the past few years, the ASP market has become a well-established business alternative to the do-it-yourself approach. This growth is driven by the increasing ease with which IP networks, with their greater bandwidth, allow for the improved delivery of software applications. ASPs offer value because they allow companies to, in effect, rent applications that would otherwise require significant resources and installation time. ASPs are attractive to companies with rapidly changing IT needs that don't require highly customized software solutions. By using an ASP, these companies can implement software more quickly, have access to IT professionals, and focus company efforts on its core product.

The earliest successes in the ASP marketplace came from ASP aggregators, or distributors, such as Corio, Breakaway, and US Internetworking. These companies take applications from other vendors and bundle them together into a product/service offering. The primary value they add is in the understanding and expertise of the integrater in a particular existing application.

ASPs offer everything from office essentials, such as word processors and spreadsheets, to multimillion-dollar financial and management applications. Large servers host these applications at the ASP's data center and are accessed by using a wide area network, usually through a dedicated connection or virtual private network.

Start-up companies are good candidates for using ASPs, as these providers can furnish ready-made applications to help a new company launch its products and services quickly. Most ASPs offer only a small selection of applications but are broadening their offerings to include sets of applications that will essentially form a complete business framework. A start-up firm can select a particular business framework and have most of its internal practices automated in a matter of days, allowing it to concentrate on growing the business instead of maintaining its software applications.

Large corporations are also looking at ASP solutions because of the time-to-market issues, lack of development resources, and a desire to lower maintenance costs. Large software applications, such as SAP, Broadvision, and Siebel, are good candidates for the ASP model, as these applications tend to be cumbersome to implement, requiring a significant amount of resources to set up and operate successfully. A typical ASP package includes limited software customization, application and database management, data backups, recovery and offsite storage, service-level agreement, secure connectivity, dedicated hardware and upgrades, and 24/7 proactive monitoring, security management, support, and help desk.

The jury is still out on the viability of running applications on a true ASP model over the Internet. It seems much more logical to run such applications from a local network server that would provide faster access. But things are changing. With increasing bandwidth and applications designed for hosting, we expect a resurgence of the ASP model.

Infostructure Management

Once the development is done, the project is ready to move into production. You come face-to-face with the enigma of many CIOs: how to provide always-on service and performance required for a successful foray into the world of e-business. Production infostructure is one of the least-understood areas of e-business. The old model of software release distribution, whereby you have to ship CDs and maintain the systems on site, just doesn't work. Most projects are totally rearchitecting solutions into hosted models, which require a heavy emphasis on infostructure management.

In our opinion, infostructure design is very much like urban planning. Urban planners design utility, roads, and transportation systems for specific carrying capacities and expand them to meet changes in demand. When plans are unrealistic, new infrastructure construction can't keep up with demand, resulting in congestion, bottlenecks, and customer complaints. When overloaded, systems either break down or operate very poorly. However, when planners anticipate growth over a certain period, they can design the infrastructure to meet it. When population increases more rapidly than expected or when zoning ordinances no longer control growth, problems ensue, and physical systems break down. This analogy is easily transferable to e-business.

In many ways, the functions of an e-business infostructure planning mirror those of urban planning. Urban planners establish the framework to plan and develop a transportation and utility infrastructure along with creating zoning ordinances to guide the physical development of the city and ensure that growth is managed. The same principles apply to e-business infostructure. The infostructure team plans for the necessary capacity, scalability, hosting, and processes that will support the overall business needs and the specific application framework elements.

This section explores a number of topics related to the infostructure design (see Figure 14.8) that make up a production environment:

- Colocation and hosting: Do I create an Internet data center for my applications? Or do I need to host in a colocation facility, such as Exodus or Level 3?

- Capacity planning: How much load is going to be on this service and at what times?

- Scalability: What techniques are available to scale this service?

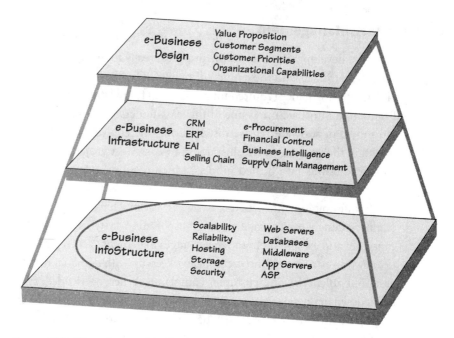

Figure 14.8: Three Layers of e-Business

- Reliability: When and where does this service need to be available?

- Availability: How can the availability of this service be increased?

- Security: How can I insure myself against hackers and denial-of-service attacks?

This section is not intended as a comprehensive analysis of all deployment topics but rather as a starting point for structuring your thinking and preparing you for deeper exploration of these issues.

Internet Data Centers

So, you've built your applications, and you're ready to go live. Or are you? Building the right production hosting solution really to do the job all day, every day, regardless of unpredictable demand can be very difficult. You need ongoing technical support, efficient bandwidth use, reliable hardware, 24/7 proactive monitoring and support, and plenty of time and money. However, a new generation of colocation firms can help their client companies build the Internet data centers they need.

The Internet has fundamentally changed the role of the corporate data center. The traditional data center has sought to maximize application availability at minimal cost by combining disciplines, processes, and procedures. Simply put, its essential focus has been on delivering predictability in performance and service. The Internet is anything but predictable. On the Internet, the demand for network services—and thus for data center systems—can be extremely volatile. For example, the Victoria's Secret online fashion show was viewed simultaneously by 1.5 million users, placing tremendous demand on the show's application network.

Newly introduced software applications can be ten times as popular as originally predicted. Also, the deployment of new data-driven applications, such as an ERP data mart, can increase storage system use beyond all analyst projections. Accurately assessing a company's need for data center resources is extremely difficult, as it must ensure that adequate capacity is available 24 × 7 × 365, while minimizing capital outlay required. Colocation facilities provide an innovative option for addressing these needs.

Colocation companies, including Exodus, Jam Cracker, LoudCloud, and Interpath, take a company's applications and group them together on dedicated servers in a state-of-the-art network operations center. Customers access the applications through high-speed Internet connections, which are protected by sophisticated firewall technologies. Asking the following questions can help you determine whether a colocation service is right for your firm.

- Can you expand your servers and connection pipe quickly enough to keep up with demand?

- Would your business be more competitive if the capital costs associated with building facilities and network architecture could be reallocated to other areas?

- Do you have the capital to support ongoing maintenance and expansion? Can you promise your customers the highest degree of service in a secure, reliable, and protected environment?

For most businesses, building and expanding the facilities that house network architecture can be a major roadblock to success. So pay attention to this facet of e-business.

Capacity Planning

Face it: Online customers—whether B2C or B2B—are an impatient lot. Make them wait too long and you may never see them again. One of the most difficult problems e-businesses face is predicting demand levels for network services. Statistical averages, such as average daily hits, are useless given the potential for enormous—and temporary—spikes in demand. An advertising campaign or a news story can increase the demand for access to a company's Web site by a factor of 10–100 times the network's normal volume.

The complexity of today's networks, with all their interdependencies, may make it difficult to isolate what is driving demand for a particular service. As a result, capacity planning for e-business solutions must be an ongoing, continuous process that follows these steps.

1. Determine whether your physical infrastructure is capable of supporting the transaction volume requirement you've defined. This includes identifying which of your services will be the first to max out as you increase the activity at each portal. By identifying the amount of excess capacity, if any, your company's network has, you will know where to focus your efforts.

2. Measure and monitor your traffic on a regular basis to verify your business model. For example, how many of the hits on your e-commerce Web site were to your search engine? How many hits did you expect? What variances in customer demand can you tolerate?

3. Use your business model for long-range scenario planning. Understand how dramatically you will have to change your capacity plan to meet your overall growth projections for upcoming years.

In capacity planning, don't think just Web transactions. Think about how rich content, such as audio and video, affects capacity. Rich content attracts more visitors, but it also places increasing demands on the Web site to deliver the content quickly and reliably. As a result, Web site owners frequently elect to constrain the amount of rich content on their Web sites, for fear of frustrating users with the site's slow response time. The quality of the user experience is sacrificed in order to maintain minimally acceptable performance levels.

Scalability

The scalability of a service impacts both the number of users that can be simultaneously supported and the service-level performance that users experience. On the Web, it is not uncommon to have a million people all trying to get into one place at one time, resulting in a huge bottleneck. Lack of scalable infrastructure can bring the Web site down, along with the network around the site, and can create a big problem. Because it is typically not cost-effective for a Web site to design its infrastructure to handle relatively infrequent periods of "flash," or sudden, demand, periods of peak network traffic and surges in traffic volumes often overwhelm the capacity of the site, causing long delays or complete site outages.

Two areas need to be considered in creating scalability: (1) attaining higher scalability directly through hardware (processors, servers, and storage systems); and (2) achieving higher scalability through indirect techniques, such as caching and replication.

Hardware scaling enables you to use more hardware to directly scale the performance of a service.

- Deploy multiple, smaller servers that operate in parallel and share the load (the "rack and stack" approach). The advantage of this approach is that it allows the use of smaller, higher-volume, less expensive servers, such as Linux. However, this approach doesn't work well for all services, and it can lead to higher support, administration, and management expenses as the number of servers increases.

- Deploy a multiprocessing server, such as Sun Microsystems Star Fire, that can support many processors and memory. By deploying a megaserver, you can scale by simply adding processors to the system, enabling you to stay with the same system longer. You also often simplify management and reduce administration costs compared with the rack-and-stack model. The initial price tag may be higher, but the total cost of ownership can be lower.[5]

Simply having a lot of hardware may not solve the problem when dealing with rich multimedia content. The combination of richer content and increasing volumes of users can significantly lengthen the time required for a user to download information from a site and may cause the site to crash. These performance problems are exacerbated during peak demand times, such as a breaking news event, Olympic games, rock concerts, an online special event, or sudden demand for a new software release.

Online traffic congestion problems called "hot spot," or "flash crowd," problems occur when too many users try to access the same site simultaneously, such as during the Webcast of a Victoria's Secret fashion show in February 1999. To solve these issues, indirect or software scaling techniques, such as caching and replication, are used.

- *Caching.* You can design your infrastructure so that portions of each service are stored at multiple places, each of which becomes an access point for the service. Typically, a company's Web site is accommodated on a single server in one location. Large companies may use several servers, but typically they are in the same location, too. In both cases, large volumes slow service down to a crawl. Caching is commonly used in Web deployments, where there are often multiple primary servers, and file systems. Examples are Akamai, Adero, Digital Island, and Keynote Systems.

- *Replication.* Under the replication method, portions of the service are copied so that users with specific needs can be moved off the main system. This approach works best for read-only users who will tolerate a time lag. Like the caching method, it makes it easier to deliver services over great distances. Replication is commonly used in deploying directory services.

Availability

Availability is the accessibility of the e-business operation: 24 hours a day, 7 days a week, 365 days a year. Face it: People do business online for real-time gratification. Achieving this goal impacts every aspect of the infrastructure, because there can be no weak links. Delays and site crashes often cause user frustration and disappointment. Jupiter Communications found that in June 1999, if response times at a particular Web site did not meet Internet users' expectations, 37 percent of users visited a substitute Web site to meet their needs. For 24 percent of users, the decision to use an alternative Web site was permanent.

The following techniques can help companies move toward maximum uptime:

- *Clustering and replication techniques.* Techniques exist for many applications and services to increase availability. Advanced high-availability cluster software, such as Windows 2000 Datacenter, includes sophisticated fault-management tools that automatically detect, isolate, and recover from single hardware or software failures.

- *Process and business practices.* High availability is more than technology. Process-related problems are a common source of downtime. There is no magic to solving process-related problems; you must establish and formalize your business practices and your education and training programs, and you must be very consistent about applying the processes you define.

- *Monitoring service deployments.* Although it is important to monitor and to measure services, it is no less critical to monitor and to measure the systems that the services are deployed on. Here are a number of things to watch for: *Is the rate that the service is being accessed consistent with the load on the systems? Are there any deviations from your models? If a service is deployed across multiple systems, are they all experiencing similar loads, or are some being accessed more than others are? If the service is experiencing periods of performance degradation, such as long access times and low bandwidth—what system activities is the degradation correlating with?*

The modularity of the infostructure is critical to attaining continuous availability, because there are so many variables and potential sources of downtime that monolithic systems simply cannot deliver adequate uptime for multiple network services. In addition, because network services are heavily interdependent, continual monitoring and measurement of service availability are important in isolating problem areas.

Security and Risk Management

Preventing potentially debilitating security threats is far easier and less costly than having to respond after the fact. For example, distributed denial of service (DDoS) attacks send a flood of IP packets from hundreds of sources (DDoS clients) to the targeted system. These DDoS clients, often PCs of innocent users, have themselves been compromised by an attacker, and the clients are controlled remotely to ensure that the attacker cannot be traced. The packets that hit the victims are generally forged, with invalid source addresses, making tracing to the client extremely difficult.

Several high-profile Web sites, including Yahoo!, CNN, and Amazon, were attacked in early 2000. In lieu of these highly visible Internet site attacks, business executives must pay attention to their companies' network security and understand what their firms' development organizations and hosting vendors are doing to identify and to solve potential security problems.

Security and disaster recovery planning go hand in hand. A company's solid reputation can be destroyed in a single day on the Internet. It is important to think through various disaster scenarios and have a plan for addressing each one.

Adoption Management

We've all been there. After months of sweat and tears, you're about to roll out your big project. It's leading-edge, feature rich, and ready for prime time. There's just one small glitch. The users aren't ready to adopt it en masse. Changing your customers' behavior is going to be more difficult than you expected.

When introducing changes to how your company interacts with its customers, it is important to remember three behavioral responses you have to overcome:

- *Denial.* "No problem. Customers just need to be educated about how comprehensive our solution really is."

- *Anger.* "Unbelievable. After all we've done for them. They just don't get it! This has to roll out! This is not optional!"

- *Acceptance.* "Okay, folks. Let me show me how our solution works. We can provide you with one-on-one training at no cost to you and on your schedule."

Acceptance is when your customers are willing to work with you to understand the new service, learn how to use it, and become clear about its benefits. Acceptance is the beginning, not the end, of a solution's adoption by its intended customer. Successful adoption requires

- A communications plan that keeps customers informed about new features and functionality occurring after their initial training

- A transition management plan

- Key performance indicators that you continuously measure to see how the company's service is performing and where it can be improved

The importance of regular, consistent project communication was discussed earlier in this chapter. However, its importance extends beyond the life of the project as a means of providing your customers with the tools they need to successfully use your e-commerce service and for obtaining valuable customer feedback.

A critical part of any e-business implementation is transitioning users from the old applications with which they are familiar to the new applications, which are as yet unknown. Transition issues can cause serious problems for a firm. For example, Samsonite, the world's leading luggage maker, had its U.S. product shipments nearly stop during the first 20 days of July 1998 because of conversion problems while implementing its new financial, manufacturing, and distribution applications. These system problems even disrupted Samsonite's invoicing and its electronic data interchange communications with its retail stores, resulting in inventory stockouts and lost sales at the retail level. The conversion problems contributed to a shocking $29.9 million loss, a subsequent drop in stock price, and numerous shareholder lawsuits.[6]

Large projects affect change in three stages. In the first stage, jobs are re-defined, new procedures are established, applications are fine-tuned, and users learn the benefits of the new information sources the technology platform pro-vides. In the second stage, new skills are executed, business structure changes occur, processes become integrated, and add-on technologies are implemented to further expand the application's functionality. During the third stage, a transfor-mation occurs; the new tools and processes become almost second nature to their users, and the benefits of the change are organizationally apparent. This is a time when the synergy of a company's people, processes, and technology reach peak performance.[7]

Measurement for Learning and Improvement

In the 1988 NBA Eastern Conference finals, the Detroit Pistons eliminated their nemesis, the Boston Celtics, winner of three NBA championships in the 1980s. Amid the postgame commotion, Celtics forward Kevin McHale confronted Pis-tons captain Isiah Thomas and challenged him to seize the opportunity to lead his team to victory in the finals rather than revel in the thought of having "arrived." Great teams are measured by championships, not finals appearances, was McHale's implicit message. The Pistons then went on to outplay the Los Angeles Lakers in nearly every game. But the Lakers won the series. They out-smarted their opponents and succeeded in the only metric that matters: *winning when the buzzer went off.*[8]

What does winning mean for your project, and how can it be measured? Many e-business companies are champions on paper. They spend countless millions of dollars on applications, hardware, advertising, and consultants to assemble a sup-posedly unbeatable Web infrastructure and strategy. But when it comes to results, they come up short.

How does a company know that it is doing well? Key measures are an impor-tant element of any new e-business process. The performance metrics that best reflect a Web site's success are the numbers of members it attracts and the conver-sion of these members into customers. However, attracting customers at a high cost is not good business. For example, Garden.com has, during the past 9 months, spent more than $80 million and has 183,000 customers. The company has spent an average of $437 per customer on the site, whereas sales per customer average only $38. How long can they continue to burn cash at this rate?

Ask yourself, *What should my company measure?* Several key performance measurement categories are

- *Risk.* How many customers are live and using our online channel?

- *Financial.* What is our revenue growth due to e-business?

- *Loyalty.* Who are the most profitable and most frequent customers to our site? Do we know our most valuable customer segments and understand their specific needs, habits, and buying patterns?

- *Fulfillment.* How do we ensure the efficient processing of orders and shipment of products to our customers? How many orders are fulfilled accurately, on time, and with the right quantity?

- *Customer satisfaction.* Are our customers returning? Is their transaction volume growing steadily?

Create measures that make sense for your business. Don't establish so many measures that they begin to distract everyone from the purpose of using metrics to align tactics and activities with a forward-looking strategic vision. There is no correct number of metrics to establish, but the rule of thumb is "more is usually worse."

Finally, this section is not intended as a comprehensive analysis of all measurement issues in e-business but rather as a starting point for structuring your thinking and preparing you for deeper exploration of these issues.[9]

Memo to the CEO

The honeymoon period for e-business is over. Today, the spotlight is on execution. Most executives are acutely aware of the need to execute their e-business strategy in order to complement their existing business models. But numerous forces continually undermine the effectiveness of these efforts. It is important to remember the following.

- *Ruthless tactical execution is becoming increasingly essential to business.* Rapid technological and market change and shorter product and service life cycles favor companies that excel at implementing forward-looking, immediately deployable strategies. If a project cannot be completed within 6 months, move on to something that can.

- *Provide strong blueprint leadership.* Many companies have no central decision maker for their e-commerce initiatives. Worse, this is a difficult position to fill, as it requires business and technical expertise in a variety of areas. In addition, e-business problems are fluid and multidimensional. This is exacerbated by the fact that many companies have multiple, department-level initiatives under way, with no blueprint strategy tying them together. Other firms are so busy making their internal IT systems work that they have little time to focus on how market forces are affecting them.

- *Communicate a clear vision.* The goal of e-business is to develop a portfolio of technical and process solutions that support a well-articulated vision of the future. Like the applications that support its achievement, an e-business vision can be developed iteratively and continuously modified and enhanced to ensure success.

- *Pay attention to your application architecture.* The e-landscape is littered with corporate failures that paid too little attention to building a foundation for a scalable application infrastructure. These companies failed because they later had to dismantle their systems in order to create a new foundation to support e-business.

- *Recruit the right talent.* New applications require new skills. A dynamic e-strategy requires a special blend of talented performers who work together, performing their jobs correctly. Talented performers dislike ambiguous project or corporate objectives. They want tasks that can be measured and evaluated and that provide a concrete sense of achievement. Given the difficulty of retaining top talent, companies need to be creative in their incentive and compensation packages.

- *Pay attention to your development methodology.* e-Business development presents a unique set of challenges. Much of the available technology used to design Web applications is immature and changes at an unprecedented rate, with new versions often released quarterly. Your software designers must cope with technology's limitations. These limitations include browser incompatibility across vendors, versions, and platforms; inadequate performance owing to network constraints; and inadequate development tools.

- *Manage adoption carefully.* Being continually customer focused means watching customers carefully as they use your product or service. Winning strategies usually embody a revolutionary way of getting feedback from a target market and target customer. Such strategies require clear metrics and measurement. Such strategies can succeed only if there is tightly integrated, sound execution followed by rapid adjustment when unexpected developments occur.

Attention to basics is fundamental to sound execution and is the foundation for a successful e-business strategy. It is the key to instinctively making the right—and rapid—responses to opportunities or problems. In any business, some people will leave over time, and competitors will copy successful behaviors. The key to long-term success is to create a legacy of leadership, revolutionary strategy, and transition to excellent execution, all supported with top talent. The great teams and the great companies sustain this kind of organization to create a lasting dynasty.

Finally, mastering e-business is not unlike building skill at other things: The more you do it, the better you get. Good luck, and happy implementing.

Endnotes

Chapter 1

1. "Dot-Coms: Can They Climb Back?" *Business Week,* June 19, 2000, p. 101.
2. Information asymmetry is a core concept in economics. Basically, it means that buyers have less information than do sellers. The business of intermediation stems from this concept, as intermediaries attempt to reduce the gap.
3. John Seely Brown, ed., *Seeing Differently: Insights on Innovation* (Boston: Harvard Business Review Book Series, 1997).
4. Jean Nash Johnson, "Internet Puts Encyclopedia a Click Away," *Dallas Morning News,* June 29, 1999.
5. Eric W. Pfeiffer, "Start Up; The Story of a Prodigy; Whatever Happened to America's First Cutting-Edge Online Service?", *Forbes,* October 5, 1998, p. 19.
6. Morgan Stanley, U.S. Investment Research, "The Internet Retailing Report," May 28, 1997, from http://www.msdw.com/
7. "Microsoft Moves to Rule On-Line Sales," *Wall Street Journal,* June 5, 1997.
8. Online travel agents charge $10 commissions, whereas traditional agents demand $50.
9. The term business webs (BW) was first introduced by the Alliance for Converging Technologies in its multiclient study "Winning in the Digital Economy." The study has been published in the book by Don Tapscott, David Ticoll, and Alex Lowy, *Digital Capital: Harnessing the Power of Business Webs* (Boston: Harvard Business School, 2000).
10. The largest purchase item is a home. According to the National Automobile Dealers Association (NADA), the industry's largest dealer organization, U.S. consumers spent more than $300 billion in 1999 on new vehicles, representing 15.8 million new units.
11. Clinton Wilder, "Online Auto Sales Pickup," *Information Week,* February 9, 1998.
12. BellSouth outsourced its entire IT function to EDS and Andersen Consulting in a contract worth more than $4 billion.
13. Georgie Raik-Allen, "Staples Collates VC Funding," Redherring.com, November 13, 1999.
14. "Procter & Gamble and Institutional Venture Partners Launch reflect.com, the First Interactive, Personalized Beauty Company; New Company Combines the Power of the Fortune 20 with the Prowess of Silicon Valley to Usher in a New Era in Consumer Business," *PR Newswire,* September 13, 1999.

15. e-Business architecture design and implementation has emerged as one of the fastest-growing consulting businesses of the decade because it helped firms to transition to e-commerce.

16. In mid 2000, FDX lost the National Semiconductor account to UPS. UPS logistics signed a $150M five-year deal to handle National's shipments.

17. For more examples of market leaders that responded and those that did not, see Gary Hamel and C. K. Prahalad, *Competing for the Future* (Boston: Harvard Business School Press, 1997).

18. Credible social and business prophets, notably Peter Drucker and Alvin Toffler have been anticipating this business environment of ever-increasing rate of change for decades. Therefore, no organization, no manager, no person should be caught off guard. (Peter Drucker, *Managing in Turbulent Times,* New York: HarperBusiness, 1980; Alvin Toffler, *Future Shock,* New York: Bantam Books, 1970).

Chapter 2

1. Michael Eisner, chairman and chief executive officer, Walt Disney Co., in address to the shareholders, annual stockholders meeting, Kansas City, Missouri, February 24, 1998.

2. A 1997 report by the U.S. Department of Commerce estimates that overall data traffic on the Internet is doubling every 100 days.

3. Eileen Shapiro, *Fad Surfing in the Boardroom,* New York: Perseus Press, 1997.

4. "Trend-Spotting: Anyone Can Play," *Business Week,* March 2, 1998, p. 12.

5. Evan I. Schwartz, "How Middlemen Can Come Out on Top," *Business Week,* February 9, 1998, p. 4.

6. Annalee Saxenian, "The Origins and Dynamics of Production Networks in Silicon Valley," working paper, Institute of Urban and Regional Development, University of California, Berkeley, April 1990.

7. "Sara Lee's Plan to Contract Out Work Underscores Trend among U.S. Firms," *Wall Street Journal,* September 17, 1997, and "Sara Lee to Retreat from Manufacturing," *Wall Street Journal,* September 16, 1997.

8. Nuala Moran, "Chemical Industry Applications: The traditional business practices of the larger producers are increasingly being challenged by new Internet-based distributors," *Financial Times* (London), October 20, 1999, Survey Edition 2, Survey: Electronic Business.

9. Bob Violino, "Technology Spending—The Billion Dollar Club," *Information Week,* November 25, 1996, p. 27.

Chapter 3

1. Bruce Upbin, Kodak's Digital Moment, August 21 2000.

2. Sanford C. Bernstein & Co., "Investment Report: Retailers and the Internet," June 18, 1999.

3. Peter Sinton, "Electronic Postage Debuts," *San Francisco Chronicle,* April 1, 1998, final edition.

4. Katherine Hobson, "Out to Lunch? Webvan/HomeGrocer Deal Doesn't Deliver All the Answers," http://www.thestreet.com/tech/internet/977452.html

5. Rusty Weston, "Webvan: Return of the Milkman," *Upside,* February 18, 2000.

6. Greg Farrell, "Clicks and Mortar World Values Brands," *USA Today,* October 5, 1999, final edition.

7. The company provides music in its name-sake format MP3 (Motion Picture Experts Group-1, Audio Layer 3). The technology compresses high-quality audio files to a more manageable size—roughly one twelfth their original size—thereby reducing the time it takes to download near-CD-quality music. As a result, a song that takes more than 40 minutes to download in CD format using a 56K modem would take less than 4 minutes to download as an MP3 file using the same modem.

8. In 1998, the WAP Forum published technical specifications for application and content development and product interoperability requirements based on Internet technology and standards.

9. Robert Poe, "Akamai Dishes It Out," *Upside Inside,* January 17, 2000, http://www.akamai.com/news/media.html

Chapter 4

1. "The New Rules," *Business Magazine,* August 1999, p. 52–56.
2. "Point and Click for Prozac," *Business Week,* October 19, 1998, p. 156.
3. Elizabeth Corcoran, "The E Gang," *Forbes,* July 24, 2000.
4. Geoffrey Moore, *Crossing the Chasm* (New York: Harperbusiness, 1999).
5. A. A. Milne, *Winnie-the-Pooh* (New York: Puffin, 1992).
6. Richard Lueckie, *Scuttle Your Ships Before Advancing* (New York: Oxford University Press, 1994) pp. 165–166.
7. This strategy was quite common in the 1960s and 1980s. Between 1959 and 1979, American Express acquired a staggering 350 companies, including Avis, Continental Baking (Wonder Bread, Twinkies), Sheraton, and Hartford Insurance.
8. Anthony Bianco, "The Rise of a Star," *Business Week,* December 21, 1998, p. 60.
9. "The Power of Virtual Integration: An Interview with Dell Computer's Michael Dell," *Harvard Business Review,* March/April 1998, p. 72.
10. Lynn Cook, "Requiem for A Business Model," *Forbes,* July 24, 2000.
11. "The Model for B2B Integration: Dell Computer Corporation and webMethods," white paper, www.webmethods.com.
12. Suzie Amer et al., "America's Best Technology Users," *Forbes,* August 24, 1998, p. 63.

Chapter 5

1. Bill Gates, "The Digital Nervous System," http:/www.microsoft.com/dns/overviews/DNSoverviews.htm.
2. Source: Meta Group Research
3. Helen Atkinson, "ERP Software Requires Good Planning," *Journal of Commerce,* December 9, 1999, p. 14.
4. Clinton Wilder, "Booksellers' Battles Head for the Web," *InformationWeek,* March 3, 1997, pp. 62–63.
5. Source: SAP Case Study
6. Norwest Mortgage has been acquired by Wells Fargo Bank. The new company is called Wells Fargo Mortgage.
7. "America's Best Technology Users," *Forbes,* August 24, 1998, p. 63. Norm Payson, a physician-turned-business manager, brought Oxford back from the brink. Most observers agree, it has been a spectacular turnaround.

8. James Niccolai and Martin LaMonica, Whirlpool latest to hit ERP production snags InfoWorld, November 8, 1999.

9. Craig Stedman, "The Complexity Sound Familiar? Make Room, ERP; CRM Now Confounds Staff," *Computerworld,* November 22, 1999.

10. Steve Konicki, "Nestle Taps SAP For E-Business," *Information Week,* June 26, 2000.

11. Bob Wallace, "IT Revamp Fuels Auto Parts Maker's Expansion," *Computerworld,* November 02, 1998.

12. "Appliance Firm Gives Pricing System a Whirl," *Computerworld,* March 23, 1998.

13. Carol Sliwa, "Procurement App Tracks Expenses," *Computerworld,* October 12, 1998.

14. David Orenstein, "Enterprise Application Integration," *Computerworld,* October 04, 1999.

15. H. Ford, *Today and Tomorrow,* Doubleday, Tage, and Company, (Garden City, NY: 1926, reprinted by Productivity Press, Cambridge, MA, 1988.)

16. "Wal-Mart's IT Secret: Extreme Integration," *Datamation,* November 1996.

17. "Wal-Mart CIO Leaves Retailer an IT Leader," *Computerworld,* March 6, 2000.

Chapter 6

1. "Sybase Customer Asset Management Solutions," http://ww.sybase.com/.

2. Rebecca Quick, "The Lessons Learned," *Wall Street Journal,* April 17, 2000.

3. As e-commerce and CRM come together, they are creating the next generation of CRM, also or enterprise relationship management (ERM).

4. "BlueGill Saves Companies Millions of Dollars with Internet Billing," http://www2. software.ibm.com/casestudies/.

5. For more information on billing application service providers, see Internet billers Derivion, Just-in-time Solutions, iPlanet's BillerXpert, and BlueGill.

6. "Live to Ride," *Financial World,* September 26, 1995, p. 6.

7. "Biggest Sales Mistake: Asking Your Customers," *American Salesman,* November 1996, p. 22.

Chapter 7

1. Michael Fitzgerald, "Xerox Bets Virtual Office," *ComputerWorld,* October 31, 1994.

2. "Signing Suppliers for Ariba," http://www.onlink.com/customers/ariba.html.

3. "We Sure as Hell Confused Ourselves, But What about the Customers?" *Marketing Intelligence & Planning,* April 1995, p. 5.

4. "Hewlett-Packard Printing and Digital Imaging," http://www.selectica.com/customers/stories/hp.shtml.

5. "Producing Unique Goods—and Headaches," *Inc.,* May 1998, p. 24.

6. "Smart Managing/Best Practices," *Fortune,* 10 November 1997, p. 283.

7. For more details, see "Customer-Focused E-Commerce at Cisco Systems; Creating Competitive Advantage Through E-Commerce," http://www.cisco.com/warp/public/779/ibs/solutions/ecommerce/.

Chapter 8

1. Tim Minahan, "Enterprise Resource Planning," *Purchasing,* July 16, 1998, p. 112.

2. Legend has it that IBM turned down a contract to customize the production planning software of ICI's German subsidiary. The five programmers took the contract on themselves, founding SAP as a result.

3. "3Com Corporation: Success Story," http:/www.sap.com/success/index.htm. File: 50020231. pdf. After its merger with U.S. Robotics in 1998, 3Com, headquartered in Santa Clara, California, now employs 13,000 people across 160 R&D, manufacturing, sales, and service sites worldwide.

4. "GM Picks SAP to Improve Information Technology," *Wall Street Journal,* November 13, 1997.

5. Bob Francis, "The New ERP Math," *PC Week Online,* October 26, 1998.

6. Glovia International, http:/www.glovia.com/about/direction.html.

7. April Jacobs, "Business Process Software Pays Off, *Computerworld,* August 31, 1998.

8. Joseph B. White, Don Clark, and Silvia Ascarelli, "Program of Pain," *Wall Street Journal,* 14 March 1997.

9. "The Software that Drives Microsoft," SAP case study, SAP, Palo Alto, California.

10. Thomas H. Davenport, "Putting the Enterprise into the Enterprise System," *Harvard Business Review,* July/August 1998.

11. Analyst Reports, Investext CD-ROM Database.

12. Todd R. Weiss, "PeopleSoft Launches Browser-Based ERP Suite," *ComputerWorld,* July 11, 2000.

13. "Managing the ERP Equation," *PC Week Online,* October 26, 1998.

Chapter 9

1. Carol Hildebrand, "Beware of the Weak Links," *Enterprise CIO,* August 15 1998, p. 20.

2. Andrew E. Serwer, Michael Dell Turns the PC World Inside Out, *Fortune,* September 8, 1997, p. 76.

3. *Journal of Business Strategy,* November/December 1997, p. 25.

4. Andy Reinhardt and Seanna Browder, "Fly, Damn It, Fly"; *Business Week,* November 9, 1998, p. 150.

5. "America's Best Technology Users," *Forbes,* August 24, 1998, p. 63.

6. "Toys 'R' Us Falling Short on Christmas Deliveries," *Bloomberg News,* December 23, 1999. In July 2000, seven e-tailers, including Toysrus.com, agreed to pay a total of $1.5 million in fines related to FTC charges over shipping delays last holiday season. The FTC alleged that the online stores did not give shoppers enough notice of impending shipping delays or that they continued to promise deliveries they could not make during the holiday season.

7. Margaret Kane, "Online Booksellers Look for Fulfillment Wizardry," *ZDNet Interactive Investor,* July 7, 2000, and Larry Mcshane, "Kids Line Up for 'Harry Potter,'" July 8, 2000, Associated Press.

8. Jennifer Bresnahan, "The Incredible Journey," *CIO Magazine,* August 15, 1998, p. 56.

9. Greg Sandoval, "Furniture.com a Case Study in E-Tail Problems." CNET News.com, July 31, 2000, http://yahoo.cnet.com/news/.

10. Firms providing early versions of advanced planning capability include SAP (Advanced Planning and Optimization (APO) Engine), I2 Technologies, Manugistics and Logility. More sophisticated systems that integrate production planning and transportation planning are under development.

11. Damark International, 10 K Filing with the Securities and Exchange Commission.

12. It's estimated that companies spend about $500 billion owning, holding, and moving inventory, including wrapping, bundling, loading, unloading, sorting, reloading, and then transporting goods.

13. "Gaining a Competitive Edge," Speech by M. Anthony Burns, Ryder Systems, Economic Club of Detroit, April 21, 1997.

14. Marshall Fisher, "What Is the Right Supply Chain for Your Product," *Harvard Business Review,* March 1997, p. 80.

15. Starbucks is North America's top specialty coffee roaster and retailer. This king of café lattes has experienced more than 60 percent sales growth for 8 consecutive years, including retail store growth from 11 stores in 1987 to more than 1,500 in August of 1997. Starbucks serves more than 4 million customers in its retail stores every week. In fact, the company has gone international, with locations in Tokyo and Singapore. Starbucks has elevated drinking coffee from a mundane morning exercise to a social experience.

16. An Interview with T.R. "Ted" Garcia, Starbucks Senior Vice President, Supply Chain Operations, in the August 1997 Issue of *APICS—The Performance Advantage,* p. 45.

17. The wholesale drug distribution network is the most cost-effective means for pharmaceutical manufacturers to get their product to market. The two principal factors driving growth are a general increase in the size of the pharmaceutical market and a realization by manufacturers that drug distributors are able to service customers more efficiently than manufacturers, which frees manufacturers to allocate their resources to R&D, manufacturing, and marketing. At the same time, the drug wholesaler's role is changing from providing only cost-effective logistics to also providing marketing and information services to suppliers and customers.

Chapter 10

1. "Holding the Line on SG&A," *CFO Magazine,* December 1996.

2. Fara Warner, "Ford Motor Uses the Internet to Slash Billions of Dollars from Ordinary Tasks," *Wall Street Journal,* October 14, 1998, p. 4.

3. "Automotive Trade Exchange to be Called 'Covisint,'" *PR Newswire,* May 16, 2000. The name Covisint is a combination of the primary concepts of why the exchange is being formed. The letters "Co" represent connectivity, collaboration, and communication. "Vis" represents the visibility that the Internet provides and the vision of the future of supply chain management. "Int" represents the integrated solutions the venture will provide the international scope of the exchange.

4. "Reaping 'Net Savings—Microsoft's Online Buying App Slashes Costs," *Internet Week,* August 4, 1997.

5. Microsoft Web site, www.microsoft.com.

6. Ariba Technologies Web site, www.ariba.com.

7. Amex Consulting Services, T&E Management Process Study, 1997, retrieved from www.extensity.com.

8. Merril Lynch, The B2B Market Maker Book, 3 February 2000.

9. e-Procurement *Industry Report: A Guide To Buy-Side Applications,* Stephens Inc. December 27, 1999.

Chapter 11

1. "NCR More than Doubles Data Warehouse for World's Leading Retailer to Over 100 Terabytes," *PR Newswire,* August 17, 1999.

2. Exchange Applications, S 1/A prospectus filed with the Securities and Exchange Commission, 1999.

3. Norbert Turek, "Decision into Action—Closed-Loop Systems Are Making Retailers More Responsive to Inventory Adjustments," *Information Week,* October 26, 1998.

4. John Dodge, "Tiny SeeCommerce Carves Out Supply-Chain Management Niche," *Wall Street Journal,* May 31, 2000.

5. Steve Alexander, "Printer Manufacturer Tracks Your Inventory," *Computerworld,* November 16, 1998, p. 67.

6. Creative Good, Business Week and the Boston Consulting Group.

7. Janet Novack, "Database Evangelist," *Forbes,* September 7, 1998, p. 66.

8. Sun Microsystems, "British Telecom," http://www.sun.com/products-n-solutions/telco/ success.stry/ss10.britele.html.

9. Marina Bidoli, "Managing a Giant," *Financial Mail,* October 16, 1998, p. 80.

10. Janice Maloney, "Healtheon: Internet-Based Health Care Information and Services," *Fortune,* July 8, 1996, p. 88.

11. W.H. Inmon. Building the Data Warehouse, 1992.

12. Lawrence S. Gould, "What You Need to Know about Data Warehousing," *Automotive Manufacturing & Production,* June 1998, p. 64.

13. *DBMS,* August 1998, p. 36.

Chapter 12

1. Securities and Exchange Commission Form 10-K405 for OfficeMax, filed on 21 April 1998.

2. Niccolo Machiaveli, "The Prince," Oxford University Press, 1998.

3. Source: The Juran Institute.

4. Stephen J. Wall and Shannon Rye Wall, "The Evolution Not the Death of Strategy," *Organizational Dynamics,* September 22, 1995, p. 6.

5. David Diamond, "Hold on Tight: Trends in Electronics Industry in 1998," *Electronic Business,* December 1998, p. 70.

6. Peter Drucker calls this set of interrelated assumptions the "theory of the business." Gary Hamel and C.K. Prahalad, in *Competing for the Future* (Boston: Harvard Business School Press, 1994) expand this concept, maintaining that "every manager carries around in his or her head a set of biases, assumptions, and presuppositions about the structure of the relevant 'industry,' about how one makes money in the industry, about who the competition is and isn't, about who the customers are and aren't, about which technologies are viable and which aren't, and so on" (p. 35).

7. Evan I. Schwartz, "OK, Retailers, Why Do Your Own Marketing When You Can Make 100,000 Other Web Sites Do It for You?" *New York Times,* 10 August 1998, sec. D.

8. Robert Hiebeler, Thomas Kelly, and Charles Ketteman, *Best Practices: Building Your Business with Customer-Focused Solutions* (New York: Simon & Schuster, 1998).

9. Ruth Owades, interview by John Metaxas, *In the Game,* Cable News Network, transcript, June 1997. Calyx & Corolla was acquired in August 1999 by Gerald Stevens, a leading integrated retailer and marketer of flowers, plants, and complementary gifts and decorative accessories.

10. Scott Kurnit's talk at the Esther Dyson Adventure Conference, 1997.

11. Gary Hamel and Jeff Sampler, "The E-Corporation," *Fortune,* December 7, 1998, p. 80.

12. Joseph C. Picken and Gregory G. Dess, "Right Strategy—Wrong Problem," *Organizational Dynamics,* June 22, 1998, p. 35.

13. See Adrian J. Slywotzky and David Morrison, *Profit Patterns: 30 Ways to Anticipate and Profit from Strategic Forces Reshaping Your Business,* (New York: Random House, 1999) for an exhaustive list of brick-and-mortar business designs. We highly recommend this book.

14. "Not Just Clicks Anymore," *Business Week,* August 29, 2000, p. 226.

15. Quoted in Stephen Harper, "Leading Organizational Change in the 21st Century," *Industrial Management,* May 15, 1998, p. 25.

Chapter 13

1. *Information Week,* May 15, p. 42; source: www.informationweek.com/786.chase.htm

2. Clinton Wilder and Beth Davis, "False Starts, Strong Finishes," *InformationWeek,* November 30, 1998.

3. Saul Habsell, "Citibank Sets New On-Line Bank System," *New York Times,* 5 October 1998, sec. C.

4. Clinton Wilder, "E-Commerce—Myths & Realities," *Information Week,* December 7, 1998.

5. Stage 5 is predicated on the assumption that business models have a powerful predisposition to mutate and to evolve. This idea is similar to so-called business ecosystems, made popular by James Moore in his book *The Death of Competition* (New York: Harper Business, 1996).

6. W. Edward Deming, *The New Economics,* (Cambridge, MA: MIT Center for Advanced Engineering Study, 1993), pp. 50–51.

7. Clinton Wilder and Beth Davis, "False Starts, Strong Finishes," *Information Week,* November 30, 1998.

8. Robert Frost, *The Road Not Taken* (Dover Publications, 1993).

9. Robert Cooper, Scott Edgett, and Elko KleinSchmidt, *Portfolio Management for New Products,* (Reading, MA: Addison-Wesley, 1998).

Chapter 14

1. Richard C. Morais, "Bullterrier Banking," *Forbes,* July 24, 2000.

2. TPN Register, GEIS.

3. Personal Interview with Lynn Lorenc.

4. The data for this figure came from the Gartner Group.

5. Dave Douglas and Greg Papadopoulos, "How to .com Your Business: The Survivior's Guide to the New Net Economy," (http://www.sun.com/dot-com/wht/).

6. Frank Hayes, "The Main Event; IT's Sideshow Days Are Over. Our Projects Can Make or Break a Company," *Computerworld,* November 8, 1999, p. 86.

7. Bruce Caldwell and Tom Stein, "Cultural, Organizational Shifts Move Beyond Software," *Computer Reseller News,* 7 December 1998.

8. Robert Preston, "It Takes More than Flash and Money to Win on the Net," *InternetWeek,* June 12, 2000.

9. See Kaplan and Norton, *Translating Strategy into Action: The Balanced Scorecard,* (Boston: Harvard Business School Press, 1996) for a roadmap to measuring customer satisfaction, quality, profit attainment, and continuous learning.

Index